CLASSIC CAR RESTORATION GUIDE

LINDSAY PORTER

THE COMPLETE ILLUSTRATED STEP-BY-STEP MANUAL

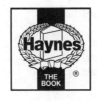

Haynes

THE BOOK ®

First published in 1994
Reprinted 1996, 1997 and 1998

British Library Cataloguing-in-Publication Data:
A catalogue record for this book is available from the British Library

ISBN 1 85010 890 0

Published by Haynes Publishing, Sparkford,
Nr Yeovil, Somerset BA22 7JJ, UK.

Tel. 01963 440635 Fax 01963 440001
Int. tel. +44 1963 440635 Fax +44 1963 440001
E-mail: sales@haynes-manuals.co.uk
Web site: http://www.haynes.com

Printed and bound in England by J. H. Haynes & Co. Ltd

Jurisdictions which have strict emission control laws may consider any modifications to a vehicle to be an infringement of those laws. You are advised to check with the appropriate body or authority whether your proposed modification complies fully with the law. The publishers accept no liability in this regard.

While every effort is taken to ensure the accuracy of the information given in this book, no liability can be accepted by the author or publishers for any loss, damage or injury caused by errors in, or omissions from the information given.

Contents

Introduction

Hundreds of thousands of classic car enthusiasts can't all be wrong! There is enormous interest in classic cars and in restoring them, but never before has there been a comprehensive guide to their restoration in the useful step-by-step style of this book.

As the author of quite a number of books on the restoration of specific models of classic cars, I have brought together all the experience I have accumulated into this one book on restoration techniques. My wife and I owned innumerable MGBs, Morris Minors, 'Frogeye' Sprites and cheap Jaguars in the days when they were just a slightly eccentric and low cost way of getting about. Keeping them going and keeping bodywork and soul together was something you picked up as you went along, with the assistance of the Haynes manual and friendly advice from those in a similar predicament. But when I turned to writing, I rapidly learned that I was in a privileged position to acquire 'inside' knowledge!

Paul Skilleter, then Managing Editor of *Practical Classics* or Tony Dron at *Classic Cars* would ask me to write about Subject Y: I would realize that I didn't know an X about it so I would go and set up camp, armed with my camera, on the doorstep of the finest specialist I could find. I would use my background as a trained metalwork teacher and DIY nut to ask all the relevant questions – and one of the results is this book! It's a compendium of facts, inside information and knowledge gleaned from the finest specialists on classic car restoration in the land, with a little of my own experience – I later ran a restoration workshop – thrown in.

As you will see, the book is divided into logical chapters covering various 'departments' of restoration work. However, there is another complete set of techniques that is not covered in detail even though it's a crucial part of doing the job. It's to do with using the toolbox in your head. Whenever you watch an athlete at work – a long jumper at the start of the run up, for instance – you'll see the way he or she takes a moment to concentrate on the job in hand. The idea is to wrap the mind totally in what needs to be done to the exclusion of all else. I'm not suggesting that you sit cross-legged on top of the bonnet meditating before each session in the workshop – you'd get a cold posterior for a start – but I am saying that having the right frame of mind is essential if you are to properly carry out restoration work. Here are one or two traps and how to avoid them:

▲ *IN1. Whether your car is ancient or modern, remember that the stripped down parts will take up three or four times as much space off the car as they did when on it.*

Rushing to finish causes poor work, accidents and annoyance when things don't get finished on time. Turn things on their head. Tell yourself all along that you are not doing the work in order to get the job finished; you're doing it just for the sake of *doing it*, and doing it properly. If you have to stop and come back to it later, if you have to start again from scratch, if you spend days rather than hours getting something right, that's all OK. The point is that you are doing restoration work because you want to do it, right? So enjoy doing it: it'll be finished when it's done and not before.

▲ *IN2. Take your time, take photographs and make notes and sketches as you strip the car, and reassembly will be a thousand times easier. You'll also know what new parts to order, and what to have repaired by specialists, well in advance of when you need them.*

Being a perfectionist, taken literally, is just as bad. There's no such thing as perfection. The smoothest surface will be like the mountains of the moon if you look closely enough – with a microscope if necessary. (Even molecules are fairly bumpy!) Be reasonable with yourself: aim to do your best; then be happy with what you have done.

▲ *IN3. Working out of doors is OK if the weather is fine. Don't expect to be able to complete a very major project without under-cover facilities. An electricity supply is essential, too.*

Work comfortably, even out of doors when you have no alternative. Don't let your circumstances be totally inappropriate to the level of work you are aiming to carry out. I learned my motor apprenticeship in the biggest garage in the world – the roof was the sky – and I've even rebuilt bodywork and resprayed a car out there. But in terms of frustration and extra problems, I don't recommend it. Even if all you can do is rig up a temporary timber and plastic sheet shelter, I suggest you do it.

Poor tools and equipment set the wrong standards to start off with. A cheap Chinese adjustable wrench might look just as shiny as one made in Europe or the USA but it will almost certainly be tacky to handle and adjust, and will very likely break at an early age. A non-manufacturer's replacement panel will be a lot cheaper than the 'genuine' part but it will only fit where it touches and, even after you have spent many hours bringing it up to an acceptable standard, you will still know that you have fitted something below standard to your car. Use your common sense, your discretion and, while not just buying the most expensive for the sake of it, aim always to buy good quality.

Big stoppers are sometimes best worked round rather than tackled head on. You can have a stubborn nut refuse to go on to a concealed thread for what seems like hours. Walk away, drink coffee, come back and you'll find that it will either spin straight on or you'll have sussed out why not (wrong thread, weld spatter, or whatever). I have known – on more than one occasion – a notoriously difficult MGB engine refuse to slot on to the splines on a gearbox. You curse, swear, sweat, realign everything and end up convinced that someone must have added a Ford gearbox to your car while you weren't looking. Next morning, the engine slips in a treat. Why? Who knows, although it's certain that the more determined/annoyed/anxious you get, the more the problem will stand up to you instead of quietly evaporating away.

▲ *IN4. Even if you don't tackle every part of the restoration yourself, you can save a very significant sum of money by doing the labour-intensive, semi-skilled jobs.*

All hobbies and interests have to have a challenge built into them in order to make them worthwhile, and the business of restoring a classic car certainly is a fascinating challenge, no matter whether you just want to improve the car you've got or carry out a total rebuild. I have aimed to include just about all the information I could within these pages. There will always be unique and individual problems to encounter of course – that's all part of the interest of classic cars – but the idea of this book is to supply the foundations of facts and information which you can develop to suit your own particular case.

1979 when I started writing about motoring, my wife and I were still teaching, and we were also in the midst of building our own house. There was a lot of hard work in those days (there still is!) and throughout it all, Shan has been an invaluable ally and all round best pal in every way. She has also taken quite a few of the photographs that appear in this book as well as having helped with collating some of the material. My assistant Zoë Palmer has also been marvellous in organizing both me and material, and she has put in a lot of hard work on this project. So many other people have been involved in supplying help and advice over the years that the best way of thanking them has been to do so in each separate section of the book, and this I have tried to do. I hope that you, the reader, gain as much use and pleasure from this book as I have gained from my association with classic cars over the years – happy restorations! But watch out: it's habit forming!

Lindsay Porter
Bromyard, Herefordshire

▼ *IN5. There's nothing more satisfying than to enjoy a special trip in a car you've just restored yourself!*

Chapter 1
Buying & getting started

CLASSIC BUYING CHECKLIST

When it comes to choosing which model of classic car to buy, there's just one piece of advice to bear in mind before committing yourself to a particular model – DRIVE ONE FIRST! I remember a true story of a man who bought an E-type and had it restored at huge expense, using the money from a legacy. The first time he got in it he was full of excitement and drove off wearing a big smile. Half an hour later he returned with a look of abject disappointment. Stunning though it is, not even an E-type drives like a modern car. Just imagine how you would feel if you had spent years of your spare time restoring a car, only to find that you hated it! Driving a classic can be an acquired taste: you have to want to enjoy the 'olde worlde' sensation, not be cossetted as you would in the latest Fordmobile.

Other key points to bear in mind when deciding which classic to go for are:
– Was the car reliable when new? (Inherently unreliable cars don't improve with time, unlike vintage port!) Read up contemporary road tests.
– Are spares readily available? Join the appropriate club and find out.
– Do other members of your family like it? Shared enthusiasm is so much more enjoyable and enables you to spend more time on your chosen hobby.
– Do you have the skills, space, tools, cash and determination (a crucial factor!) to restore the car you have

your eye on. If not, lower your sights and buy something less demanding, in terms of work to be carried out, so that you can enjoy the car!

HOW MUCH TO PAY?

There are a number of good price guides in magazines, such as *Practical Classics* and *Classic Cars*. Sometimes they are a fair way off beam, but usually they will give you a good guide to the going rate. Compare them with actual advertisement asking prices and make an allowance for the fact that *asking* prices aren't necessarily *selling* prices.

But there is a better way to judge what cars are really selling for, if you've got the nerve. If you ring up about a car only to find that it has been sold, ask the vendor if he/she would mind giving you an idea how much these cars tend to actually sell for because it will help you to judge, etc., etc. You can't use dealers' prices as a guide because they are including their overheads – as indeed they should and must – in the asking price. On the other hand, if you find an optimistic private seller asking the same as would a local dealer, you'll know that there's something wrong! This could be an ideal candidate for a phone call two weeks later. If the car isn't sold by then, the owner will be far more likely to talk turkey!

HOW TO INSPECT A USED VEHICLE

Even if you know nothing at all about cars, use this section, or the bits of it that you feel you can cope with, to root

out the obvious no-hopers from your list. Then, if you're really keen, arrange for a local main agent to carry out an inspection for you, or ask the RAC or AA to do so. Alternatively, take someone with you who *genuinely* knows what he is talking about. It is sometimes said that there are just two things that every man will claim to be a total expert in: one of them is cars .... So if you doubt the expertise of any of your acquaintances, and you don't want to pay the cost of a full inspection, see if a mechanic from a local garage will look over a few cars for you. His (or, increasingly, her) expertise will probably just cost a few pounds an hour and will be money well spent.

STAGE ONE: Before you get heavily involved, a few quick checks will tell you whether the car is even worth considering. No matter how new or old the car, you would be best avoiding a car that has suffered heavy crash damage, and you certainly want to avoid a car that has been daubed full of filler. So:
– Catch the light down the sides, roof and bonnet of the car. Can you see any ripples in panels? (Panels that have been crash repaired usually remain rippled after the event. But not always!)
– Has the car been resprayed in a totally different colour? Check inside the door openings. (Ripples and other crash damage is easier to conceal on cars with light colours, especially white. Black, maroon and other dark coloured cars are more difficult to repair without blemishes and ripples showing.)

– Stand back from the car. Does the colour and finish of the paintwork look the same all over? Check especially that front wings and bonnet, or tailgate/boot and rear wings are the same as the doors and roof. Metallic paints are especially difficult to match properly. You must find out why any respray work has been carried out.

– Check the following for 'overspray': Sprayed paint that has clung to other bits of the car by mistake when a cheap respray is carried out; edges of windscreen rubbers, especially the corners where it is particularly difficult to persuade masking tape to 'stick'; mud flaps and tyres; door seal rubbers and chrome work; inside the engine bay, inside the front wings or even over the engine itself; inside grille apertures; on the edges of door mirrors. (Bad overspray indicates that a cheap-'n'-quick respray has been carried out. It might soon fail – frost may cause it to blister, rust might soon break through – and you may wonder (1) why it was done at all and (2) why a poor quality job has been carried out and what that tells you about the way the car has been looked after.)

– Look *very carefully* inside the engine bay and inside the boot for evidence of rippling in the metal. You will usually have to look quite low down, mainly in the vicinity of structural box-section members designed to carry the strength of the car from the ends towards the centre. They are also designed to crumple under impact. This area may still look shiny, and folds or ripples may look at first as though they should be there – check the other side of the car! Crash damage repairers often leave tell-tale signs such as these in the knowledge that most people will just look at the condition of the outer panels. You want to know more! The car may not be 'true', there might be collateral suspension damage and the car could be unsafe to drive. Walk away from these cars.

– Look at the gaps between panels. Doors with tight or wide-open gaps are a strong indication that something may be amiss. Also check bumper alignment, comparing one side of the body with the other.

STAGE TWO: If the car gets past these early stages you should start looking a little more closely. When looking at older cars, your first area of concern should be the condition of their bodywork:

– The most important structural areas are usually the sills. Check them by lifting the carpets just inside the doors and looking at the area where the outer edges of the floors join the sills. Also check the footwells, especially around the edges, whilst you are at it.

– Look inside the engine bay, if you haven't already done so, checking now for corrosion. Look especially at the tops of struts, where cars use strut-type front suspension. Check inside the boot, as well, looking at the outer edges of the boot floor, where they join rear wings/inner wings.

– Check the bottoms of wings, the 'skirts' beneath front and rear bumpers and the tops of wing panels for corrosion. Corrosion that has been filled over with filler will burst through again and be worse than virgin rust – look out for large blisters of painted filler coming loose.

– In all of these places, ensure that filler hasn't been used to 'bodge' a repair. You can usually tell with a visual check: filled surfaces often appear slightly rippled, and edges, especially where they butt up against seams, are often poorly finished. To be on the safe side *take a magnet with you*. It will 'stick' to steel but not to plastic filler.

– Other crucially important areas are beneath the car. If you don't know what you are doing in this area, or if you don't have the means to get safely beneath the car, leave the check to someone who does.

NEVER GO UNDER A CAR SUPPORTED ONLY BY A JACK! Jacks are for wheel changing only. See if you can hire the use of a local garage's hoist and, best of all if you're not an expert, have one of their mechanics look around the car with you.

– Check around spring mountings, the joints between floors and sills, all box-section 'chassis' members and anywhere that suspension components are fixed to the car's body structure.

– Check all brake pipes and hoses. None should show any signs of corrosion.

– Look at the shock absorbers. Any fluid leakage means failure.

– Is the exhaust rusty, patched or holed? For the most part, suspension checks are difficult to carry out unless you know what you are looking for, although a recent MOT should ensure that everything is OK.

– You could try 'bouncing' each corner of the car. If the shock absorbers are good, the car will not bounce up and down after you stop.

– Try jacking up each of the front wheels in turn. Spin them. A 'shot' wheel bearing will produce a graunching sound – but only if it is really quite bad!

– Try grasping each wheel with the car jacked off the ground. (Don't get under the car, in case it falls off the jack!) Push and pull each wheel, top and bottom. If there is clunking or obvious free movement, expect severe suspension or wheel bearing wear.

– Do examine each wheel very carefully. Any bulges or splits in a tyre's sidewalls mean that it will be scrap and not even fit to drive the car home safely or legally. If tyres are badly worn on one side more than the other it *might* mean that the car's tracking – easily adjustable, although the tyre may be scrap – is out of alignment, or it might indicate suspension damage, maybe from an accident.

If you are buying a classic car which needs work doing to it – and this may be an excellent way of buying your car more cheaply, provided that the work is not structural – try making the owner an offer 'subject to MOT test'. Then, you can have the car MOT tested: an inexpensive (though not necessarily complete) check on the overall condition of the car. You will also know the worst that you can expect, and you will know just what you have to do in order to make the car roadworthy. If you shop around, you will also be able to find an MOT testing garage that doesn't charge extra, or only charges a nominal amount, for re-tests, but do check on the time limit between tests.

MECHANICAL COMPONENTS

The mechanical components are the least vital part of the car in many ways! You can buy parts for most modern classics at a sufficiently low price to make almost anything repairable at low cost, while 'consumable' items such as shock absorbers, clutches and brake parts can still quite often be bought at low cost from motorist shops or, at worst, from your one-make club. Imported cars can sometimes be an exception to this rule.

Some mechanical checks are best carried out with the engine cold, and there are some tell-tale signs that you can look for without even hearing the engine running.

– Before starting up, remove the oil filler cap and take a look inside. Grey sludge around the cap is a certain indicator that the engine is on its last legs.
– Pull out the dipstick. Is the oil level very low? Is the oil a dirty black and does it feel gritty between finger and thumb? (*Not* a well maintained car!) Does it have droplets of water on it? (If so, this spells big problems – probably a blown head gasket! Or worse, a cracked block or head!)
– Check inside the radiator cap (**ONLY if the engine is cold!**). Do you see a pleasant colour of anti-freeze? Good! Do you see rust? Bad! Do you see droplets of oil? Disastrous! (See previous paragraph.)
– Start the car and note whether the starter motor sounds lively or whether it is struggling to keep up. These days, a new battery won't come much cheaper than some brands of overhauled starter motor for the most popular, modern classics! Then, when the engine is running, let checks commence!

– Undo and remove the oil filler cap again. (N.B. Overhead camshaft engines spray oil around in *copious* quantities. Ensure that you don't get covered if the filler cap is in the camshaft cover!) If you can feel, hear and see oil mist chugging out, the engine bores are badly worn. You will also certainly see smoke from the exhaust (see later).
– Does the oil pressure warning light flicker with the engine cold? (If so, low oil pressure is likely and an engine rebuild could be near.)
– Bonnet open. Does the 'top' of the engine rattle on start up? (Mechanical tappets could be out of adjustment, or hydraulic tappets worn. Not likely to be expensive in the case of mechanical tappets but, if the rattle continues after the first 30 seconds or so and the car keeps rattling, a more expensive replacement camshaft may be called for.)
– Rev the engine. Does it rattle in a deep, growly way, from low down in the engine? If so, the big end and/or main bearings are gone and it's time for a replacement engine.
– Go to the back of the car. You'll probably see steam, especially in colder weather, and even water dripping out. This is no problem, although it should go away after the car has been driven, except in really cold weather. Rev the engine, hard and several times, blipping the throttle. If you see anything from puffs to clouds of *black* smoke (as opposed to *grey* steam), you have another indication that the engine is on the slippery slope.

STATIC 'RUNNING' CHECKS

You can't always take a test drive, and if the car is cheap enough and desirable enough, you may be prepared to put up with that. However, the price would have to be *very* right because there are always more fish in the sea. But there are certain simulations that you can try out in the driveway:

– If the drive is a few yards long, slip the car into first gear, then into reverse and move it as far as you can. Do

gears 'grind' badly? Is the clutch stiff? Does the gearchange shift OK? Is the steering wheel or seat loose (ideal time to find out, as you shift your position and push down on the clutch)? Does the brake pedal feel spongy and head for the floorboards? (If you find lots of problems at this stage then, oh dear, you *have* got problems!)

– Pull on the handbrake, put the car into second gear, rev the engine a little and slip the clutch. Does the handbrake work? Does the clutch slip without showing signs of moving the car?
– As the car moves back and forth, try turning the steering as far as possible this way and that. Does it have any tight spots, or is there a lot of free play or are there graunching sounds? (Worn steering rack or steering box.) Does the steering column move from side to side, or is the wheel so loose that you can move it up and down? (Worn column bushes – not expensive but an MOT failure and possibly a few hours work)

Far more can be determined by driving the car on the open road, however.

INTERIOR CHECKS

Disregard this part of the car and you could end up hating it! When a car is running well and looking fairly sound, you forget about its functional qualities. But if the car is fundamentally uncomfortable, it will become your enemy. Be sure to check each of the following:

– Examine the carpets: If they're wet, water is probably leaking in somewhere, unless someone has been getting in with snow on their boots! One of the world's most irritating occurrences is to have a leak that drips cold water on to your accelerator leg – it's *always* that leg. The second most is when you turn the heater on and the water *inside* the car evaporates, then condenses on the windscreen so that you can't see where you are going. Water coming around a windscreen seal can often easily be cured if the car is newish. If it's oldish, it is likely that the screen surround steelwork has corroded, making chances of a repair-in-a-tube just about nil, and requiring some major, awkward and expensive welding repair work. Alternatively, water ingressing from beneath suggests that the car's lower structure has as much future as an old car park ticket. Take water leaks seriously! An alternative source of water leaks is the heater radiator (invariably well hidden from view) or the heater piping or screenwashers. The heater can be expensive and tricky to replace.

- Examine the seats. Rips can be a pain, although they are not impossible. Do realize that they will invariably get much worse, and finding the right replacements for the more unusual cars could be impossible. Check especially for sagged seats. If your knees come up as your backside goes down, the seat springing has sprung its last. Feel underneath. If you observe the remnants of Pirelli webbing strips, replacement is slightly fiddly but relatively cheap: if there's a split membrane or sheet of rubber, finding replacements might be impossible. Check with specialist suppliers.

- Look at the headlining. Can you live with rips or severe discoloration? If it's there, that is more or less what you will have to do because it's almost impossible to clean easily and replacement is usually the sort of job that drives strong men to drink. If the car you're really keen on has scrap headlining, obtain a quote from a trimmer before going ahead.

- Take a *close* look at seat belts and mountings. Pull on inertia reel types – they should lock up when you tug hard – and check that buckles click shut and come free easily. Replacements can be expensive.

- Check that the heater works properly. On a sunny day in June, you forget how damned miserable life can be on a cold spring day when the heater doesn't function! Check that the heater controls turn the tap on *and* off; that the controls direct air where you want it (especially, does the demister work?); that the heater gets really hot when on full; and that the fan works. You will want them all to

function properly, as on some cars repair can be very time-consuming, tricky and expensive, especially on more up-market cars.

You can be sure that the seller already knows about 'odd' faults and things that don't work. He/she probably also knows how much it will cost to put them right – could this be why they are selling? To be safe, don't accept lame excuses when things don't work! If things are *so* easy to fix, why haven't they been done already?

OTHER EXPENSES SPARED

Take time to check every accessory and electrical fitting on the car. If it's fitted with a radio set, ensure that it works and that it is included with the price. If you forget to check that the reversing light works, the car might fail the MOT test. Repair could conceivably require a new lamp unit, if the old one has corroded, or replacement of a particularly difficult to reach switch on the gearbox. Or you might even need to call in an auto-electrician if there is a more awkward fault. On the other hand, it might just be a bulb.

- With the help of an assistant, check every item of lighting on the car to ensure that all the lamps illuminate as they should. If a fuse has blown it is important that you know why – it could be because there is a serious and potentially dangerous 'short' somewhere.

- Methodically go through every switch on the dash, the column controls and the centre console. Open every cubby hole and check that everything functions properly.

- Check door seals for bad wear: They are surprisingly expensive to replace!

- Don't forget to check the condition of the spare wheel, the condition (and existence!) of the jack and toolkit and, while you're at it, the state of the spare wheel well or spare wheel carrier.

- Open and close all of the windows and sunroof. (Also look for stains around the sunroof aperture – they can leak unremittingly!) All should function smoothly, without forcing and without grinding noises. Electric windows and central locking should be checked particularly carefully because

repair/replacement costs can be high! All of this seems like a huge amount to go through, but it is well worth it when you bear in mind the expense you will be committing yourself to and the potential for problems if you make a bad purchase. And do remember that, with a private sale, you can buy at the best prices, but you can't take it back if you make a mistake!

Finally, but perhaps most important of all, make sure that the person who is selling you the car actually owns it!

- Ask to see the Registration Document. If it's not available it could be that the 'owner' has (a) lost it; (b) has it but it doesn't show the 'owner's' name because he/she is a trader masquerading as a private seller; (c) he/she does not have title to the car because it is leased or for some other reason that means the car doesn't properly belong to the seller. If you can't see the Registration Document, *walk away!* Or at the very least, ask to see the owner's original purchase receipt, and check that the car is owned by the 'owner' rather than subject to a Hire Purchase agreement. Your local Citizens Advice Bureau (see telephone directory) should be able to check it out on your behalf.

N.B. If you pay for a car that is subsequently found to belong to someone else, you will lose the car as well as having lost your money!

BUYER'S CHECKLIST

If you want to be as sure as you reasonably can about the condition of your chosen classic car, the following checklist should be taken with you on your car hunt, and the car or cars at the top of your list should be examined with a fine-tooth comb. The following sequence doesn't claim to be totally exhaustive. The only way you can find out key information on any particular model of car is to talk to a specialist about 'your' chosen model of car's trouble spots.

Checking over a prospective purchase can be, and should be, very time consuming if the 'right' car is to be bought rather than a glossed-over heap of trouble. What follows is an elimination sequence in three separate parts, each one taking longer and being more thorough than the last – this approach having the virtue of saving the purchaser both time and embarrassment. It is always easier to withdraw at an early stage than after an hour spent checking the car over with the aid of the owner's comments and mugs of coffee! Thus, Stage A aims to eliminate the obvious 'nails' without having to probe too deeply. Stage B takes matters somewhat further for cars that pass the first stage, while Stage C is the 'dirty hands' stage, the one you don't get into on a snowy February evening unless you are really serious.

TOOL BOX

Old, warm clothes (if the ground is cold); an old mat or a board if the ground is wet; a bright torch; a pair of ramps; a screwdriver or other probe; copies of the following pages and a notepad and pencil; a bottle, trolley or scissors jack and axle stands.

Safety: Safety should be carefully considered and any necessary steps taken. In particular, when inspecting a car don't forget safety. NEVER rely on the handbrake to hold a car that is on a slope or up on ramps. Ensure that the wheels are chocked when using jacks or ramps. Use axle stands if you have to inspect the underside of a car. Do not use a naked flame or smoke when inspecting the underside of a car. Wear goggles when lying on your back beneath a car, poking at body and components above.

USING THE CHECKLIST

The checklist is designed to show step-by-step instructions for virtually all the checks to be made on a car offered for sale. After each check, the fault indicated is shown in brackets. For example, the instruction: 'Look along wings, door bottoms, wheel arches and sills from front to rear of car' is followed by the fault, shown in brackets, as (Ripples indicate filler presence/crash damage. £££). The pound sterling signs require some explanation. They are

intended to give a guide to the cost of rectifying the fault if it exists. '£' indicates that the cost is likely to be less than the cost of a new tyre, '£££' stands for the cost of a new set of tyres, or more, while '££' means that the cost is likely to be between the two. The cost guide relates to the cost of the component(s) only, other than in the case of bodywork – allow more if you have the work done for you.

When examining a car you are advised to take this book (or copies of the relevant buying checklists) and a notebook with you. As each item is checked, a record can be kept in the notebook. You may wish to record a running cost total for necessary repairs as faults are discovered – this could be a useful bargaining tool at the end of your examination.

It is strongly recommended that the repair and restoration sections of this book, a copy of a Haynes *Guide to Purchase and DIY Restoration* for your car (see Chapter 2, Section 1) and also the Haynes *Owners' Workshop Manual* relevant to the car you are examining so that you are fully familiar with every component being checked.

STAGE A – FIRST IMPRESSIONS

1 Is the car 'square' to the ground and are bonnet, bumper, grille, door to hinge-pillar gaps even and level? [Closed-up door gaps and rippled front wings usually indicate poorly repaired crash damage – £££+] ☐

2 Look along wings, door bottoms, wheel arches and sills from the front and rear of the car. [Ripples indicate filler presence – £££] ☐

3 Check quality of chromework, especially bumpers, where appropriate. [Dents, dings and rust ££] ☐

4 Turn on all lights, indicators and reversing lights and check that they work. [Sidelights/marker lights rust in their sockets – ££]
Rear license/number plate lamps earthing/grounding problems plus other specific component problems. ☐

5 'Bounce' each corner of the car. Worn shock absorbers cause the corners to feel springy and bounce up and down. [Each damper – £] ☐

6 Check visually for rust – gain an overall impression at this stage. [From cosmetic to dire! – £ to £££+] (See following sections.) ☐

7 Check for parking damage to areas above and below bumpers, front and rear. [Damage ££ to £££] ☐

8 Examine general condition of interior at-a-glance. [Rips, dirt, parts missing. [££ or £££] ☐

9 Check fit of both bumpers. [Accident damage – possibly £££] ☐

10 Quality of paintwork. Does it shine when dry? Are there scratches beneath the shine? Is it chipped? [Neglect and poor-quality, cover-job respray – £££] ☐

11 Does the seller and his/her surroundings look like those of someone who is likely to have maintained his/her car? [Maintenance – £££] ☐

STAGE B – CLEAN HANDS!

If a car doesn't match up to requirements after Stage A, don't be tempted – reject it! There are always more cars to be seen. Stage B decreases the risk of making a mistake without even getting your hands too dirty!

Check hard for body corrosion in all the places shown below. Use a magnet to ensure that no filler is present – magnets will only 'stick' to steel. (Obviously this doesn't apply to those cars with aluminium or fibreglass bodywork.) Work carefully and methodically.

BODYWORK

1 Front apron, beneath grille. [Accident damage, corrosion, cheap repair – ££] ☐

2 Front wing, headlamp area.
[Corrosion; filler – £££ if severe] ☐

3 Lower front wing – continuation of sill line. [Corrosion; filler; damage – £££ if severe because hidden corrosion indicated] ☐

4 Tops of front wings and area around scuttle/dash pan. [Filler – £££] ☐

5 Sills. [Corrosion; filler; damage – £££ to replace] ☐

6 Door bottoms. [Corrosion; filler – ££ or £££] ☐

7 Door skins – outer panel. [Corrosion; filler – ££] ☐

8 If the car is open-topped, measure door fit along the rear, vertical edges. [Open at bottom, closed at top means sagging bodywork – virtually terminal – £££+] ☐

9 Rear wheel arch. [Corrosion; filler – £££] ☐

10 Open door. Lift up and down and note 'looseness'. [Hinge wear – £. Corroded door – £££] ☐

11 Check the area along the length of any chrome trim strip and finishings. [Corrosion around trim clips. Unless severe, usually cosmetic – £] ☐

12 Check the bottom corners of the windscreen apertures. [Corrosion – £££] ☐

13 Fibreglass bodywork. Check for star crazing – deep damage requiring more than just filling over – and for cracks and splits, especially around hinges, door/bonnet/boot shut points and wing/bonnet/boot top. [Repair – £££] Also for chassis corrosion where fibreglass is bonded on top. [Repair – mega-£££!] ☐

14 Aluminium bodywork. Corrosion where the aluminium touches steel panels or chassis. [Major structural repairs needed – £££] ☐

INTERIOR

1 Examine seat and backrest. [Worn, thin or split covers: leather – £££; cloth/plastic – ££] ☐

2 Tip seat forward on two-door cars. Check for damage. [Scuffing and tears: leather – £££; cloth/plastic – ££] ☐

3 Check dash. [Cracks, tears or scratches. 'Wrong' instruments – £ to £££] ☐

4 Check condition and cleanliness of headlining. [From £ if dirty to £££ for replacement] ☐

5 Examine steering wheel/gearknob. [Correct parts fitted? – £/££] ☐

6 Test inertia reel seat belts for looseness, fraying, correct operation. [Should hold when tugged sharply – £ to ££] ☐

7 Check door trim and door/window handles. [Wear and scuffing at bottoms, buckling of hardboard backing, broken handles – £ to ££, if parts available] ☐

8 Ensure that the seats fold forward (two-door cars), that the 'paddle' allows different backrest positions (where fitted) and that they slide and lock. [Failure to slide easily, especially on the driver's side, is sometimes an indication that the floor is corroded – £££] ☐

9 Wind both windows up and down – there should be no restriction. [Usually lack of lubrication – £] ☐

10 Is rear parcel shelf there (hatchback cars) and in good condition? [££ for trimmer to remake/purchase replacement] ☐

MECHANICAL

Ask owner to start up engine. Let it idle – thorough warming-up takes quite a while on the road – this will help. Does he/she leave it to idle on choke? Harmful practice!

1 Pull and push the steering wheel and attempt to lift and lower at right angles to steering column. [Clunking indicates: wear in column bush, loose column connections – £. Wear in steering column U/J – £] ☐

2 Pull bonnet release. Is it stiff? [Seized mechanism or cable.– £] ☐

3 Open bonnet. Check for non-standard air cleaners, rocker cover, etc. [If originality is important – £ to ££] ☐

6 Check engine/engine bay for general cleanliness and presence of oil. [Leaking gasket/lack of detail care – probably £] ☐

7 Listen to the engine. If top-end tapping it could be anything from tappet adjustment to 'shot' camshaft. Bottom-end rumble; timing chain tinkle – worn engine. [Timing chain and sprockets – ££. Worn crank – £££+] ☐

8 Is paint peeling around clutch/brake cylinders? [Carelessly spilt fluid strips paint – £ plus time; leaking cylinders – ££] ☐

STOP ENGINE AND LEAVE IT TO COOL DOWN.

9 Remove radiator cap SLOWLY with rag and beware of spurting, scalding water. Inspect coolant level and its general cleanliness. (Orange indicates rust and a long time since it has been changed. Check for oil on top of water. Remove dipstick. Check for water droplets in oil. [Head gasket problems – probably £££] ☐

CHECK MANUAL FOR SPECIFIC CAR'S SAFETY REQUIREMENTS: HOT WATER MAY BOIL AND 'BLOW' OUT AS PRESSURE IS REMOVED!

10 Remove engine oil filler cap. Look for yellow or brown slimy sludge, or foaming. [Severe bore/valve guide wear – £££] Look for white foaming or 'goo' inside cap. [Faulty ELC (Evaporative Loss Control system) where fitted – £]

11 Inspect the fins of the radiator. [Exchange radiator – ££ to £££]

12 Examine engine mountings, if visible, for signs of previous removal. [Engine removal is not necessarily a bad thing, but it would be interesting to know why!]

13 Jack both front wheels off the ground together. Turn steering wheel from lock-to-lock. [Roughness indicates wear in steering rack or mechanism. Replacement or overhaul – ££ to £££]

ROAD TEST
Only carry out the following tests on traffic- and pedestrian-free roads. Keep a constant look-out for other road users.

If you (the tester) are driving, ensure adequate insurance cover. Otherwise, simulate the following tests with the owner driving.

1 Start up. Is starter noisy on engagement? [Worn starter dog – £; or worn starter – ££ to £££]

2 Is it difficult to engage first gear? [Worn clutch and/or worn selector mechanism – £££]

Drive for three or four miles to become familiar with the car and to warm the engine.

3 Drive at 30 mph. Brake gently to a halt. (a): Does car 'pull' to one side? (b): Do brakes rub or grind? [(a): worn pads or shoes – £; seized callipers – ££. (b): worn pads or shoes – £, but more if discs or drums are ruined.]

4 Drive at 30 mph in 3rd gear. Apply, then release, accelerator four or five times. Listen for transmission 'clunk'. [Worn universal joint – £; worn differential – £££; worn halfshaft/driveshaft – ££; worn wire wheel splines (when fitted) – ££]

5 Drive at 40 mph. Lift off accelerator. Listen for differential whine. [Worn differential – £££ if severe or unbearably noisy.]

6 Accelerate hard in 2nd gear to 40 mph, then lift off. Listen for engine knocking. [Worn engine bearings – £££] Also ...

7 ... does gearbox jump out of gear? [Worn internal selector mechanism – £]

8 Drive as in 6 and 7 above, but lift off in third gear. Does gearbox jump out of gear? [Worn internal selector mechanism – £]

9 Drive at 50 mph in fourth gear and change into third gear. Does gearbox 'crunch'? [Worn synchromesh – £; faulty/worn clutch – ££]

10 Drive at 30 mph in third gear and change into second gear. Does gearbox 'crunch'? [Worn synchromesh – £; faulty/worn clutch – ££]

11 Do front wheels flutter or shake at 40 mph? [Wheels out of balance – £; worn front suspension – ££ to £££]

12 Check that road conditions are suitable. With ratchet knob or button depressed (don't let it go!) pull the handbrake on whilst travelling at 10 mph maximum. Don't risk a skid! (If the car pulls to one side it means a faulty handbrake on that side (see 20 below) [If handbrake has no discernible effect, rear brakes probably oiled or worn – ££]

13 In second gear at about 30 mph accelerate hard, then decelerate hard – don't brake. (If car veers to left or right, a rear wheel drive car's rear axle may be loose, or the springs are faulty or subframe mountings (front or rear wheel drive cars) are loose, soft or corroded. [New axle U-bolts – £; new rear springs – ££; mountings £ to £££++ if bad corrosion] Also, check tyre pressure and tyre types.

14 When stationary, operate the brake pedal. Apply light pressure in repeated strokes. [If the pedal slowly works its way to the floor – even over a period of a minute – the master cylinder may be faulty. Dangerous fault! – ££]

15 Accelerate from about 1000 rpm in top gear, full throttle. [Pinking/spark knock probably indicates maladjusted timing and this can cause piston damage over a long period – ££ or £££]

16 At highway speeds, climb a slight hill with a very light throttle. [Hesitation, coughing, snapping or spitting indicates an over-lean carburettor setting, which can cause valve damage over a long period – ££]

17 Does automatic gearbox 'clunk' heavily going into 'Drive' or does it change up and down very slowly/lazily? [Clogged filter, low oil level – £ unless damage has occurred. Worse faults: investigate! – up to £££+, although not that common.]

18 Stop car. Apply parking brake firmly. Engage second gear. Gently let out clutch – but depress again as soon as car shows any signs of distress. [If car pulls away: worn rear brakes.– £; oil in brake drum – ££. If car remains stationary but engine continues to run – worn clutch – ££+]

BOOT/TRUNK INSPECTION

1   Is the spare tyre inflated and with a good tread? [Replacement – £ (obviously!)] ☐

2   Does the jack work? [Replacement – £, or lubrication.] ☐

3   Is there a key for the boot/trunk lock? [Replacement key if right number can be found, or even replacement lock – £] ☐

4   Does the boot (trunk) light illuminate – if fitted? [Switch, bulb or wiring fault – £] ☐

5   Is the door key the same as the ignition key? [Ask why, if not. Can be inconvenient!] ☐

STAGE C – DIRTY HANDS

This is the level at which the car – by now being seriously considered – is given the sort of checks that make as sure as possible that there are no serious hidden faults which could still make the purchaser change his or her mind. It might also throw up a few minor faults to use as bargaining points with the seller!

While Stage A took only a minute or so and Stage B took quite a while longer, Stage C involves a lot more time, inconvenience and effort. But if you want to be sure, it's the most vital stage of all. **Safety: Ensure that wheels are chocked when using jacks or ramps. NEVER go under a car supported only by a jack.**

1   Jack rear wheels off ground, one at a time. Grasp wheel, twist sharply back and forth – listen for 'clunks'. If wire wheels fitted, do wheels move relative to brake drum? [Worn splines on hubs/wheels – £££; otherwise worn differential – £££] ☐

2   Jack up front wheel at wishbone, partially compressing front suspension. Spin wheel and listen for roughness in wheel bearings. [Imminent wheel bearing failure – £ to ££] ☐

3   Grip roadwheel top and bottom – ensure car weight cannot fall on to your hand – and rock in the vertical plane. [Play indicates: wear in wire wheel splines – £££; wear in wheel bearing – £; wear in kingpin or suspension joints (see manual) – ££ to £££] ☐

4   From beneath car, examine rear of rear brake drums and insides of wheels for oil contamination. [Failed oil seal/block differential breather – £] ☐

5   Lift carpets, check floor for rusting, particularly adjacent to inner sills in footwell. [Significant corrosion – possibly £££] ☐

6   Feel inside front inner wings for corrosion, especially at front and rear. [Severe corrosion – £££] ☐

7   Remove mud, if present, from around rear spring hangers. Probe for presence of corrosion with screwdriver. [Significant corrosion – £££] ☐

8   Examine and probe around inside of rear wheel arches and area inside boot/trunk in line with rear wheels. [Corrosion – £££] ☐

9   Sniff around fuel tank from beneath and look for evidence of fuel staining, especially from front of tank and from around the sender unit. Tanks usually corrode from above, from outside. [Replacement – ££ to £££] ☐

10   Probe around jacking point(s), chassis sections and under-sill areas with a screwdriver. Check visually for distorted jack points and supports and general corrosion. [Severe corrosion – £££] ☐

11   Examine insides of front apron, particularly at ends. [Corrosion – ££] ☐

12   Examine insides of rear apron, particularly at ends. [Corrosion – ££] ☐

13   Inspect the engine for oil leaks. N.B. There will almost invariably be some with an older car!

    Front seal on timing chain cover. [£] ☐

    Rear seal. Leaking oil usually comes through gearbox bellhousing drain hole. (Sometimes a gearbox oil leak is to blame. Both require engine and/or gearbox removal, depending on model). [£] ☐

    Side covers – tappet inspection plates – on side of engine. [£] ☐

    Around the oil filter. [Spin-on canisters can come loose as can bolt-mounted type. Badly fitted rubber seal on bolt-mounted type – £] ☐

    Camshaft/rocker cover on top of engine. [£] ☐

14   Examine the rear axle for oil leakage and oil thrown onto the body. [Slight leakage not uncommon. Heavy leakage suggests a faulty seal, clogged vent or overfilled differential casing – £] ☐

15   Grasp each shock absorber in turn and twist and shake. [Worn bushes, linkages or shock-absorbers – £ each] ☐

16   Look for evidence of grease on grease points. [Lack of servicing – £ to £££] ☐

17   Condition of exhaust system and exhaust mountings. [Replacement exhaust – ££ or £££] ☐

18   Check brake discs for deep scoring. [Replacement or reground discs – £ to ££] ☐

19 Check the insides (as well as outsides) of each tyre for bulges, cracks or splits, and the wheel rims for damage. Also, check older alloy wheels for obvious cracks around stud holes or rim. [£ to £££] ☐

20 Check visually from above the condition of the battery, and look at the battery mountings from below. [New battery/batteries – £ to ££; corroded mountings – ££ to £££] ☐

21 Determine the free play of the clutch pedal. [If more than an inch or so, the clevis pin in the pedal/master cylinder pushrod is worn – £] N.B. Springs should usually be attached to both pedals. Move the pedals from side to side. [More than slight movement indicates worn pedal bushes, or the bolt holding the pedals is loose – £] ☐

22 Check the steering wheel for excessive free play by attempting to rotate it lightly with the car stationary and the front wheels on the ground. Normally, more than one to two inches at the circumference of the wheel is excessive (check manual). [Severe wear in steering mechanism – £££] ☐

BUYING A STATIC CLASSIC

In an ideal world, buying a classic car would be a pleasurable experience. The vendor's honesty would be overwhelming, a few happy hours could be spent examining the car (in brilliant sunshine of course, with the added advantage of all the workshop facilities most of us can only dream about), and an extended test drive at the wheel of our prospective purchase would be the very least we could expect. We would negotiate a price and drive off, sunset behind us and Blandings Castle to the right, secure in the knowledge that we had bought a classic bargain.

Life's not like that, of course. There are pitfalls when buying *any* used car, multiplied many times in the case of a 'classic' – a prime target for the attentions of the fill-'em-and-spray-'em brigades that can still be found lurking in many a back street.

For many, though, buying a 'classic' involves looking at a car that, for one reason or another, cannot be driven on the open road; it may not be MOT'd and taxed, it may be a non-runner, it may be in need of restoration or it may be at an auction.

Whichever category it falls into, the car you're looking at requires extra careful examination if you are to avoid being taken advantage of, although the difference between a genuine car and a lemon can be no more than paint deep. Remember to take along with you a healthy dose of scepticism.

Under these circumstances, it's still possible to make a thorough examination of the bodywork and chassis of the vehicle, but everything else requires a different set of examination priorities. Buyer beware!

HOMEWORK
Before going to view any car, irrespective of its condition, take heed of this advice – *do your homework*! It will pay dividends if you turn up to view a car armed with a head, or a notebook, full of facts and figures about that particular make and model. In fact, it pays to read as much about it as you possibly can. If there's time, you might like to obtain copies of old or reprinted road tests, but more important is the need to read as many buying guides as possible. Most of the classic car magazines offer a back-issues service and will be happy to supply details of when (and if!) they ran a buying guide on the make and model you're interested in.

In addition, the Haynes *Guides to Purchase & DIY Restoration*, written by 'Yours Truly', and the excellent MRP *Collectors' Guides* give full model-by-model details of what to look for. They're all an excellent investment when you compare the cost of a book with the cost of a car – or an unexpected restoration!

It is always a good idea to contact a club or specialist before you even think about viewing a car. They will confirm the major problem areas to look for but, more important, they will also give you an idea of the price of some of the spares that may well be needed. Take a note of some prices, making the list as comprehensive as you can. It should cover as broad a range as possible, from body panels like front wings, sills, doorskins and so on, to obvious mechanical items like clutch, steering box, trackrod ends and track control arms, brake shoes and pads, gaskets, dynamos and alternators, starter motors, general service items and so on. Armed with all this information, you're ready to join the fray!

BODYWORK
Whether or not a vehicle can be driven on the road is broadly irrelevant when inspecting its bodywork. Try to find out as much as possible about the car's history, though, and bear this in mind when examining the car. If you're told that 'your' car has been stored for years, you may well find it to be in surprisingly sound condition ... but don't depend on it! Even stored in a garage a car can carry on rusting (the condensation and humidity found in many garages will simply encourage any rust already present to continue its process of gradual disintegration!) So, check carefully for the usual signs of rust and rot.

The same applies to the underside of the vehicle, whether it has a separate chassis or is of monocoque construction, and so you must be prepared to don your dirty clothes and crawl underneath. There is little point in going into minute detail here about the major 'rot-spots' to examine, for they are exactly the same as if a vehicle is on the road and can be test-driven. On a car with a separate chassis, whether it's a '60s Triumph Herald or a '30s Morris Eight, it is essential to thoroughly examine the chassis for signs of rot – often easier said than done, for the top of the chassis is invariably hidden from view and can be disguising all sorts of potential problems. It's best to adopt the iceberg principle.

For all the rot you can see there will be 90 per cent that you can't. With a monocoque construction, many of the outer panels are structural and should be examined with great care.

Check everywhere for signs of corrosion, paying particular attention to any areas that are notorious for rot on that particular model. If spares availability for 'your' model is impressive and you have both the equipment and the skill to carry out your own welding, then it's up to you to decide how much importance to place on the condition of body panels. As long as the structure and inner panels of the car are solid and generally free from corrosion, you may not object to having to replace some panelwork ... but do be realistic about your own limitations, in terms of both talent and time! If an MG Midget, MGB or MGB GT is the order of the day, it will inevitably be less expensive and easier to purchase a brand new Heritage bodyshell if you are planning a complete restoration. For the rest of us, it is essential that we know our respective spares situation inside out to avoid much heartache later.

Checking out a car at an auction can be physically awkward. While most classic car auctions leave a fair amount of space round each vehicle to enable it to be fully examined, the same cannot be said for the more mundane, 'everyday' auctions that take place in many major towns and cities. If you're fortunate enough to find an interesting or 'classic' vehicle at such an event, you must be prepared for *very* cramped conditions in which it will be extraordinarily difficult to carry out a proper bodywork and underside check. If you can't carry out a satisfactory inspection, don't be tempted to ignore this fact and jump in at the deep end; you must never rely on first impressions only, and the best advice is to leave well alone unless you've got lots of time and space to inspect the vehicle thoroughly. And the old rule about never getting carried away at auctions still applies – decide a maximum price that you'd be willing to pay for a particular car and *stick to it*!

However, you *might* find that the rules applicable to the auction you are attending may work in your favour. Sometimes, at local auctions, you are entitled to a one-hour 'guarantee' period. This might enable you to carry out a road-test later. But check! *Is* there such a 'guarantee' period? An hour from when? And does it work in practice, without unbelievable hassle? Check with the auctioneer's office.

ENGINE

When you can't drive a prospective purchase, its examination now starts to get rather more tricky.

If the car is a runner, then the situation isn't too bad, except that you won't be able to fully 'warm up' the engine and gearbox. Start the engine and carry out the usual checks. Note whether the engine starts easily; and have someone standing at the back of the car to report on any excesses of blue smoke (which may indicate worn piston rings and a full engine strip-down and rebuild – or it could be worn valve guides, or perhaps just valve stem seals. Play safe; assume the worst! It is often a good idea to ask the owner himself to start the engine for you, so that you can see his starting 'habits'. Check whether he lets the engine idle on choke for long, as this can be harmful and an indication that the car has been somewhat mistreated, albeit unintentionally.

Even without moving the car, having it running can tell you much about the state of its engine. It is advisable before starting the engine, however, that you remove the radiator cap and check the colour of the coolant. An orange colour suggests rust in the system and a long time since the coolant and antifreeze (if there is any!) were changed. Check, too, for oil in the water (and, for that matter, water in the oil by checking the dipstick) which inevitably means head gasket problems – expensive to rectify if the head itself is also damaged.

When starting, does the engine turn over very slowly? This could be caused by a worn starter motor, tired battery or poor electrical connections. Listen carefully for any clues about the state of the engine. A top-end tapping sound

could mean tappet wear; a bottom-end rumble can indicate crank wear; and a front-end 'tinkle' may mean a worn timing chain. All these problems could be expensive to put right and will inevitably result in major engine work and a rebuild in due course. Check for these faults while varying the revs of the engine and make sure that a reasonable tickover can be achieved. If not, you may need to invest in a carburettor overhaul. With somebody else operating the accelerator, listen for the above faults with the bonnet open.

Don't forget the obvious tell-tales of oil pressure and water temperature gauges. Oil pressure that drops off *badly* as the engine warms usually spells serious trouble – but not with every engine (this is where a good buyer's guide comes in). A water temperature gauge that resolutely stays low could suggest a missing thermostat – which should lead you to ask why! Is it because a blocked radiator led to overheating and thermostat removal. An overheating engine could be worse. It might be a stuck thermostat, or a leaky radiator cap, but the wise buyer is a pessimistic old owl. Assume a blowing head gasket (i.e. a damaged head and/or block face).

While in the underbonnet area, check for general cleanliness. Freshly cleaned engines can tell some fascinating tales. Is the engine an unreformed oiler, a lapsed member of Oilers Anonymous? Look for dribbles around rocker box or camshaft gaskets, oozes around front oil seal/timing chain cover and drops at the oil filter. And if the engine is not incontinent it could *appear* to be incompetent. A freshly cleaned engine may miss and splutter because of no more than moisture in the distributor cap introduced when the engine was washed off. If you're feeling brave you'll bid where others stand back or better still, take a look first.

Be on the lookout, too, for corrosion in the engine bay – on the bulkhead, inner wings and front panel and on the engine ancillaries themselves: rocker cover, radiator, air cleaner and so on. These latter items are not crucial but will give an indication of how much use the car has had in recent years and how well it has been stored if it hasn't been used. While carrying out these checks, it is worthwhile looking for any non-original parts (special air filter or a different carburettor, for instance) which again may provide indications of the sort of use and driving styles the vehicle has endured over the years.

The age-old advice about buying within your means is all the more important with a car that you aren't able to try. That doesn't just include purchase price but potential troubles too. You may be able to afford to buy an old Jaguar XJ12 instead of the immaculate Morris Minor you've had your eye on, but a replacement engine for the former will mean *big* money!

If the car you're looking at has been standing for a long time and is a non-runner, you'll be relying heavily on Lady Luck! You should buy such a vehicle only if it represents *outstanding* value for money (bearing in mind that it may need a lot spending on it mechanically, basically because the state of the mechanicals will be so unknown) or if the bodywork and underside are in exceptional condition, or if the thing is so rare that you simply can't resist!

Assuming that you're fortunate enough to be able to spend a considerable amount of time checking an 'as-found' old car, don't be tempted just to fit a new battery and plugs and then try starting the engine. Remove the spark plugs, pour a releasing agent into the engine via the plug holes and leave for a week. Then, with battery charged and spark plugs still out, crank the engine on the starter until the oil pressure comes up on the gauge or the warning light goes out. You can now replace the plugs and start up, secure in the knowledge that bearings are well lubricated. Then, if the car has been standing for years, replace the petrol or jury-rig a (safe!) temporary supply. Old, smelly petrol won't allow the engine to start or run. It's at this stage that you'll begin to get an idea of the state of the engine. You can carry out all the usual checks, but don't be surprised if the engine starts, ticks over, but hates being

asked to pick up revs. Try the cheap option of changing the condenser before assuming a major fault.

GENERAL MECHANICALS

Obvious underbonnet checks that apply to any vehicle should be adopted (with even greater thoroughness!) with a car that's off the road. Check all the fluid levels (oil, water, brake and clutch fluid, battery level and so on) to give an idea of how well-maintained the car has been. Remove the oil filler cap and check for yellow or brown slimy sludge or foaming inside the cap – this possibly indicating severe bore or valve guide wear.

With one end of the car carefully supported on axle stands (*never* crawl underneath a vehicle that's simply lifted on a jack) and, with the other wheels securely 'chocked', have a good look underneath for signs of general wear and tear. This is not as foolproof a method as being able to test drive the vehicle as well, but you can still check for such potential problems as worn track rod ends, track control arms, wheel bearings, steering box and components, prop. shaft universal joints (insert a screwdriver between them and lever), holed exhaust and silencer ... and, of course, you should have another very careful look at the general condition of the underside and its structural box sections and crossmembers.

Having studied all the potential areas of trouble, you should work out roughly how much they will cost to put right ... taking into account the price of parts and labour, even if you intend to do the work yourself. It is wise to include a price for labour in any approximate costs, because restoration and maintenance work always works out more expensive than you first anticipate, and it is essential to cover all eventualities. As mentioned earlier, you should always do your homework before going to see a car.

With the car still on axle stands (or even over an inspection pit if the vendor has one), continue the 'check, check and check again' process. I cannot over-emphasize the importance of this, for you won't have the obvious advantage

of being able to test drive the vehicle and consequently pick up all sorts of indications as to its general condition and driving 'feel'. During your process of examination (both with the vehicle on the ground and supported securely on axle stands), don't forget to:

- Check the steering for excessive play by moving the wheel slightly with the front wheels on the ground. 'Read up' to find out how much free play is acceptable.
- Whether or not you can start the engine, move the car backwards and forwards slightly (pushing it if necessary, but ideally under its own power) to show whether the brakes are seized.
- Check thoroughly the condition of the brakes, from the brake pipes (if the car has stood for long, assume that you'll need to fit new copper brake pipes) to the drums (are these rusty?). Also check that the discs, if fitted, and drums are not badly scored.
- Even with the car stationary, operate the brake pedal. Apply light pressure in repeated strokes and, if the pedal slowly works its way to the floor (even over, say, a minute) then you can assume a faulty master cylinder.
- Pull on the handbrake and check for excessive play before it begins to 'bite'. Does the handbrake ratchet hold?
- Check the ease of operation of the gearchange, even if the engine won't start. If the car is a runner, try selecting each gear with the engine running and listen for 'crunching'. (This could be because of gearbox wear or a clutch that needs replacing.)
- Assuming the car is a runner again, engage second gear with the handbrake fully on, and gently release the clutch ... but depress it again as soon as the car shows any sign of distress. If the car pulls away easily, you can assume worn rear brakes, or even oil in the brake drum. If the car remains stationary but the engine continues to run, you should suspect a worn clutch.
- 'Bounce' the shock absorbers to see how much movement there is (a full set of new dampers could prove expensive), and examine them

carefully for any signs of oil leaks.
- Carefully inspect the rear axle for oil leaks. A quick test drive would reveal all sorts of noises if the back axle is worn but, of course, you don't have that luxury at your disposal! This is the biggest pitfall when your prospective classic is static.
- When switching off the engine, note whether it 'runs on'.

INTERIOR

An area of car inspection that is often placed bottom of the list, and yet it is something that can be very expensive to put right. Examine minutely for discoloured, sagged or split headlining, which can be very expensive to replace. Check that seats are sound, and make a point of removing seat covers and over-mats. Check door trims for scuffing, loose-fittings and warped back-boards, and cast an eye over dash condition, steering wheel and carpets. GO TO TOWN on the interior; it can be horrendously expensive to put right. And, most important, check that the trim that is there is right for the car – swaps are quite common!

It is always advisable to make the most of any unfortunate situation, and using the lack of test-driving facilities to your advantage is essential when negotiating a price. You can embark upon some strong bargaining by capitalizing on this fact, stressing the 'unknown quantity' aspect of buying such a vehicle when you're talking money. Even if the car you're looking at is claimed to be '... professionally restored, immaculate condition, one of the best available, full MoT ...', you should be wary about not actually being able to drive the car prior to purchase. It might well have a new MOT, but that's no guarantee that the car is mechanically sound. After all, as the Department of Transport rightly point out on the back of each certificate, an MOT pass should not be taken as an indication of condition.

If the sole reason for not being allowed to test-drive a car is your own lack of adequate insurance (and don't be tempted to take the risk of pretending you're insured to drive a stranger's car

when, in fact, you're probably not) at least you can insist on being taken for a drive by the owner.

Even if you're not driving the car yourself, you can still take notice of the car's general feel. Study the owner's driving style, not only to give you an indication of how the car has been treated in the past but also to show you whether he needs to adopt any special 'techniques' to compensate for the car's shortcomings. For instance, does he keep his hand on the gearstick to prevent it jumping out of gear? Does he conveniently avoid any steep hills to hide the fact that the clutch is slipping badly? And don't be afraid to ask the owner to head for a section of road where he can demonstrate the car at speed, for you need to be sure that all is well when the car is being driven other than sedately. Look out for poor acceleration, wheel judder, excessive engine noise and any other problems that may arise when driving on a motorway at motorway speeds. It may not be an ideal situation, being driven in your prospective purchase by its current owner, but it is preferable to not being allowed out in the car at all! And do remember to turn off the radio, turn down the chat and listen hard for untoward noises, especially when accelerating and braking, cornering or covering bumpy ground.

When inspecting any car, particularly one that has perhaps been standing for a long time and is not road legal, it is imperative to remember *safety first*. You should ideally take with you an old board or a blanket (it will inevitably be cold and wet when you're crawling underneath a car in someone's driveway!), a torch, a pair of ramps or axle stands, a jack, a hammer and screwdriver, a notepad and pencil, a rough draft list of any areas of the car to which you've decided you must pay special attention and a photocopy of any buyer's guides that you've managed to get your hands on. You'll find all of these items absolutely essential if you carry out a really thorough examination of the vehicle.

▲ BSC1. Cars that have been standing often deteriorate faster than cars that are on the move. Check chrome and lamp backs as well as the usual bodywork rust and rot points.

▲ BSC2. Pay special attention to interiors and especially to under-carpet areas where condensation or leaking-in can cause corrosion.

▲ BSC3. Added difficulties will appear if half the car is in bits. (See next section: 'Unfinished Restoration Project'.)

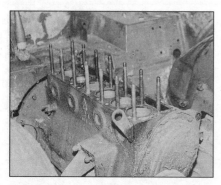

▲ BSC4. A stripped down engine is a better guide to condition than one that is complete but won't start – provided that you know what you are looking for. Turn to the section of this book on engine rebuild, where faults and problems in a stripped-down engine are described.

▲ BSC5. The mileage reading on the odometer may be entertaining but will almost certainly provide you with no useful information. Older odometers are even easier to 'clock' than those fitted today. Assume the worst, and in 99.9% of cases, you will be right!

▲ BSC6. Do ensure, if you are looking for an original car, that all the numbers match. Easiest numbers to check are the chassis number and engine number, while the number stamped on the rear axle may also be quite easy to find.

A number of publications list chassis number changes – this author's books on the restoration of individual cars among them (see Appendices for full list of models covered) – and your one-make club should also be able to provide you with the detailed information you require. Assemble it well before you go a-hunting! (Pictures in this Section, courtesy John Fletcher)

UNFINISHED RESTORATION PROJECT

If you take care when buying an unfinished project, you can save yourself a considerable amount of time and expense – but only if you watch what you buy!

The sort of 'unfinished' project to buy is one where work carried out has been done to a high standard and all parts are available. Let's look at what to avoid.

– Ensure that door, boot, bonnet, wings, windscreen surround (if a sportscar) and other panels fit properly. A car that has been welded in a distorted condition is *to be avoided at all costs*. Spend some time checking this over. Also, check obvious things such as the condition of welds and the general standard of work carried out.

– Make certain that you can check that all the parts you will need are available and identifiable. If the car is at all rare or unusual, bear in mind that you will have no way of knowing what goes where without carrying out an awful lot of research. A collection of 'before' photographs and dismantling notes would be ideal – but you'll be lucky! If you can't even see all of the parts, because they are in some impenetrable pile, you must assume that many will be missing, that many will be useless and will have rusted or seized during storage – so you must make suitable allowance. Unless the car is very rare – not unusual; *rare*! – or unless it is very cheap, forget about it.

On the plus side, you will be able to see a part-restored car at its worst, and buy it at its cheapest. A poor-condition but complete car invariably conceals the worst of its faults; a part-restored vehicle usually exposes them for all the world to see. At least you shouldn't be taken too much by surprise! But do bear in mind that you have got to get the vehicle home. You'll probably have to free off seized brakes before you can load it on to a trailer, and the parts may well require the services of a separate van.

There will *always* be problems with missing or badly fitting parts with projects of this sort, but if you buy wisely – preferably from someone who has run out of cash rather than someone who has run out of competence – you could save a lot of money. Here's how the author went about tackling an almost finished project that still took months of work. (It's always the unforeseen things.)

Many years ago Len Ball built 90 per cent of a Ford 'Convair' Special. The author finished the job off in 1988. Here's how it went:

In 1957, Len Ball bought his wife a 1939 Ford Ten E93A. At that time Len was a rep. with Girling, the brake manufacturers, and so he and his wife enjoyed the luxury, unusual at the time, of being a two-car family. Unfortunately, the little side-valve Ford must have been quite near to the end of its natural life because, by 1959, Len decided that the car was too rusty to continue in active service, and took the dramatic decision to rebuild the car completely – but not as a boring old Ford Ten. As those of us who pored longingly over the pages of *Practical Motorist* and *Car Mechanics* of the time will remember, there were pages and pages of advertisements for incredibly sleek and sexy motor cars which, almost incredibly, had metamorphosed out of cheap and boring bangers such as Austin Sevens and 'upright' Fords, any of which could be bought in a running but ropy state from £5 upwards.

At about the same time, a young man by the name of John Haynes, smitten by the special builder's bug, but dismayed by the lack of published and useful material on the subject, was wearing out his right arm running off Gestetner pages of his *Special Builder's Manuals*, the first efforts of Haynes Publishing.

Smitten by the same bug, and guided by the works of John Haynes and 'G. B. Wake' (actually JH again, writing under a pseudonym because, having joined the Air Force, it seemed wise not to make his business activities too public), Len Ball looked around for a suitable special body. During his travels on behalf of Girling, Len came across a company known as Convair Developments, described by 'G. B. Wake' (aka John Haynes) as 'the first concern in this country to introduce and market a ready-made glassfibre bodyshell'. Wake/Haynes describes several different bodyshells as being on offer from Convair: an open model, costing £79-0s-0d and a saloon body costing £117-0s-0d, complete with window frames, door locks, striker plates, etc. Len Ball recalls Convair Developments as being in the midst of breaking up the company when he went there in 1959. Apparently, the two brothers who ran the company were arranging to go their separate ways, and so Len was able to buy everything he needed at cut prices. Indeed, Len's recollection is that the saloon body had proved to be one of the causes of the company's demise. It had cost quite a lot of money to develop but, Len claims, only two or three of them had been built, demand having been poor. And when one considers the cost, which must approximate to a four-figure sum today, the lack of demand is not surprising.

Anyone who had looked at the specials of today with any degree of interest will have been struck by the disparity between the cost of the basic shell and the cost of getting the car actually on to the road. Yesterday's specials were no exception! As the invoice dated '9th July 1959' shows, the boxed chassis Len purchased, along with new wheels and spacers, silencer and radiator, cost him a further £58-0s-0d. Other bills which he passed on to me (including one for 'one wood rim steering wheel, boss, etc' at £6-0s-0d) added another £134-16s-9d to the cost, and that wasn't taking account of things like tyres, shock absorbers (and brake components?) for which there are

delivery notes – but no invoices! It seems that, within the motor trade at the time, there were wheels within wheels among representatives, and Len was able to scrounge quite a few bits and pieces which were brand new all but for a little testing, which had rendered them unsaleable in the normal way.

The boxed chassis Len purchased was a necessary feature of all Ford Specials of the time. As 'G. B. Wake' pointed out, the original chassis was only sufficiently rigid when the all-steel Ford body was perched on top of it. Replace the original with a flexible fibreglass body, and the shifting and shaking would have been prodigious. The usual answer was to take the existing chassis – Len's wife's car was too far gone, which was why he bought new – and weld flat steel along the open faces, the original chassis consisting of channel sections turned on their side.

Len began work on the car straight away that summer, stripping down the old car and having the mechanical components reconditioned. The engine was rebuilt by Flanders Garage in East Ham at a cost of £34-11s-6d, including a new clutch, spark plugs and oil. The gearbox was stripped and rebuilt (with close-ratio gears, Len thinks) and, at the same time, Len started collecting other 'just in case' spares – a complete set of new valves, springs and tappets came to me with the car, as did a complete set of gearbox internals. As Len became more and more involved with the job, he became more and more determined to do the job properly. He fitted a new carburettor (and bought a spare); a new distributor (and bought a spare) and new coil (and spare), until everything imaginable had either been rebuilt – the suspension being rebushed and the springs re-set – or replaced with new. Even the dash instruments, the wiring loom, shock absorbers and tyres were bought new. All of the glass (perspex in the rear body) was new, of course. And he bought spares.

Len had the rear lower spring softened, to match the lighter body, and flattened to lower the body over the wheels, which were in a smaller size

than standard. He fitted a high-ratio final drive to overcome the problem described by 'G. B. Wake': 'when a lightweight aerodynamic shell is fitted ... the car becomes very undergeared unless a new crown wheel and pinion with a higher ratio is fitted,' and 'these may be purchased for about £6.' Len also bought and fitted a multi-branch manifold, a water pump in place of the basic car's syphonic system, plus a shallower radiator mounted further forwards, and he converted the car to 12-volt electrics.

All of this takes considerably less time to say than it does to do, as anyone who has carried out a restoration, never mind a ground-up new car construction, will know. By 1965 Len had the car running. The new, reclining, Triumph GT6 seats (no, he didn't buy spares!) were not in place, but the engine ran, suspension and brakes worked fairly well and the Nordec Engineering (a company connected in some mysterious way with Convair) remote gearshift would find the gears with a bit of a hefty shove. First, there was a problem – or rather, yet another problem, because any saga of this sort is a catalogue of problems which have to be tackled, one by one – when the suspension was found to foul the chassis quite badly. Then, while Len was having a breather from the project, personal tragedy struck. Len's wife, the owner of the car in the first place, fell ill and died. This was, of course, a body-blow to Len; one that knocked him sideways and which took him a long time to begin to come to terms with. Naturally, all work on the car stopped, and by the time he came to think about it, Len just couldn't bring himself to do anything about the car. It was pushed into a dry shed in his garden and left, and left. On one occasion, a few years ago, a neighbour's son heard about the car and offered Len a silly small amount of money for it, but Len felt that he couldn't part with it for so little. Then, out of the blue, he contacted me through a mutual friend. I saw the car, but instead of instantly deciding to buy it, I was torn!

I vividly remembered the

advertisements of my youth and my longing to build a special out of my first car, also a Ford Popular; but with 20 more years of water under the bridge, I knew what massive undertakings apparently simple 'finishing off' jobs can be. In the end my heart won, and Len's car was transported to my garage, with a promise that he would be the first to ride in it when it was finished.

Not quite knowing how much I had let myself in for, the first job was to unpack the heaps of spares, piled up in cardboard boxes made shapeless by their loads and their age. The first surprise was a pair of brand new E-type Series I headlamp glasses, rubbers and chrome surrounds, along with a pair of perspex covers marked 'Lotus'. Len explained that he had hoped to be able to fair-in the headlamps, but that it proved impossible. Another surprise was to find the 'new' duplicates mentioned earlier. There were lots of door hinges in the box and various bits of door gear that were yet to be fitted. Then the car itself was examined. The doors didn't shut, the stuck-on headlining was sagging down and, when I sat inside the car, I seriously doubted whether there was going to be enough headroom – and that was without seats! (As it turned out, the seats allow you to recline in a way that you can't when sitting bolt upright on the hard wooden floor, so that was a false alarm.)

I decided that the first job would be to start the engine, but how was I to do that when no petrol would come through to the carburettor? The fuel pipes were blocked solid and the smell inside the fuel tank – new only 25 years earlier! – had to be experienced to be believed. When it was drained, the stench lingered on hands and floor, where some was spilled, for days. Although the outside of the tank was perfect, the inside was full of all manner of junk. I threw a handful of pebbles into the drained tank and shook it until my arms ached, dislodging most of the rust and gunge in the process. A small slag heap of the stuff poured out! The inside of the tank was then sealed with some of Paul Beck's excellent Slosh Tank Sealant before the tank was left for several days for the sealant to cure.

After stripping and cleaning the carb, the engine fired almost first time – but sounded horrible and wouldn't rev. Points were clean, plugs had been replaced (we took Lodge plugs out; remember them?), so the culprit was almost certainly the condenser. There would be no point in buying a 'new, old stock' condenser, because it is often the simple passage of time that causes them to break down, so I adapted a later Ford condenser to fit, mainly because it was the only one I could find that was a good fit in the distributor body. But still the engine wouldn't run properly. A compression tester revealed that there was no compression on number two cylinder, and I felt mildly cheesed off at having to disturb the cylinder head, although that is hardly a major task on a side-valve engine. Graham Maclaren, a friend of mine, was giving me a hand by now, and I suggested taking out the plugs to find out if we could see if there was a stuck valve. Not only could we see it, but it could be reached with a screwdriver. A squirt of releasing fluid, a sharp rap with the hammer and the valve was free. You couldn't do that with an overhead valve engine! At the third time of asking, the engine fired up again and this time, after blowing out clouds of choking black smoke, revved freely and ticked over amazingly sweetly. Len *thought* he might have had the engine balanced; he had!

For some reason, Len had used what seemed to be badly worn second-hand door hinges, which meant that it was impossible to persuade the doors to shut without fouling. In addition, the driver's door glass channels proved impossible to fit properly and, instead, I had to reshape the fibreglass bodywork. After considerable thought, we got hold of a pair of second-hand Mini van door hinges, re-bushed them and, reversing them left-for-right, Graham found that he could make them fit after a great deal of regrinding the angle at which they sat against the doors. He actually achieved wonders in getting the doors to shut perfectly and with as near to a 'clunk' as GRP special's doors will ever achieve!

I took the rear spring away to a 'specialist' in Bristol who returned it with a bill for £30 and settings which seemed identical to those it had started off with! Then, luckily, I found a Ford specialist in Ludlow, Shropshire, which specializes in 'new-old stock' Ford parts, and bought an original rear spring from them. In order to fit this spring it has to be flattened out and pushed hard against its prodigious strength, and here again it was Len's foresight to the rescue! His father-in-law, a blacksmith, had made a spring fitting tool with hand-forged shackles and hand-formed threads; a masterpiece of the blacksmith's art. After experimenting for several hours I was able to use the device to fit the original-type rear spring, along with shackle drop plates to restore the rear body to an appropriate height with no residue of suspension thump.

After making a dummy rear floor to take out undulations in the steel original, carpets were fitted and door trims, made also from carpet, were cut and glued to fit the hardboard door casings Len had provided. The car was now ready for a test-drive.

The engine started, the remote change was forced to find a gear and an alarming 'square tyred' ride took place! The tyres had got flats on them from standing in one place for so long with little air in them. I inflated them to 40 lb and, with use, they have reverted to more-or-less round, while the gearchange has also become slightly more civilized now that it has been used a few times.

I took the car for an MOT test before telling Len that I had finished it, three years after taking it from him. When I rang to invite him over, his excitement was as great as mine! The day he came over for his drive in the car was one of the most enjoyable I have had as a motoring writer. Len didn't say much as his memory returned him to the engineering tricks and wrinkles he had pulled all those years ago, but it was obvious that he was, quite naturally, a little moved that the car which he had feared might have gone for scrap, but which he couldn't bring himself to finish, was finally on the road.

On the road, FT 4909 is, quite frankly, awful! Clutch and gearchange co-ordination is an acquired art, steering is something that the Ford Convair Special seems to like doing by itself, and the seating position is strange, though not impossible – although, if you get into the car at the wrong angle, your left foot becomes trapped under the clutch pedal and can't be extricated unless you get right out of the car and limbo down into the cockpit once again. On the other hand, I think the body styling is fabulous, and the Convair is certainly one of the best looking of all the Ford specials. The quality of fixtures and fittings, while a joke by modern production car standards, is superb by the standards of the genre, and paintwork and body are excellent. Surprisingly, the engine pulls responsively as well as purring satisfyingly on tick-over; and, in addition, the car is undoubtedly the finest condition Ford Special in existence and a piece of history to boot. Martin Ortell-Shaw of the Ford Side-valve Club tells me that only three surviving Convairs are known, while this is the only known closed Convair and was clearly the last.

'Convair Developments,' G. B. Wake/John Haynes tells us in *The Ford Special Builder's Manual*, 'were the first concern in this country to market a ready-made glass fibre bodyshell ... and [they] are of an extremely high standard.' How fortuitous that this one has survived. Best of all, however, is the happy ending to this little tale. Unfortunately, I can't afford my own motor museum and, in any case, although I enjoyed doing the work (partly so that Len's earlier endeavours were not in vain), I wouldn't have enjoyed keeping the car. When John Haynes heard about the Convair, he immediately offered to buy it on behalf of his museum – The Sparkford Motor Museum. I am delighted with the outcome, and Len is looking forward to his visit to see 'his' car in Somerset. Arch enthusiast John Haynes is also delighted with his latest purchase and assures me that my misgivings are misplaced. 'Not only is it a superb example of its type, it also drives perfectly well,' he assures me, 'for a Ford Special ....'

▲ URP1. The car as 'found' appeared to be complete and was in unpainted fibreglass. Len Ball had kept all of the parts logically collected in cardboard and wooden boxes.

▲ URP2. The Ford fuel tank was completely clogged with residue. We used Paul Beck's Slosh Fuel Tank Sealant to trap most of the bits and to stop them getting through to the carburettor.

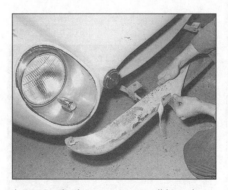

▲ URP3. The bumpers were all brand new but, after a quarter of a century of storage, the wrapping materials had glued themselves well in place! The bracketry required adapting before the bumpers would fit the car.

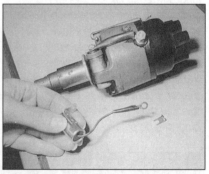

▲ URP4. One of our first priorities was to get the engine running. It would start, but missed badly, so we replaced the condenser in the distributor with one of a later type. The problem is that condensers often fail in storage whether they are being used or not, and you're often better off using a 'wrong' brand-new condenser than trying to struggle along with another old one that could also fail.

▲ URP5. The single transverse leaf spring had to be flattened out so that the eyes in the spring would release the shackle pins. Len had made a DIY special tool which just goes to show how ingenious you sometimes have to be to get over one-off problems.

▲ URP6. For some strange reason, the hinges fitted to the car by Len were very badly worn, allowing the doors to sag and catch on the sills. We took a lot of time finding suitable replacements, and eventually used Mini door hinges with the side of the hinge that bolted against the car ground down to the correct angle to allow the hinge pins in both of the hinges to be parallel with one another.

▲ URP7. The car was re-sprayed by Graham Macdonald, using two-pack paint which is definitely not suitable for home use because of its toxic nature.

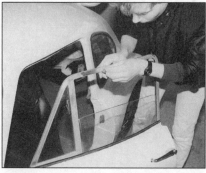

▲ URP8. The aluminium door frames were restored to a brushed finish using wire wool.

▲ URP9. The Triumph seats that Len had purchased back in the early sixties fitted perfectly – but only when bolted directly down to the floor! There was insufficient head room in the car to use the seat runners. This is the trouble with classic specials: they simply don't function as well as production cars.

▲ URP10. The rear floor of the car consisted of the rear floor pan of the original Ford on which the car was based. The hollows in the pressing were to be covered with a wooden board. I first made a cardboard template ...

▲ URP11. ... then transferred the shape to a piece of plywood ...

▲ URP12. ... covering the board in foam carpet underlay and a single piece of carpet to trim out the whole of the rear of the vehicle. The cheapest cord carpet looked the part!

▲ URP13. Door trim panels were made out of hardboard and covered in the same material as the rear floor: cord carpet.

▲ *URP14. Len Ball was the first person to inspect the finished car, 25 years after he had started work on it. The Convair Special now lives in the Haynes Motor Museum at Sparkford to celebrate the fact that John Haynes' second ever book was all about how to build a Ford Special – including this very model.*

GETTING THROUGH THE MOT

Whether you buy a classic car to use while you carry out a 'running restoration' or you buy a car to take off the road to restore, one of the first jobs you will want to carry out will be to obtain an MOT certificate so that you can use the car on the road.

Why, if you want to totally restore a car, would you want to use it first, you may ask. Well, the first reason is that, if you haven't driven this model of car before, you want to be sure that you will at least *enjoy* using it! Since you have, presumably, bought the car by now, you really are drinking at the last chance saloon: but better to find out the truth now, before you spend years of your time and a fortune in cash. You could at least resell the beast – *with* an MOT certificate!

The second reason for MOT-ing a restoration project is that, by driving the car, you will gain a better idea of what needs doing to it, short-term, long-term, structurally and – once the car is in use – cosmetically. Take notes. Get your preparation right. It could make all the difference in carrying out the sort of rebuild you will be happy with. There is nothing more frustrating than to 'complete' a long restoration only to find that the starter motor sticks or the wipers fail when the motor has been in use for a few minutes.

One problem with the MOT for classic car owners is that the test is aimed primarily at newer cars. Hazard warning light: So what! Diesel emissions: Who cares? Catalytic converters: What are they? So, whether you are MOT-ing before or after the restoration, you will want to be sure that your car doesn't fail just because the examiner doesn't understand the rules.

The British 'MOT' annual test has been designed primarily for newer cars, although the powers-that-be recognize that certain exceptions have to be made for older vehicles. Where legislation has changed after a vehicle has been built, it may be unrealistic to insist on compliance with the later law. For instance, no one would seriously propose that your side-valve Morris Minor should be fitted with a catalytic converter!

The problem with classic cars, however, can stem from the fact that MOT examiners can hardly be expected to be familiar with every aspect of MOT regulations. There are many regulations and exemptions and, while the examiner will be familiar with the main ones, there are many that could well escape his mind. The best approach is for the owner to familiarize him or herself with the regulations as they apply to the individual car, and to gently point them out to the examiner should the need arise. You would be well advised to buy the 'bible' on the subject, *The MoT Inspection Manual for Cars and Light Commercial Vehicles*, published by HMSO and available through branches of HMSO or by order through most bookshops.

The excellent Federation of British Historic Vehicle Clubs has published a list of some common areas of confusion as they relate to older cars, along with a reference to page numbers and sections of the MOT tester's manual. The following is reproduced from their 1993 Newsletter, but do watch out for subsequent legislation and changes to the MOT test.

HOW TO PROMPT YOUR MOT EXAMINER

The MoT Inspection Manual for Cars and Light Commercial Vehicles is divided into six sections. Most of the sections have subsections which, in turn, have paragraphs. Each page is divided into three columns: Information, Method of Inspection and Reasons for Rejection. These are abbreviated below as 'Info', 'Method' and 'Reason'. Page numbers restart at 1 for each section. 'Appendices' come at the end of the manual. Should you want to draw an examiner's attention to any one of the allowances prescribed for our sort of car the following list may help you.

For quick reference take the first number shown which is the section number and the page number at the end of the entry. Thus, for brakes with a corroded cable go to Section 3, page 5.

Chapter 2

The workshop

TOOLS AND EQUIPMENT

There is no such thing as the fully-equipped workshop! No matter how many tools you possess, there always seems to be a need for more, especially as your skills and aspirations increase. On the other hand, there is a certain basic level of tools without which you cannot hope to proceed – and that applies whether you plan to work in the most palatial of workshops or the front drive.

The cheapest of tools are a complete waste of money. They may look similar to more expensive tools (but do avoid those that look rough and poorly finished) but their strength and fit will cause a lot of problems. Badly fitting spanners are prone to round off nuts, especially since cheap spanners tend to 'spring' their jaws open, while screwdriver ends rapidly lose their edges and become unserviceable. Worst of all, many cheap tools are made of a type of steel which is simply not strong enough for the job. As a result, they often break at their weakest point. Since the time when they break is when you are applying the most force, such tools are potentially dangerous as well as being damned annoying, preventing you from completing a job just when you are in the swing of things.

TOOLS OF THE MIND

There's another, rather more subtle but just as important reason for buying good quality tools. If you hope to carry out a high standard of work, high quality is something that must surround the whole job. Once the basic skills have been learned, high quality work is a state of mind. *Determination* is a key component. Without it, you simply won't get through the inevitable low points in any project of this sort. *Patience* is another essential part of the tool kit. Any piece of restoration work must take as long as it takes. We all know the feeling of 'must get this bit finished before the six o'clock news/dinner is ready/Christmas, or whatever' but it really is the way to make mistakes and second-class compromises. A useful mental trick is to tell yourself that the best part of carrying out the job you are involved in is the doing-of-it rather than the finishing-of-it. Of course, it's great to have the job finished, but you should just let that happen in its own sweet way, not treat it as a major objective – *the* major objective – around which your work takes place.

So what has that got to do with high quality adjustable spanners, you might ask. Have you ever tried using one of those dreadful cheap Chinese adjustable wrenches where the adjuster screw goes alternately tight then loose? Picture yourself in the middle of taking off an oil union from your engine. The nut size is obscure and you have to turn to the spanner of last resort. Because you are having to use the adjustable wrench you are making a big effort not to damage the nut on the union but, in trying to get the spanner to fit the nut as perfectly as possible, you're having to fight the adjuster screw. Turn it here, and the jaws are loose and not holding their position; here and the screw is tight and you have to back it off and tighten it against the pressure in the screw. By the time you've got it just right – if ever you do – you feel like braining the person who produced a lousy wrench and an odd size of union nut. These are not the best of conditions in which to carefully and painstakingly introduce the spanner to the nut and ease it off (back and forth, perhaps, if it is especially tight) without shearing the threaded stub on which it is mounted, or rounding off the flats on the nut. It might sound like high-fallutin' philosophical nonsense, but it's bog standard common sense really! Surround yourself with materials, equipment and a state of mind that are all high quality, and the work you do will be so much better for it.

TOOL SELECTION

Quite apart from the equipment that you will need for special jobs, such as a panel beating set or a valve grinding tool, you will need a basic set of hand tools to use in almost all aspects of restoration. A basic set of spanners will comprise both combination spanners – with a ring spanner at one end and an 'open ender' at the other – and a socket set. Half-inch drive socket spanners are stronger and will be essential for jobs such as tightening down cylinder head nuts, for example, but ⅜ inch drive socket sets are cheaper and provide slightly better access. If I could afford only one type, I

25

would definitely go for the larger size.

Be sure to buy the right size for your car. Almost all British and American classic cars use AF (across flats) sized spanners, while European and Japanese cars use metric. Unfortunately, the older a car, the more likely it is that you will find some 'odd' sized nuts and bolts. Older Morris Minors, for instance, use a number of Whitworth spanner sizes, and it is not unknown for BSW (pipework sized) spanners to be needed for some of the car's plumbing, such as on the fuel system. For the odd spots, use a good quality adjustable spanner with discretion. If your car is an odd-bod with lots of Whitworth spanner sizes needed, find a specialist tool supplier in the pages of one of the classic car magazines and invest in a set.

Having said that cheap tools are not worth having, here is one case where they can be worthwhile. If you have a seized nut with flats that have become well rounded, you may wish to use a cheap-cheap spanner socket of *just* too small a size, heat it up to expand it, hammer it on and have another go.

Haynes manuals each contain useful advice on the purchase of workshop tools, and this information is repeated below. However, there is more to be said on the subject when it comes to restoration work. You will need to be able to easily lift the car, and for that purpose you can't beat a trolley jack. Shop around, and you'll find them at ridiculously low prices. Do bear in mind my earlier strictures about the safety of cheaper tools, and take even more care than normal never to go beneath a car supported by one of these jacks. You will also need some means of supporting the car off the ground. Buy a set of four axle stands with as broad a base as possible to give you the maximum amount of security against the car toppling. ALWAYS ensure that at least two wheels are on the ground and properly chocked before going down-under.

You will find a vice and workbench invaluable tools, although a Black & Decker 'Workmate' can be most versatile and useful in place of a fixed bench if you haven't got room. You will need to

buy or hire an engine hoist at some stage in the proceedings and you will also need some means of cleaning gungy mechanical components. A drip tray, such as the type available from Holden Vintage & Classic (see Appendix) would be excellent because you can then manoeuvre a whole engine into it, whilst on the floor, without risk of damaging the flexible plastic of which the tray is made. Pour a little paraffin into the tray, set to with scraper and brush and you can carry out one of the most disgusting and yet satisfying jobs in any restoration project. Once you have stripped parts down, cleaned them up or painted them, you must cover them up with a dust sheet. They will stay neat and clean for much longer, ready to be refitted in the fullness of time.

To help the average owner to decide which tools are needed to carry out the various tasks detailed in Haynes owners' workshop manuals, there are three lists of tools under the following headings: 'Maintenance and minor repair tool kit', 'Repair and overhaul tool kit', and 'Special tools'. Newcomers to practical mechanics should start off with the 'Maintenance and minor repair tool kit' and confine themselves to the simpler jobs around the vehicle. Then, as their confidence and experience grows, they can undertake more difficult tasks, buying extra tools as and when they are needed. In this way, a 'Maintenance and minor repair tool kit' can be built up into a 'Repair and overhaul tool kit' over a period of time without any major one-off cash outlays. Experienced do-it-yourselfers will have tool kits good enough for most repairs and overhaul procedures, and will add tools from the 'Special tools' category when they feel the expense is justified by the amount of use these tools will be put to.

MAINTENANCE AND MINOR REPAIR TOOL KIT

The tools listed below should be considered a minimum requirement if routine maintenance, servicing and minor repair operations are to be undertaken.

Ideally, purchase sets of open-ended and ring spanners, covering similar size

ranges. That way you will have the correct tools for loosening nuts from bolts having the same head size, for example, since you will have at least two spanners of the same size.

Alternatively, a set of combination spanners (ring one end, open-ended the other) give the advantage of both types of spanner. Although more expensive than open-ended spanners, combination spanners can often help you out in tight situations by gripping the nut better than an open-ender.

AF combination spanners – $\frac{3}{8}$, $\frac{7}{16}$, $\frac{1}{2}$, $\frac{9}{16}$, $\frac{5}{8}$, $\frac{11}{16}$, $\frac{3}{4}$, $\frac{13}{16}$, $\frac{7}{8}$, $\frac{15}{16}$ in
Metric combination spanners – 8, 9, 10, 11, 12, 14, 15, 17, 19mm
Adjustable spanner – 9 in
Engine sump/gearbox/rear axle drain plug key (where applicable)
Spark plug spanner (with rubber insert)
Spark plug gap adjustment tool
Set of feeler gauges
Brake adjuster spanner (where applicable)
Brake bleed nipple spanner
Screwdriver – 4 in long x ¼ in dia (crosshead)
Combination pliers – 6 in
Hacksaw, junior
Tyre pump
Tyre pressure gauge
Grease gun (where applicable)
Oil can
Fine emery cloth (1 sheet)
Wire brush (small)
Funnel (medium size)

REPAIR AND OVERHAUL TOOL KIT

These tools are virtually essential for anyone undertaking any major repairs to a motor vehicle, and are additional to those given in the basic list. Included in this list is a comprehensive set of sockets. Although these are expensive they will be found invaluable as they are so versatile – particularly if various drives are included in the set. We recommend the ½ in square-drive type, as this can be used with most proprietary torque wrenches. On the other hand, ⅜ in drive are better for working in confined spaces and, if of good quality, will be amply strong enough for work inside the engine bay. If you cannot afford a socket set, even bought piecemeal, then inexpensive tubular box spanners are a useful alternative.

The tools in this list will occasionally need to be supplemented by tools from the 'Special tools' list.

Socket (or box spanners) to cover range in previous list

Reversible ratchet drive (for use with sockets)

Extension piece, 10 in (for use with sockets)

Universal joint (for use with sockets)

Torque wrench (for use with sockets)

'Mole' wrench – 8 in

Ball pein hammer

Soft-faced hammer, plastic or rubber

Screwdriver – 6 in long x ⁵⁄₁₆ in dia (plain)

Screwdriver – 2 in long x ⁵⁄₁₆ in square (plain)

Screwdriver – 1 ½ in long x ¼ in dia (crosshead)

Screwdriver – 3 in long x ⅛ in dia (electrician's)

Pliers – electrician's side cutters

Pliers – needle nosed

Pliers – circlip (internal and external)

Cold chisel – ½ in

Scriber (this can be made by grinding the end of a broken hacksaw blade)

Scriber (this can be made by flattening and sharpening one end of a piece of copper pipe)

Centre punch

Pin punch

Hacksaw

Valve grinding tool

Steel rule/straight-edge

Allen keys

Selection of files

Wire brush (large)

Axle stands

Jack (strong scissor or hydraulic type)

Light with extension lead

SPECIAL TOOLS

The tools in this list are those which are not used regularly, are expensive to buy, or which need to be used in accordance with their manufacturers' instructions. Unless relatively difficult mechanical jobs are undertaken frequently, it will not be economical to buy many of these tools. Where this is the case, you could consider clubbing together with friends (or a motorists' club) to make a joint purchase, or borrowing the tools against a deposit from a local garage or tool hire specialist.

The following list contains only those tools and instruments freely available to the public, and not those special tools produced by the vehicle manufacturer specifically for its dealer network.

Valve spring compressor

Piston ring compressor

Ball joint separator

Universal hub/bearing puller

Impact screwdriver

Micrometer and/or vernier gauge

Carburettor flow balancing device (where applicable)

Dial gauge

Stroboscopic timing light

Dwell angle meter/tachometer

Universal electrical multimeter

Cylinder compression gauge

Lifting tackle

Trolley jack

Rivet gun

BUYING TOOLS

Tool factors can be a good source of implements, because of the extensive ranges which they normally stock. On the other hand, accessory shops usually offer excellent quality goods, often at discount prices, so it pays to shop around.

The old maxim 'buy the best tools you can afford' is a good general rule to go by, since (as I have said) cheap tools are seldom good value, especially in the long run. Conversely, it isn't always true that the MOST expensive tools are best. There are plenty of good tools available at reasonable prices, and the shop manager or proprietor will usually be very helpful in giving advice on the best tools for particular jobs.

CARE AND MAINTENANCE OF TOOLS

Having purchased a reasonable tool kit, it is necessary to keep the tools in a clean serviceable condition. After use, always wipe off any dirt, grease and metal particles using a clean, dry cloth, before putting the tools away. Never leave them lying around after they have been used. A simple tool rack on the garage or workshop wall for items such as screwdrivers and pliers is a good idea. Store all normal spanners and sockets in a metal box. Any measuring instruments, gauges, meters, etc. must be carefully stored where they cannot be damaged or become rusty.

Take a little care when the tools are used. Hammer heads inevitably become marked, and screwdrivers lose the keen edge on their blades from time to time. A little timely attention with emery cloth or a file will soon restore items like this to a good serviceable finish.

WORKING FACILITIES

Not to be forgotten when discussing tools is the workshop itself. Some form of suitable working area becomes essential if anything more than routine maintenance is to be carried out.

It is appreciated that many an owner mechanic is forced by circumstance to remove an engine or similar item without the benefit of a garage or workshop. Having done this, any repairs should always be done under the cover of a roof, if feasible.

Wherever possible, any dismantling should be done on a clean, flat workbench or table at a suitable working height. Engine dismantling, though, is safer carried out on an engine stand (they can be hired sometimes) or on a large cardboard box opened out to give a clean surface on the workshop floor.

Any workbench needs a vice – the larger the better – and one with a jaw opening of 4 in (100mm) is suitable for most jobs. As mentioned previously, some clean dry storage space is also required for tools, as well as for lubricants, cleaning fluids, touch-up paints and so on, all of which soon become necessary.

Another item which may be required, and which has a much more general usage, is an electric drill with a chuck capacity of at least ⅜ in (10mm). This, together with a good range of twist drills, is virtually essential for fitting accessories such as wing mirrors and reversing lights. Cordless drills are far more convenient to use and don't carry any electrical risks in use. Last, but not least, always keep a supply of old newspapers and clean, lint-free, rags available, and try to keep any working areas as clean as possible.

SPANNER JAW GAP COMPARISON TABLE

N.B. Using a badly fitting spanner – one of the incorrect size, worn or with 'sprung' jaws – can be dangerous.

AF size	Actual size	Nearest metric size	Metric size in inches
4BA	0.248 in	7mm	0.276 in
2BA	0.320 in	8mm	0.315 in
⁷⁄₁₆ in	0.440 in	11mm	0.413 in
½ in	0.500 in	13mm	0.510 in
⁹⁄₁₆ in	0.560 in	14mm	0.550 in
⅝ in	0.630 in	16mm	0.630 in
¹¹⁄₁₆ in	0.690 in	18mm	0.710 in
¾ in	0.760 in	19mm	0.750 in
¹³⁄₁₆ in	0.820 in	21mm	0.830 in
⅞ in	0.880 in	22mm	0.870 in
¹⁵⁄₁₆ in	0.940 in	24mm	0.945 in
1 in	1.000 in	26mm	1.020 in

Whitworth size	Actual size	Nearest AF size	AF Actual size
³⁄₁₆ in	0.450 in	⁷⁄₁₆ in	0.440 in
¼ in	0.530 in	½ in	0.500 in
⁵⁄₁₆ in	0.604 in	⁹⁄₁₆ in	0.560 in
⅜ in	0.720 in	¹¹⁄₁₆ in	0.690 in
⁷⁄₁₆ in	0.830 in	¹³⁄₁₆ in	0.820 in
½ in	0.930 in	⅞ in	0.880 in
⁹⁄₁₆ in	1.020 in	1 in	1.010 in

Whitworth size	Actual size	Nearest Metric size	Metric size in inches
³⁄₁₆ in	0.450 in	12mm	0.470 in
¼ in	0.530 in	14mm	0.500 in
⁵⁄₁₆ in	0.604 in	15mm	0.590 in
⅜ in	0.720 in	18mm	0.710 in
⁷⁄₁₆ in	0.830 in	21mm	0.830 in
½ in	0.930 in	24mm	0.945 in
⁹⁄₁₆ in	1.020 in	26mm	1.020 in

HEAVY PLANT

These days, it is almost impossible to carry out any major restoration work without the assistance of power tools. The most common and obvious is an electric drill. A good quality rechargeable drill will be best because of the way in which you will be able to reach tricky spots without the inconvenience of trailing cables, and because they are far safer to use than mains equipment where you might be working out of doors or lying on the ground. Next in the list will be an angle grinder, useful for jobs as diverse as sanding filler off a panel, cutting through steel or even resharpening your cold chisel.

A compressor comes fairly high up the list of required tools once you start getting really serious, as will welding equipment of some sort. Indeed, if you plan to restore a car, you simply won't be able to get by without carrying out welding, unless you have a welder come in to your workshop and do the work for you. So important is welding equipment to the restorer that the next section looks closely at the choices available.

TOOLS AND EQUIPMENT

▼ T&E1. Obtain a suitable fire extinguisher for workshop use. Dry powder may be best; water-filled is unsuitable where an electrical fire may be concerned. Contact Chubb Fire for advice on which type to use (see Appendices).

▼ T&E2. A good selection of hand tools will prove invaluable. Buying the cheapest type of tools is a false economy, and you would be well advised to invest in a medium-to-high quality range such as those from Sykes-Pickavant.

▲ *T&E3. Only used now and again, but a godsend when it's needed, this is the Sykes-Pickavant ball joint splitter.*

▲ *T&E4. SP also produce this range of toolboxes and lockers to enable you to keep your hand tools in an orderly style.*

▶ *T&E5. More useful hand tools from Sykes-Pickavant: this is the bench folding tool which enables you to make accurate folds when constructing steel panels. Two pieces of steel clamped together would do the same job, although in a far more long-winded way.*

◀ *T&E6. Two more sheet metal bench tools: the bench wheeled guillotine which slices through steel far more easily than tin snips; and the flanging tool which places a shoulder on the edge of a piece of metal, enabling two pieces to be lap jointed giving a flush finish on the outside.*

◀ *T&E7. The Pencut sheet metal cutter gives distortion-free sheet metal cutting without the expense of an aching hand! It is operated by your electric drill and has the added advantage that no swarf or filings fall down into box sections or on to the upholstery. (Courtesy: Frost Auto Restoration)*

◀ *T&E8. There's no competition when it comes to domestic-sized gas welding kits. This is the BOC Portapac.*

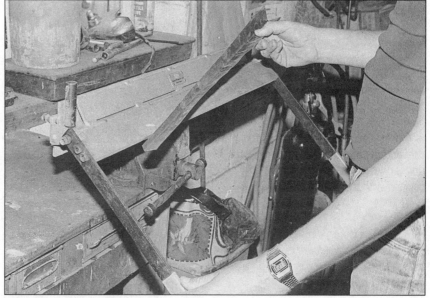

▲ T&E9. The kit and exchange cylinders are available from BOC cylinder centres throughout the UK and similar establishments are to be found in Australia, the United States and most other countries.

▲ T&E10. If you have any more than a tiny amount of welding to do, it is not worth considering anything but a MIG. Clarke now claim to be the UK's largest supplier of MIGs suitable for home and garage use, and the cost of buying a small MIG unit is considerably less than equipping yourself with a BOC gas welding set-up.

▶ T&E11. For factory-finish welds, you will need a spot welder. It can't, of course, be used when you can't obtain access with the welding tips.

▲ T&E12. Very upmarket are these two SIP plasma cutters. They enable you to cut out sheet steel quickly, cleanly and without distortion; and the smaller model, the Plasma 25, is about the same price as a mid-range MIG welder.

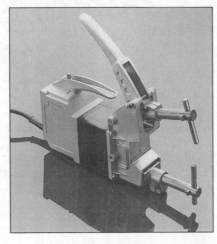

▲ T&E13. If you're going to carry out your own respraying, you will need a compressor. The SIP Air Mate range has the right combination of performance and affordability, and the cost could be recouped on the first job you carried out.

▲ T&E14. The same company also produces a full range of spray guns right up from the least expensive DIY model to the full-size professional gun.

▲ T&E15. This Clarke random orbit sander enables you to rapidly sand filler and primer during the respray process without the scratches and marks that would be left by ordinary electric-type sanders. It is specially designed to consume a smaller amount of air than a full-scale professional sander and is thus eligible for use with the larger DIY compressors.

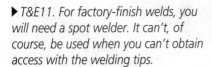

▲ T&E16. A range of electric hand tools will be absolutely essential. Shown here, from left to right, are the following Black & Decker tools: random orbit sander; mini-grinder; electric sander; rechargeable electric drill, which enables you to get into odd spots around the car without having potentially dangerous cable trailing along the floor.

▲ T&E17. An electric drill is an absolute 'must' and will be used a thousand and one times. Bosch make what is probably the best quality range of drills available, and include cordless drills-cum-power screwdrivers in their line-up. Cordless tools are safer and far simpler to use, while the power screwdriver feature can save a great deal of time when it comes to removing screws, nuts and bolts.

▲ T&E18. Machine Mart, a company with retail outlets throughout the UK, sell a huge range of workshop equipment, such as this Clarke engine stand. Only worth buying if you carry out a lot of such work, but an engine stand may nevertheless be available from your local tool hire centre.

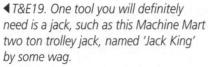

◀ T&E19. One tool you will definitely need is a jack, such as this Machine Mart two ton trolley jack, named 'Jack King' by some wag.

▲ T&E20. Another invaluable set of tools are these axle stands. Some owners make do with old bricks, oil drums and the like, but it is most important that you do not do so! Bricks can crumble, cans can topple, and the results of a car falling on you could be very terminal indeed.

▲ T&E21. Part of your preparation should be the purchase of as many nuts, bolts, washers and clips as you think you might need. We have often used packets of Namrick fixings – all of them of bright zinc-plated steel, except for those that we purchased for use in the most vulnerable parts of the car, which were made of stainless steel. **Nuts and bolts associated with suspension and steering should be of original specification because of the specified tensile strength required. Non-specified bolts may shear and cause a component to fail.**

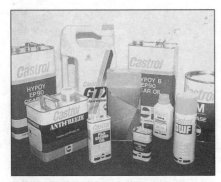

▲ T&E22. You will also need the fullest range of lubricants, and Castrol will be able to supply you with lubrication information, free of charge, if you contact their Customer Relations Department (see Appendices).

▲ T&E23. Having completed the restoration of your pride and joy you will want to prevent any future corrosion. Machine Mart sell workshop dehumidifiers which keep the humidity level down and thus dramatically reduce the incidence of corrosion.

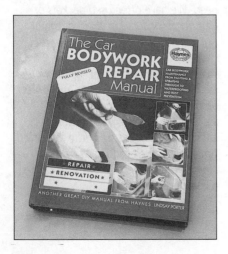

◀ T&E26. The Car Bodywork Repair Manual, also by Lindsay Porter and published by Haynes, contains over a thousand illustrations and covers every aspect of car bodywork repair techniques, including detailed information on welding, panel beating and spraying.

▲ T&E24. Haynes Guide to Purchase & DIY Restoration books give specific information on individual models of classic cars. The series was initiated by the author of this book and most of them have been written by him.

▲ T&E25. Tin snips are available for cutting left-hand or right-hand curves or in 'universal' pattern.

▲ T&E27. Essential after welding, spraying or before any reassembly, is the need to clean all threads. A set of taps and dies or, as shown here, a re-threading kit, will be needed.
 (Courtesy: The Eastwood Company)

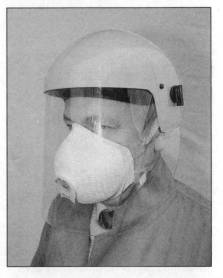

▲ T&E28. Protective visor, industrial-thickness gloves, face mask (different types needed for dust and for solvent-based products), ear defenders: all will be needed at different times.
(Courtesy: Frost Auto Restoration)

SAFETY EQUIPMENT

In many parts of this book, various items of safety equipment are specified. Obtaining them must take top priority for the health and safety of the user and those around you. To start off with, purchase safety goggles, industrial leather gloves, cotton overalls and ear plugs for use with noisy power tools.

Safety: At the start of many sections is a 'Safety' note. Naturally, safety is the responsibility of each individual restorer or repairer, and no responsibility for the effectiveness or otherwise of advice given here nor for any omissions can be accepted by the author or publisher. After all, the jobs you will be carrying out will be *your* responsibility, so do take care to familiarize yourself with safety information available from the suppliers or manufacturers of the materials or equipment which you use. 'Safety' notes are intended to supplement this information with useful tips, as is the additional information on workshop safety and workshop practice in the Appendix – you are strongly advised to read the Appendix before beginning any of the tasks detailed in this book.

Take note of information in the text on safety hazards. NEVER drain petrol over a pit nor anywhere where a spark could ignite the vapour, e.g. near a central heating boiler – outdoors is best. For obvious reasons, attempting to weld a fuel tank can be lethal and should be left to a specialist. Never use a flame near the fuel tank or lines. Drain fuel only into suitable containers. Do not use plastic containers which are attacked by petrol. The battery should be taken out prior to fuel tank removal, to prevent accidental shorting in the presence of fuel vapour. When storing the battery, take care to ensure that no object will fall unnoticed across the terminals and become a potential fire risk. Paint stripper is damaging to the skin and eyes – read instructions before use and wear gloves, goggles and protective overalls. Ensure that the vehicle is firmly supported when lifted off the ground – a jack is NOT safe enough. Wear goggles when probing beneath the car, and beware of rusty, jagged edges. Never work beneath a car supported on a jack: use axle stands, ramps or a roll-over cage (see Suppliers section) and, in the former case, securely chock the wheels that remain on the ground.

WELDING EQUIPMENT

Probably the most difficult choice to make when it comes to workshop equipment will be knowing which type of welding gear to purchase. MIG, TIG or MAG? Carbon-arc or oxy-acetylene; Mapp gas, electric arc or spot? There are now so many types of welding system available that the choice can seem overwhelming. First, a little background information:

In the beginning there was the weld; just one type and none of your fancy nonsense. A big bloke with hands like hams inserted two pieces of iron into the white heat of the forge and when the iron was as soft and white as dripping on a slice of toast, the two pieces were placed overlapping, one on top of the other and hammer welded until their contiguity became continuity. These days it's a fairly difficult operation to carry out, mainly because of the nigh impossibility of getting hold of the low carbon – virtually *no* carbon – iron necessary to enable the metal to be heated to a sufficiently plastic state. Steel burns and self-destructs in the forge well before the requisite white hot putty emerges from the flames.

Working at the forge is one of the most satisfying of all the manipulative skills. It's redolent of the days when men were men, it puts blisters on your hands where the callouses ought to be and, when you're doing it for fun, you can stop for a drink just before the two arrows are fired into the bench behind you, as in all the best adverts. On the other hand, it's not a lot of use if all you want to do is to change a front wing on your Mini Cooper. The nearest a Mini ever gets to hammer welding is when it goes through the crusher at the end of its days. The amount of heat you will need in order to weld a wing is very similar to that found in the middle of the forge, but it's a bit more subtly applied. The difficulty lies in choosing the system with which to apply it.

BRAZING

Before the various types of welding proper are explored, it's worthwhile mentioning brazing, or braze-welding as it's sometimes called. True welding involves the fusion of the two or more pieces of metal to be joined together. An analogy can be made with the fusion of the various pieces of a plastic model aircraft kit. Here, the fusion is caused by a special type of cement that melts the surfaces to be joined together so that by the time the solvent within the cement has evaporated, the melted surfaces of the plastic components have flowed and fused together. In the case of metal welding, the 'cement' is the heat applied to the surfaces being welded together (and more often than not, some extra metal is flowed into the joint to help strengthen it), and the process of evaporation, which allows the melded surfaces of the plastic to set, is replaced by the process of freezing of the metal once the heat source has been removed. As soon as the metal cools below its freezing point, you are left with a joint which consists of a more-or-less continuous piece of metal where previously there were two; in other words, a weld.

Brazing is certainly capable of joining the same two pieces of metal together and, superficially, the process is the same, but beneath the surface there are great differences. A heat source is used to heat the two pieces of metal, in a similar way to that of true welding, except that the metal is not heated to melting point. A filler rod of bronze alloy (hence 'braze'; cf. 'brass') is then also heated at its extremity and, because its melting point is lower than that of the steel being brazed, it melts, 'flushes' into the joint and adheres to both pieces of metal. The braze actually 'sticks' extraordinarily well because there is molecular bonding between the brazing material and the steel which gives, in effect, something between a glue and the total fusion you obtain with a welded joint.

Brazing has the major advantage that it is simpler to carry out than true welding, but it has two major disadvantages. One is that the heat required, although of a lower temperature, is 'softer' and spreads over a wider area. Consequently, there is often a great deal of distortion in unstressed steel panels. Secondly, the joint is relatively weak because the joining substance, the braze, is itself weaker than the pieces of steel which it is holding together. MOT testing stations will not accept brazed joints on major structural components of the car, although outer body repairs are acceptable. Door skins – no problem! Spring hangers – no chance!

Hardly anyone would purchase any sort of welding gear just in order to carry out brazing. However, as a sometimes useful adjunct to conventional welding, it may be worth bearing in mind that brazing *can* be carried out with oxy-acetylene welding gear, with the addition of no extra equipment, and it *can* be done with arc welding gear, although the carbon-arc brazing kit that is added to the welder gives a very widespread heat source. This causes a lot of distortion, and the wide spread of heat means that the braze itself tends to flow far and wide – and a flood plain of braze comes expensive! Brazing *can't* be carried out with MIG or spot welders, of course.

Brazing has its limitations, but also its uses. If I wanted to fix a broken joint in a steel gate, I'd braze it. Less cleaning up is required, it's quicker and simpler to do and the odd dribble of braze won't matter. If I had a short seam to seal on a body panel I *might* braze it, because the braze would flush into and seal the joint. But, then again, I probably wouldn't, because of the distortion risk, and because all traces of the braze's flux have to be meticulously scrubbed away to prevent future corrosion beneath the paint. And in any case, tack welds and modern seam sealers would do at least as good a job.

ELECTRIC ARC WELDING

Arc welding equipment producing alternating current is the cheapest type of welding system to buy, and also the easiest to set up. Unfortunately for car bodyworkers, it's just not suitable for welding thin steel, although the

aforementioned carbon-arc brazing kit can be added to it. The thinnest steel that an arc welder will handle comfortably is, for instance, the sheet steel on a Land-Rover's bulkhead. Anything thinner and the weld blows right through. Another snag is that it takes a bit of practice to get it right, although that shouldn't be a major disincentive to anyone who wants seriously to go into welding. The equipment consists of a welding machine, or transformer, which takes the ordinary household current and transforms it into the type of current suitable for safely welding steel. Leading from the machine are two heavy-duty cables: one, the 'earth' cable, has a clamp on the end which must be clipped on to the workpiece, and the other runs to a handgrip into which a welding rod is clamped. The welding rod is little more than a piece of steel covered in a sheath of flux which, as the welding takes place, flows over the top of the weld and lies as a glassy 'slag' on top of the weld until it is chipped away later. Without the slag, the weld would form in a blobby, pock marked state, known in the presence of maiden aunts as 'chicken droppings'. With the slag in place, air is excluded for as long as it takes for the molten weld metal to freeze, which allows a smooth weld.

In order to carry out the process, the machine is turned on, set to the appropriate amperage, and one end of the rod is touched on to the workpiece. The light created by the arc welding process is both intensely bright and strong in ultraviolet radiation. It is necessary to protect the skin from the carcinogenic effects of the glare and to protect the eyes from the uv and from the intensity of the light. A mask incorporating a piece of darkened glass is held in front of the face – and that's where your troubles start, because until you start welding, you can't see a thing!

The first touch of the welding rod usually results in the rod 'sticking' to the workpiece, a furious buzzing from the transformer and a welding rod that rapidly glows red hot. Furious shaking has no effect and the only solution is to turn off. A new rod is inserted, the amps

turned up – and you blow a hole right through the workpiece! But when you get it right, there's a satisfying steady crackle and a successful weld takes place – and you *can* see what you're welding once you start!

The 'sticking' effect can only be overcome by turning the amperage up until the current is too high for thin sheet steel and the welder blows holes right through it. A direct current arc welder is far less 'sticky' – you haven't got to contend with the 'on-off-on-off' effect of alternating current, as it goes from one polarity to the other 52 times per second – but such machines are very much more expensive to buy, and you may as well purchase a MIG welder.

MIG, MAG AND TIG

Electric arc welding is the least sophisticated form of electric arc welding. If you took the same principle and designed a better way of carrying out the job, you may come up with what is known as MIG welding.

Because I believe that the correct use of language is the way in which it is used and not the way in which some say it should be used, I will continue to refer to MIG as MIG, even though it is more technically correct to call it 'MAG', except for those times when it really is MIG. Confused? You soon won't be.

MIG stands for Metal, Inert Gas while MAG stands for Metal, Active Gas. The 'Metal' bit is rather tautological, because it's obvious that that is what we're talking about. And in the case of MIG, the 'Inert' bit is just plain wrongly applied. But, first of all, here's how they work:

MIG welders have an earth cable, just like ordinary arc welders. They also have a hand grip which controls the welding rod. However, the 'rod' consists of bare, thin wire which starts on a drum in the welding machine, passes along an umbilical cord between machine and hand grip and out of the end of the hand grip like water from a hose. A motor in the machine pushes the rod out of the grip, and is activated when a trigger on the grip is squeezed. Also, when the trigger is squeezed, two other things happen. One is that the current is turned 'on' (much less risk of an unexpected 'flash' from catching the rod on the workpiece than with arc welding), and the other is that gas is passed down an adjacent tube in the umbilical cord and over the workpiece as the weld takes place. If you were to weld aluminium alloy, the wire would be of aluminium alloy and the gas would be pure argon. Argon is inert – it doesn't burn, it doesn't act as a catalyst, it doesn't react in any way with the molten metal – and that is what makes it perfect, because it allows the aluminium alloy weld to form without atmospheric interference. In welding with argon, you would most certainly be carrying out Metal, *Inert* Gas welding. If you were to use the same gear for welding mild steel, which is far more likely, the wire would be of steel, and the gas would probably be Argon mixed with a small quantity of carbon dioxide. CO_2 helps the weld to penetrate deeper into the steel, whereas argon may leave the weld too shallow. And since the CO_2 *does* something, that makes it, strictly speaking, Metal, *Active* Gas.

Apart from the small safety advantage already mentioned, MIG welding is streets ahead of arc welding where car body repairs are concerned, for a number of reasons. One is that it works very well indeed on thin steel. Used with discretion, virtually no distortion need take place because the shielding gas cools the work down as you go along. In addition, less trim needs to be stripped out of the car, because the smaller amount of heat does not travel so far. MIG is quicker, because you don't have to keep stopping to change rods, and it's cleaner because there is no slag to chip away. Argon and argon-mix gases are available from gas cylinder rental companies and in very small throw-away cylinders from companies such as Machine Mart, who are the country's leading suppliers of all types of electric welding equipment.

In some ways MIG is more limited than any other type of welding. It won't braze, can't be used for freeing nuts or for cutting metal; it just welds. But MIG is so much better for general welding that it must be regarded as the prince among sheet metal welders.

TIG welding (Tungsten, Inert Gas) is being used more extensively in well-equipped body shops for welding aluminium panels. As well as the ubiquitous earth clamp, there is a hand set with a tungsten tip and, once again, an umbilical cord, along which passes only argon gas. The tungsten tip is presented to the workpiece and an incredibly bright electric arc is formed which melts the aluminium at the point of weld but not the tungsten, which lives to weld another day. With his other hand – it is necessary to wear a full head mask – the welder introduces the end of a welding rod into the molten weld pool and so forms the weld. TIG is expensive, highly specialized and not at all a DIY proposition.

PLASMA CUTTING
Of course, this isn't welding at all, but it's closely related to arc welding. It's because it does such a magical job of cutting sheet steel, in a way that avoids distortion and messy edges, follows any shape and gets on with it in a flash – almost literally – that I'm mentioning it here. Plasma cutting involves passing an arc combined with a flow of air through the panel to be cut. The resulting 'plasma' cuts through so smoothly, rapidly and with so much ease, that it has to be seen to be believed. Your instincts tell you to expect some resistance – as if you are using, say, a jig saw – but there isn't any; the cutter just passes along the sheet steel, blasting a pencil thin cut with what seems more like light and sound than substance jetting on to the floor beneath.

OXY-ACETYLENE WELDING
For a time it seemed as though the two 'bottled' gas giants, BOC and Air Products, were deliberately discouraging the use of oxy-acetylene in the home workshop. There were justifiable fears about safety, but the nettle has now been grasped and BOC in particular, in association with welding 'hardware' suppliers Murex, provide for sale the 'Portapak' gas welding set and small cylinders for long term rental.

Oxygen and acetylene are mixed in the welding torch and the flame, once ignited at the end of the nozzle, burns at a very high temperature indeed. The flame is played on to the steel being welded and when a molten puddle begins to form, a thin rod of steel is fed into it. The rod melts and helps to build up a good thickness of steel around the joint. The process demands a huge level of hand-eye co-ordination! Your right hand is playing the flame on to the steel, not too close and not too far away, building a weld pool without going right through the steel and without hanging around so long that you cause more distortion than is necessary, while your left hand is feeding in just the right amount of rod at just the right time. The flame also has to be swirled a little, to push the molten rod into an even covering, and fed along the line of the weld. It's quite a skill but so very satisfying when mastered, although it takes the skill of a true master not to create panels that resemble washboards.

Oxy-acetylene does not require the scrupulous cleanliness of MIG (although the cleaner the metal, the better the weld can be). It can cope with steel where there may be a thin surface coating of rust, whereas MIG cannot, but it is a much harder task to perform; distortion is an ever present threat and safe storage and usage are even more crucial. On the other hand, it is far more versatile, allowing you to cut through quite thick steel with a cutting nozzle, or even with a large welding nozzle used with excess oxygen – and until you've seen its ability to heat seized nuts up to red heat and so allow them to come away without shearing, you've missed a treat!

It is still possible to purchase what you might call 'oxy-mapp' welding gear. The oxygen comes in the small disposable containers used for argon-mix and the mapp gas, (and a concoction of other gases, to give a combination that burns almost-but-not-quite as hot as acetylene), comes in another similar container. The 'pros' are cheapness, ease of storage and the relative safety that comes from having less gas around; the 'cons' are the very high cost of the gas on anything more than the smallest job, and the fact that mapp doesn't reach the temperature of acetylene and so struggles with thicker steel or where a heat sink pulls away the heat.

SPOT WELDING

Where two pieces of metal overlap, such as at a seam, and where there is access, use a spot welder to almost totally eliminate distortion. There is very little skill involved in using a spot welder. As long as the metal to be joined is clean and close, and as long as you have tried a few spot welds on similar metal to gauge how long each weld should be carried out, there is nothing more to it than to just do it!

The two overlapping pieces being joined are held close with clamps, the spot welder arms are cleaned and honed down to the recommended size if they have become flattened out with use, the points of the arm are pinched on opposite sides of the join-to-be and the trigger is pressed fully home. The machine buzzes, the proximity of the weld may glow red, the spot weld is fused and the arms removed – and that's all there is to it. Robots are stupid, and if they can do it, anyone can!

The 'pros' are obvious, but the 'cons' do need considering. The joint will not be sealed and you should always use a spot weldable primer, one that allows the weld to happen without burning away. After welding, the seam should be Waxoyled and/or seam sealed on the inside, where it is prone to moisture ingress. Spot welding can't, obviously, be carried out where the arms can't reach, although dear old MIG can be used to make a series of welds through small pre-drilled holes to emulate the process. The very serious home restorer, determined to follow production methods where possible and to eliminate distortion in every conceivable instance will buy a spot welder. Others will just envy those who have done so, or hire!

WHICH SYSTEM?

No single welding system will suit every need and so, for most of us, it's a matter of making a compromise decision. Here are three rather different possibilities:

CHEAP GAS WELDING KIT

If all you want to do is the occasional emergency repair, or if you want to have a go at welding before committing too much money, you may wish to consider this option. It's too expensive and too difficult to operate for regular use, however: cylinders give minutes of welding, not hours!

ARC WELDER WITH CARBON-ARC ATTACHMENT

This would enable you to carry out emergency body repairs with the brazing attachment, to weld the odd chassis repair (although it's difficult for a beginner to weld on to old steel, especially when working upside-down) and to carry out the *very* occasional bit of domestic welding that may become necessary. Not capable of much more, but cheap to buy and run.

CHEAP ARC WELDER PLUS PORTAPAK OXY-ACETYLENE KIT

This would enable you to carry out every aspect of bodywork restoration, with the reservations mentioned earlier regarding gas welding. Portapak cylinders give 10 to 20 hours welding per pair of cylinders, and BOC require pre-payment of a *one* year rental period, in advance.

CHEAP GAS WELDER PLUS MIG

This one is my favourite combination, although MIG plus Portapak would be the expensive ideal, of course. MIG has all the advantages outlined above, plus you would have access to gas welding for those few occasions when it really was necessary.

▲ WE1. This typical SIP MIG welder consists of a case containing a transformer in one half and storage for a wire drum and a wire feed mechanism in the other.

▼ WE2. Start arc welding by first learning to tack weld.

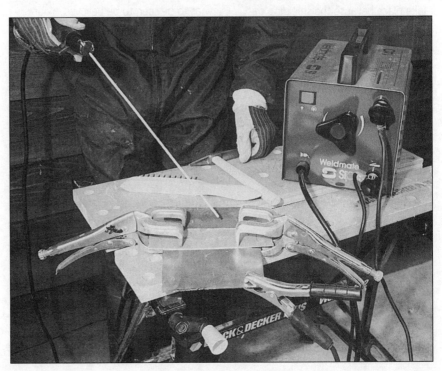

▶ WE3. The light given off is dangerous to eyesight and skin which is why you must wear the correct type of face shield. Sparks can burn if they fall down sleeves or collar! Welders from Clarke and SIP are among the best known for home and light pro. use.

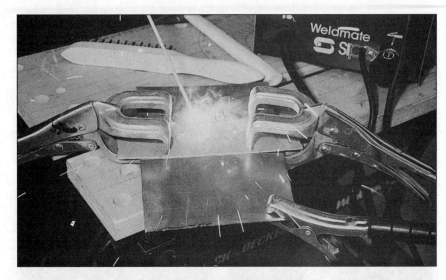

▶ WE4. Carbon-arc kits look somewhat Heath Robinson! The two carbon rods (left) are moved together with the slide on the hand grip until they strike an arc between themselves.

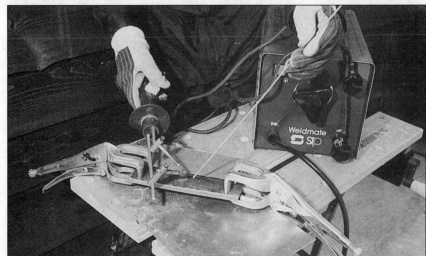

▲ WE5. This extremely bright arc provides the heat for conventional, if messy, brazing

▶ WE6. Brazing with oxy-acetylene is best saved for short runs where distortion will be minimal. Always wash off flux when cool.

▶ WE7. Here's how MIG and spot welding can be used in the fitting of an MGB lower rear wing repair panel; used when replacing a complete sill.

▼ WE8. The panel should be made to fit perfectly, and then the bottom seam can be spot welded into place.

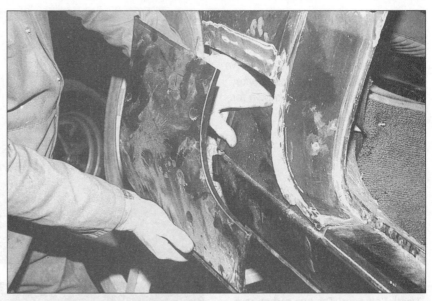

▶ WE9. Just to ensure that the gap is as tight as possible, a hammer handle is used to 'lean' the panel into place, leaving one hand free for welder; the other for face mask. You should wear gloves when MIG welding to protect the hands from uv. Many garage welders don't understand the risk and so don't bother.

▶ WE10. You should weld for an inch or two, stop, weld another part of the joint, stop, switch to another section until you return to 'fill in' the gaps. This spreads the heat around in an even way and reduces further the risk of distortion.

▲ WE11. It is best never to force a repair panel into place to be held there by welding; the stresses included will add distortion. Here, a professional body shop wheels an XK repair panel to a perfect fit.

▲ WE12. Cutting sheet steel with a Clarke plasma cutter – expensive, but quick, easy and clean.

▲ WE13. Heat-resistant putty helps to stop distorting heat from spreading as you gas weld. This is 'Cold Front' putty in use. (Courtesy: Frost Auto Restoration)

▲ WE14. This Frost welder demonstrates how, as one end of this steel sheet was heated to melting point, the other was cool enough to hold. (Is **this** why they're called Frost? Perhaps not!) Heat distortion and damage of nearby components should be greatly reduced. (Courtesy: Frost Auto Restoration)

▲ WE15. Clamping to-be-welded panels in place can be tricky! These 'aviation industry' clamps act like temporary pop-rivets and are taken out for re-use once welding is complete. (Courtesy: Frost Auto Restoration)

▲ WE16. Inter-grip clamps are excellent for butt-joints, although they can be a bit of a fiddle to set in place. (Courtesy: Frost Auto Restoration)

▲ WE17. The Lumiweld system lets you weld cracked aluminium, alloy and 'pot metal' parts. Also shown here is 'jigging putty' which allows you to hold the parts together as you weld them. (Courtesy: The Eastwood Company)

▼ WE18. The Kel-Arc welder is an inexpensive arc welder accessory. It has a 'pulsing' action which allows you to arc weld thin car bodywork steel – not normally possible with a home arc welder. (Courtesy: Frost Auto Restoration)

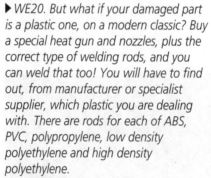

▲ WE19. This spot weld gun is another inexpensive accessory for your home arc welder, and is ideal for tricky to reach areas since it welds from one side. (Courtesy: Frost Auto Restoration)

▶ WE20. But what if your damaged part is a plastic one, on a modern classic? Buy a special heat gun and nozzles, plus the correct type of welding rods, and you can weld that too! You will have to find out, from manufacturer or specialist supplier, which plastic you are dealing with. There are rods for each of ABS, PVC, polypropylene, low density polyethylene and high density polyethylene. (Courtesy: The Eastwood Company)

▼ WE21. Practice on scrap first, if possible! Clamp the broken pieces together, set the heat gun so that it just melts panel and rod, and 'dip' the rod into the plastic weld pool. Follow **to the letter** the makers' instructions on toxic gases. Best of all, work out-of-doors. (Courtesy: The Eastwood Company)

WORKING CONDITIONS

I once knew a chap whose first restoration was of a Porsche 911 – nothing like starting with something simple! – carried out in a garage with no heat or light and which was so narrow that, in order to get from one end of the car to the other, he had to crawl beneath the bodyshell which was standing on axle stands. The amazing thing was not the quality of the finished job which, to be honest, wasn't that brilliant, but that he finished it at all. Most people in such circumstances would have given up well before the end. But, in general, you can lay down some fairly simple minimum guidelines for suitable working conditions.

Your chosen workshop will have enough room for you to be able to open the car's doors, and for you to get all round it. There will be enough room at one end for you to lift an engine and withdraw it. It will be free from severe draughts and, of course, leaks, and there will be an adequate supply of electricity and light. You can help the lighting situation by the simple expedient of painting all the walls with cheap white emulsion paint, and you are strongly recommended to fit strip lights – say four per car-area. They are cheap to run and give lots of revealing light.

Having said all that, I also knew someone who carried out all of his mechanical and bodywork repairs out of doors, right down to stripping an engine, removing bolt-on wings and even a complete respray which, while being below professional standards, was quite acceptable and not at all bad for the work of a 20-year-old. That someone was me! Provided that you pick your time of year (or that you're tough enough to work with frozen hands), you can do tolerable work out of doors if there is no alternative. The main secret is not to be too ambitious. Only plan to carry out a limited, self-contained amount of work at a time. If you are pretty sure that you will be able to complete a job in a week or so, give it a try. It is when you have to leave an unfinished job outside in the cold, cold snow that disillusionment sets in and the car ends up being disposed of in its unfinished state. I know because that has also happened to me.

THE IDEAL WORKSHOP

Over 20 years after my out-of-door exploits, I was fortunate enough to be able to buy my ideal workshop. If you have space to build a garage, this type could be ideal for you, too. Whether you need a garage to supplement the existing one, or whether you are a 'first time buyer', the requirements remain the same. You will need a sound concrete base that will stay free of cracks in spite of the weight of a car supported on a trolley jack; a weatherproof structure and one that does not allow condensation to form, and the whole thing really ought to be reasonably attractive to look at, since you will be well and truly lumbered with it once it is in place! Other points worth considering are the time it will take to get the garage in place, the amount of maintenance required and – not least – the cost.

Doug Pound, whose company sold me the garage, sees timber-framed buildings as one of the best solutions for classic car enthusiasts. His company, D. W. Pound Garden Buildings, specializes in the supply of timber sheds, garages and the like, so perhaps he is a little biased, but he certainly raised some interesting points. Not least is the speed with which one of these buildings can be erected. Even the large structure that I was invited to photograph took less than a day to erect, and for a structure that allows you to park and work on two good-sized cars, that's amazing – especially when you compare it with the amount of classic car time you would have to give up in order to build your own conventional, brick-built garage. In addition, the timber-framed building could be put up by someone without specialist building skills, or the Pound erectors will do it for you. Other points in favour of the timber job include: freedom from condensation; the possibility of taking it with you when you move house and the pleasant appearance of wood. The garage shown being erected here is built of cedar which will not rot, although it will discolour down to a boring grey if not treated with Cuprinol at least every two years. The felt roof will also require replacement every few years – something between four and seven years being the norm, in my experience.

DIY garage erection may well be within the scope of the average car repair enthusiast – and smaller garages can be considerably simpler to erect than large ones – but there are a number of absolutely critical points that must be borne in mind.

▲ IW1. If Pound are going to erect the building, they insist that the concrete base is in-place first. The size has to be spot-on: correct to less than half an inch, and so it is essential that the wooden formers into which the concrete will be poured are (1) straight; (2) dead level, using a builder's spirit level to be sure; (3) firmly pegged, so that the great weight of the mix and the force of 'tamping' the concrete level do not force them apart. With an area measuring 20 feet across, you have to have an intermediate plank at the same level as the surrounding ones from which to work. Use scaffolding planks, building them up a day or two before the ready-mixed is delivered, and sitting them on hand-mixed concrete. Once the ready-mixed is in, you can pull out the planks and bucket in enough mix to fill the gap where the planks have been. Leave the timber formers in place for several days after laying the concrete, to allow it to go hard and resist edge breakage.

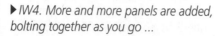
IW4. More and more panels are added, bolting together as you go ...

IW5. ... until the entire 'ground floor' structure is in place. Panels with doors or windows in them come ready built. The entire front consists, in this case, of just two complete panels. Also provided are sufficient Rawlbolts to fix the structure down to the concrete pad. This is simply a matter of drilling through the base of the frame and into the concrete, followed by hammering the bolt through the timber, into the base. As the bolt head in the top is tightened, the base of the bolt expands, gripping the base in a pretty immovable way.

▲ IW2. Before starting with the assembly, Pound's experienced erectors placed all the bolts and other fittings to be used around the concrete pad within easy reach – essential if the wind is blowing half a gale and the panel you are trying to erect feels like it's emulating a mainsail. Note the clean edges to the accurately built concrete pad. You should always start with one corner, placing both corner panels in place on the edge of the pad before pushing the coach bolts provided through the pre-drilled holes in the timber framework and spannering them tight. I was fascinated to see that all the holes really did line up!

▼ IW6. Eaves panels come in two separate sections for each end, while the 'overhangs' are separate and nailed on from above. Note the way in which Dave has placed a length of timber against the outside of the eaves to take the weight of his ladder placed against the inside. Roof

timbers are also pre-fabricated and are intended to sit one on each of the timber uprights in the wall sections. They are nailed on at the eaves, but just to hold them secure, a temporary strip of timber is nailed across the top. This will be removed when the roof proper is fitted.

▲ IW3. This is why the pad has to be so precisely measured: The prefabricated panels sit over the edge of the concrete pad, giving a weatherproof joint against the floor. Impressively done!

◄IW7. With eaves dead vertical and roof timbers properly spaced, the pre-cut sheets of ply are nailed straight on to the roof. In this case, narrow strips have been nailed on to the front edges to give an exact fit with the full-sized sheets to follow.

▼IW8. Roofing felt is fitted, starting with the bottom and overlapping each strip as you progress up the roof to give a weathertight seal, nailing down every two inches with galvanized felt-nails. One of the last jobs is to fit fixtures and fittings, such as door bolts and window catches.

▼IW9. Dusty garage floors are a bane, especially when restoration work is to be carried out. Old fashioned-type floor paints wear off rapidly. This is a 2-pack floor covering called Reuseal which is as superior as 2-pack car body paint is to cellulose. Until you have worked on a properly finished garage floor, you can't fully appreciate the difference it makes to good working practice.

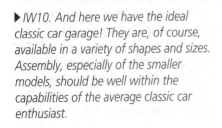

►IW10. And here we have the ideal classic car garage! They are, of course, available in a variety of shapes and sizes. Assembly, especially of the smaller models, should be well within the capabilities of the average classic car enthusiast.

Chapter 3
Bodywork restoration

The majority of classic cars are repaired in the traditional way, and it's for them that this chapter has been written. However, there are sometimes alternatives, and these are touched on first.

It is almost impossible to carry out the total restoration of a classic car without repairing a car's bodywork. I say 'almost' because there are one or two exceptions. One is that the car you are restoring has spent all of its life, mainly under cover, in some virtually dry part of the world such as Arizona. Nice if you can get it! The other is if you are able to obtain a replacement bodyshell for your car. A very small number of companies make complete, replacement bodyshells from scratch. One of them makes a replacement body for the MGA; another makes bodies for E-types; yet others will no doubt come and go. These bodies are, theoretically, ready to use (or, in the case of the MG, ready to bolt straight on to your MGA chassis). In practice, however, such bodies may require a lot of work before they can be used. Original bodies are made on factory jigs and variations in dimensions are kept within acceptable tolerances. 'One-offs' of this sort are never in the same category, and invariably require skilled adaptation before they fit properly. The choice you have to make is whether the frustratingly large amount of work is worthwhile in order to have a brand new body without a shred of rust in it. The

best bodies, in terms of fit and finish, are those for the MGB and Sprite/Midget made by Heritage, a subsidiary of Rover Group. They are made using many of the original tools and, while the shape may not be perfect in every detail (you may have a struggle to fit the MGB's windscreen frame, for example), they are by far the best replacement bodies available and will last for far longer than any vehicle with repaired panels.

PLANNING THE WORK

For most restorers, however, body restoration is an integral, essential part of the process. It is sometimes tackled as a complete car-off-road project; less often whilst the car is on the road, taking the car out of action just for as long as the repair work takes to carry out. Most people who follow the latter route get the work back to front. They start by repairing the most obvious, outer corrosion first, only moving on to the more deep-seated stuff as time progresses or as it becomes obvious that, say, a new wing can't be bolted back on because of the corrosion beneath. Charles Ware, classic car guru and proprietor of the famous Morris Minor Centre in Bath, takes a different view. In fact, he starts his thinking on classic car restoration from the opposite angle to most people.

You should bear in mind Porter's First Law of Restoration: 'A stripped down car always needs three times more work doing to it than you thought it needed when it was in one piece'. And this means, of course, that the corollary: 'It

will therefore need three times more money spending on it', also holds true. Charles Ware believes that you should restore a classic because of its intrinsic values: it's easier to understand and to repair than a modern; it wastes less of the earth's resources; it was built with more individual pride, and you can take pride in owning it.

He also realizes that few people can afford the true cost of restoring a classic in one go. Unfortunately, many professional restorers lead their customers up the garden path. They quote for the work required to repair what you can see to be wrong with a car, ignoring Porter's First Law. They must know, if they have any experience as restorers, that things will be more complex, but they choose to ignore it. Then, when the work is carried out, the poor customer receives a bill that shocks, and/or the restorer cuts corners. It is better by far to plan not to do all the work in one go, but to phase the work.

Phase one will, unconventionally, ignore the outer panels, interior trim, chromework and other cosmetics, and concentrate on making the car structurally sound. With the majority of cars, this involves looking at the underside of the car, the suspension mounting points, the sills and the structural box sections. The brakes, suspension and steering would also be tackled at the same time, along with the electrics. The result will be a car that looks little different from the way it looked before. In fact, it might even look worse! There will invariably be some bits of structural work that show up on the top side: welding that has burned paint off a panel for instance. Grit your teeth, brush paint over it and put up with it, in the knowledge that your car is now sound, it will pass the MOT, it is less likely to let you down because the electrics have been sorted (they're the cause of 90 per cent of all breakdowns) and you can save up for the next phase in the work.

Phase two will see the outer body panels worked upon: wings, chromework, respray – producing a car that now looks as sound as you know it to be. You must, of course, do as much as you can to preserve the car as the work is carried out so that you're not having to repeat the work in the foreseeable future.

Phases three and four will cover the mechanical components such as engine, gearbox, axle and so on, and the interior trim. These, of course, can be carried out more easily as you go along, with less need to take the car off the road for lengthy periods.

The sort of restoration that is carried out all in one go presents different sorts of problems, of course. You will still find that there is more work than you had originally planned and that the cost will be greater. It will all take longer than you envisaged, too, but rushing and restoration can never go together.

Probably the biggest blunder that you can make when restoring major bodywork components would be to weld panels in place, locking the car into a distorted shape – and it's not as difficult as you might think! If your car has a body and separate chassis, it is essential that the body is repaired whilst still on the chassis. Otherwise, it will probably never fit again! In the case of monocoque, chassis-less bodies – the majority of modern classics – it is equally important that the car is supported evenly on jacks or axle stands, and it is *crucial* that bonnet, boot and doors (*especially* doors!) are tried and fitted before major components such as front flitch panels (the large area behind the front wings) and sills are welded into place. See later sections in this book for more details.

The following sections each deal with a major part of the car and/or a major technique that is specific to classic car restoration. Haynes' *Car Bodywork Repair Manual* by the same author as this book, covers in detail all the specific workshop skills for which there is not room here, such as spraying, welding and so on.

SAFETY

At the start of many sections is a 'Safety' note. Naturally safety is the responsibility of each individual restorer or repairer and no responsibility for the effectiveness or otherwise of advice given here nor for any omissions can be accepted by the author. After all, the jobs you will be carrying out will be *your* responsibility, so do take care to familiarize yourself with safety information available from the suppliers or manufacturers of the materials or equipment which you use. 'Safety' Notes are intended to supplement this information with useful tips, as is the additional information on workshop safety and workshop practice in the Appendix – you are strongly advised to read the Appendix before beginning any of the tasks detailed in this book.

Take note of information in the text on safety hazards. NEVER drain petrol over a pit or anywhere where a spark could ignite the vapour, e.g. near a central heater boiler – outdoors is best. For obvious reasons, attempting to weld a fuel tank can be lethal and should be left to a specialist. Never use a flame near the fuel tank or lines. Drain fuel only into suitable containers. Do not use plastic containers which are attacked by petrol.

The battery should be taken out prior to fuel tank removal to prevent accidental shorting in the presence of fuel vapour. When storing the battery, take care to ensure that no object falls unnoticed across the terminals and becomes a potential fire risk. Paint stripper is damaging to the skin and eyes – read instructions before use, and wear gloves, goggles and protective overalls. Ensure that the vehicle is firmly supported when lifted off the ground – a jack is NOT safe enough. Wear goggles when

probing beneath the car, and beware of rusty, jagged edges. Never work beneath a car supported on a jack: use axle stands, ramps or a roll-over cage, and in the former case, securely chock the wheels that remain on the ground.

QUALITY NOTE
The sparks from an angle grinder 'burn' themselves immovably into glass, whether in the car or in your workshop windows. Take a note of the direction in which the sparks are travelling, but always cover up window glass, mirror glass and paintwork if you are using an angle grinder within spark-travelling distance of the car.

GLASS – REMOVAL AND REPLACEMENT

FRONT AND REAR SCREENS AND FIXED SIDE WINDOWS
The basic procedure is the same for all types of windscreen held in with conventional rubbers, but different models of car may be fitted with different types of trim or moulding around the screen. This must be removed before the glass is taken out. Some cars are fitted with bonded-in windscreens where the glass is, in effect, glued directly to the windscreen frame. Removal and replacement is a job for a windscreen specialist.

Make sure you know which type of glass is fitted before attempting to remove it. 'Toughened' glass will stand a certain amount of thumping before breaking, but other types crack or shatter much more easily.

Safety: The dangers of broken glass should be self evident! The Haselock mechanics photographed in the following sequence were happy to work without gloves or goggles; you should wear both. Also, be sure to apply masking tape to the windscreen demister vents to prevent any broken glass from dropping in. It could blow out later and get into your eyes with pretty dire consequences!

▲ W1. After removing any trim or mouldings (and after taking off the windscreen wiper arms if the front screen is to be removed), you should use a chisel-shaped piece of wood with a rounded end to ease the rubber free all the way around both inside and out, taking care not to split the rubber if it is good enough to be re-used. (It rarely is: a new rubber is strongly recommended for ease of fitting and because it will be far less likely to leak.) You may, if you wish, use detergent in water brushed into the inside of the joint to help the rubber to slide. With two assistants on the outside to prevent the screen from plopping on to the floor, push the screen carefully but firmly from the inside (use your foot if you like!), starting with one top corner and then the other.

▲ W3. When the glass and rubber start to come free, they can be pulled clear from the outside. With the screen out of the way, clean off any stuck-on remnants of rubber or adhesive, scrape off any rust back to shiny, bright metal before painting – and don't be amazed if you even have to carry out a small patch repair, cutting out corroded metal and replacing it. And be sure to seal the screen properly next time to prevent this happening! Make sure there are no sharp edges on the screen aperture (see W5 onward).

▲ W4. Thoroughly clean the edges of the glass to be fitted. Old rubber which has gone hard and started to crack is no use, so be prepared to replace it. Fitting is much easier with new rubber, too!

▼ W5. Identify for yourself the flap in the rubber that folds over the metal screen aperture. Take some thin cord – nylon is ideal – and push it under the flap all the way round. (A 'quick-tip' is to use a short piece of brake piping through which you thread the end of the cord. Push the end of the tube under the flap and draw it along, laying the cord into place.)

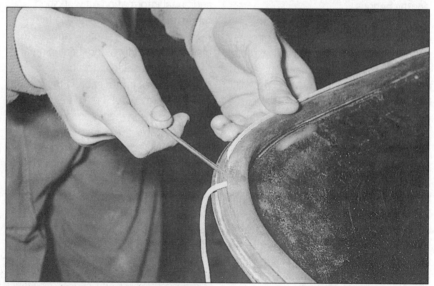

▲ W2. The safest way of working is to cover the glass with broad masking tape, which is what Haselock did when removing the screen from this fully restored Beetle. Then, even if the glass should crack or shatter – and you can never guarantee that it won't – the danger, to say nothing of the mess and inconvenience, will be much less. Note that a cloth has been used to cover and protect the bodywork.

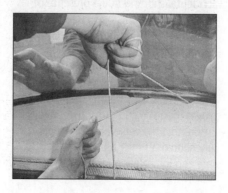

◄ W6. Aim to make the two ends of cord join, then slightly overlap at the base of the screen. Have the screen propped into place from the outside, locating the base of the screen as well as possible. Whilst the screen is pushed inwards fairly hard at the bottom, pull one end of the cord ...

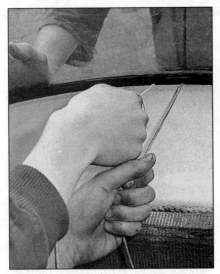

▲ W7. ... so that your hands cross and the rubber lip is pulled over the edge of the metal window aperture.

▲ W9. The tricky point will come when you go round the corners and into the finishing straight at the top. It will help enormously if your assistant gives the screen regular (careful!) smacks with the heel of the hand (wear thick industrial gloves!) to push the rubber well into position, otherwise the cord may easily pull out of the rubber lip without it having been pulled over the steelwork. Finally, refit any chromework or trim to the screen surround. New rubbers should not be prone to leakage, but VW used to recommend the use of windscreen sealant on the screen surround. If you wish, you may inject screen sealant into the rubber where the screen glass is seated, before pushing it on to the glass, and into the rubber where it flaps over the screen aperture, before inserting the cord. Needless to say, this will create a lot of mess on hands and glass! After you have finished, scrape the excess off the glass with a plastic scraper and wipe the glass clean with paraffin/kerosene followed by a strong mix of detergent and water.

▲ W10. When refitting the screen, you may have to refit the rubber or 'chrome' plated plastic trim and spreader insert. It's very tricky and time-consuming without the correct, inexpensive special tool. (Courtesy: Frost Auto Restoration)

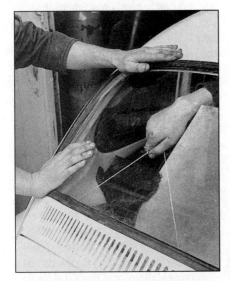

▲ W8. Your assistant (or better still, two of them) can make all the difference between success and failure here. The glass must be pushed downwards so that the lip is held well on to the window aperture, while first one end of the cord is pulled for a few inches and then the other. Two snags are likely to occur unless you're forewarned. One is that you may tug too energetically on the cord and pull a cut into the rubber, and the other is that the cord may catch on a snag on the metal aperture and break, although this is less likely with nylon.

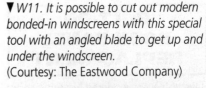

▼ W11. It is possible to cut out modern bonded-in windscreens with this special tool with an angled blade to get up and under the windscreen. (Courtesy: The Eastwood Company)

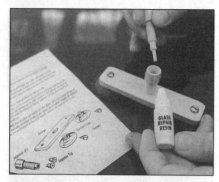

▲ W12. Chipped screens – an MOT failure in Europe, if the chip is in the driver's eye-line – can be repaired with glass repair resin and a suitable repair kit. (Courtesy: Frost Auto Restoration)

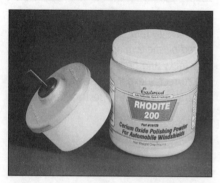

▲ W13. Scratches on glass can be polished out with a polishing mop fitted to your drill and a special polishing compound. (Courtesy: The Eastwood Company)

BOLT-ON BODY PANEL REPLACEMENT

Have you ever wondered just what sorts of people write workshop manuals? Let me tell you now that they are the sorts of people who, if you were ever unfortunate enough to accompany them at dinner, would take you warmly by the arm just as you were about to savour your last, saved-up morsel off the plate, so that you dropped it embarrassingly on to your lap. They are the kinds of drivers who always park their cars at an angle, so that you can't quite squeeze into the last parking space, and they are the very people who pay for their grub at motorway services with a credit card so that you, who are standing next in line, have to put up with food that is

disgustingly bland, grossly overpriced *and* cold, to boot. In short, they are blots on the landscape, and as such are prone to taking their blottishness into their professional lives. Allow me to prove my point.

You turn to your official reprinted Manufacturer's Workshop Manual for divine guidance on how to remove a suspect recirculating poppet valve. 'One,' says the Manual, 'detach the Recirculating Poppet Valve Cluster from the car after removing the retaining bolts. Two,' it continues optimistically, 'dismantle the Cluster and replace any faulty Poppet Valves after inspection.' Wallop! That's it! No hint as to *where* it is, how to find the hidden fixings, or to bear in mind that the brake servo will be in the way and has to be removed first. *Those* are the sorts of people who write workshop manuals; my advice is to steer well clear of them!

In particular, you should never ask one of them how to remove and re-fit bolt-on body panels, whether to an ancient or a modern classic. It will only encourage them. It's best to face it right from the start: bolt-on body panels only ever bolt-off after more hassle than you can shake a stick at and never, ever willingly go back into place.

On the other hand, bolt-on panels are far better for the DIY repairer to work with than weld-on panels, if only because they require fewer specialist tools and less in the way of specialist skills. As long as you don't expect bolt-on panels to go together as easily as a Meccano set, they are ideal for the home repairer to have a go at. There is just one major proviso, but I'll come to that later.

First comes the question of what you are going to use as a replacement for the old panels. With many classics, you just thank your lucky stars if there are replacement panels of any sort available. With others you have no choice at all, since there is none available, or you have a choice between relatively expensive OE (original equipment) panels, or cheaper 'pattern' panels. If you possibly can, my advice is almost always to go for OE panels. *Don't* expect them to fit first time (although with Porsche and

Mercedes you stand a better chance), but you can almost guarantee that pattern (non-original) parts will only fit where they touch. They usually require skilled work to make them fit fully, which makes them more expensive and usually less good-looking, in the long run. One example of this is Beetle panels, and another is Mini panels. Both are plentifully available, and both are vastly better as OE panels than as 'pattern' parts.

Where panels are simply not available, there is a different set of choices to hand. You can either try to repair rusty panels yourself, have them repaired, or have someone make new panels as one-offs. The latter course is fraught with difficulties, unless you have the maker fit the panels for you. (Not the least of your problems will be in finding someone *capable* of making the panels for you!) But then, if you have the parts fitted, you will hardly need an article of this sort. If you want to try to repair the panels yourself, DON'T try to carry out all the repairs with the panels away from the car and then expect the panels to go back on again. More about this later.

OFF WITH THE OLD

Removing old bolt-on body panels is good fun! Everything happens relatively quickly and you can see results more rapidly than at any other stage of a restoration project. However, don't skimp the safety steps, and do ensure that you are properly prepared in other ways, too. Have strong industrial gloves handy, because old, rusty panels can be dangerously sharp, and there will be a lot of hand tugging involved. Have goggles handy, too, because you'll have to work beneath the car for at least part of the time and the risk of rusty particles in your eyes is very real.

Make sure also that you have got plenty of room! If you've ever taken a clock apart, you'll know how the 'innards' seem to take up more space than you would have believed possible. It's just the same with a car's bodywork, except that the sheer volume of space required can be enormous, especially in the case of pre-war cars. Earlier cars usually have sweeping front wings, running boards, rear wings with flanges and great folding bonnets. Ensure that you have something like a spare room, or even an empty garage or shed in which to store the parts you take off. Best of all, have assistance when it comes to taking the bits off. A complete door, even on a modern car, can be a surprisingly heavy lump, and many cars have large wing panels that can be difficult to manoeuvre – there's no point in creating more damage than is necessary.

PANEL REMOVAL

'Open your Manual to page H56 where you will learn all about how to remove the front wings. Disconnect all appropriate wiring, disconnect all the retaining bolts and lift the wing away,' it says, or words to that effect. Trouble is, it won't be like that, so don't be taken in!

Problems often start with, and also end with, the wiring. After disconnecting the battery, try disconnecting the wires from the lamps themselves or by pulling apart the bullet connectors, if fitted. In the latter case, don't just grab the wires and pull: take two pairs of pliers; one for the bullet connector tube and one for the wire where it emerges from the tube. If you're lucky, you won't pull the wire out of the 'bullet' itself, but don't bank on it!

Don't rely on the workshop manual's wiring diagram to tell you how to re-connect the wires when you fit the replacement wing. All too often, colour codes have faded, wires have been replaced with 'foreign' cables of random colour coding, or extras have been wired in, such as flashing indicators where none were fitted originally. It only takes a few moments to tag each wire ending with a piece of masking tape on which you can easily write with a ballpoint pen, and it will save you so much time and frustration later.

Before you can remove most front wings, bumpers have to come off and, for some reason, bumper bolts are especially prone to rusting solid. On the other hand, they are invariably of generous dimensions, so you can apply lots and lots of grunt without risk of a bolt shearing. Life will be made so very much simpler, however, if you have the foresight to soak the bolts a good couple of days before you are due to begin work. It sounds a fiddle, but you won't believe how much easier the job will become, and how many of the smaller bolts you will be able to save that you would otherwise have sheared. In fact, several good soakings are better than one, but it's a job that most people can't be bothered to do, believing that bolt removal will be all right on the night. Unfortunately, it won't, and persuading reluctant bolts to shift will, without a shred of doubt, prove the biggest challenge when it comes to panel removal. But back to the bumpers: you can use an extension tube on a ring spanner (*never* a socket or open-ender!), but the best and safest way is, (with the car on the ground, not on a jack, ramps or axle stand), to lie down and push the spanner with your foot. If you need to develop extra 'shove', just imagine that a certain ex-Prime Minister has stepped out in front of you whilst you're driving your car. Which pedal you choose is up to you!

One step you can take to make nut and bolt removal easier, is to chisel off the old wing before tackling the fixings. Somehow, your mind gets into a pattern of thinking: 'It's bolt-on, therefore I've got to take all the bolts out first.' Not so! Just think how much easier it would be to get at all those bolt heads tucked up inside the wing if the wing wasn't there in the first place! Using a cold chisel, you don't have to be especially neat about removing the old wing, but do wear the thick, industrial gloves I mentioned earlier. Those edges will be razor sharp!

A few panels are held on with screwdriver-head screws. You may feel that you won't have a hope in hell of moving them, but that isn't necessarily so. An essential tool in anyone's tool kit is an impact screwdriver. Before using it, ensure that the screw head is thoroughly cleaned out, locate the impact screwdriver firmly in place and give it a good thump with a heavy hammer. It's no good using a toffee hammer; you've really got to shock a stubborn thread free. In order to prevent panel damage, you may have to support the other side of the panel with another hammer – using your third hand, of course. By this means, the screw will come free. Or it won't. And if it doesn't? ...

SEIZED FIXINGS

Removing nuts, bolts, machine screws and captive nuts that have stripped, sheared or seized is, unfortunately, an inevitable consequence of having to replace bolt-on body panels. Approach seized bolts and captive nuts calmly and logically. Do not, at this stage, throw your spanner through the car's windscreen. You may regret it later. Instead, read *Zen and the Art of Motorcycle Maintenance* once more and take one of the following steps:

If you have found a nut that won't budge and you're certain that all you will do is shear a bolt, you can take off the nut by other means. You could heat it with an oxy-acetylene torch – or even a butane torch – which may well break the rust bond – but do take the usual and vital safety precautions and *never* use heat near inflammable fluids or materials. You could try sawing down the nut, or chiselling it down with a really sharp cold chisel, or you could use one of those amazing and invaluable tools, a nut splitter.

Once you've gone and sheared the thing off, you have got to remove the old stud, and the best – possibly the only – option is to drill it out. Turning captive nuts is another story. You may be able to close up the cage from behind, to remove the cage and use a nut, or you could buy a new one that taps in from the front. Try your local motor factors or independent VW dealers – Beetles are riddled with the things! (See caption No. BOB18.)

The best solution of all, of course, is not to have to struggle to get nuts and bolts undone in the first place! I have taken to doing two things with all restoration nuts and bolts. One is to use stainless steel nuts and bolts (available from people such as Namrick) in all the most vulnerable places, while other screwed fixings all have their threads wiped before assembly with Comma's 'Copper Ease', which appears to be grease with a high proportion of copper particles contained within it.

SUBTERRANEAN ACTIVITIES

The stripped-down car will be both satisfying and daunting to look at. Satisfying because it was a dramatic thing to carry out; daunting because you can now see for real how bad things are!

Your first job will be to dig down into what you have exposed, cleaning, scraping and preparing to repair any corrosion damage that you may find there. In the case of a complete strip-down car, you'll be able to apply a pressure washer to all those important little places, although I strongly recommend that you don't try the sand-blasting attachment. The sand will end up everywhere, including engine internals, suspension components and brakes. There are many brands of corrosion-inhibiting primer on the market from people such as Finnigans, Comma and Corroless, and while I don't know how well they work as rust inhibitors, you've got to use something.

Your biggest problem will come from having to cut away and repair rusty panels, and it's here that you will find the major snag I mentioned earlier, because you will be at no advantage whatsoever over the person whose car is fitted with weld-on panels. However, if you are not a welder, you could always bring in an expert to do the job for you, or you could decide that, since you will be working on hidden panels, now would be a good time to learn. Do remember that your new or repaired bolt-on panels will have to fit the stuff that you have welded in. Lots of test fitting will be called for before any tack welds are turned into the real thing. If you have to fabricate complete inner panels, it's best to build them, or at least test-fit them *in situ*. An inner wing, if it's of typically simple pre-war construction can be constructed piece by piece, clamping and screwing the assembly into place as you go until, when final assembly takes place, you can be sure of a good, tailor-made fit.

You may now be ready for reassembly. Now, you remember all those notes, sketches and photographs you took as the job was coming apart? ('What do you mean? What notes?')! Parts that look as if you could never forget what they are or where they go as they come apart can take on a mysterious existence as reassembly takes place. You're never quite sure whether the strangely shaped thingie you have found *is* actually off your car, or whether it dropped out of the peg bag.

REFITTING THE PANELS

'They came off, so they'll go on again.' But if you've worked on the old panels, or the inner panels, or if you've bought new, then like heck they will! You'll have to start, obviously enough, by test fitting the panels to see where the worst of the gaps are to be found. The most likely problems will be where flanges have become distorted, which will involve dressing them back again with hammer and dolly, or where repairs have been carried out and the fit is less than perfect. In spite of all your panel-by-panel test fitting, you may still find that you have to change the shape of some panels or to grind down any excessively high welds where they are getting in the way. With new panels, it is quite common to have to file out some of the mounting holes so that the wing can be moved backwards or forwards, and in or out. Be absolutely certain that you are fitting panels around the relatively fixed points of doors, bonnet and boot lid. They will, of course, have some adjustment built in to them, but they and the totally fixed items such as bulkhead and sills are the standard starting points around which the other bolt-on panels are assembled. You will also have to check that the grille fits the front wing shape on cars such as the MGB, for instance, before you bolt everything firmly into place. Make no mistake about it, this can be a time-consuming part of the work, but it's essential if your car isn't going to look very odd when it has been resprayed, which is when all the badly fitting gaps will show up!

Before the car can be painted, any blemishes must be filled and spot primed, and then any remaining tiny blemishes can be taken out with polyester stopper, rather than the dreadfully outdated cellulose variety which shrinks as it dries. And then, of course, you should take the whole thing apart again for painting!

FINAL ASSEMBLY

After paint, and not before, is the time to apply rust prevention treatment. Waxoyl contains loads of silicones and they really are the painter's enemy. They cause 'fish-eye' cratering, where the paint is repelled by the silicone and the only answer is to strip off the paint and start again. They can be removed with silicone wipe, but since you can't see the stuff, you can't be sure whether it has all gone or not until it is too late. Better by far to keep anything containing silicones away from the car until after painting is complete. Also on the rustproofing front, try to use bright zinc-plated nuts, bolts and washers if you can't afford all stainless steel, and coat all flange mountings, the undersides of flat washers and any other potential moisture traps with an appropriate sealer. You can buy it from motor factors either in tubes or as strips on a roll.

Before you finally fit and adjust the doors, make sure that the door seal strip has been fitted to the aperture first; it makes an enormous difference to the fit! Also ensure that the door gear is all in place, because the extra weight will invariably make the door sag, and don't be afraid of having to give the door a bit of a twist to make it line up with the door opening.

Replacing bolt-on panels is by no means as straightforward as dismantling and reassembling a Meccano kit. There is a lot of work and a great deal of care required to carry out the job, although arguably less specialist skill needed than for the replacement of weld-on panels. The trouble is that one can make it all sound *too* daunting – maybe workshop manual writers have got the right idea, after all.

▲ BOB1. The Porsche 911 and 912 feature many bolt-on panels. This beautiful 912 was restored entirely by home restorer Peter Monk.

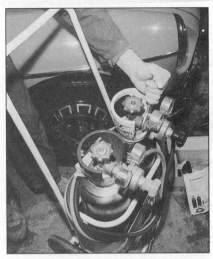

▲ BOB4. Oxy-acetylene may prove useful for inner panel repairs and will be invaluable for shifting stubborn nuts.

▲ BOB2. Some wiring will have to be fed through body panels. Tag each one clearly.

▲ BOB5. A pressure washer, such as this Clarke machine, will prove its worth at this early stage, enabling you to see clearly every fixing.

▶ BOB6. Never put new panels over bare or rusty metal. The new panels themselves are often poorly protected, too. Spend time cleaning off, painting and Waxoyling: much of what you can now see will later be impossible to reach.

▲ BOB3. Be prepared to drill out impossible-to-shift studs.

▲ BOB7. There will always be rust present beneath rusty outer panels. Be prepared in advance for the time you will have to spend cutting out and replacing rusty panelwork that will only be revealed once outer panels are out of the way.

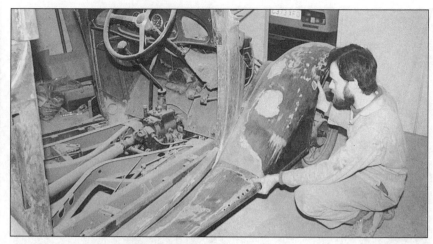

▲ BOB10. The repaired panels must be fully trial-fitted before painting.

▲ BOB8. When you have to build up replacements yourself, build up complex inner panels in sections.

▲ BOB11. Don't tighten any of the bolts until all are in place, otherwise manipulating panel positions will be impossible and some bolts won't line up with the holes.

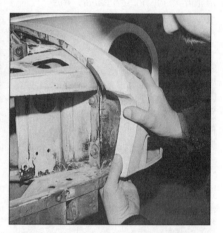

▲ BOB13. Front wings have to fit doors and bonnet, and in many cases they also have to suit the grille, front bumper and front valence. Trial fit all of them.

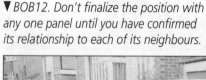

▼ BOB12. Don't finalize the position with any one panel until you have confirmed its relationship to each of its neighbours.

▲ BOB9. When it comes to putting the sections together, spot welding is best, MIG a good second best, while gas welding takes real skill.

▲ BOB14. Filler will take out minor blemishes but must not be used to cover up mis-matches in panel fit. You'll need to remove panels again for painting.

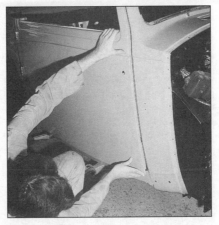

▲ BOB17. Fit door seals before fitting doors and bear in mind that doors may take a degree of twisting to make them fit.

WELD-ON WING REPLACEMENT

The following picture sequence covers the fitting of a typical weld-on wing and shows how to replace a complete Austin-Healey 'Frogeye' Sprite rear wing. The general principles can be applied to most weld-on wings, although, if anything, some are even easier to fit because there is no inner wing to which they are attached. The crucial thing with all weld-on wings is that you must be certain of their fit to relative door pillar and sill line (and bonnet, where applicable) before welding in place.

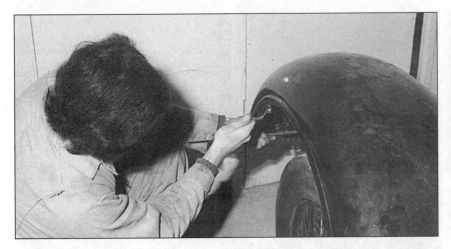

▲ BOB15. After painting, the fitting process must be carried out all over again – but take care to protect that paintwork!

▲ ROW1. This Frogeye rear wing had appeared fairly sound until we sanded – and sanded and sanded! – and found that it was, in fact, full of filler. It had to come off!

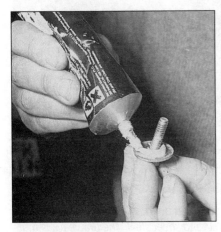

▲ BOB16. Use seam sealer around panel fitting washers and to stop moisture getting in to joints.

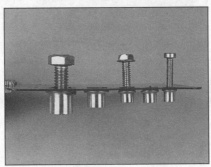

▲ BOB18. It is quite common to have captive nuts detach themselves or come loose. They are best removed – you may have to work **very** carefully at the back of a panel to remove the old cage – or drill new holes an inch or so further along. These replacements are fitted from one side of the panel using a special 'pop-rivet' tool after drilling a hole of an appropriate size. A godsend! (Courtesy: The Eastwood Company)

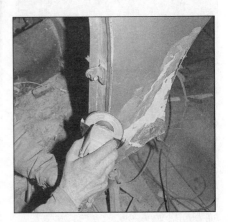

▲ ROW2. The angle grinder was used to take off most of the corner, where the wing flange joined the door shut pillar.

▲ *ROW3. Then what remained of the wheel arch flange was similarly ground away. Both edges were then opened up with the bolster chisel. The edges created in this way are really sharp – take great care and always wear thick leather industrial-type gloves!*

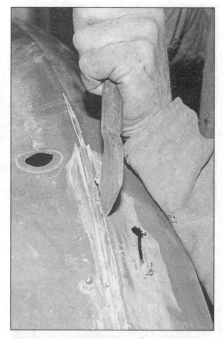

▲ *ROW5. Distortion wasn't a problem here, so we showed how a bolster chisel can do the job. It's quite a lot faster but harder to control. A power jig saw would be another alternative.*

▲ *ROW7. Rather than risk melting the aluminium trim rail, the last part of the cut was made with a bolster chisel.*

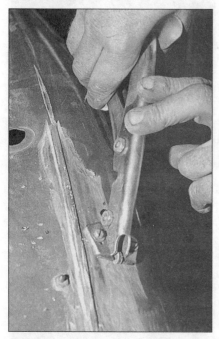

▲ *ROW4. Next, the wing has to be cut near its join with the centre panel. There are a number of ways of doing it. One is to drill a hole in the panel and use a panel cutter such as this Monodex. This curls a thin swarf of steel upwards between the two anvils which lie flat on the steel. It doesn't distort the steel at all, but it's very slow. You can buy an electric-drill-powered alternative or use a jig saw with a blade for sheet steel. Wear ear defenders!*

▲ *ROW6. This welder ended up using the oxy-acetylene cutting torch. Used at an angle, so that the flame is cutting through the maximum amount of steel at a time, it's quick and, with practice, it*

becomes a remarkably clean method of cutting sheet steel. The drawback is that it's an expensive way of doing it and you introduce more distortion into the metal.

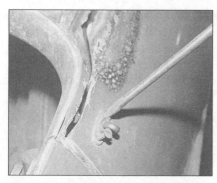

▲ ROW8. Remember to take off any fixtures and fittings such as, in this case, the hood fixing turnbuckle before the panel is scrapped.

▼ ROW9. There's something very satisfying about lifting away a panel that has just been cut off.

▲ ROW10. With the wing out of the way, the end retaining bolt for the aluminium trim strip could be seen. It is incredibly difficult to get at with the wing in place. Many such fixtures and fittings – lamps for instance – are best left until this stage.

▲ ROW11. The trim strip was removed to avoid any risk of damaging it later on.

▲ ROW12. The remains of the wing and the wing beading were held by spot welds. The centre of each spot weld was drilled out.

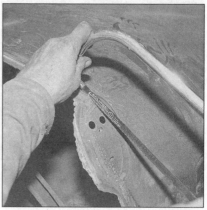

▲ ROW13. A hacksaw was used to cut through the wing remnant at the top of the rear light mounting.

▲ROW14. The spot welds around the rear light mounting and around the rear flasher mounting were drilled out.

▲ROW15. Similarly, the spot welds at the door shut pillar were weakened. It is usually necessary to use a ⅛ inch drill and then to make the final break with a bolster chisel.

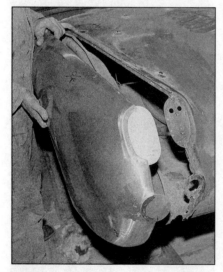

▲ROW16. The new rear wing was, for a handmade wing of its shape and curvature, an acceptable fit, but do remember that hand-made wings will never just slot into place. Quite a lot of work will be required!

◀ROW17. The actual wing fitting is quite a fiddle but not especially difficult. It is necessary to use lots of clamps and/or self tapping screws to ensure that the wing is a perfect fit before welding it in place.

◀ROW18. Unfortunately, there is no escaping the fact that on this car, the top flange/beading has to be welded from inside the boot, the welder having to work in a very confined space. When carrying out work in a space of this size, great care must be taken to avoid toxic fumes. MIG welding, in particular, is known to produce fumes which can be dangerous under these enclosed conditions. Hire and wear a compressor-supplied air-fed mask.

▲ROW19. Tack-weld the wing top, taking care not to damage the beading at all, or spot weld/tack it from inside the car.

◀ROW20. Here is where we had to carry out the biggest modification. We had to cut a slot in this wing and bend the bottom flange upwards by almost half an inch to make it fit properly: all par for the course where hand-made (and even some pressed non-original) panels are covered.

▲ ROW21. The best way of removing spot welds is as follows. Use a sanding pad on the angle grinder to go lightly over the line of welds. This will remove the paint, except in the 'low' areas of the spot welds. Use a spot-weld cutter in your drill: the centre pin locates the cutter. (Courtesy: The Eastwood Company)

▲ WR1. If the rear lower section has to be renewed, fit the repair panel for this area first, but make absolutely sure that its front edge is in line with the normal position of the wheel arch flange which may have rusted away.

▼ WR2. Here, the wheel arch repair panel is seen fitted and tack-welded in position.

▲ WR3. On the other side of the car, you can see that the bottom of the repair panel supplied has to be cut off when a rear lower section (see WR1) has been fitted first. This is most certainly a point in the favour of this repair section – it's better to have too much, so that you can cut some off, than too little.

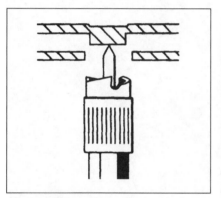

▲ ROW22. This allows the blades to cut through the panel to be removed, leaving the inner panel intact. All you have to do is grind away the remaining dimple of spot weld. (Courtesy: The Eastwood Company)

▼WR4. After placing the repair section against the wing and drawing round it. The old steel has to be cut away leaving a suitable overlap.

WING-LOWER PATCH REPAIR

It is usually much simpler to repair an existing wing, provided that it is not too far gone, than to fit a complete new one. Manufacturer's panels can be tricky to fit, not because of poor fit but because they were designed for the production line. Consider cutting them down so that you just use what you need. When considering whether to repair or replace, find out what repair sections are available and ensure that your existing wing will have enough left to weld to. If not, replace!

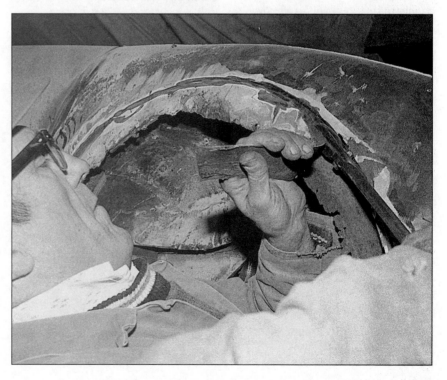

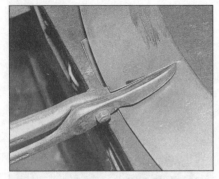

▲ WR5. Occasionally, such repair panels have to be tailored to fit. Here the panel is being snipped prior to opening it up a shade. If the adjustment is very small, the imperfection in the curvature will not be noticeable.

▲ WR6. This repair panel was slipped behind the cut edge of the old wing, forming a small overlap. An effective way of carrying out the work is to produce a stepped edge so that the two panels sit flush with the overlap behind the wing. ⅛ inch holes were drilled at regular intervals ...

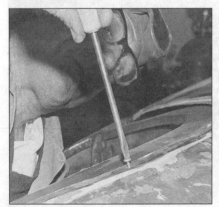

▲ WR7. ... and self-tapping screws used to ensure a good, tight fit.

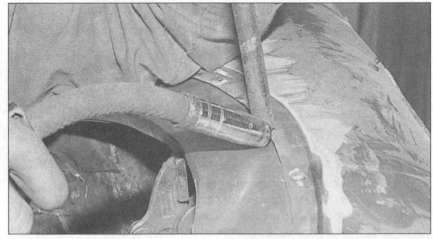

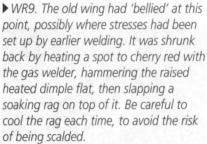

▲ WR8. Where small gaps existed, they were held closed while the SIP MIG welder seamed them into place.

▶ WR9. The old wing had 'bellied' at this point, possibly where stresses had been set up by earlier welding. It was shrunk back by heating a spot to cherry red with the gas welder, hammering the raised heated dimple flat, then slapping a soaking rag on top of it. Be careful to cool the rag each time, to avoid the risk of being scalded.

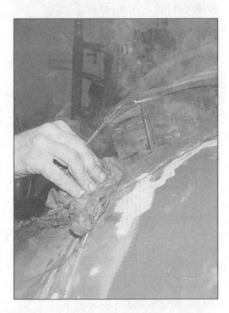

▼ WR10. On the other side of the car it was necessary to make a flat patch to fit between the repair section and the door shut pillar. This was simply marked up in situ, cut out, and welded in place.

▲ WR11. You can only weld successfully on clean steel. At the risk of highly abrasive sand dust all through the workshop (work outside?) or in every nook and cranny of the car (only use it on a stripped-out body?) you could use a spot-sandblaster with your compressor, provided that it's a powerful one. (Courtesy: Frost Auto Restoration)

WHEEL ARCH REPLACEMENT

Whenever an outer wing corrodes, you can bet your life that any inner wing to which it is attached will also be rusted away. You can purchase inner wing repair panels for the most popular cars: MGBs, Triumph sports cars and the like, but for many cars you will have to fabricate your own.

Fortunately, using this simple system devised by the author, you can easily fabricate an inner wing repair section for most cars.

▶ FRI1. With the whole rear wing out of the way, it was easy to see just how rotten a typically rotten wheel arch can be. Virtually all of the corrosion had taken place in the flange and the vertical section leading from it.

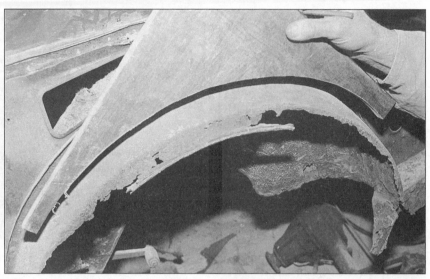

▲ FRI2. No repair sections were then available for this area of a 'Frogeye' Sprite, so we set about developing a DIY method of making one. First, we cut a piece of 10mm thick plywood into the exact curve of the wing. Note that we only attempted to make it half the circumference of the wing arch. Handling a piece any larger than this would have been difficult and wasteful of steel.

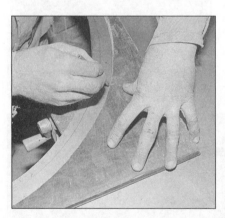

▲ FRI3. The wooden former was used to mark out a piece of steel to the correct shape and size ...

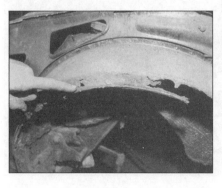

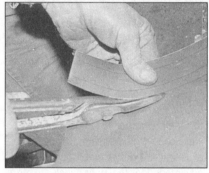

▲ FRI4. ... and the steel for the repair section was cut out.

▲ FRI5. Using a combination of the bench vice and grips, the steel was clamped to the wooden former and the flange folded over. The other pencil line which can be seen here is for a fold to cope with the curve in the inner wing.

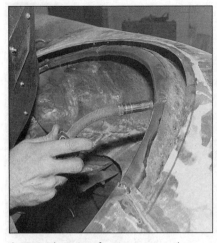

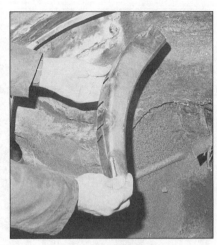

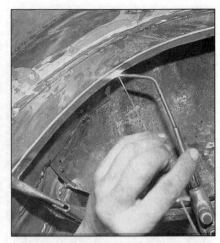

▲ *FRI6. The same former was used to create these inner repair sections where only a wheel arch repair section was being used.*

▼ *FRI7. These repair sections MUST be fitted with constant reference to the shape of the new outer panels by offering the outer panel up at regular intervals. An alternative preferred by some people is to fit the outer panel first and then fit the inner panel from beneath. For the less experienced this has the distinct advantage that the inner panels are more likely to fit properly and from that point of view the method can be recommended. But it does mean that the panels are far less 'get-atable' and therefore more difficult to weld into place.*

▲ *FRI8. A note regarding the rearmost inner wing section, where the double curve almost turns back on itself: try snipping the innermost fold to help the steel to curve, then trim and weld up the steel neatly.*

▲ *FRI9. The final step is to weld the inner and outer wing flanges together. They can be spot welded – and indeed that is by far the quickest way of doing the job, but be sure to use seam sealer. Another solution is to neatly seam the two flanges together with a small nozzle and flat, unobtrusive welds; or better still, use MIG.*

◀ *FRI10. There are various models of shrinkers and stretchers available. Almost any combination of curves and angles can be reproduced. They're not cheap but if you have a lot to do ...*
(Courtesy: Auto Restoration)

PANEL BEATEN PATCH REPAIRS

Nothing illustrates the evolution of the motor car's bodywork better than the shape and the structure of car wings. As soon as car bodywork began to be fitted lower down relative to wheel centres, rather than up high in the fashion of the horse drawn carriage, wings became a somewhat architectural combination of function and styling, both stopping the mud and setting the tone for the visual appeal of the whole car at the same time. But with the development of monocoque construction, wings metamorphosed into aesthetic components of the shape of the entire car, and with the change in deployment came a change in structure.

Consequently, the techniques for repairing the wings of, say, a 1920s

Silver Ghost and an MGB have important differences, quite apart from the fact that you can buy off-the-peg replacements for one but not for the other! On the other hand, many of the techniques and the materials are interchangeable, a fact that was brought home to me most vividly when I was recently privileged to spend some time with David Felton, proprietor of the most highly skilled and accomplished car bodywork restorers I have ever encountered, and his leading panel beater, Pete Mulroy – a man of almost magical skills. David Felton's abilities are of such a high level that I can recommend them unequivocally. (See Appendix.)

In no time at all, Pete knocked up some extremely high quality samples of his craft as demonstration pieces for this section of the book. He started off by taking a scrap MGB wing 'out of the skip' and made a patch repair for a corroded area in the top. Now, hardly anyone would want to make a patch repair for a very badly corroded MGB wing since new ones can be bought for half the cost of repairing one, but the principles are interesting. The first point Pete made is that patch repairs should NEVER be lap jointed because the overlap in the metal becomes a focal point for corrosion. For the complete beginner, butt welds are certainly harder to carry out than lap welds but that is, quite rightly, no concern of Pete's! Until you are experienced enough to set up the welding torch correctly and to judge hand-eye co-ordination to a nicety, you would be well advised to spend some time practising butt welding on pieces of spare steel until you have got it right. On the other hand, pre-war wings are often easier to weld than later panels because unless they have been significantly thinned by rust, the extra thickness of steel reduces the likelihood of just burning through.

Quality note: In spite of the advantage of gas welding to someone as accomplished as Pete, the great majority of home restorers are strongly advised to use MIG for their butt welds. The chances of carrying out a sound weld are increased, and those of creating distortion are decreased.

Pete's approach to making the MGB patch was coloured by the fact that he wanted it to fit perfectly onto the repair area without it having to be pulled into position as it was tacked. This is the most difficult thing of all to do and, while it is absolutely correct and desirable for reasons that I will shortly be going into, it's not something that the majority of so-called 'panel beaters' would even attempt. Pete started off by making what happened to be the easiest part of the patch first. He measured the size of the flange on the original wing with his callipers and marked out the positions for the two folds, for the horizontal and the vertical sections of the flange, onto the piece of steel to be used for the repair which he had previously cut to just the size he wanted it. The two flange folds were made by Pete just by hammering the steel over the edge of his steel bench and then, to make the corners of the folds nice and sharp, he actually struck the edge of the steel square-on. All of this obviously takes great skill and judgement if the job is not to be spoiled before it has properly started, and lesser mortals are advised to use a pair of tinsmith's folding tongs, which look rather like a giant split-pin but are made out of flat steel and are gripped in the vice after the steel sheet has been inserted to the fold line; or two pieces of 'angle iron', similarly gripped in the vice; or, in order to replicate the softer fold at the top of the wing, two pieces of planed hardwood.

As I said, this part of the operation was the easiest part and is something that any tyro should be able to carry out provided that he/she remembered to fold the steel gradually, taking several passes working from one end to the other to get the fold square. Otherwise, if the fold is made all in one go, the metal being folded will stretch and could easily end up wrinkled. What Pete did next would be a bit more challenging! He pointed out that the MGB wing top has a convex curve, looked at from above, forming the main dome but that it also has a concave curve between the crown of the dome and the inner flange. But then, just to make things really

awkward, there is a slight curve running from front to rear. A slight digression here will illustrate the reason for this bit of apparent cussedness on the part of the Abingdon designers: the sloping tops of Rolls-Royce radiators look flat, but only because they are convex! If they were flat, they would actually appear concave, and the same visual trick – that of making the top surface of a structure convex in order to make it appear flat – had been carried out in the design of the rear part of the MGB front wing.

Pete made the side-to-side convex curve by the apparently simple means of bending the sheet over his knee, bending and offering up the emerging patch panel to the wing several times until he had the curve just right. The lesser, concave curve was made by holding the sheet over a large dolly held in the vice and panel beating the curve into place.

The curve in the other direction could only be made satisfactorily in a more sophisticated way and by using the correct equipment. The panel had to be passed back and forth between the rollers of a wheeling machine until just the right degree of front-to-back curvature had been attained. Then, as I said earlier, the patch had to be made to sit perfectly flat on the wing top to the extent that no matter where the panel was pressed down, there was no tipping and no gaps underneath. This took up very little of Pete's time but the amateur would be well advised to take as long as necessary to ensure that this sort of fit is attained because otherwise there will be stresses built into the panel as it is fitted. The more ham-fisted approach is to take part of the panel in place and to twist and hammer it to fit, tacking it down as you go along, but the stresses which are built up in this way will be a major contributory factor to rippling and distortion.

It is vital to cut out the old wing to exactly the same dimensions as the repair because any excessively wide gaps will be so very much more difficult to butt weld successfully. At the same time, it is demoralizing to spend ages making a superb repair panel, then to cut out the old panel and to find that there is more corrosion under the paint or beneath the panel that necessitates a larger panel. Avoid this by stripping all paint from the panel around the rust area so that you can be sure just how far back the corrosion extends, and sand the underside of the panel back to bare metal as well, which you will have to do in any case before you carry out any welding to ensure that the weld is nice and 'clean'. In the knowledge that the repair is of the right size, you can place it over the wing and, after clamping it securely into place, scribe around it very accurately. Cut around it with tin snips or a nibbler tool, or some other non-distorting tool, cutting through awkward shapes such as flanges with a hacksaw. If you're not 100 per cent sure of your aim, cut slightly under-size rather than over-size and hand file the wing until the repair fits snugly into place. Clamp it adequately and tack weld it every three or four inches at first, followed by closer tack welds later. Don't try to weld the panel in place from one end to the other, but weld just part of one edge. Then, after cooling the panel down as described here, weld part of an edge on the opposite side to balance out the stresses, shifting the attention around from one part of the panel to another until the welding is complete.

Forcing a mis-shapen panel into place is not the only reason for distortion: another is the unskilful application of heat. Most people don't have the training or the instinct born of experience to know how to avoid heat distortion from an oxy-acetylene flame, so other precautions have to be taken. The first option is to avoid using 'gas' welding at all! MIG welding has some distinct advantages for the amateur, not least that it cuts down dramatically on the amount of heat introduced into the panel – although it does have disadvantages which will be mentioned later. Oxy-acetylene melts steel perfectly well, of course, but since steel is an excellent conductor of heat a very large amount of the heat is drawn away from the weld area. You can partly alleviate the problem by placing wet rags around the weld, remembering to turn them

and re-wet them as often as necessary to prevent them catching fire, and I reckon that it's a good idea to stop every few minutes and to wipe the panel over with a wet rag to cool it down – but take care not to scald yourself and always make sure that you have an adequate fire extinguisher to hand.

Even when using MIG, it's a good idea to cool the panel down every now and again because there is obviously going to be some heat transference from metal that has been raised to white heat in order to weld it. Then you have to be careful about splashing water around electrical equipment, and the obvious risk of electrocution. Keep the two apart!

I have occasionally come across another type of damage in the panels of earlier cars that has nothing to do with corrosion. Fellow motoring writer Paul Skilleter once owned a Standard Swallow with a neat, oval hole in the inner face of each front wing. This came about because the Swallow's steering lock had only been limited by the tyres pressing on said front wings and, as a result, the tyres have actually rubbed right through the steel! The problem will be solved by letting-in a simpler version of the wing patch repair already described, making sure that the full extent of the friction damage has been cut out.

However skillful a welder you are, a weld will contain high and low spots. If you have used 'gas' welding, you will now have a distinct advantage over the user of MIG because, instead of having to sand the weld's high spots off, you can actually do something to consolidate the strength of the weld. Hold a dolly beneath the weld and planish the top of the weld with a panel beating hammer so that the high spots are spread down and, to an extent, into the low spots. Not only does this save the removal of metal from the very place where you want to retain strength, it also has the beneficial effect of re-work-hardening the steel in the immediate vicinity of the weld.

Two words of caution: if your welding has been very lumpy, you won't be able to bash the lumps out of existence and the worst will have to be sanded off; and don't hammer the steel for too long

because each hammer blow not only pushes the steel down, it pushes it outwards as well and too much hammering will stretch the panel and reintroduce that old enemy – distortion! After hammering the weld, a large rubber-backed sanding disc on an angle grinder should be used to sand excess weld off or, if your budget doesn't run to a large angle grinder, a disc on a mini-grinder or electric drill can be used, although the latter two are more likely to put ripples into the panel. But then, cheaper still and even less likely to cause distortion: a file and body rasp.

Wings on more modern mass-produced cars have softer lines which generally consist of more complex combinations of curves than earlier wings, but changes of shape on earlier wings – for instance the curvature between the top and sides of the wing – can often be more sudden. And there are often other problems which are peculiar to more venerable automobiles. Cars fitted with aluminium wings, for instance, would usually have had inner wings which took the form of liners beneath the wings proper, and which prevented stone damage from showing through and ruining the appearance of the upper wing. Before any significant repair work can be carried out to the main panel, and that includes panel beating as well as letting in a patch repair, the inner wing may have to be removed.

Pete made a demonstration patch repair for one of the Rolls-Royce wings too. To get over the problem I have already mentioned, that of the rapid change of shape between the top and side of the wing, Pete made the repair section in two pieces. One further complication was that the material used was aluminium, although Pete didn't actually see this as a problem at all, and I think it likely that the difficulties of welding aluminium are sometimes over stressed. Pete cut out two flat sections, one for the wing top and one for the side and, after bending the top section to the curve of the wing top, used the wheeling machine to make a curve which approximated to half of the radius at the top corner of the wing and followed it up by putting a similar radius in the appropriate part of the side piece. He offered both pieces up to make sure that they matched both the shape of the wing and that their jointing edges fitted exactly, and then he welded the two together. The weld was panel beaten and finally, to equalize the two curvatures, the jointed area was passed once again through the wheeling machine.

Aluminium welding is, strictly speaking, a form of brazing. The rod usually has 10 per cent silicon and 4 per cent copper combined with the aluminium which gives a lower melting point than that of the aluminium alloy used for car bodywork. Both surfaces to be welded should be painted with flux but only along their edges – you should avoid using too much flux – and, once the workpiece has been set up, the end of the rod is heated and dipped in the flux, or more flux can be painted along the rod. The workpiece is heated with the welding torch in the normal way but it is here that you can encounter a major problem. Aluminium doesn't turn red before it melts, so you have no visual guide to the temperature of the material as you have with steel. And moreover, it doesn't slowly become plastic but melts in a bit of a rush and blobs all over the floor or bench! The answer is to use the state of the flux as a guide to the correct welding temperature: as soon as it begins to flow along the joint, feed in the rod but don't feed the rod in too soon because, although it will melt, it won't bond properly to the workpiece. Once again, MIG is easier to use. You need a specially coated liner to prevent the aluminium wire from sticking in the feed pipe, and you have to use argon – not argon-plus-carbon dioxide – as the shielding gas. You'll use a lot of power, too, and the smallest mini-migs may not be able to cope. Even the smallest full workshop models have to be used in short bursts. If you've stuck with oxy-acetylene welding, you absolutely must spend several minutes washing every trace of flux from around the joint with warm water, otherwise the extremely caustic qualities of the flux will attack the aluminium in no time and blister paint.

Pete's final demonstration to me was the addition of a wired edge to the wing repair to match that on the car. He scribed a line around the edge of the panel and proceeded to hammer a right angle fold all the way around the edge, holding the repair patch over a flat dolly and taking the metal over gradually so as not to stretch it. Then he cut out a length of soft iron wire coated with copper, purpose made for the job and of the appropriate diameter and carefully laid it inside the fold with the panel placed flat on the bench. Holding the wire tightly into place with one hand, Pete hammered the folded up flange gradually over the wire until, when it was most of the way over, he used the edge of a cross-pein panel beater's hammer to bring the flange tightly around the wire. The panel was then turned over and the remaining visible signs of the original right angle bend carefully hammered out. After a little filing, the new edge of the panel looked as attractive as it was strong.

Ordinary paint will not adhere to aluminium for very long. In the old days, aluminium had to be carefully wire-brushed all over in order to key the surface, the arm-aching job being given to long-suffering apprentices. Nowadays there are few apprentices, but there is self-etch paint to use as a quicker way of preparing to paint. But that, as they say, is another story ....

▲ WPR1. This is the ultimate panel-beater's challenge! This 1920 Silver Ghost with Barker body is being restored by Scott-Moncrieff. Trouble is, it had been fitted with a pick-up rear body and used to take vegetables to Derby market. There was none of the original rear body, no patterns and no drawings. To say the least, Pete coped admirably! The Ghost also has a nasty dent in the nearside wing to add to the problems of incorrect shape.

▲ WRP2. There's rather more to panel beating than can be described in print and there is no substitute for learning by doing. Pete first 'roughed' out the dent by holding a dolly beneath the dent and hammering just 'off the dolly' ...

◄ WRP3. ... followed by a more careful version of the same thing ...

▲ WRP4. ... and finally by a session with the hammer only, feeling for levelness carefully with a flat hand.

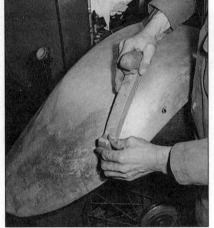

▲ WRP5. Minute imperfections were taken out using the panel beater's rasp.

▲ WPR7. Wheeling is a rare skill, and well beyond most DIY enthusiasts.

▶WPR8. Pete actually butt-welded the panel in place without using rod. Unless you've had 40 years experience, don't try it!

▲ WPR9. This type of repair, with a tight radius included, is best made in two parts ...

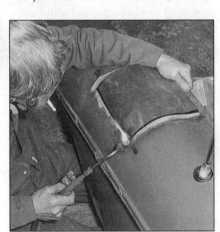

▼ WPR10. ... which can then be welded into one. Aluminium welding is strictly a form of brazing, but it is trickier to carry out than the welding of steel.

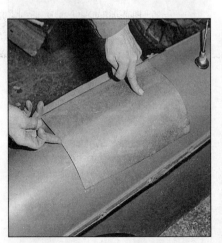

▲ WPR6. The MGB patch panel was made to sit on the wing perfectly so that when it was welded in it didn't induce warpage into the panel. Here's how Pete did it.

▲ WPR11. In order to wire an edge, you have to start by folding a right angle ...

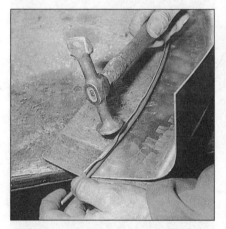

▲ WPR12. ... then, with the coated soft-iron wire in place, begin folding – see main text.

▼ WPR13. The cross-pein end of the hammer is then used to 'tuck-in' the flange around the wire.

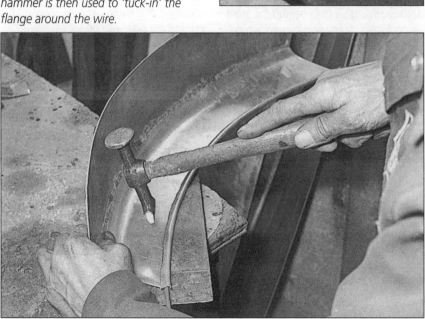

◄ WPR14. The real pros., such as David Felton, use these special tongues to give the wired edge its perfect shape.

The remaining information and photographs in this section are by David Felton himself, and here, he describes the way in which his workshop overcomes some common patch repair problems. This is the sort of work that will be required for the very large number of cars for which off-the-peg replacement panels are not available.

◄ WPR15. This is the underside of the end of an MG TD wing at the point where it bolts to the running board. The reinforcing plate illustrated acts as a moisture trap, and both thicknesses commonly corrode through.

▲ WRP16. David makes a point of specifying 20 gauge mild steel with a reference CR4. It is important to specify the correct type of steel because the wrong types may be too springy and will be difficult to work. Here the repair section has been cut to size and the corroded metal cut away. Note that the end 'flap' has been shaped but not yet folded down. In WPR19 you will see the importance of not simply hacking through the section to be cut away. Please read on! The edges to be welded between the repair section and the original metal must be an exact and even fit with no gaps. Try not to distort the edge of the wing – use small bites with the snips and never close the handles.

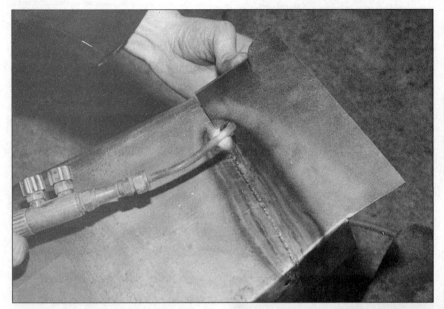

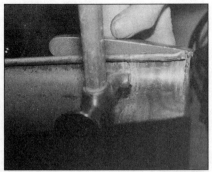

▲ WPR20. After straightening the wire, the wired edge can be reformed around the original wire.

▲ WPR17. Note that before beginning work, the inside edge of the wing had been folded down but it was not to be welded first. The trick to lessen distortion is to prop the main body of the wing securely, hold the patch in one hand and the torch in the other (wear heavy duty leather industrial-type gloves. Only the highly skilled can have enough confidence in their own manipulative ability not to cause a burn!). Hold the patch in the correct place and, starting from the nearest edge of the wing in the picture, play the flame (nozzle No. 1, neutral flame) on the join until the edges flow together, working towards the outer edge of the wing. The repair piece can be manipulated manually to keep the two edges together: something that you wouldn't be able to do very easily if the end fold had been made or if the nearest fold in the picture had been welded down. Don't let the edges overlap, but on the other hand, if they start to draw apart, let the weld cool until they draw back together again. Should an overlap occur, stop welding and hammer and dolly the weld until a gap appears in the unwelded section. Finally, you can weld the inner edge.

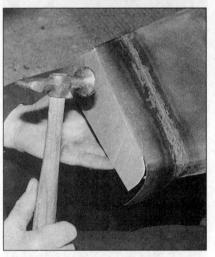

▲ WPR18. The rear edge is now folded down with a dolly held behind the steel being folded. Many non-experts would ensure that the fold takes place neatly and accurately by clamping two pieces of hard wood, one above and one below the fold. The fact that David Felton's workshop achieve this degree of accuracy in this way and as a matter of course is yet another testimony to their high level of skills.

▶ WPR19. Now, here is the reason why the rusted metal could not simply be hacked away. It is vitally important when dealing with a wired edge that the metal is unpicked from around the wire leaving it intact so that it can be incorporated into the repaired section.

▲ WPR21. After priming both hidden surfaces with a zinc-rich weldable primer, available from good quality paint factors and suppliers of bodyshop materials and equipment, the new end reinforcing plate can be spot welded into place.

▲ WPR22. There was fairly limited corrosion, shown here as pin holes in the top of this TD wing.

▲ WPR23. After cutting a rectangular patch, Pete uses the wheeling machine to shape the patch so that it fits precisely on top of the wing with no rocking, and covers the area to be replaced.

▲ WPR24. After scribing around the patch, Pete used a plasma cutter to cut away the bulk of the metal, and then his trusty tin snips to finish the job off precisely. Other alternatives spring to mind such as a jig saw fitted with a metal cutting blade and then using a file to take off the last bit of metal. Most of us wouldn't trust ourselves to use tin snips with Pete's degree of accuracy!

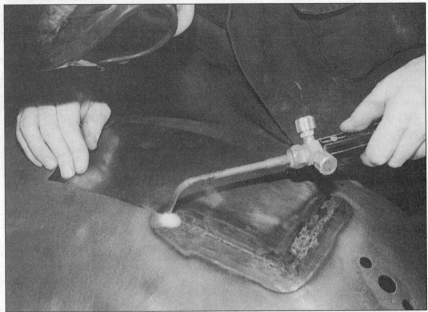

▲ WPR25. Michael Riley is the other craftsman involved in the repair of this wing and he can be seen here welding in the patch repair. Note the way in which he is applying pressure to the top of the patch, encouraging it to sit perfectly level with the wing as the weld is flowed into place. If you make the joint tight enough, you may find it relatively simple to carry out this type of gas welding without the use of filler rod. Then, if you 'blow through' in a few places, you can go back with rod and fill in the gaps later. Once again, the majority of non-specialists would find it much simpler to carry out a job like this with a MIG welder.

▼ WPR26. Then it's back to Pete again, and after using a hammer and dolly as previously described to remove minor imperfections from the weld (albeit in this case the dolly used is called a head and is mounted on a stand) any small distortion can be completely removed in the wheeling machine. You can see that by this stage, there are two patch repairs in place taking care of two separately identified areas of corrosion.

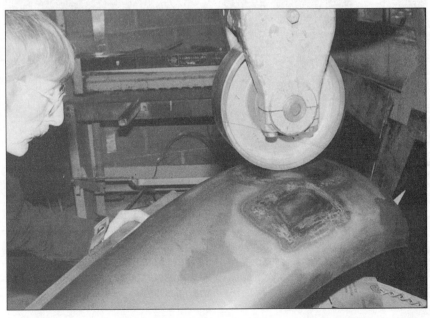

▶ *WPR27. If you've ever wondered how the holes are ever relocated, here's how! Using a flexible rule, a line is scribed through the centres of each hole making sure that the start and finish of each line extends beyond both sides of the area to be removed. Two lines are required at about 90 degrees from each other. When the new area is in place, simply pick up the lines and continue across the new patch and the intersection will locate the centre. Here the location for the bracket to take the wiring harness for the head and side lamps is being established. (Unfortunately, David, Pete and Michael don't give all their secrets away, but this is a good one!)*

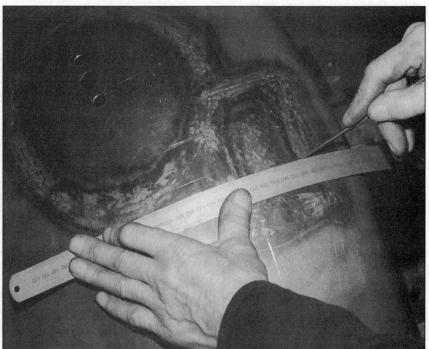

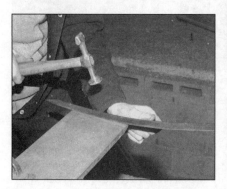

▲ *WPR28. Pete fabricates a simple looking repair section for another part of the wing, but note the curvature – the reason why it couldn't be done in the folders!*

▲ *WPR29. Once again, the repair section is used as a template for marking out and then cutting away the rusty section of steel.*

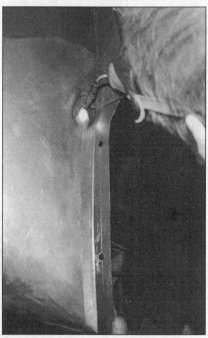

▲ *WPR30. The repair section is welded into place, carrying out the long weld first, getting the shape and fit right and then finishing the ends off only after the repair is in place. Note that the mounting holes have been drilled prior to welding the repair section into place. Those slightly less confident of their abilities to create and fit repair sections with great accuracy might wish to drill the holes later!*

▲ *WPR31. Typical of wings fitted to cars made in the 1950s and earlier is this cumbersome mounting bracket. It is shown being removed here by drilling out the spot welds. The section underneath was to be built up and replaced, and so the welds could be drilled right through. If you wished to save the metal underneath, you could either take enormous care and only drill through the top piece of metal or else use a specially made spot weld cutter which looks rather like a mini tank hole cutter much used by plumbers. (In fact, that's exactly what it is!) Sykes-Pickavant, for instance, produce a suitable one. Its only disadvantage is that it makes a far bigger hole than is strictly required.*

▲ *WPR32. Here a new wing support panel has been made and is being checked for fit prior to being clamped and spot welded into place on the wing. The captive nut cages were replaced at this stage. In David Felton's workshop they make their own using a purpose made press. You may possibly be able to buy replacements from a specialist supplier, and they are certainly available for Volkswagen Beetles from VW specialists, although in that case you will have to use metric bolts, of course.*

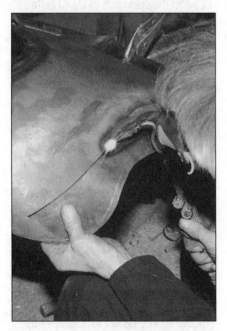

▲ *WPR33. Yet another repair section is welded into place with an extra allowance made for the wired edge. Pete says that this is a perfect example of why it is better to make and use larger patches rather than smaller ones: small ones get too hot to handle and can distort!*

▲ *WPR34. The job done, and both front wings are as good as new, or even better with the assistance of modern rust inhibitors. Lead load if you must, although fluxes are highly corrosive and must be washed away very thoroughly. Modern plastic fillers are probably better, but these wings don't need either. (The latter may certainly be true of panels produced in David Felton's workshop, but for mere mortals the use of filler will be essential. It is interesting to see David blowing away the myth that plastic fillers are intrinsically worse in some way than lead loading.)*

Rather interestingly, the MG TD to which these wings were to be re-fitted was from a complete and original left-hand drive American import shipped to David Felton in England for repair on its way to a new home in Austria.

Felton's footnotes:
1 It is important to note that the smaller amount of MIG-induced distortion is in fact far harder to correct than the distortion caused by gas welding. This, we think, is because of the introduction of a much harder grade of steel in the case of MIG.
2 A further digression. Here is a quote from Rolls Royce's booklet *Makers of the Best Car in the World*. (It relates to the fact that so many car body panels have curves in them when we think of them as 'straight'.)
'The shell of the grille appears to be

perfectly rectilinear. In fact, to achieve this effect, every line and surface has been slightly curved. This strange property of lines and shiny surfaces was known to the Greeks, who called it ENTASIS. The architect of the Parthenon made use of entasis when he designed the graceful curves into its Doric columns.'

3 Aluminium welding. The 'rod' used should be a strip of the parent metal, as care must be taken not to introduce dissimilar metals, particularly in areas likely to need reworking. (Traditionally 16G SICH 4 or BS 1470 (1987) 1.5mm, as it is today.) SICH 4 is 99.5% pure aluminium BS 1470 is down to 99.2% There is a form of aluminium brazing using lower temperature rods, but different fluxes are needed. Even specialist welding retail outfits get confused – the usual response being 'nobody gas welds aluminium any more'.
  Murex Saffire aluminium welding flux and Sifflux are both suitable, mixing only sufficient with water to form a thin paste – enough to do the job in hand. Apply with a small stiff brush.
4 The easiest way to learn to weld, is to take a long strip of metal about 6 inches wide (for aluminium nozzle No. 3, and a slightly acetylene-rich flame, i.e. double cone showing). The hottest part of the flame is just beyond the blue cone – concentrating this part on

the edge of the strip and, being the edge, this will melt quite soon – the trick is to progress right across the strip – taking the metal to melting point, but not beyond, otherwise you will blow holes in it. At the end of the run, the edge is even more vulnerable, so where to stop must also be learned. Don't try to use too small a piece of metal – it will vanish before you've learned anything. Working down the strip, go across again and again. Next, try, with a rod in the other hand, to lay a thin strip of molten metal off the rod into the pool you're making with the torch in the practise strip. The rod, being thin, soon melts, so this is kept in the flame, but further away from the hottest point – a slight oscillating motion being developed by the rod into the pool and out, whilst the flame is oscillated across the imaginary joint. The aim is to use as little rod as possible. When confidence has been gained, the strip may be cut across, and an actual join attempted.

Three hands are useful, but not compulsory. Fasten one piece in the vice, torch in one hand, piece of metal to be joined in the other (flux paint aluminium edges first). Hold the edges together. Starting just away from that vulnerable edge, play the flame across the joint, trying to achieve that vital first tack. Just carry on, again and again and again. The holes must be filled with rod (again, as little rod as possible). To fill a hole, start welding about half an inch before the hole, rod ready as you work towards the hole – a quick dab to fill the hole and stop about half an inch past. It really is not as hard as you might think. Our 10-year-old daughter became quite proficient; your average apprentice takes about three weeks. Interestingly, during the Second World War some of the very thin aircraft alloys (which really do require a deft and delicate touch) were successfully welded by young ladies with no previous experience, having been recruited specifically to weld these alloys, as apparently it took less time to train them than it did for skilled welders to

learn the deft-touch required!

N.B. (i) Wash flux from aluminium panels whilst still hot, and dry completely before further work. The fumes from hot flux will rust adjacent tools – hammer heads and dollies are usually polished for aluminium work, so keep them out of the way!

N.B. (ii) Of interest is that a perfectly good aluminium weld (just after joining) has a wavy black line right up the centre – it looks just like a crack, but it should wash off! Don't be tempted to weld it again just in case.

5 Generally, distortion is minimized by not clamping – hence the 'wangling' with the free hand described earlier by Lindsay. Referring to the MGB front-wing patch, the patch would be seam welded corner to corner, outer longitudinal seam first. It depends whether you're left or right handed as to where you start! If distortion gets out of hand, stop and allow to cool, straighten up with hammer and dolly if required, and start again until the other corner is reached. Straighten again with hammer and dolly, and then work up from whichever corner to the bonnet/wing edge, cooling and hammering as required. The general rule – longest weld first, welds to the edges of panels working outwards, last. Tacking as described would be very difficult using gas. A disadvantage of the wet rags is that they confine the thermal gradient to a smaller area – increasing local distortion and increasing stress. A good idea, though, for protecting rubber or glass, but we usually remove them first! The other drawback that springs to mind, is that the more rapid the cooling, the harder the weld, which is undesirable, as I said earlier. However, having said all that, the *absolute* novice might be better doing it, as described, with a MIG welder!

6 For rapid cooling – a plasma cutter concentrates intense heat on a very narrow area, but the edges left will blunt any file in seconds.

7 Composition of aluminium sheet. The minute differences in iron content, and possibly manganese, do alter gas

welding characteristics and can be identified by the skilled welder.

8 Lead is still the appropriate medium for forming edges or apertures – these areas are also better able to take the heat required, without distortion. They must, however, be cleaned and painted immediately. Elsewhere, I would unhesitatingly recommend plastic (polyester) filler.

DIY PATCH REPAIRS

Most home restorers would struggle to reproduce a standard even approaching that portrayed in the previous section – but that is no reason not to try! Repairs to this standard, though, are easier to carry out on those cars with separate chassis and bodywork, and where the steel originally used was of a far heavier gauge than that used on modern cars. The one huge advantage that home restorers have over the so-called professionals, who themselves can rarely aspire to the standards of David Felton and his team, is that they have no pressure of time, and usually they take far more pride in the job.

In this section we look at patch repairs to a relatively exotic motor car carried out in such a way that the accomplished home restorer would be able to attain a satisfactory standard of work. Please note carefully the safety notes at the start of this chapter, and take particular care not to weld panels where there is any inflammable material hidden from view on the other side of the panel on the vehicle. Look out for trim boards and carpets, wiring, brake and fuel lines, underseal or fresh Waxoyl, the presence of a fuel tank, a carburettor float bowl, a battery or indeed anything else of an inflammable nature. Be sure to have an efficient workshop fire extinguisher to hand whilst welding.

Mark Marwood took the plunge and bought himself his dream car, a Maserati Merak SS. As in all the best cliches, Mark's dream turned into a nightmare after just a few months of ownership, during which time the car was off the road for longer than it was on it. When he bought the car, the bodywork looked absolutely fine with none of the tell-tale ripples indicating the presence of filler, no unfinished edges or anything else that would suggest the bodywork was anything other than perfect.

However, within a period of months rust buds were breaking out in full blossom as layers of filler unfolded themselves from around all the wheel arches. Then disaster struck. As Mark slowed down towards the end of a long, fast drive, he felt a little shimmy through the rear of the car, and the rear nearside wheel came adrift, carving an ugly slash into the wheel arch before bounding away. Fortunately, no structural damage was done, but a new driveshaft assembly was needed, and something had to be done about the bodywork. Now, Mark is a bit of a perfectionist and so decided there and then to fit four new wings and to consider fitting a pair of doors too. The decision came unstuck when the Maserati importer quoted an unbelievably high price for the parts – so much so that it was clearly going to be cheaper to employ a highly paid, high-cost specialist and have him make the parts, or at least repair panels for the parts.

In the event, the car was found to be less corroded than expected once it was stripped down – an unusual circumstance, to say the least – so a relatively small area of each wing had to be cut out and replaced. Here the approach is totally different from that of full panel replacement, the 'knife-and-fork' techniques being applicable to any car, and in particular those where panels are difficult or horrendously expensive to obtain.

▲ DPR1. It's sometimes easy to forget that aggressively sculpted body lines and whiplash acceleration are no proof against corrosion. Like most Italian cars 'of a certain age', the Merak is prone to corrode!

▲ DPR2. This rear wheel arch was decorated with a few scabs along its rim. There was no rust apparent, only white filler which, because it was being pushed out by the corrosion beneath, was an even more ominous sign. At least when you see rust beneath the paint you are usually aware of the extent of the corrosion. When you see filler, you wonder where it stops.

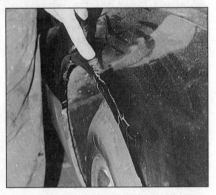

▲ DPR3. The front nearside wheel arch was starting to develop a split all the way round, which suggested that there wasn't a great deal of steel there at all, just a lot of filler being pushed outwards by the great pressure that rust exerts as it grows and expands. Just a couple of months earlier, this wheel arch had looked absolutely perfect, which demonstrates the lengths to which it is economically possible to go in order to 'bodge' an expensive or exotic car. The doors had begun to corrode in one or two silly little places, such as beneath the mirrors close up to the chrome trim, which was to involve carefully dismantling the expensive trim before letting-in repairs.

◀ DPR4. By now looking very dejected, the car with wheel re-attached (we'll skip the fact that it took Maserati six months to get round to delivering the parts!) was taken to the home workshop of experienced panel beater Ray Walker. After stripping off bumpers and trim and covering up the glass, for reasons which will become apparent, work began.

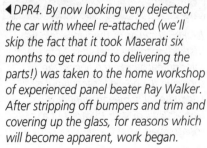

▲ DPR5. With all the filler out of the way, it was found that the wings were quite rusty around the outer lips of the wheel arches, but none of them suffered from corrosion in its main body or in the inner wing. Here's how the corrosion was repaired. After the rusty metal was carefully cut away, a strip of steel was cut out to follow the contour of the wing as accurately as possible, but wider than necessary to allow a flange to be turned under. Templates had previously been cut to show exactly the curvature of the wing and, just as a double-check, one side of the car was completed before the other was begun. That is a basic ground rule where repairs involving panel fit or panel shape are involved, especially with a car like the Merak where it is not so easy just to get hold of another car to check things out.

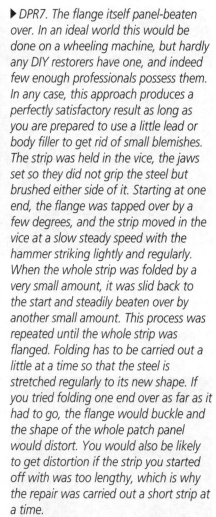

▶ DPR7. The flange itself panel-beaten over. In an ideal world this would be done on a wheeling machine, but hardly any DIY restorers have one, and indeed few enough professionals possess them. In any case, this approach produces a perfectly satisfactory result as long as you are prepared to use a little lead or body filler to get rid of small blemishes. The strip was held in the vice, the jaws set so they did not grip the steel but brushed either side of it. Starting at one end, the flange was tapped over by a few degrees, and the strip moved in the vice at a slow steady speed with the hammer striking lightly and regularly. When the whole strip was folded by a very small amount, it was slid back to the start and steadily beaten over by another small amount. This process was repeated until the whole strip was flanged. Folding has to be carried out a little at a time so that the steel is stretched regularly to its new shape. If you tried folding one end over as far as it had to go, the flange would buckle and the shape of the whole patch panel would distort. You would also be likely to get distortion if the strip you started off with was too lengthy, which is why the repair was carried out a short strip at a time.

▼ DPR8. Before attempting to weld the outer patch panel in place, it may be necessary to build up a part of the inner wing. It is best to replace them both together, but what you must NOT do is make the outer wing a perfect replica of the original, then use it to clamp and pull inner wing patches into place, because this will distort the outer wing shape. **Safety note: Always wear gloves when MIG welding (in spite of what you see here) as well as a full-size welding mask. All skin and eyes must be protected against the strong and cancer-forming UV rays given off by the weld process.**

After offering up the strip and making sure it fits properly (and in real life if the strip is just how you want it first time you

▲ DPR6. The line of the flange fold was marked on to the steel strip. Note that this approach lacks the fine accuracy shown in the previous section but is adequate for someone without the highest level of skills to carry out a sound repair.

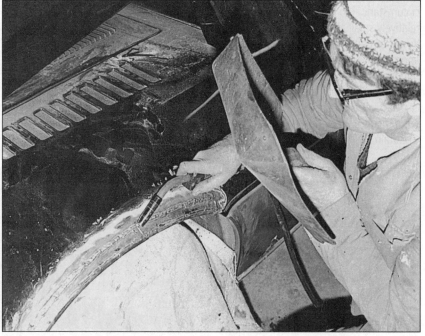

will be extremely lucky – you will probably have to make several trips to and from the bench) the strip can be tack welded into place. With all the strips accurately lined up, they can be seam-welded in. Here the enormous advantages of the MIG welder come into their own. The lack of excess heat generated is obvious from the close proximity of unburned paint, and the practical outcome is a lack of distortion – a vital point on the relatively large, flat Merak panels.

▲ *DPR9. The only significant disadvantage of a MIG weld is its high build-up on the outsides of car panels (it doesn't matter on hidden sections of course). On the other hand, the welds are always clean, with virtually no weakening inclusions (unless a lot of rubbish has been welded over) and they can be simply linished (sanded) back flush. Don't hold the linisher too long in one place, otherwise you will put more widespread heat into the panel than you did with the MIG! Now you can see the point of protecting all glass: sparks from the linisher will pit glass if they are allowed to hit it, making a scattering of little black specks that are sharp to the touch and impossible to remove.*

▶ *DPR10. After power sanding all the welded joints flush, a wipe of polyester body filler can be applied to the panel. Some people throw their hands up in much-practised horror at mention of the word 'filler', but in this instance there are absolutely no practical advantages in using lead, and a good many advantages in using polyester filler which, I am convinced, is an excellent material whose reputation has been marred only by the fact that it is so frequently mis-used. Over a sound rust-free base it can be excellent!*

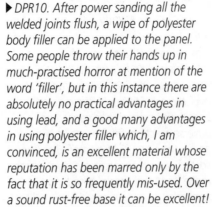

▶ *DPR11. One of the greatest plus-points of polyester filler is the fact that it can be so readily sanded with less of a health risk than that attached to lead, and it can be easily built up over minor depressions. Mind you, it is not meant to be used in any situation where structural strength is required. At this stage, coarse 40 or 80 grit can be used, the scratches themselves being flatted out with 120 grit prior to priming.*

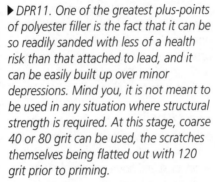

▶ *DPR12. Where complex mouldings have to be formed, a shape gauge (such as the one shown here) is a valuable tool, enabling you to match curvatures exactly. Once the basic structural work had been carried out, Mark took his car to Autotech at Belbroughton, on the south-western edge of Birmingham, for the refinishing to be carried out.*

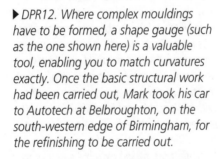

▼ *DPR13. Autotech's first job was the removal of the fixtures and fittings left in place by Ray Walker, such as the grille on top of the luggage compartment lid at the front of the car. The grille, in two halves, was forcefully held down with 16 cross-*

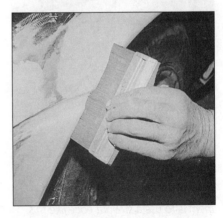

head screws. The rear styling struts (shown here) were also removed, to be prepared and painted separately. They were held to the rear of the cockpit by the one stud, pointed to here, and two bolts through the top of the rear wing. Note that the engine cover grilles have also been unscrewed. Removing and refitting window glass is always a risk, especially with the bonded-in type used here, and so a decision was taken to leave this very expensive piece of glass in place as there was no sign whatever of rust forming around the window apertures. It was, however, masked off very carefully.

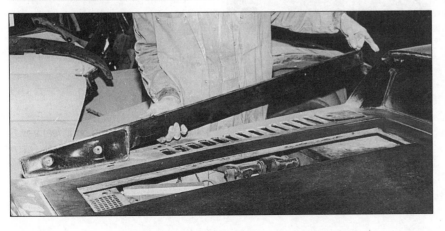

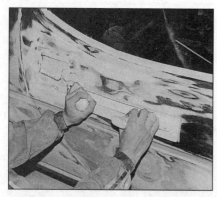

▲ DPR14. The whole car was flatted (sanded) over by hand using a long flat tool like this to hold the self-adhesive strips used. The advantage of this type of flatting, slow though it can be, is that it shows up all the high-spots and low-spots in each panel so that the former can be sanded down and the latter built up with a further skim of filler or polyester stopper in the case of tiny blemishes.

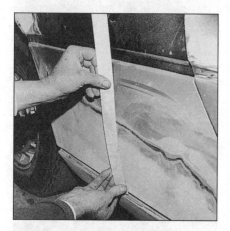

▲ DPR15. Large panels show ripples very badly. The best way to check against them is to use a straight edge like this and hold it against the panel, scraping it lightly from front to back. You must also crouch down by the straight edge and squint closely for any gaps between straight edge and panel, just as your woodwork teacher demonstrated at school after planing a face-side. Then carry out the same check with the straight edge held horizontally. As the panels were flatted and bare metal exposed, the car was spot-primed to prevent any surface corrosion from setting in. When all the flatting and levelling was finished, the car looked like a patchwork quilt.

▶ DPR16. The next stage was to spray a coat of primer-filler which could be given a final, careful flat all over before the car was painted. Disastrously, the primer-filler reacted badly with the paint coats beneath, producing vicious crazing all over the car. Strangely, the cellulose-based spot priming had caused no adverse reaction with the paint beneath and yet the two-pack primer-filler (the sort of paint that requires a hardener to make it set and special breathing apparatus to apply) crazed badly except where it was applied over the cellulose primer. Strictly speaking, just a little primer-filler should first have been tried on a small area, but cellulose primer is usually more prone to reaction than two-pack, so it is not surprising that Autotech had felt safe to carry on.

▶ DPR17. Of the two possible solutions, either to strip everything – primer, paint and filler – back to bare metal and start again, or spend hours sanding back to the base paint with a random orbit sander, only the latter was an economic possibility. Before the coat of primer-filler was re-applied, the whole car was sprayed with a paint with a neutral base, known as an isolator, to prevent the risk of reaction happening again. Often a paint with a wood-alcohol base similar to meths is used, but Autotech chose a water-based paint. Then came the tedious task of hand-flatting, taking extreme care not to break through the isolator and expose the angry paint beneath.

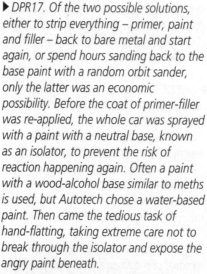

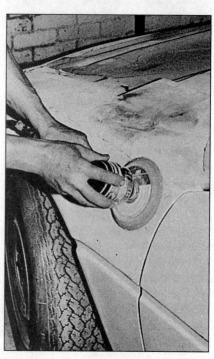

◀ DPR18. Mouldings and body features can be difficult to flat satisfactorily. Often the best solution is to cut out a piece of wood of the right shape and size and wrap the flatting paper around it.

▲ DPR19. After flatting, which took a good number of hours, the car was prepared for the spray booth. Before taping paper across the door aperture, strips of broad masking tape were placed right across the opening in both directions as a support for the paper: useful tip! The Sikkens paint technical rep for the area came in to paint the car, to show Autotech just how good he believed his company's paint to be. He spent some time going over the car with a tak-rag (a specially made piece of sticky cloth) and an 'air duster' on the air line to chase off and catch every speck of dust from every nook and cranny in the masking tape and paper, door channels and so on.

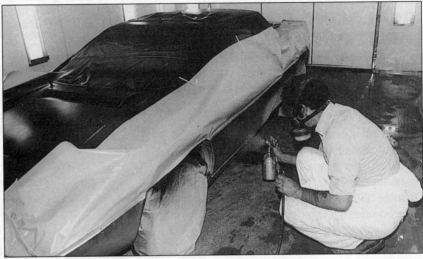

▲ DPR21. In this shot, the top colour has been sprayed, hardened and masked off. You can see that it has dried to a semi-matt finish. Note the wet floor – it was soaked with nothing more exotic than a watering can before spraying began – and also the mask being worn by the man from Sikkens. He should have worn an air-fed mask, supplying him with fresh air from outside the booth, but familiarity in his case bred something approaching foolhardiness as he chose to wear only a charcoal mask, which cannot possibly be as efficient, and in any case does not protect the eyes from the iso-cyanate in the two-pack paint. It is also ESSENTIAL to protect head, eyes, hands – all skin in fact – when using this material, which is NOT SUITABLE FOR HOME USE UNDER ANY CIRCUMSTANCES!

Once both coats had flashed off, the clear gloss coat was sprayed over the top in four separate coats. As the first one went on, the car took on a superb vibrant appearance. It is important that there are no blemishes beneath the clear coat because they obviously cannot be polished out afterwards. The other difficulty is that, to an inexperienced sprayer, it is difficult to tell how much clear coat is going on, with the consequential risk of paint runs or dry patches. There was none in this instance, and the spray job was carried out to a superb standard.

▼ DPR22. Fitting up, polishing glass, wheels and tyres and general valeting consumed another large slice of time, but to do justice to a highly satisfactory paint job and an extraordinary beautiful and now perfectly sound motor car, the effort was worth it!

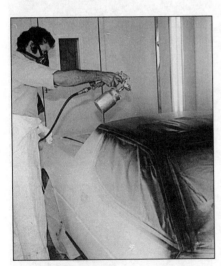

▲ DPR20. The paint used was of the two-pack clear-over-base-coat variety, which means that the colour coat or coats are applied first, 'flashed off' in the booth (i.e. the booth is turned up to a high heat level so that the solvent in the paint is sprayed on top. The base coat looks shiny here, but that is only because it is still wet.

REPLACING FRONT FLITCH PANELS

BUMPER MOUNTING AREA

On many cars the front 'inner wings' are known as the flitch panels. They form the side walls of the engine bay in front-engined cars and are always of great structural importance. Often you can repair; sometimes you need to replace. On some cars there are also rear flitch panels in place of the inner wings shown earlier. Replacement is similar to the sequence shown here on a VW Beetle.

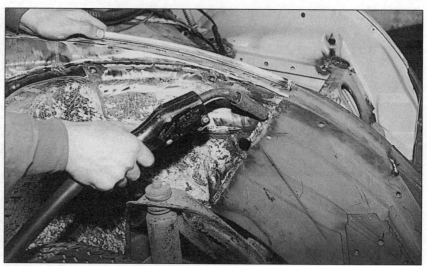

▲ FQ1. Here there's a similar situation to that at the rear end of the car. There's a choice between fitting the complete, excellent quality and very expensive full quarter panel, or a repair panel. This is the front bumper repair panel being offered up by body man Stuart after the old one has been cut away.

▲ FQ2. After the paint has been sanded off the weld edges, the new panel can be fitted into place – always check it at this stage against the luggage bay cover line and the front panel.

▲ FQ3. Then, when everything is perfectly lined up, the panel can be welded in place with a long seam weld; one which will keep out damp and thus corrosion ..

▼ FQ4. ... and you can see that the front panel/spare wheel well has been welded to the new metal all along its inner flanges, too. Seal all welded joints with seam sealer as extra protection against corrosion.

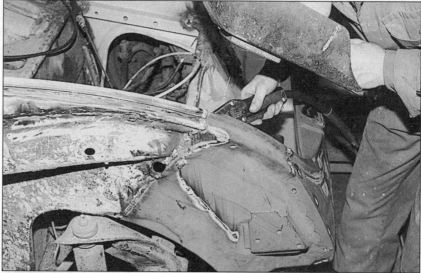

▲ FQ5. Corrosion is quite common in this area and you can see where a plate has been welded on here in the past.

▲ FQ6. And the suspension towers and tower tops on models with MacPherson strut front suspension can corrode, too.

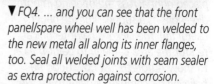

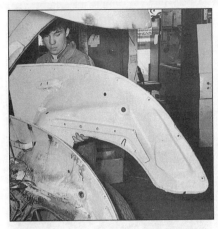

▲ FQ7. Where severe corrosion is found, it may be best to cut your losses and fit a full manufacturer's front quarter panel, if available.

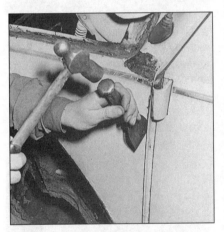

▲ FQ8. After comparing the new panel with the attachment points of the old, you can start cutting the old one away. Here the first cut to remove the old panel is made ahead of the door hinge pillar seam.

▲ FQ9. It's essential to study the new panel closely to find out which struts and box sections are part of the new unit and which have to be left in place. Stuart is using a special tool to drill out the spot welds before tapping in a thin bladed, sharp bolster chisel to finally make the break, although in the event this box section had to be taken out anyway. A twist drill handled carefully will do the job just as well, as long as you (i) centre punch and drill as close to the centre of the spot weld as possible and (ii) when you can, drill through the spot weld in the panel you are taking off, but not the one that remains. Of course, this is not always possible, in which case the hole should be used to make a strong plug weld with the MIG or gas welder.

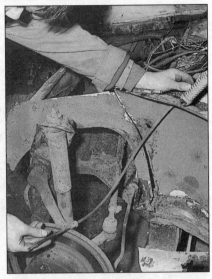

▲ FQ10. Before the wheel arch part of the panel can be removed from the left hand side of the car, the speedo cable which is driven off the front left-hand wheel bearing dust cover, must be removed.

▲ FQ11. Then, after more drilling out of spot welds, the wheel arch can be cut free ...

◄ FQ12. ... leaving all the weld flanges on the inner panels in place.

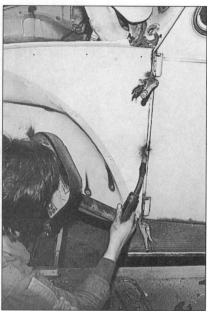

▲ FQ13. When all of the old panel has been removed, the weld flanges can be sanded back to bright metal and trued up very carefully with the hammer and dolly after patch-repairing any other areas of corrosion that may be found, such as at the end of the heater channel. Note that if the spare wheel well (early models) has to be replaced, it is best done with the old front quarter panel still in place so that it can be perfectly aligned before cutting the quarter panel away.

▲ FQ16. After clamping the panel securely in place and, where necessary, re-dressing the flanges with the hammer and dolly to ensure a good fit, he tack welds the panel to the hinge pillar seam. The best way of joining these two together is actually with a spot welder.

▲ FQ15. ... and checks the fit against the luggage bay cover, the spare wheel well, the door hinge pillar and the body flanges left in place. You must also be **certain** that the door hinge pillar has not moved out of position at this stage, especially on convertibles which are inherently far less stable, of course.

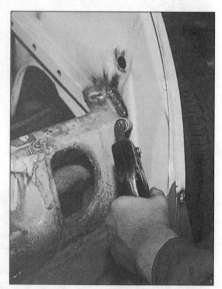

▲ FQ14. Stuart offers the new panel up to the car ...

▲ FQ17. Seam welds are the order of the day where the new panel meets internal members.

◀ FQ18. Where you're joining new metal to existing like this, it is essential that the old metal is bright and clean, otherwise the weld will be untidy and weak, being full of impurities.

▲ FQ19. Another joint is to be found where the footwell heater channel (sills) meet the new panel.

▲ FQ20. Always seal all welded joints with seam sealer, brushing into the joint, after it is piped on, with a brush dipped in the correct solvent for the seam sealer – check with your supplier.

DOOR STRIPDOWN

STRIPPING OUT DOOR GEAR

Sometimes you have to take out door gear because the mechanism goes wrong, and sometimes you have to remove it to repair a door. There are several different types of door gear, and it isn't possible to cover every different make. However, most types of door trim and window gear are shown here, so there should be enough information contained in this section to apply to

whatever car you are working upon. Before removing any type of window mechanism, remember to prop the glass up, or have an assistant hold it there, or it can crash down and cause a nasty injury. Also remember that there is often a lot of force contained within window winder gear springs. With glass removed and/or part of the operating mechanism detached, the winder arm can whip round with considerable force. Check your manual.

When replacing glass channels and winder mechanisms, remember to replace everything without tightening up. Then make sure that everything operates smoothly before finally tightening nuts and bolts.

STRIPPING MGB-TYPE DOORS (LATER TYPE)

▲ DSD1. Start by removing the trim rail at the top of the door (two crosshead screws at each end), then remove the single screw which holds the window winder in place.

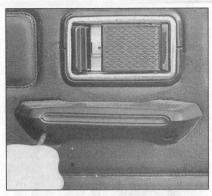

▲ DSD2. Unscrew the two crosshead screws holding the door pull in place (lift the fold-down handle on earlier models).

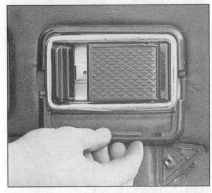

▲ DSD3. Door catch bezels 'break' in the middle – they clip apart then slide out.

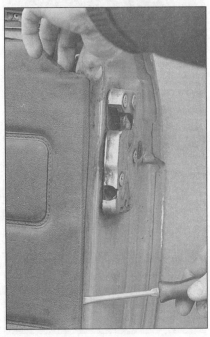

▲ DSD4. The door trim clips forwards and off. Take care, if the trim is an old one, to lever near to the spring clips.

▶ *DSD5. The protective plastic sheet (if still fitted) should be carefully removed and reused later if not damaged. If it's missing, replace later. This now gives access to the door's internals.*

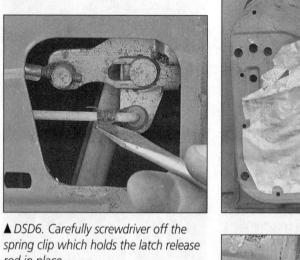

▲ *DSD6. Carefully screwdriver off the spring clip which holds the latch release rod in place ...*

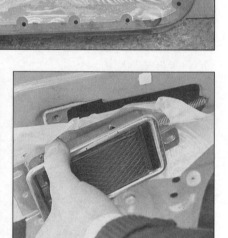

▲ *DSD11. Remove the four screws holding the latch pull in place and remove it.*

▲ *DSD7. ... and the one which holds the locking lever.*

▲ *DSD9. Take out the screws holding the latch unit in place.*

▼ *DSD12. Take out the window runner top screw.*

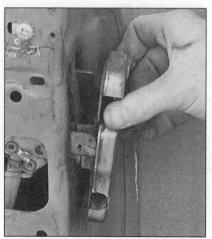

▲ *DSD8. Pull them forwards and out of location with the latch.*

▲ *DSD10. Remove the latch unit.*

▲ *DSD13. Unbolt the bottom of the runner, either inside the door ...*

▲ *DSD14. ... or from outside, removing the bracket as well. Leave the runner loose, inside the door.*

▲ *DSD15. Remove the window regulator extension screws.*

▲ *DSD16. Remove the regulator securing screws. Slide the rollers out of the bottom of the channel fixed to the bottom of the window glass.*

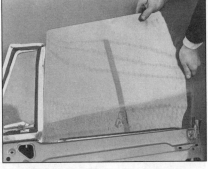

▲ *DSD17. Lift the glass up and out of the door.*

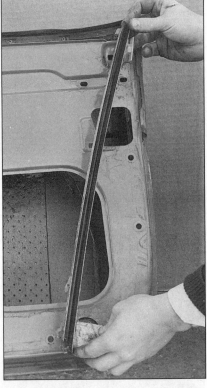

▲ *DSD18. Now you can lift the rear glass channel out of the door.*

▼ *DSD19. 'Persuade' the regulator assembly out of the holes in the door.*

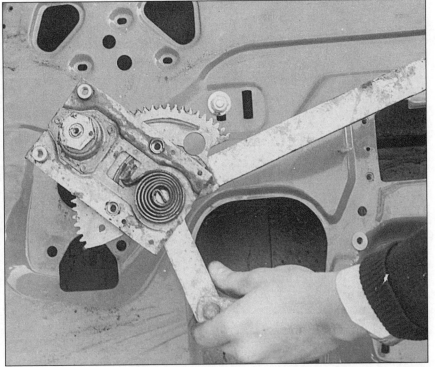

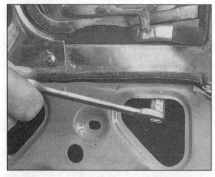

▲ DSD20. Lever the grommets, if fitted, out of their holes in the front of the door. Remove the two nuts which hold the quarterlight from beneath and the one which holds it from the front of the door.

▲ DSD21. Undo the two nuts which hold the front window channel (an extension of the quarterlight).

▲ DSD22. Lift the quarterlight assembly out of the door.

▶ DSD23. The chrome trim clips forwards and off (be very careful not to distort it). The door push is held by two nuts – two screw threads protrude from the handle, backwards through the door skin – and the lock is held by a spring clip which slides into a groove in the lock, tight against the inside of the door skin.

▼ DSD24. Voila! The now denuded door skin is ready for whatever work is to be carried out.

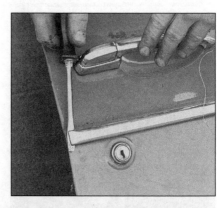

STRIPPING MINI DOOR TRIM (EARLY TYPE)

▼ DSD25. Start by taking out the trim finishers which simply push into each end of the door pocket.

▼ DSD26. Take out the screws that hold the trim into the base of the door pocket.

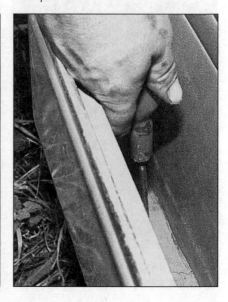

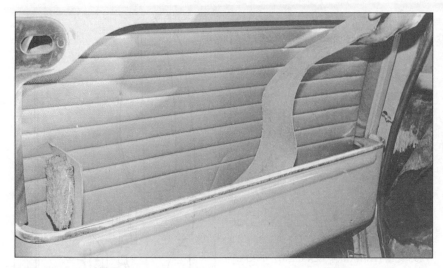

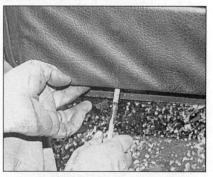

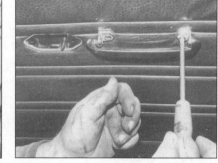

▲ DSD27. Take out the card trim, taking care not to rip it.

▲ DSD28. Next, ease your arm behind the main door trim and push it forwards in the centre so that it bows forwards and comes clear of the door frame at one end. Lift that end upwards and lift out the main trim board as shown.

▲ DSD30. Next the door pull handle is removed by taking out the two screws which hold it in place.

▲ DSD31. The trim board is held to the door by a ring of clips which snap into holes in the door frame. Carefully ease a screwdriver behind the trim board and snap the clips out one at a time. Avoid snatching at the clips or they may pull out of the trim board, especially if it has started to age and lose its strength. When the two sides and bottom of the trim panel have been snapped away, the top of the panel is eased downwards out of its retaining flap at the top of the door. Once again, there should be a waterproof covering behind the trim panel, and if this has to be removed, re-glue it into place before refitting the trim panel.

▼ DSD32. Exploded view of Mini van, pick-up and early saloon models' door lock and handle assembly. Start by taking off the screw which holds the lock handle spindle in place (Item 1). Use a straight point screwdriver.

▲ DSD29. Take out the cross-headed screws that hold the window winder knob and the door catch handle (top right). Each handle then pulls off its square shaft.

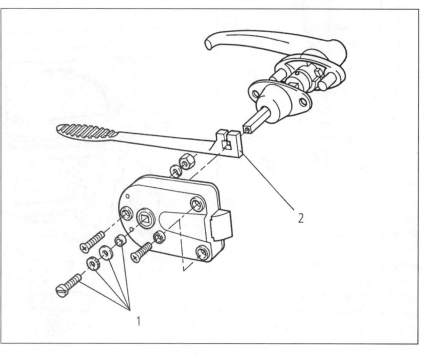

▶ *DSD33. The exterior handle can now be removed, but not before the interior handle (see DSD32, Item 2) has been eased off the spindle with a screwdriver. Some are held in place with a pinch screw, and this is being undone in the photograph.*

▲ *DSD34. Keep the oddly sized, oddly threaded retaining screws their washers safe by putting them straight back into the end of the spindles.*

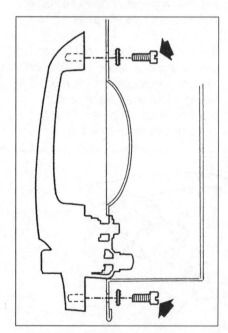

▲ *DSD35. This is the later type Mini door handle assembly. With door trim out of the way, later-type door handles are removed by unscrewing the two screws arrowed here. The screws holding the internal handle and lock in place are also clearly visible with the trim out of the way, while the latch assembly is screwed to the rear closing face of the door.*

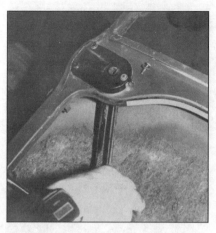

▼ *DSD36. Front door lock removal: note that clips at A and B have to be removed after all three mechanisms have been disconnected from the door. With the handle taken off, the lock barrel and push button can be dismantled as follows: (1) Prise off the retaining clip which holds the lock barrel to the handle. (2) Insert the key into the lock and use it to pull out the lock barrel. (3) Undo the screw that fixes the retaining plate to the exterior handle. (4) You can now take out the push button after lifting off the retaining plate, operating link, washer and spring.*

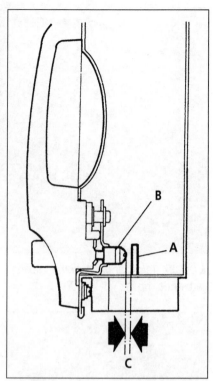

▲ *DSD37. On earlier models the plunger cap (B) can be adjusted by screwing in or screwing out to give around 1mm to 1.5mm of free movement before the door lock release begins to move.*

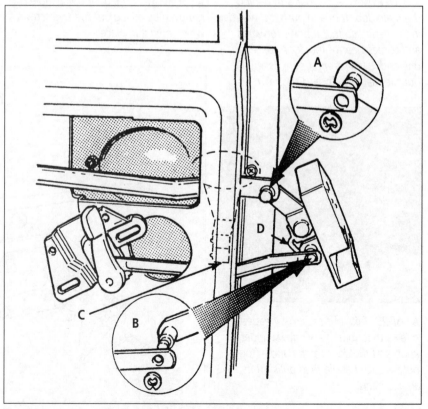

VOLVO DOOR STRIP

▼ *DSD38. The top of the door trim is held in place with self-tapping screws. Be sure to retain the cup washers.*

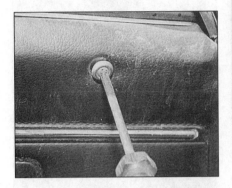

▲ *DSD39. Door handles push onto a splined shaft and are held in place with a spring 'hairgrip' clip.*

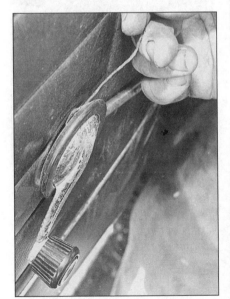

▲ *DSD40. This is best removed by 'fishing' for the loop end of it with a wire hook, whilst the door trim panel is pushed back far enough to give access.*

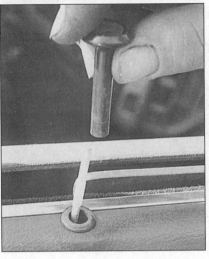

▲ *DSD41. The door lock button simply unscrews, leaving a threaded pin protruding.*

▲ *DSD42. Around the interior latch handle, the plastic bezel springs on – and off.*

▼ *DSD43. Now, like most door trims, the concealed clips around sides and base are eased away leaving the trim panel free to be lifted up over the door lock pin and away.*

▲ *DSD44. Next, the four bolts holding the mechanism to the door casing can be removed, but ensure that the glass is supported.*

▲ *DSD45. Now, this is cheating! This clip is found on the assembly at the bottom of the glass, inside the door casing, facing away from you (i.e. facing the outside of the car), so there's no other way to photograph it! By feeling up inside the door casing, the spring clip has to be raised over the pin and pushed off ...*

▲ DSD46. ... followed by a spring and washers. All the while the glass must be supported, preferably by an assistant.

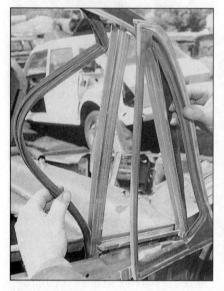

▲ DSD47. Next the quarter light and door glass channel rubbers are eased out (use washing up liquid to help ease them back in, using a blunt screwdriver for 'persuasion').

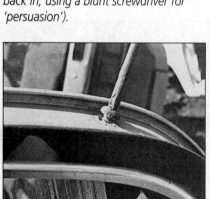

▲ DSD48. Take out the top screw holding the glass guide in place ...

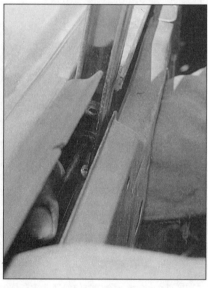

▲ DSD49. ... and the screws holding it just below the top of the door frame. This tightly-squeezed view is through the gap from whence the glass appears when wound upwards.

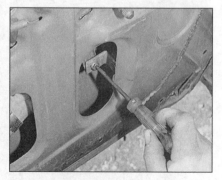

▲ DSD50. Then remove the bottom attachment screw ...

▲ DSD51. ... leaving the channel to be lifted upwards and clear.

▲ DSD52. Now the glass is free to be lifted up and away through the top of the door and the mechanism can be taken out through one of the bottom apertures.

FIAT DOOR STRIP

This is a cable type of winder system and is, if anything, easier to dismantle than any other because there are no bulky and mischievous mechanisms to handle.

▲ *DSD53. The chrome bezel around the base of the door handle is carefully levered off.*

▲ *DSD56. The window channel is held at the top of the door frame by a screw ...*

▲ *DSD58. The channel can be removed through the bottom of the door.*

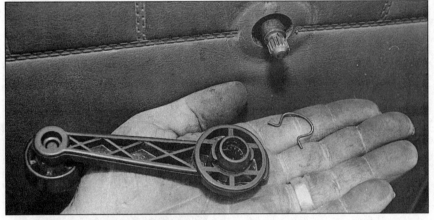

▲ *DSD54. Once again, the handle is of the splined shaft/concealed spring clip variety.*

▲ *DSD55. The door pull/armrest comes away after unscrewing the two retaining screws.*

▲ *DSD57. ... and at the bottom, inside the door casing, by a bolt.*

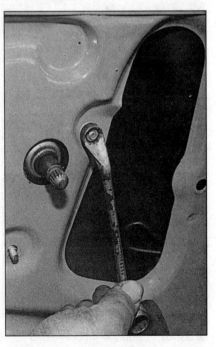

▲ *DSD59. The winder regulator is held to the door frame by three nuts ...*

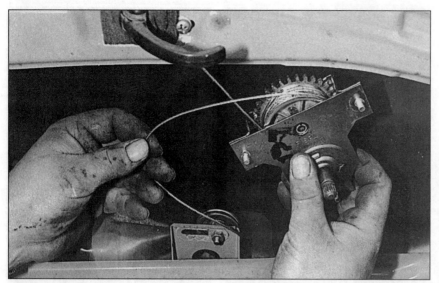

▲ DSD60. ... but when removing, be careful not to get the cable itself into a tangle.

▲ DSD61. The cable can be removed from the bottom pulley ...

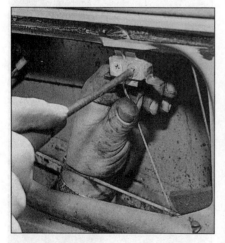

▲ DSD62. ... and the window eased down far enough at least to expose the cable clamp. One of the screws must be taken out completely but the other need only be slackened.

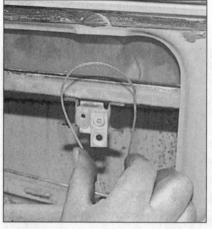

▲ DSD63. The cable comes clear of the clamp and can be removed from the concealed pulley up inside the door frame.

▼ DSD64. Carefully lower the glass to the bottom of the door and lift it over the bottom edge of the frame and out.

FORD DOOR STRIP

▼ DSD65. This particular Ford system is neither unconventional nor difficult to remove. Remove the three screws holding the regulator arm support from the door, after propping the glass in the ¾-down position.

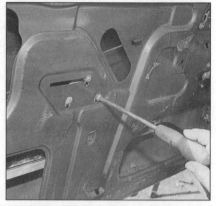

▼ DSD66. Take out the screws holding the regulator winder mechanism to the door.

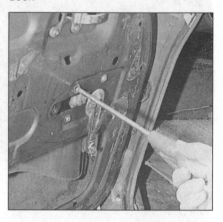

▲ DSD67. With the mechanism free inside the door casing, slide the rollers out of the channels on the bottom of the window glass.

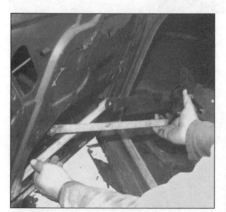

▲ DSD68. Ease the mechanism out of the bottom of the door ...

▲ DSD69. ... and the glass out of the top as shown.

GENERAL DOOR STRIP

▼ DSD70. Remember that old doors will undoubtedly have had a good few gallons of water pass through them! Soak all fixing nuts, bolts and screws with a spray-on releasing fluid well before starting work.

▲ DSD71. On some older cars, quarter light or vent assemblies were often attached to the glass runner so look out for screws holding the whole thing in place and not just the runner.

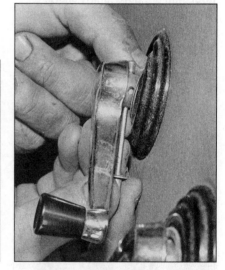

▲ DSD72. Some internal door handles are held on in a way that's a bit difficult to understand at first. Push the trim inwards and behind the bezel you may find that the shank of the handle and the squared shaft it pushes onto have a pin passing through them. It may or may not be a tapered pin, but if it is tapered, push from the narrow end, of course. Push the pin out with a thin punch or nail as shown – you may need to give it a tap with a hammer.

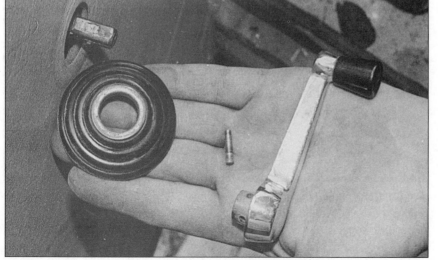

◄ DSD73. Then the handle and bezel just pull off. The trim may have a spring behind it placed around the squared shaft, to keep the assembly up tight.

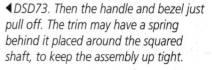

DOOR RE-SKIN

DOOR SKIN REPLACEMENT

This is the basic procedure for removing and replacing door skins on most cars. You don't have to strip out all of the door gear in most cases, although there are two things to bear in mind: (1) Remember that door handles and other fittings may be easiest to remove after taking off the door skin; (2) *Always* remove the door glass – even if access is not impossibly difficult, you will be almost certain to damage the glass with grinder sparks and weld spatter.

Safety: The edges around a cut-off door skin are particularly sharp. Wear industrial-type leather gloves. Wear suitable goggles when using an angle grinder.

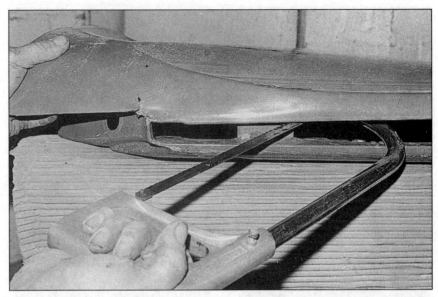

▲ SGD2. On this type of door, then, remove the skin by first sawing, grinding or drilling out the spot welds of the connecting bridge.

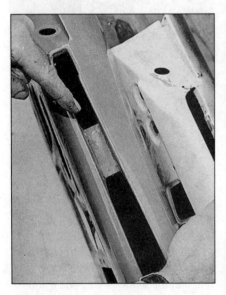

▲ SGD1. As with a number of classic cars, GT6 door skins have a bracing bar between the skin and door frame positioned underneath the quarterlight. Having full width windows, a number of other cars do not.

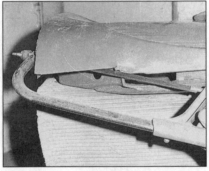

▲ SGD3. The corner can also be sawn through rather than ground if desired. It's best to remove all the glass to protect it against hot metal sparks.

▲ SGD5. The half inch wide return lip can then be separated from the frame ...

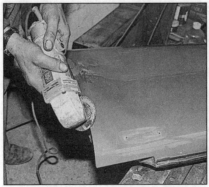

▲ SGD4. Grind around the door skin edge just deep enough to remove the folded-over edge.

▲ SGD6. ... and stripped off. Remember it's razor sharp so wear gloves.

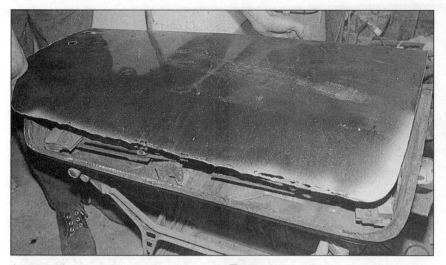

▲ SGD7. The outer skin can then be lifted off.

▼ SGD8. Rather than take the chance, refit the frame into the car and double check for any distortion.

▼ SGD9. Any such distortion can now be easily corrected with a panel beating hammer and dolly.

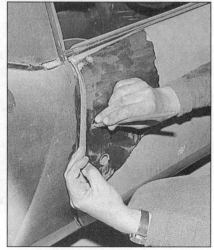

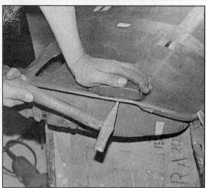

▲ SGD10. All being well, lay over the new skin and tap over the return lip as shown using a supporting dolly, or use a door skinner tool.

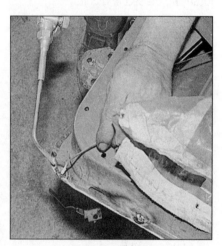

▲ SGD11. All that's needed now is just a few weld or braze tacks made in key places around the edge. Brazing has the advantage that it can be more easily softened and the panel moved. It has the disadvantage that too much heat from the welding torch can cause distortion. As usual, MIG is best unless you're confident of your skills.

◄ SGD12. Nowadays, most door skins come complete with lock and handle holes already formed. If there aren't any, a good way to ensure correct placement is to cut out a section from the old skin (avoiding distortion) and mark around the inside of the relevant holes. Suitable start holes can then be drilled and joined up to complete the desired cut out with a file after which the door can be resprayed and the handle refitted and tightened home.

▲ *SGD13. Once back on the car, the door fit can be adjusted by slightly loosening the securing bolts ...*

▲ *SGD14. .. and levering up and down ..*

▲ *SGD15. ... and backwards and forwards before finally retightening the bolts. You might wish to do this before tack welding the skin in place just to ensure that it fits the frame properly.*

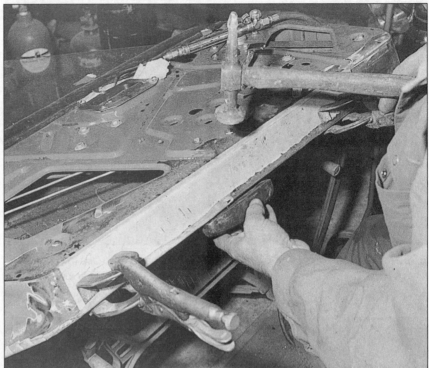

▲ *SGD16. Incidentally if, as is likely, the door frame base has corroded, you could fabricate (using a Sykes-Pickavant bench folder) a repair section, letting it into the new door skin as the skin is fitted ...*

▼ *SGD17. ... then welding or brazing it in place after the door skin is in place. MIG welding would be better for most DIY welds.*

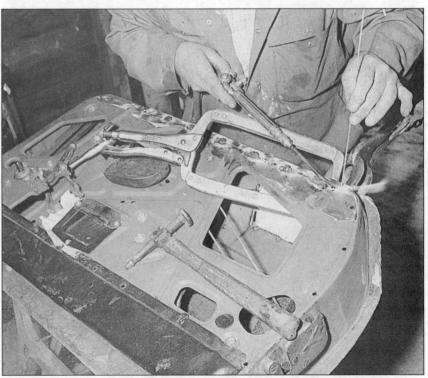

SILL REPLACEMENT

For the great majority of cars, rusting sills are the equivalent of sinking foundations in the structure of a house. They are essential to the strength and well-being of a car, particularly if it's a sports car where little more than sills and transmission tunnel link the front of the car to the rear.

The following sequence shows how even the most technically complex of cars come down to the basics – at least in the area of sills. Here's how to replace sills and inner structures on a Porsche 911. Remember, no matter what sort of car you are working on, to ensure that both ends of the car are held off the ground in such a way that the structure remains true. And check, check and check again before finally welding in the replacement panels. The door makes the best template of all for checking alignment and fit.

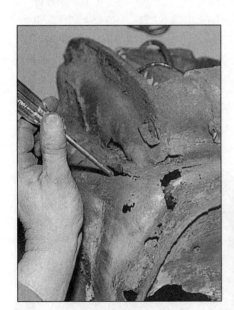

▲ SR1. Corrosion ahead of the sill itself is common on pre-galvanized Porsche 911s and can be patched separately, using scrap sections or trimmed original panel. This sort of repair is not likely to be found on other models of car.

▲ SR2. Further corrosion at the rear and in the adjacent floor pan, also requiring patching.

▲ SR3. For the 911 and for many other cars, full or half floorpans are available, but fitting one is a specialist task on the 911, needing a chassis jig. On almost any car, if the inner sill is rusty, some repairs to the floorpan are almost certain to be needed.

▼ SR4. Cut away the corroded metal here, at the rear of the sill/body rocker, to assess the extent of the repair.

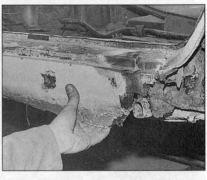

▲ SR5. Drill through the spot welds and use an air chisel or tin snips to remove the outer sill/body rocker. **(Wear heavy duty gloves!)**

▲ SR6. With the outer sill/body rocker removed assess the condition of the outer side member. Probe the metal surrounding the jacking point. This picture shows a new outer side member being offered to the old structure. This determines the amount of metal to be cut out. Note that rear outer sill/body rocker support and the jacking flange have been removed.

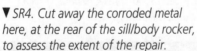

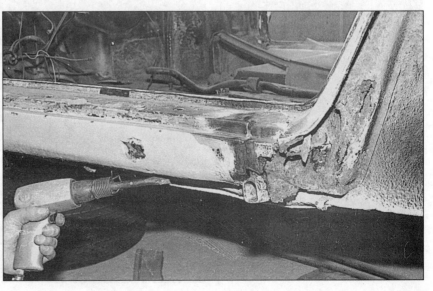

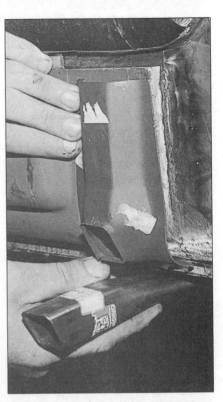

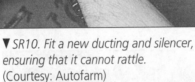

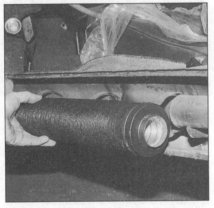

▲ SR7. If the outer side member is in poor condition, remove this also ...

▼ SR10. Fit a new ducting and silencer, ensuring that it cannot rattle. (Courtesy: Autofarm)

▲ SR8. ... to reveal the heater ducting, peculiar to 911s and VW Beetles. (Courtesy: Autofarm)

▼ SR11. Ensure that the curvature and fit are good and that all surfaces to be welded have been sanded back to bright metal. (Courtesy: Autofarm)

▲ SR12. New jacking point supports are fitted after the inner panel but behind the outer sill/body rocker. The jacking tube itself is fitted with reference to the outer sill/body rocker. (Courtesy: Autofarm)

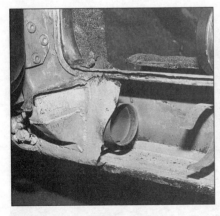

▲ SR9. This shot shows the rearmost extent of cutting away and simple repairs to the base of the door pillar. (Courtesy: Autofarm)

▶ SR13. The side member should ideally be spot welded to its mating inner member at the top edge, but careful MIG welds produce a satisfactory result, and they can be ground to a better finish if required. If the jacking point is to be replaced, drill out its spot welds and use these as the position indicator to locate the new item. Again, careful MIG welding can replace the spot weld. Wire brush, rust proof and then zinc prime the outer member at this point.

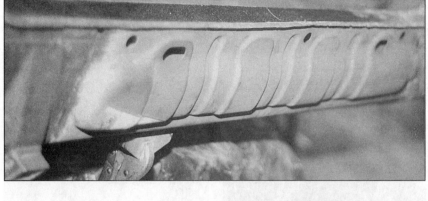

▲ SR14. Cut off the corroded rear sill/body rocker support with reference to the new one.

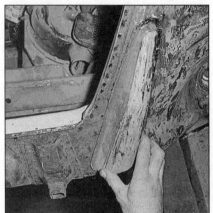

▲ SR15. Offer up the rear sill/body rocker support and determine its position by using the spot weld drillings from the previous item. If the inner wing/fender had been patched in this area, then clamp the new sill/body rocker in the correct position (see next paragraph), and tack the support to the inner wing/fender. When satisfied remove the outer sill/body rocker and finish welding the support to the inner wing/fender.

▶ SR16. The door bottom gap is determined by the sill/body rocker position. Use clamps to hold it in place and move the sill/body rocker around until the correct position is found. The front joint face of the sill/body rocker with the front wing/fender should be 2mm in front of the door edge. There should be a 4mm gap between the sill/body rocker and the lower edge of the door. The sill/body rocker should form a uniform contour with the door when viewed from above. When satisfied with the position tap down the proud edges of the panel to the surrounding structure. Weld the sill/body rocker to the hinge pillar, using additional patching in this area as necessary. Do not weld on to rusty metal.

▼ SR17. Additionally, weld the front of the sill/body rocker to the front wing/fender support flange, the undertray seam, the rear sill/body rocker support and the jacking point flange. (Courtesy: Autofarm)

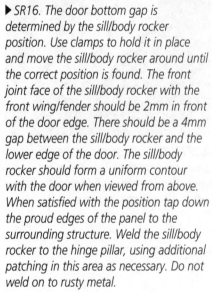

▲ SR18. Replacement of the door latch panel requires careful positioning, not only for the door latch itself, but also because it locates the rear outer wing/fender at its front. The panel should be tacked on and the rear wing/fender offered up, to ensure that the correct 4mm door gap can be achieved. When satisfied with the position of the panel, the rear wing/fender is removed and the welding completed. Use of a MIG welder will require careful work and grinding-off of excess weld before further finishing, such as lead loading or plastic filling.

▲ SR19. This picture shows the door lock panel ready for welding. The rear wings/fenders are sound and have been left in place in this instance.

▼ SR20. In order to thoroughly seal this joint, you could well lead load it. (See relevant section of this book for details).

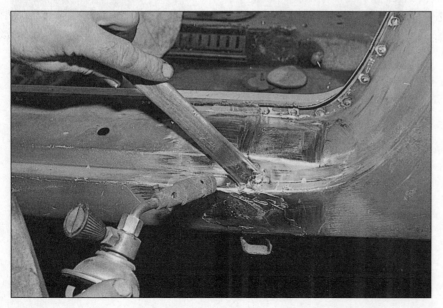

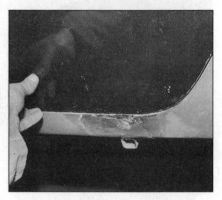

▲ SR21. File the lead so that the contour ..

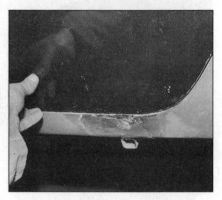

▲ SR22. ... fits that of the door. Whilst fitting the new sill/body rocker, be sure to temporarily re-hang the door before welding the new panels in place, as a sure check that the position is absolutely correct. Also, do so if new floor and/or inner wing sections are fitted, checking before welding each one in place.

PANEL ALIGNMENT

Having repaired outer panels and gathered together new replacements, it is essential that all the panels are fitted up and properly aligned before preparing for paint. The time you spend at this stage in getting the panel alignment right and ensuring consistency of panel gaps will make all the difference between an 'ordinary' restoration and a good looking one. Be prepared to spend as long at this stage as it needs, fitting and re-fitting panels as necessary. This sequence shows a typical panel fitting sequence on an MGB.

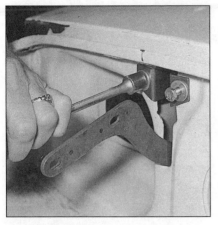

▲ PA1. The first step is to fit bonnet hinges. Two bolts into captive nuts inside the engine bay here ...

▲ PA2. ... and two more inside the cockpit beneath the scuttle.

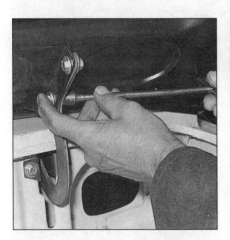

▲ PA3. The bonnet fits to the hinges with nuts, bolts and washers and there are slotted holes to allow adjustment.

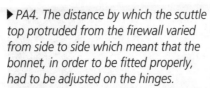

▶ PA4. The distance by which the scuttle top protruded from the firewall varied from side to side which meant that the bonnet, in order to be fitted properly, had to be adjusted on the hinges.

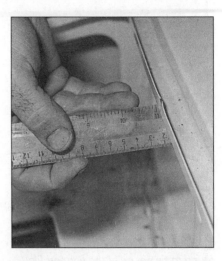

▼ PA5. The Rover Group Heritage experts fitting these panels use flat steel levers to force the bonnet position and the bonnet hinges to take the required shape. When done skillfully, work of this sort is **not** a bodge! After all, you are only working with what were once flat pieces of metal; this is the process of bending them a little more one way or the other.

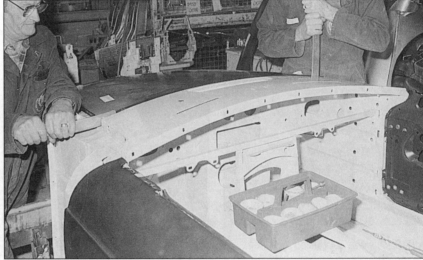

▼ PA6. With the bonnet propped open, a new wing is offered up for fit. Needless to say, it doesn't!

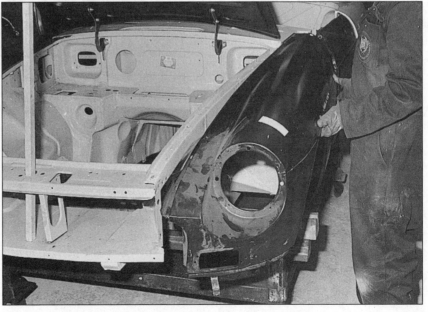

▲ PA7. The rear end of the wing was found to be not quite the right profile.

▲ PA8. This was countered by panel-beating the wing shape to make it match that of the scuttle.

▲ PA9. The scuttle was also given the treatment to enable the wing to fit snugly against it.

▲ PA10. When fitting the front wing, be sure to fit a spacing washer between wing and scuttle at the point of this bolt. The wing should not be pulled tightly against the scuttle. If you can't find the original, cut a new thick washer with a slot in it.

▲ PA12. With the wing fitted but none of the bolts tightened up. The wing position can be altered by placing a wooden block in **exactly** the position shown here and tapping the wing backwards. Use the block anywhere else and you stand a chance of distorting the wing.

▶ PA13. Another similar adjustment can be made to the shape of the back of the wing once the bolts have been tightened up ahead of this position or to move the whole wing forwards a touch.

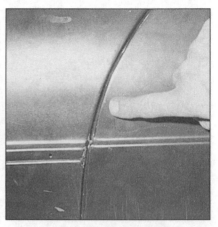

▲ PA11. It's crucial to get the gap between the rear of the wing and the front of the door as accurate as possible. Door adjustments can be made as shown earlier, of course.

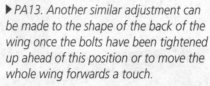

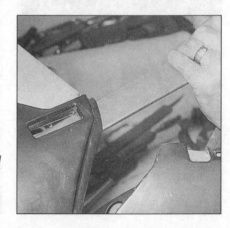

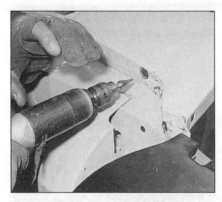

▲ PA14. More movement will be afforded if the mounting holes in this position are opened out. This might or might not be necessary – it depends on the individual vehicle.

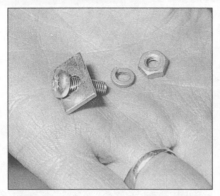

▲ PA17. The bottom of the wing fits to the body with a small nut, bolt and washer and a special square-shaped washer as shown.

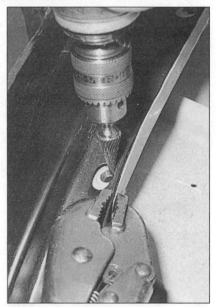

▲ PA19. Where holes in the wing don't align with the holes in the body, you could grind away unwanted steel with a rotary cutter or remove the wing once again and file out the slot.

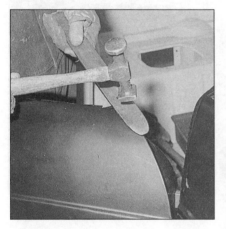

▲ PA15. Don't forget that you can also adapt the shape of the top of the front of the door to match the wing, although it's best not to hammer directly onto the door for fear of marking it.

▼ PA18. Clamp the wing in position and tighten all nuts and bolts in turn.

▼ PA16. It's crucial that the moulding that runs along the side of both wing and door are in complete alignment – check with a straight edge.

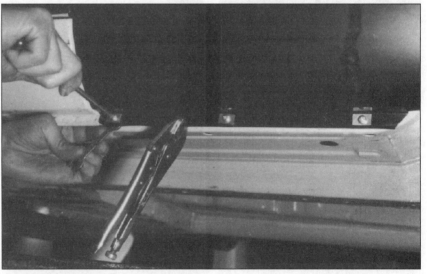

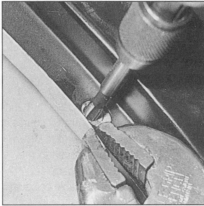

◄ PA20. It's a good idea to put a tap through every hole to make sure that all the threads are clear.

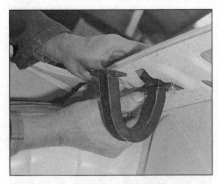

▲ PA21. Boot lid hinges bolt simply to the inside of the rear bodywork.

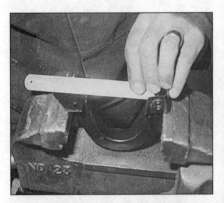

▲ PA22. The hinges themselves may need some adjustment in order for the boot lid to shut in the correct position. You can place in the vice and squeeze in order to close them up, as shown (measure carefully at each stage to ensure that you don't overdo it) or to lengthen the hinge, find a suitable piece of wood with a diameter larger than the V of the hinge, and hammer it into the hinge opening.

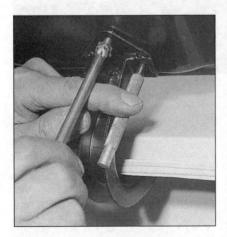

▲ PA23. Using an odd length of steel to align the holes, start with the first screw and fit the boot lid to the hinge.

◄ PA24. Fit all the bolts but, before tightening any of them, check boot lid fit.

▼ PA25. Once the limits of adjustment have been reached on the hinges, extra movement can be gained by levering the boot lid, as with the bonnet in PA5.

CHASSIS/ STRUCTURAL MONOCOQUE

Safety: Above all, be sure that work is done to a good professional standard. It would probably be wise to have anything but the simplest work checked over by a body repair shop approved for repairs by one of the major car manufacturers or a leading car insurance company. Also, follow the usual safety rules (see Appendices), especially if working under the car.

It is an established fact that it is not corrosion but accident damage that ends the lives of most sports cars. Of course, most of those which are written-off by the insurers will have corroded to the stage where any accident damage sustained is no longer capable of being repaired at a realistic cost, but the point is still there: that they end their lives crashed into oblivion. Sprites and Midgets are no less susceptible to this unhappy event than any other sports car, and when front-end damage has taken place, the front chassis rails are prone to buckling. We use this car as an example of how to repair exposed chassis rails.

Even heavy damage is repairable with a professional body jig which holds the body firmly in the required shape. The jig includes a set of guides against which to check the body for correct alignment in every direction.

Light damage can be repaired by the home enthusiast, especially if it is possible to hire a hydraulic body ram of the type illustrated here – they're the sort of thing that a half-decent tool hire shop ought to stock. We show how a lightly kinked chassis rail was pushed back into place, with precision.

▲ CD1. *The kink in the right-hand chassis rail can clearly be seen here, towards the top of the picture. We began by establishing just how far out of alignment the rail was. We took one of the shock absorber bolt holes as a datum point on one side, and the bonnet locating hole on the other.*

▶ CD2. *We took a further check, this time back from the shock absorber mounting to the upright corner of the bulkhead ...*

▼ CD3. *... and then, once again, the opposite diagonal was measured.*

▲ CD4. *Lastly – and logically – the actual gap between the rails was measured, comparing front, rear and damaged areas.*

▲ CD5. *Before carrying out any remedial work, it is essential to check that the car is on axle stands and on a level floor. Check the floor with a long spirit level along the line of the car ...*

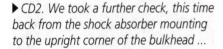
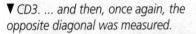

▲ CD6. *... and across the line of the car.*

▲ CD7. Then check that the axle stands – and thus the car (or bodyshell as in this case) – are dead level all round.

▲ CD9. Of course, the footwell end-plate is nowhere near strong enough in itself to take these sorts of loads, so it was reinforced with two baulks of strong timber: one between the toe board and the floor crossmember, and another back from the crossmember to the heel board.

▲ CD10. Meanwhile, back in the engine bay, things were moving fast! We used a bottle jack, supported with a timber on one side and with a steel plate to spread the load a little on its 'top' surface, to help push the rail back into place.

▲ CD8. The inner wheel arch strengthening gusset, which is being pointed to here, was found to be kinked, a result of the front axle line having been pushed back. We used the hydraulic ram, pushing forwards from the footwell end-plate, to push it back again. Chains and fixing pins should be part of any kit of body ram parts. Here, the right-hand end of the ram has a chain taken from it to the outer edge of the chassis rail mounting. As the ram is pumped up, the chain pulls the mounting point back into place.

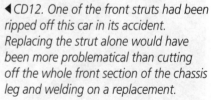

▲ CD11. Alternatively – even preferably, since far higher loads can be exerted – a professional tool can be used.

◀ CD12. One of the front struts had been ripped off this car in its accident. Replacing the strut alone would have been more problematical than cutting off the whole front section of the chassis leg and welding on a replacement.

Of course, after every stage in the procedure shown, alignment checks were taken and notes made of any movement found. In practice, it will almost certainly be necessary to carry out all the necessary pushing and pulling a number of times. It is far better to attempt to move each area a little at a time rather than trying to push it all the way in one go. The different parts are dependent upon one another and so are likely to move in sympathy with each other. If any doubts remain as to the thoroughness or accuracy of the work, or if home DIY methods do not completely achieve the desired effect (and don't forget to also check the height of chassis rails – all too often one will lift relative to the other in an accident), take the car or bodyshell to the professionals. A misaligned bodyshell can be a lethal danger on the roads – don't take chances! In any case: YOU ARE STRONGLY ADVISED TO HAVE YOUR LOCAL BODYSHOP – ONE WITH BODY ALIGNMENT EQUIPMENT – CARRY OUT A FULL ALIGNMENT CHECK ON YOUR CAR. Have them check the quality of any welding you may have carried out, too. You simply can't afford to cut corners at this stage.

CHASSIS MEMBER REPAIRS

The majority of so-called chassis repairs to the more modern classics are in fact repairs to the structural parts of the bodyshell. *Most classic cars do not have chassis!* (The only cars with chassis are those from which the entire body can be removed, leaving a denuded but 'useable' vehicle. Examples include Land-Rover, MGA and Triumph Spitfire/GT6 and Herald/Vitesse: the latter being anachronisms even in their day.) We show here an outline of the sorts of 'chassis' repairs that you might carry out on an MGB.

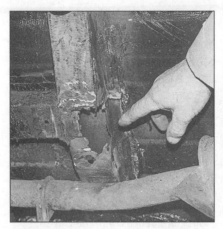

▲ *CMR1. Strictly localized chassis corrosion can be cut out, going straight back to sound metal and letting in a repair section which can easily be fabricated in the vice. Usually, however, corrosion like this is not localized, other than at the outer extremities.*

▲ *CMR2. As often as not, a patch repair like this is no better than a sticking plaster on a broken leg. What is really needed is for the complete area to be cut out and replaced. This is often a far bigger job than is at first apparent.*

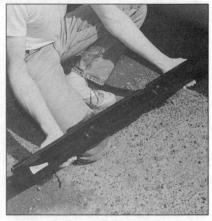

▲ *CMR3. Corrosion in the main crossmember should be met by replacing the whole section, although how you would stop at the crossmember and not have to replace the floors and the sill I can't imagine! Going this far is really a job for the experts in order to ensure that the crucial body structure does not become distorted.*

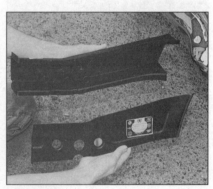

▲ *CMR4. On the subject of the extremities, the rear end of the chassis rails, where the spring hangers bolt through, are prone to corrosion, and Heritage repair panels are available from specialists such as Moss. Replacement of these outer panels is certainly viable for the careful DIY repairer ...*

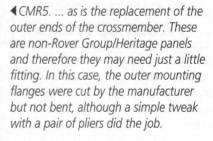

◀ *CMR5. ... as is the replacement of the outer ends of the crossmember. These are non-Rover Group/Heritage panels and therefore they may need just a little fitting. In this case, the outer mounting flanges were cut by the manufacturer but not bent, although a simple tweak with a pair of pliers did the job.*

▲ CMR6. The front end of the spring hangers seen in the floor replacement section are available as accurately made Heritage parts; although, if they are corroded, they would need to be mounted on a much wider repair than is included in this section. However, this is the vital part, and the floor repairs that surround it are relatively straightforward to fabricate.

▲ CMR7. Hydraulic body pullers are expensive but can be hired from most tool hire centres. Far more affordable is this type of mechanical puller (and pusher!) which incorporates a jack head with, in this instance, a 3,000 lb (around 1,400kg) capacity.
(Courtesy: The Eastwood Company)

BODY REMOVAL FROM CHASSIS

If your car is one of those with a separate chassis, you will have to remove at least some of it if you are carrying out a total restoration or if you intend carrying out certain chassis repairs where you wouldn't be able to weld the top of

the repair with the body still in place. However, DON'T REMOVE A RUSTY BODY IN ORDER TO REBUILD IT OFF THE CHASSIS! If you do so, the chances of its fitting back on again will be pretty slim! The correct working order is as follows:

1 Check the bodywork for strength. Will it literally fall apart if lifted from the chassis? (Leave the doors on for sure! They provide a lot of structural strength, especially to an open-topped car.) If necessary, carry out basic structural repairs or, if the chassis is sagging, weld or bolt in some temporary structural supports fabricated from square section tubing, just to enable you to lift the body in its component form.
2 CHECK YOUR MANUAL before lifting the body. There is bound to be *something* you need to know! You will find that very many bodies come off in sections.
3 Repair the chassis, having the alignment checked by a specialist (see previous section).
4 Refit the body, repair it *in situ* so that it fits the chassis!
5 Remove the body again for finishing off any 'hidden' welds before painting and rustproofing prior to final fitting on the chassis.

In order to give an idea of what is involved, we take the last volume-produced sports car to be fitted with a chassis, the Triumph Spitfire and GT6.

Removing the body tub from a Spitfire or GT6 shouldn't present any problems at all, except perhaps if a few of the bolts have rusted themselves in solid – in which case grind or cut them off, then drill and re-tap later. Fortunately, there are few bolts holding the tub in place and the shell isn't particularly heavy. So, if you haven't any lifting gear just ask a few friends round. One on each corner will be quite sufficient. There's no particular order in which the following operations should be carried out, but the main ones required for removing the body tub are illustrated below. Always remove the windscreen first: otherwise it stands a very good chance of being broken!

Safety: The dangers from broken glass should be self-evident. Tape up screen vent holes. If the screen breaks, glass particles may be blown out later when the blower is turned on.

▲ BRC1. Make sure that all wiring, earth cables, gearbox reverse and overdrive leads etc., are removed. Double check prior to lifting the body, and check again as the body is being lifted. Have a 'spare' bod assigned to dashing around the car checking connections, clearance and generally getting on everyone's nerves as the body is lifted. There always seems to be just another something-or-other that you have missed!

▲ BRC2. Brake and clutch pipes should be disconnected and freed from the body. Drain the systems first.

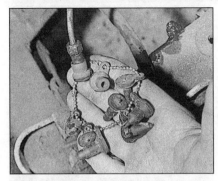

▲ BRC3. If the hydraulic pipes are to be used during the rebuild, it's useful to plug each pipe as it is disconnected to ensure they do not get contaminated with general muck. However, new pipes aren't expensive, so preferably throw the old ones away and consider fitting non-rusting new ones, such as Kunifer or copper sets.

▲ BRC4. Prior to cleaning up the top bulkhead, the brake and clutch master cylinders will have to be removed. Often, because of leaking fluid, this area will be rusty as paint is stripped off under the attack of brake fluid. To free really locked in nuts, a sharp tap with a cold chisel is often the answer. Alternatively, fit a socket spanner to the square drive on an impact screwdriver and shock it free that way.

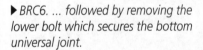

▲ BRC5. Continuing around the engine bay, disconnect the steering column by first loosening the two clamp arrangements inside the car – this shot shows the top one (earlier models are a little different) ...

▶ BRC6. ... followed by removing the lower bolt which secures the bottom universal joint.

▼ BRC7. The column can now be slid out of the way. Steering columns invariably have to be removed since they have to pass through the bulkhead.

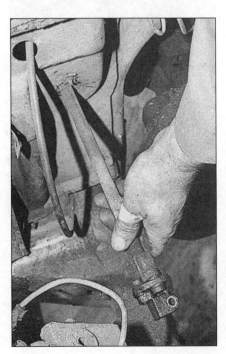

▼ BRC8. Don't forget to remove the speedometer and throttle cables. In this sequence the engine has already been removed, so choke cables, etc., have been disconnected previously. However, the engine doesn't have to be removed to lift the body off.

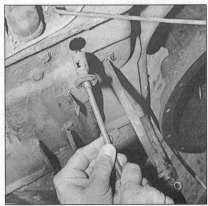

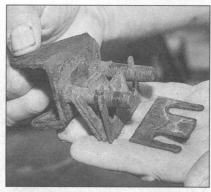

▲BRC9. Moving inside, ensure that the rear radius arms are disconnected from the body by undoing the two securing nuts on each side ...

▼BRC10. ... and tapping the bolts through.

▲BRC12. Off the car, the shims used between the radius arm bracket and body are clearly seen. Because of tolerances during manufacture, different cars will have different numbers of shims each side of the car. Label!

▲BRC13. Don't forget to disconnect the handbrake assembly.

◀BRC14. Twelve bolts secure the body on the chassis. One each side on the front bulkhead brackets ...

▼BRC11. The brackets could be totally removed, as shown here, or left on the ends of the radius arms – in which case the other end of the arms would have to be disconnected from the rear vertical link.

▼BRC15. ... with a further bolt at the end of each front over-rider. Once loosened or cut off ...

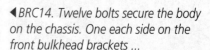

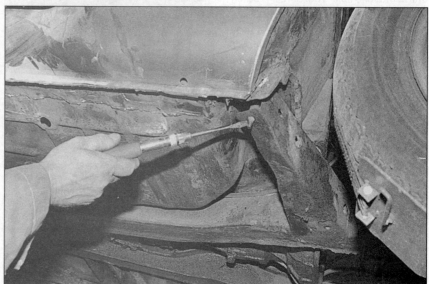

▲ *BRC16. ... these bolts can be tapped into the driver and passenger's footwells.*

▲ *BRC17. A further pair of bolts are found on each side, just forward of the seats. These bolt into the chassis' central stub outriggers.*

▲ *BRC18. Moving back, the inner seat belt mountings also bolt into the chassis, so remove these followed by the final two bolts situated on the transverse stiffening bridge.*

Before lifting, go through your manual once again, ticking off that everything that should be detached is free. Favourite to forget are throttle, choke, speedo and bonnet release cables, and also earth cables connecting engine or gearbox to the bodywork. Make certain that your car hasn't been given a non-standard earth connection: check gearbox area from underneath the car.

▼ *BRC19. As mentioned above, lifting the main tub doesn't require specialist lifting gear, but one way to do it could be to lift, then prop up the back end using a bar passed through where the transverse spring sits followed by lifting the front end.*

▲ *BRC20. The rolling chassis could then be pushed out from underneath ...*

▲ *BRC21. ... and pulled out of the way.*

It is very important to bear in mind that **THE BODY TUB MUST NOT BE RESTORED WHEN OFF THE CHASSIS**. If it is, it is highly unlikely that you will ever get it back on again! It will probably be fairly difficult, in any case, to align all the bolt holes easily.

▼ *BRC22. Whether repaired or not, the opportunity should be taken to pressure wash the chassis and to paint it with a zinc-based primer and a top coat. The 'correct' finish is body colour, but your choice of paint will depend on whether you want to be show-original or go for ultimate longevity.*

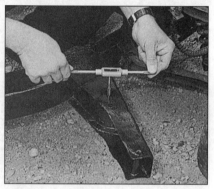

▲ *BRC23. After painting, but before refitting, use a tap to clear all the mounting threads. Fit the body and insert each bolt a couple of times. This will enable you to lift, shove and lever the body until all the bolts can be inserted. You can swear, too, if it helps.*

CHASSIS REPAIRS

Chassis repairs can generally be divided into two groups. There is the simple patch repair or replacement of outriggers. And then there are more extensive repairs of a structural nature. In the latter case the chassis will generally be stripped bare. It should then be scraped manually back to bare (or more often, rusty!) metal. Use engine cleaner to soften grease. After rinsing off with water, use a DIY-type blowtorch and scraper (wear gloves and goggles) to soften old underseal. Scrape off with a Chinese (i.e. cheap and all it's good for!) wood chisel. Then have the chassis professionally sandblasted to remove all traces of rust – see your Yellow Pages. But do note that grease and underseal *won't* be removed by sandblasting, although paint will. Important! DON'T leave any mechanical components whatsoever on the chassis: the sand will find its way in and rapidly destroy them.

Before carrying out a major chassis restoration, have it checked by a specialist for alignment (see ads. in classic car magazines). If it is badly distorted, it may be best to have them realign and repair the chassis – the route I would generally recommend. If you are a total DIY fanatic BE SURE TO HAVE CHASSIS ALIGNMENT CHECKED BY A SPECIALIST WITH AN APPROPRIATE JIG before putting it back into use. Note that the greater amount of heat required to weld the thicker steel in a chassis can itself cause distortion unless the work is carried out by a skilled practitioner.

Patch repairs are another matter, of course, and are usually eminently DIYable. Do check and double check alignments of fixings and mountings before driving and after welding.

This sequence is based on the repair of one of the most rugged of all 'classic' chassis – the Land-Rover's. For smaller chassis repairs of this kind, it may only be necessary to take off part of the bodywork. See the second sequence of pictures in this section showing simple patch repairs to an MGA chassis.

▲ CR1. This repair was carried out after removing the front floor. Shown here are an outrigger and bulkhead, with the bolt being undone (it's usually rusty!). The nut and bolt rust themselves into the socket and removal is far from easy ...

▼ CR4. When encountering rusty nuts and bolts, you can always resort to a hand-grinder or a hacksaw. Hard work but often the only way to deal with these stubborn fellows!

▲ CR5. A bolt is shown here being drifted out, while the bracket is still on the outrigger, even though this can often lead to the bracket simply falling away because of extensive corrosion!

▲ CR2. ... so much so that you may need to apply heat or, as in this instance, even drift out the bolt.

▼ CR6. This crossmember has to be chiselled off, but a hacksaw is needed to get a starting point for the air chisel.

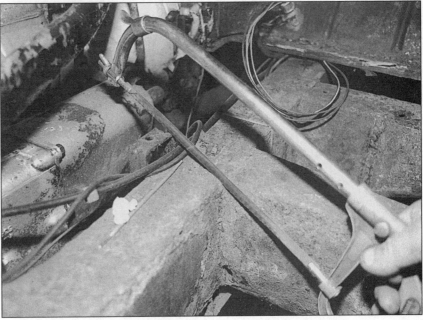

▲ CR3. The stay that holds the bulkhead outrigger to the chassis (an important 'steadying influence' on each of these parts!) is cut away; as the stay is going to be replaced at a later stage, it is easiest just to saw through it, particularly as it's a very simple, easy-to-replace component.

▲ CR7. An air-chisel is shown here actually cutting away the original weld. If you don't have access to an air-chisel, you can hacksaw down as far as possible and finish off the process with a hand chisel. One of the problems with an air-chisel (even if you do have one) is that it can sometimes cut away some of the **good** metal that you intended keeping!

▲ CR8. Another method of removing an outrigger is to carefully cut away the old weld with oxy-acetylene equipment. The beauty of this method is that it avoids the risk of 'tearing' the chassis, something to watch out for when chiselling, but all the safety points connected with oxy-acetylene **must** be remembered during this process. Best of all for the DIY repairer might be an angle grinder with cutting disc. Wear goggles and meticulously follow the safety rules that should be supplied with the grinder.

▲ CR9. The old outrigger is compared here with a (reproduction) brand new one, complete with base plate for going on to the chassis. This does in fact put the outrigger eye-bolt about ³⁄₁₆ inch further out, so do be careful when fitting this that you don't incorrectly position the bulkhead socket in relation to the bulkhead. You may be able to surface-mount this new outrigger or you may have to cut out the side of the chassis and sink it in.

▲ CR10. The bulkhead bolt described earlier is seen here (a long, thin bolt through the socket, with a washer and lock nut) prior to assembly.

▲ CR11. The chassis side must be cleaned up before attempting to fit a new outrigger. The side is being 'scurfed' here with a grinder to ensure the weld can be made against clean, bright metal. **Do** invest in an angle grinder if you don't already have one, as it will save a tremendous amount of sanding and filing in an instance like this. **Safety: DO wear goggles (essential, as shown here) and heavy industrial gloves whenever working with old, jagged edges of metal and/or grinding stones (important, as NOT shown here!).**
There's no point welding over rusty areas – you'll simply be hiding the damage rather than repairing it, only to experience even greater problems later. An angle grinder can be used to cut out rust before welding in a patch repair.

▲ CR12. The main chassis section to which you intend welding a new outrigger should be thoroughly prepared. Clean it off carefully. All paint and surface rust should be removed from the area before welding begins.

▲ CR13. You can see clearly how the mounting back-plate on this reproduction outrigger could affect the position of the hole for the bulkhead bolt. The main chassis section will need measuring and scribing prior to fitting the bulkhead outrigger, to ensure correct location. On this particular example, the chassis has not been cleaned and de-rusted properly, something which will doubtless be regretted in future years! Needless to say, the work was **not** carried out by Dunsfold Land-Rover who carried out the work shown in the rest of this section.

▲ CR15. The DIY welder can use MIG welder but only if it is one of the more powerful models, or alternatively a medium- to heavy-duty arc welder can be used (with extreme care!). With any welding, the secret is first to ensure everything is firmly clamped ...

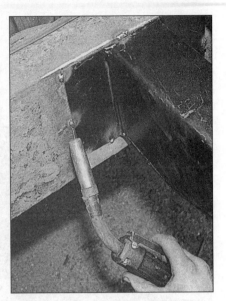

▲ CR16. ... before going on to the stage of tack-welding, at which point you must double-check for correct alignment. Once the outrigger has been tacked, the clamps can be removed. Then, when the bulkhead bolt is in position, the whole section can be seam-welded. Don't be tempted to cut corners at this stage as it is essential to retain the vehicle's original strength.

◀ CR17. Once the welding has been completed, a bracket can be fitted for the side-step. The holes are marked, taking care to ensure their correct position beforehand.

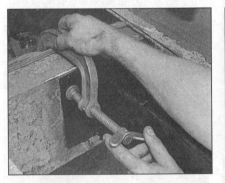

▲ CR14. Still on the same vehicle, the outrigger is clamped in place before initial tacking and final welding.

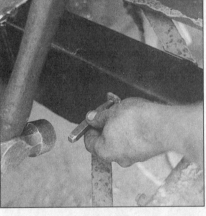

CHASSIS PATCH REPAIRS

◀ CR18. Having gone as far as to strip the chassis down, there's only one way to get rid of all the rust, and that is to sandblast it. A 'mobile' sandblaster was called in, carrying the blaster unit and sand on the back of a truck and towing a very heavy-duty compressor. Martin Griffiths, the fella doing the sandblasting, could almost have passed for Neil Armstrong when dressed like this, which is some indication of the power of the blaster and the volumes of all-pervasive dust it gives off. Do it **well** away from the house or a workshop or any sort of machinery.

▼ CR19. The blaster hosed rust off a treat, but didn't want to know about old underseal. To save a great deal of expensive sandblasting time, always clean off all traces of underseal or other soft material beforehand.

▶ CR21. Where a complete sidewall had rotted out, it was cut out and replaced whole, the jack pushing up lightly just to hold the member true.

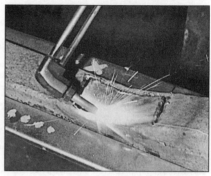

▲ CR22. A smaller area of rot was cut out with an oxy-acetylene cutting torch.

▼ CR20. Back in the workshop, a system of sturdy axle stands and chains, stretched down to hooks in the floor, was used to hold the chassis rigid. It was tuned up in all directions with a spirit level.

▲ CR23. Then a plate was tacked down at one end, tapped down flat with a hammer ...

▲ CR24. ... then, after tack-welding all the way round, seam welded with the MIG.

▲ CR25. The floor bearers had corroded into insignificance, along with one or two other small brackets. They were fabricated, generally from a thinner steel than that required for the chassis itself, and welded into place. Dimensional accuracy of every part is vital here because the chassis is literally the skeleton of the entire car. If you can't check measurements of one part from another symmetrically-positioned part (you should really measure any frail components before you have the sandblasting carried out), try to get hold of some original drawings from your specialist one-make club, or perhaps just measure another enthusiast's car. Remember that accuracy and soundness are the keynotes to your chassis-based car's safety and appearance. Have a specialist check your chassis on a jig before starting work and then again after the work is complete to ensure that the welding process has not caused any distortion to occur.

DENT REPAIR

Cars like this Triumph TR7 are typical of modern cars, with apparently simple lines, but with complex shapes and compound curves. As a result, they can be quite tricky to repair. In fact, when anything more than light damage is encountered, it makes sense to fit a whole new panel. The other complication with this particular car – and it applies to many of the most modern classic cars – is that it was

painted with a clear gloss coat of paint over a matt colour coat. Check by very lightly flatting with a fine grade wet-and-dry. If the colour you remove is the colour of the car, the finish is *not* clear-over-base; if it's a virtually colourless, perhaps milky colour, you know that you are flatting a clear coat.

▲ DR1. You can pick out the high spots of dents and distortion best by lightly running the flat of your hand over it. Use long strokes of the hand, keep it flat on the job and sense the hollows and high spots through the palm rather than the tip of the fingers.

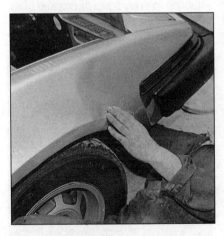

▲ DR2. It is virtually essential to have rear access in a case like this. Here, panel beater Ken Wright finds a way in to the mainly enclosed area behind the wing.

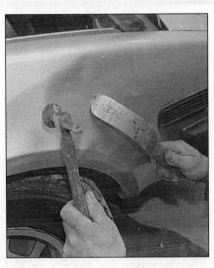

▲ DR3. He chooses a panel beating hammer with a general purpose head and a heavy spoon that will act as a dolly in this instance.

▲ DR4. Starting furthest away from the point of impact, Ken lightly taps the raised area while holding the spoon behind it. In one or two places where the panel is hollowed, he holds the hammer on the job and slaps inside with the spoon. Then he works steadily forwards, towards the point of impact. It is vitally important not to hammer too much or the metal will stretch and you could be worse off than when you started. If the metal is stretched a little, it is better to leave it slightly low and bring the surface up with a thin skin of filler than to leave it too high.

▲ DR5. In order to dress the flange, Ken chose one of the Sykes-Pickavant dollies with a shape to fit inside the wheel arch. Then, with the dolly in place, he carefully beat the flange true once again, working from the 'shock' damage which went through the panel, towards the point of impact.

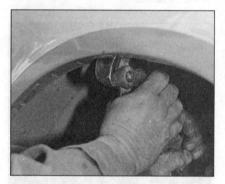

▲ DR6. In reality, you can often be wholly unconventional and yet achieve a better job. A slight kink in the flange is bent out with nothing more sophisticated than a pair of pincers.

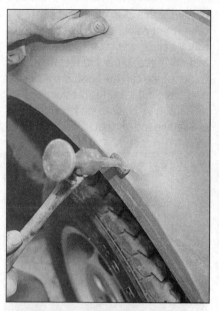

▲ DR7. With the general shape looking good, Ken now goes back and gets rid of one or two areas of very light damage. He uses a cross-pein hammer here to tap out the raised 'vee' and then, feeling that much more hammering could stretch the metal, which could take a lot more time to remedy (and perhaps more skill than most DIY-ers could muster), he looks for the couple of slightly raised areas that remain and taps them down.

▼ DR8. Next, he covers up the surrounding area, paying special attention to every scrap of exposed glass while surrounding trim areas are also masked off.

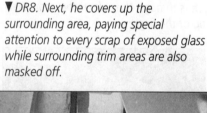

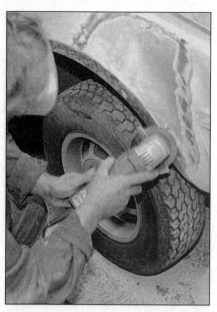

▲ DR9. He uses the angle grinder with a 40 grit sanding disc to linish the paint off, defining the full area of the repair first. Sparks from this tool can embed themselves immovably in glass, which is why it must be covered. It makes sense to keep the whole engine bay covered, too.

▲ DR10. The whole repair area is linished back to bare metal when (and this is the reality, not the textbook theory!) it is possible to discover any remaining high spots that you may not be happy with.

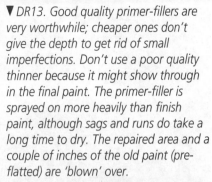

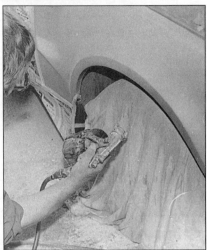

▼ DR13. Good quality primer-fillers are very worthwhile; cheaper ones don't give the depth to get rid of small imperfections. Don't use a poor quality thinner because it might show through in the final paint. The primer-filler is sprayed on more heavily than finish paint, although sags and runs do take a long time to dry. The repaired area and a couple of inches of the old paint (pre-flatted) are 'blown' over.

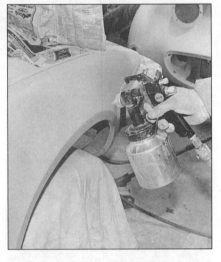

▲ DR11. Body filler has a bad name because of its use over rusty panels, but in this case, to bring the surface back smooth without hours and hours of work, it is perfectly acceptable. Indeed, for the amateur who can cause more problems than are solved by trying to take panel beating too far, the use of filler as a surfacing filling agent is highly desirable!

▲ DR15. The next job is to paint the panel with the base colour, starting with the inside of the wheelarch flange and going on to paint the whole panel in the normal way. Beware of any imperfections because they will show up right through the final coat.

▼ DR14. When dry, a very light mist of finish paint is sprayed on to the primer and flatted, the contrast in colours showing up any minor imperfections.

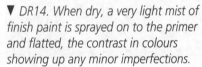

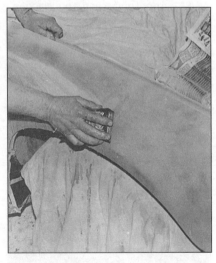

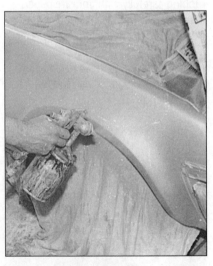

▲ DR12. Ken uses a half-round rasp to file away most of the surplus filler, before going through the grades of sanding paper, as shown in several other places in this book. On a flatter surface, it is essential to use a long flat sanding block (see previous section). When he has the surface as level and smooth as he wants it, down to a finish produced by about 120 grit dry (400 grit wet-and-dry), he chooses a high-build primer-filler.

▲ DR16. The final coat is of clear paint and this brings the matt finish up to an incredible shine and also offers some protection. Be sure to use a cellulose base paint for both coats – there is a great deal of 2-pack clear-over-base available, but it is unsafe to spray it without using quite a sophisticated spray booth and apparatus, and it is therefore totally unsuitable for DIY use.

▶ DR17. The finished result shows the car looking 'as new' again and indeed it is, with even the rust-proofing on the insides of the panel undamaged.

USING BODY FILLER

BLENDING IN WITH RESIN, MAT AND FILLER

Weight for weight, glass fibre is stronger than steel and yet is far easier to work with. It can be persuaded to adopt any shape that you wish and yet bonds with great tenacity. Its close cousin, body filler, is the ideal medium for filling gaps and smoothing out imperfections to give a perfect finish. Before applying filler or resin to a previously painted surface, remove all paint and rust back to bare, shiny metal. 'Key' a plastic surface by rubbing carefully with abrasive paper, then rub over with a spirit wipe on a clean cloth. On aluminium, either apply etching primer or use a purpose-made filler. Most 'ordinary' fillers won't stay in place on aluminium or galvanized steel for very long!

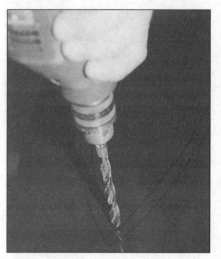

▲ UBF2. After lightly centre-punching, a hole was drilled to enable ...

▲ UBF4. We started by pop-riveting the bulge into place. Drill through both bulge and bonnet, locating the first holes with an unsnapped rivet to ensure correct alignment.

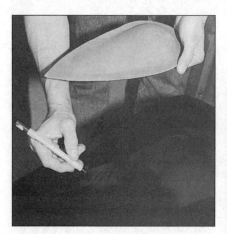

▲ UBF1. We used a Smith & Deakin glass fibre 'bonnet bulge' to demonstrate the use of plastic filler. After drawing a line around the outside of the panel, another line was drawn half an inch inside the first one.

▲ UBF3. ... the jigsaw to cut along the inner line. So that it would bond to the steel panel, the bonnet was turned over and the paint sanded off the jointing area.

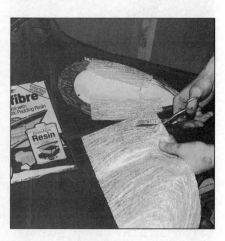

▲ UBF5. A sheet of glass mat was taken from the pack, and enough strips cut out with scissors to cover the whole area twice over, with overlaps.

A thick coat of resin (well mixed with hardener) was painted onto the panel. The mat was placed in position, and more resin was added, then stippled with a brush until the mat went floppy. The second layer was added whilst the resin was still runny.

▲ UBF6. Once the resin has gone 'off' (hard), the top can be blended in. We used car body filler and mixed in the amount of hardener recommended in the instructions.

▼ UBF7. The first coat – carefully mixed to a consistent colour – was spread smoothly over the joint. Note that the paint has again been sanded off.

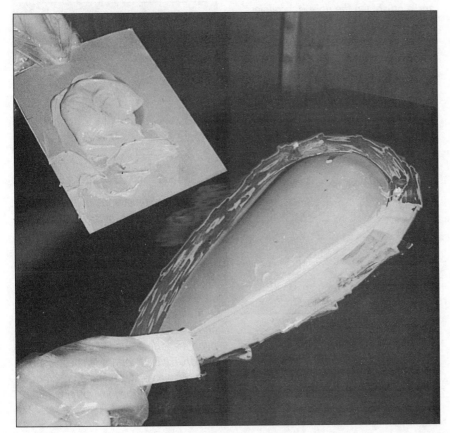

▲ UBF8. You can guarantee that a second coat of filler will be needed and, after sanding that down, probably a third coat, and possibly a fourth, in order to eradicate all blemishes. Allow the 'going off' time in your calculations. When you use filler for the first time, you will probably be amazed that an apparently smooth finish looks so awful when painted! Be prepared to carry out a lot of careful work to obtain a smooth surface – see elsewhere in this book.

Safety: Keep resin and (in particular) hardener off your hands. Wear rubber gloves or even, as we did here, plastic bags pulled over the hands. You must never sand glass fibre because of the risk of breathing in microscopic strands of glass. Always wear an efficient face mask.

If you find that you need more resin or more hardener separately (although you shouldn't if you use it in the proportions recommended on the can), there are individual cans of resin available in various sizes from your auto accessory shop. You can clean your brush in cellulose thinners followed by household washing powder. Don't leave it until the resin has gone hard; that will be too late! Only mix filler on a plastic or steel sheet. Cardboard leaves fibres in the mix.

Filler 'goes off' (sets) by chemical reaction. The warmer the weather, the quicker the reaction and the less hardener you need. It is not recommended that you use excess hardener in the mixture. In cold conditions apply moderate heat by a fan heater to start off the setting process.

LEAD LOADING

Have you ever wondered what the professional body repairer did before the days of plastic filler? In fact he did use a 'filler' of sorts for smoothing out ripples and shallow dents, and that filler was a far stronger substance than today's more common substitute. Old-style filler, known as body solder, consists of an alloy of lead and tin and has the effect of strengthening repairs, unlike plastic filler which simply sits on top of them.

Most people have seen molten electrical solder and will know that it runs as freely as water. How then can body solder be persuaded to stay on vertical surfaces without simply running in an expensive stream onto the floor? The answer lies in the properties which tin and lead develop once they are alloyed together. Tin has a melting point of 450°F (232°C) and lead melts at

620°F (377°C). Whenever tin and lead are mixed together, however, the melting point of the resulting alloy is considerably lower than that of lead. Also body solder, having a combination of 30% tin and 70% lead (and thus commonly known as 30/70 solder) has the useful property of going into a plastic, almost putty-like, state at around 360°F (180°C) and staying like that right up to a temperature of around 500°F (260°C) at which temperature it turns to a liquid.

This means that body solder can be spread around like butter if it is kept within this temperature range, but of course, there is rather more to it than that ...

WHERE TO BODY SOLDER

There's no doubt that body solder is greatly superior to plastic filler in many respects, though its advantages are often exaggerated. Plastic filler has earned some of its bad reputation for the paradoxical reason that it is so good! It can be used over any surface, and so it's frequently used to patch rusty holes which, of course, break right through again. Body solder can't be used in this way. When plastic filler is used over totally sound metal, however, it has excellent qualities. So, unless you are an out and out traditionalist, you will probably want to use body solder only in those places where it will do most good. The joint between two panels is one ideal place because the solder will run into the joint and both strengthen it and – more important – help to seal it against further corrosion. Another perfect place is where steel has become pitted on one side through corrosion, without having broken through. Here, the corrosion is sandblasted clear then the pitted area built up with body solder. A third area which is perfect for the use of the material is where a corner of a bonnet, or some other small projection, is completely missing. Again the area has to be completely cleared of any corrosion and this time a great deal of solder has to be used in one spot in order to build up sufficient material. Plastic filler would break away where

body solder has intrinsic strength.

A major disadvantage of body solder must also be considered, however, especially in relation to its use in and over joints. The flux used (see later) is highly corrosive and residues must all be washed away with meticulous care when the job is done. For that reason, *do not use it* when you are unable to reach any part of the area where flux has been applied, such as behind a concealed joint for instance.

It has been emphasized several times already that the surface of the steel has to be thoroughly cleaned before soldering. This is because the solder just will not stick to steel that is not both chemically and physically clean. One of the strengths of solder is that it combines chemically with the surface of the steel, while plastic filler just sticks on top. If any contamination is left, it forms a barrier which prevents the process taking place.

HOW TO BODY SOLDER

▼ BS1. Below are shown a few sticks of 30/70 solder, next is a pot of solder paint and a brush. On the right is a stainless steel spatula used for spreading the solder, while in between is the booklet published by the (now defunct) company which supplied the items shown here. All of the materials shown can be purchased individually from paint factors, and a spatula could be made from a piece of smooth wood. In recent years, body solder has become expensive.

▲ BS2. This is an ideal place for the use of body solder. Here a classic car's wing has been repaired using three separate repair sections. One is a replacement wheel arch panel while the others complete the front and rear of the wing. Each panel was joined to the others via a 'step' in the adjoining panel so that there was a small overlap, but the panels lay flush with one another. This left panels which lay beautifully flat and true but with joints that would be susceptible to corrosion in several years time, unless something was done about it.

▲ BS3. That 'something', at least as far as the outside of the panels was concerned, was to lead load it with body solder. Before that could be done, the joint was thoroughly cleared of any of its protective paint with a spot sandblaster run from a standard compressor. This scoured out all of the paint right from inside the joint and also removed any traces of rust that might have developed. If no sandblaster is available, it is important to spend some time scraping and sanding every bit of corrosion out of the joint, otherwise the solder just won't take.

▲ BS4. The paint was also cleared off about an inch or so back from the joint, using a medium grit sanding disc, sanding until all traces of paint were removed. Paint can also be removed by heating it until it curls, and then scraping off while it is still soft. Either the welding torch can be used with a soft flame to remove the paint or a butane torch, the sort that is mounted on top of a disposable cartridge, could be used. DON'T use too much heat at any stage of the process. You can expand and buckle steel panels all too easily.

Quite often, when metal has been dented or rippled it is extremely difficult to sand all of the paint or corrosion off the surface. A useful tip is to take a sanding disc and cut it into a square or an octagon shape. Then the 'points' of the shape will reach down into the concave parts of the panel.

▲ BS5. Old-timers would 'tin' the surfaces of the steel before starting to load the solder. This has the effect of

putting a thin coat of solder all over the surface onto which the solder can be built up. Steel does not have the same ideal affinity for solder as copper, for example, so the tinning process must be carried out thoroughly. The old-style way of doing it was to coat the surface of the steel in flux first of all. Flux is necessary to stop the surface of the steel going black as it oxidizes (reacts with the air): it melts at a lower temperature than solder, runs over the surface and keeps the air out long enough for the solder to flow over the steel and combine with it. Here, in the picture, you can see an alternative to flux and stick solder being used. Solder paint is being brushed onto the surface of the joint. This is simply flux in which powdered solder is held in suspension. Naturally it has to be stirred well before use (because the solder grains tend to sink to the bottom) after which it should be painted onto the surface fairly heavily.

▲ BS6. The next step is to play a flame over the solder paint until the solder 'flushes'. In other words, the solder has to be melted, at which point it flows across the surface of the steel. The point at which this takes place should be fairly obvious because the dull matt grey of the solder paint will be replaced by the silvery gleam of fresh solder. A common mistake when carrying out this job for the first time, especially for those who are used to welding, is to apply too much heat too rapidly. The biggest risk comes when a welding torch is being used, simply because there is so much heat 'on tap'. If the metal is overheated,

the flame will burn the flux away and oxidize (blacken) the surface of the steel before the solder has had a chance to melt. If you intend using a welding torch, choose a medium nozzle, have a 'soft' flame (oxygen turned down a little) and play the heat lightly over the job from a respectful distance, not up close such as when you are welding.

▲ BS7. No matter how hard you try to clean the metal, there will almost certainly be some impurities left – so it's a good job that flux has a slight cleaning action to go with its ability to keep oxygen out. As a result, the flux throws up a small quantity of black waste onto the surface. This must be removed thoroughly before attempting to add any more body solder. The flux itself is water soluble and so it can be removed along with the waste by scrubbing it with a wet rag when the panel has cooled.

▲ BS8. The next stage is just a little bit tricky to master and involves one of those sets of actions where you have to do and think about two different things at once. (After a while, of course, it becomes automatic – do you remember the first time you drove a car and how you seemed to have to do so much all at the same time?) The blowtorch has to be used to heat the panel over an area which covers no more than, say, the size of a playing card. At the same time, the solder has to be held on the edge of the flame so that it is being pre-heated, but not by enough to melt it. When, after a minute or two, you judge that the panel is hot enough, try pressing the end of the solder stick on to the joint. If everything is ready, the solder will become droopy and waxy and at the same time stick to the tinned surface of the steel. You should now try to deposit 'dollops' of solder at close, regular intervals along the joint or across the surface of the panel. Don't even begin to think about making a smooth surface; all you are doing at this stage is heating the solder to its plastic state (between 360°–500°F; 180°–260°C) and depositing the material on to the panel.

▼ BS9. The next stage is the one where you smooth the solder out. Throughout this, and indeed throughout the previous stage, it is best to have a piece of steel on the floor beneath the area being soldered. You can waste an awful lot of the stuff, especially if you are inexperienced: as has been pointed out

before, it's very expensive. When you have finished, collect together all the splash-shaped scraps and store it. When you have enough, make up a mould from a piece of right-angled steel and blank the ends off with lumps of ordinary household glazing putty. Put the solder scraps into a discarded can and grip the edge with a self-grip wrench. Now heat the bottom of the can with the butane torch or with a **very** soft oxy-acetylene flame (keep it moving so as not to burn through the can) then, when the solder is melted pour into your mould. Hey presto, you've got a 'free' solder stick! And you'll be amazed at how much you can save!

The spreader (or paddle) used for spreading the solder can be stainless steel, although old-timers used hardwood paddles made of beech or boxwood which they kept smooth and burnished with oil. The beginner tends to get the paddle into the flame, so perhaps stainless is best – it doesn't burn. If you look at the range of temperatures between which solder is soft, it looks pretty wide, but in practice the range seems narrow when you're actually holding the torch. Heat a blob of solder and hold the paddle close by.

Periodically, remove the flame and press down on the solder with the paddle. At first the solder will start to move but in a rather crumbly way; heat it for a little longer and it will spread like butter on a summer's day. Heat it too far, however, and it will slip in a silvery stream on to the floor – a demoralizing sight! Again, don't worry too much about having a smooth finish at this stage. Try for a consistent thickness which is slightly proud of the surface you want to finish up with.

▲ BS10. The solder can be filed down using a body file, which is a single-cut file like this one which resists clogging. It is easy to take off too much of the solder, especially if the file is new, because of the softness of the solder relative to the hardness of the surrounding steel. Professional body repairers often keep a semi-blunt file solely for filing body solder, just to prevent digging-in. An important safety point here is that body solder should never be removed with a power sander. The lead would become air-borne dust which could then be inhaled with HIGHLY INJURIOUS CONSEQUENCES! Filing should be done from all angles, working from the outside edges of the soldered patch if it is a large one, and working inwards. Long, smooth strokes should be used wherever there is room and just enough pressure should be used to prevent the file from skidding over the surface without touching. Final sanding of the solder should be carried out with 80 or 100 grit paper.

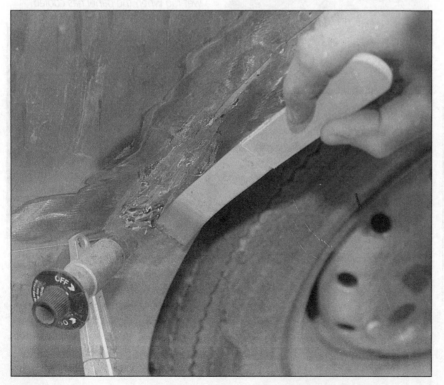

Where the solder is found to be a little low, you have three options open. You can follow a risky, perfectionist's path and attempt to build up more solder; you can console yourself with the thought that the joint is sound and strong and finish off with a skin of plastic body filler or, if the depression is really shallow, you could follow the path of the old-timers and use a skin of cellulose putty, although really this is inferior to plastic filler, with no real advantages.

Finally, a tip worth remembering in connection with the heat input involved. When applying body solder to a large, flattish panel such as a door skin for example, it is easy to cause heat buckling, especially if a wide area has to be covered. Buckling can easily be prevented by having a pail of water and a rag to hand and by soldering a small area at a time then quenching it with the rag afterwards. This restricts the flow of heat through the panel and shrinks the localized area back down to its original size, provided that it has not been expanded too far.

Safety notes: When using body solder particular attention MUST be paid to the health hazards encountered when working with lead and alloys. Whilst filing and sanding you MUST always wear a face mask and the wearing of gloves is also highly recommended.

SOLDERING ALUMINIUM

Aluminium can be soldered using ordinary 30/70 solder but it has to be prepared in a rather different way. It is possible to buy a special bar of solder which has to be used for tinning the aluminium first. The surface of the aluminium has to be thoroughly cleaned up first in the usual way and then the special tinning bar is melted on to the surface of the metal. Next, a slightly strange process has to be carried out. Whilst the tinned surface is kept molten, a sharp tool such as a scriber has to be scratched vigorously all over the area which has been tinned, reaching through the molten solder and scratching through the surface of the

aluminium beneath. This has the effect of scratching away the outer layer of the aluminium while giving oxides no chance whatever to form, and allowing the special tinning aluminium to combine with and key into the metal. From then on, the process is exactly the same as in using body solder on steel, and exactly the same materials are used.

USING METAL LOADING BODY FILLER

If you particularly want to use a metal-based filler, a metal-content plastic filler is available from specialist restoration suppliers.

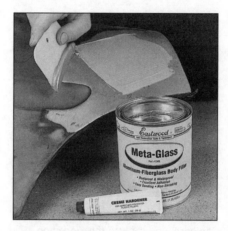

▲ BS11. It is used in exactly the same way as ordinary polyester filler and as such it is far easier to apply than body solder. The powdered aluminium it contains makes it harder than polyester filler and therefore it provides a tougher repair. It is also non-porous. The usual safety advice relating to polyester filler applies – it is very important not to inhale any of the dust caused while sanding.
(Courtesy: The Eastwood Company)

PAINTWORK

Cellulose paint is not as durable as the 2-pack paint, which is not suitable for use by DIY enthusiasts for health and safety reasons, but it has the virtue of being able to be sprayed on a DIY basis and it can also be polished to give the best shine of any paint.

Before using primer, check the existing

paint to find out whether it is compatible with cellulose. Rub a small area of paint with cellulose thinner. If the paint film dissolves go ahead; if the paint wrinkles it is affected by cellulose and will have to be sprayed all over with isolating primer 200-6 to seal it.

Safety: All filler contains skin irritants so you should wear gloves when handling it. When sanding paint or filler, particularly with a power sander, you must always wear an efficient particle mask, because otherwise the inhalation of sanding dust could damage your health. Nitro-cellulose paints, are suitable for DIY work, unlike 2-pack paints which must only be used by a professional bodyshop. However, take full note of the paint maker's own safety precautions and, in particular, never spray in other than a well-ventilated work area. Also, bear in mind that paint, thinners and spray vapour are all highly inflammable. Do not use near flames, sparks (including those created by central heating boilers), or any naked flames. Always wear an efficient face mask when spraying cellulose or aerosol paint. Take advice from your paint supplier as to the best type to buy. An ordinary particle mask is not sufficient.

PREPARATION
Tools required:
Grinder, sander, P120 and P240 grit discs, P600 'wet-or-dry' paper, dust particle mask.

Materials required:
Degreasing fluid (this is essential for removing silicones which will most certainly ruin the finished paint surface if allowed to remain on the work), stopper.

PRIMING
Tools required:
Masking tape, masking paper (such as newspaper), paint strainer, spray gun, compressor, spray mask, tack rag.

Material required:
Cellulose thinner, primer.

TOP COAT

Tools required:
The same equipment and other 'hardware' as was previously used.

Materials required:
Solid colour paint; thinner (mix 50/50). Top coat paint must be strained. Add P1200 'wet-or-dry' paper and polishing compound for polishing out any dirt particles that may get into the final coat.

Ask your stockist about the appropriate type or types of thinner to use, especially if you need to thin more than 50/50 when a different type might be required.

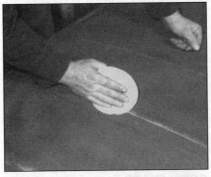

▲ P2. Hand sanding should always be carried out with the aid of a rubbing block, other than in the corners of fluted panels such as those shown here, where your fingers make an ideally shaped tool.

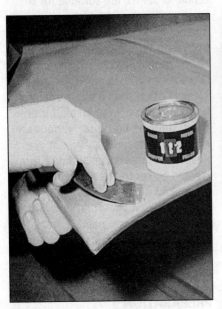

▲ P1. If many coats of paint have previously been applied, they will have to be stripped back to bare metal before being repainted. Otherwise there is an ever increasing chance, as paint becomes thicker, of one more coat being the straw that breaks the camel's back. The result will be a sudden spontaneous reaction over a small or large area, blistering and puckering the paint that lies beneath. Very minor blemishes such as pin holes or scratches in the paint should be filled with a thin scrape of 2-pack stopper which can be sanded down after hardening thoroughly.

▲ P3. With no attachment on the end of the hose, you can use the workshop compressor to blow any remaining sanding dust off the panel. You really **should** wear goggles!

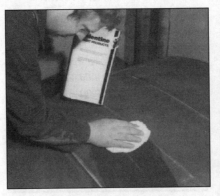

▲ P4. The degreasing fluid should be used before you start, and should be used again after sanding to remove any traces of silicones or other grease contamination. Silicones, which are contained in all domestic polishes, cause dreadful and irremovable 'fish eye' marks in the final paint finish.

▲ P5. An electric drill used with a paint stirrer in the chuck is an excellent way to stir the primer filler to an even consistency. Note the steel rule placed in the pot to aid accurate measurement when thinning the paint. Start initially with a 50/50 thinning, but be prepared to readjust to suit the requirements of the spray gun. Note that most spray guns have two adjustment screws at the rear. The top one is for the width of the spray pattern, while the lower one adjusts the quantity which comes out of the gun. Adjust the two screws so that the spray pattern and spray density are as you require. Test it out thoroughly upon a piece of scrap board or a cardboard box.

▲ P6. The edge of this panel dipped away from the user, so that part, the curved edge, was sprayed first.

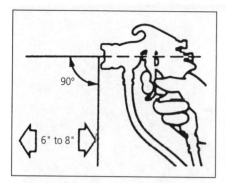

▲ P7. Always hold the spray gun at right angles to the surface you are spraying, keeping it at a distance of between six and eight inches.

▲ P10. The next day, after the two full coats of primer have thoroughly dried, a very light, heavily thinned coat of black paint can be sprayed on.

▲ P12. Before spraying the top coat, wet the floor to keep down the dust, but take care to keep water away from electrical components or connections.

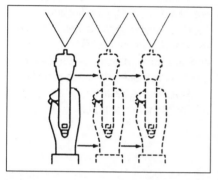

▲ P8. Keep your wrist stiff and avoid swinging the gun in an arc from your elbow, to ensure even spraying. Always spray at a steady even pace.

▼ P9. The whole panel should be painted in consistent, even bands, each one half overlapping the previous one.

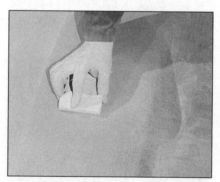

▲ P11. When the primer is 'blocked' down with medium grit paper, the thin 'guide' coat (you could use aerosol for greater speed) was sanded off as the primer filler coat was made smooth. It remained visible in the low spots, however. Block down a little further, or apply another coat of primer filler or stopper in small blemishes, as appropriate.

▲ P13. Use an air line to blow any dust from around the top of the tin before opening. You can purchase an inexpensive trigger operated 'air duster', or just hold the open end of the air line in place. Wear goggles!

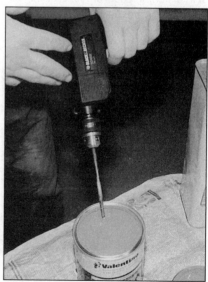

▲ P14. The cordless drill is again used for several minutes to mix the entire contents of the finish paint.

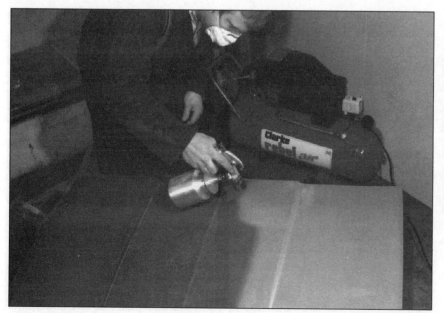

▲ P15. Use a steel rule, if you haven't got the correct painter's measuring stick, to measure the correct amount of paint and thinners.

▲ P18. An accepted way of checking that the spray gun is held the correct distance away, is to use a hand span as a measure.

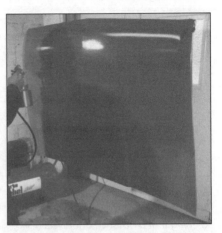

▲ P20. After this has 'flashed off' (that is, the thinners has evaporated), a full coat is sprayed in overlapping horizontal bands. Suspending the panel in this way reduces the amount of dirt contamination that can fall on the wet paint, and an open door aids ventilation – and adequate ventilation is an ESSENTIAL safety feature!

▲ P16. Pour in equal amounts of thinner and paint. Note the use of copious supplies of newspaper.

▲ P19. Spraying starts with a 'half-coat' – a thin coat to aid adhesion without causing runs – sprayed in vertical, overlapping bands.

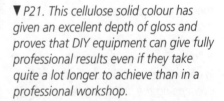

▼ P21. This cellulose solid colour has given an excellent depth of gloss and proves that DIY equipment can give fully professional results even if they take quite a lot longer to achieve than in a professional workshop.

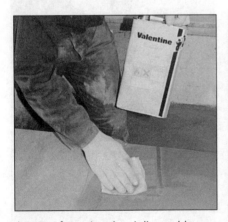

▲ P17. After using the air line to blow off the panel once more, wipe it down yet again with spirit wipe, followed by a wipe down with a tack rag to remove every trace of dust and dirt.

POLISHING PAINT

There are two particular reasons why you might wish to polish paintwork beyond the periodic rubbing down that you may give it when washing and waxing your car. One is that you have recently painted the car or a part of it and there is a little dirt inclusion in the paint, or the paint has sagged in one particular place and you have been able to remove the sag by rubbing it down

▲ PP2. You must be sure to wash the car thoroughly, removing all dirt and grit that could easily cause deeper scratching.

▲ PP5. Don't press down too hard. DON'T use the polisher near any raised edges, corners or ridges because you stand a good chance of polishing the paint right off. Keep the mop moving in a slow steady arc working your way across the area to be polished. Cover about a square metre at a time.

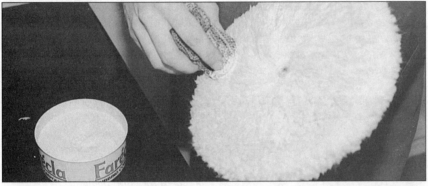

with wet-or-dry paper: the scratches have to be polished, out of course. Or another reason is just that the paintwork has become scratched or faded, and that good polishing with a machine polishing mop will bring it back to life.

▲ PP3. Fit the mop to the polishing machine and, using a rag, apply a few dabs of polishing compound around the lambswool mop. Wear your dirtiest overalls or really old clothes and make sure that if you have a fabric soft-top, it is well covered up. The mop will throw thousands of tiny specs of white polish in all directions!

▲ PP1. You will need a polishing machine – rather like a giant angle grinder but with a special slow gearing to the head, a lambswool polishing mop (far better than the foam variety in most people's book) and a tin of fine rubbing compound. This is a Black & Decker electric polisher. Professional air-driven units require the service of a really huge compressor by most home restorers' standards.

▲ PP4. The polish will go on more smoothly and be less likely to form a hard black crust which is difficult to remove if you sprinkle a few drops of water over the surface where you will be using the polisher.

▲ PP6. Be prepared to spend some time cleaning the specks of polishing compound off glass and trim – as well as the surrounding area in the workshop! Bring the paint up to a good shine with a **clean** soft cloth, turning it again and again so that it does not clog up with polish. You can do as we did here: apply a coat of long lasting sealer/polish which should help to keep the shine in place for a few weeks before it will need re-application. (If you find one that really does last for the six months advertised please let us know about it!)

SPRAYING WITH AEROSOL

Safety: Aerosol paint has many of the safety hazards associated with conventional paint spraying. Read carefully the safety instructions on the can. In particular: use only in a well-ventilated area; keep sparks and flames away from spray vapour; do not puncture the can or apply heat to it. Wear gloves and keep wet paint and mist away from skin and eyes.

▲ AP1. 'Wet-or-dry' paper was used with water to feather out the filler, leaving no trace of a hard edge.

▲ AP2. Before starting to spray, the primer can was taken outside, shaken vigorously, and the nozzle cleared.

▶ AP3. The can was held about six inches away and red oxide primer sprayed on to the bare metal.

▲ AP4. High build spray putty was sprayed on to the whole area and then, extending a little wider than the area of the original red oxide primer, a second coat of spray putty was applied after the first had dried.

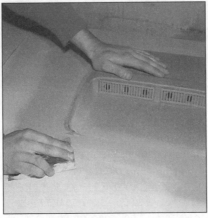

▲ AP5. Provided that the filler work was carried out properly, the use of high build spray putty will allow you to remove every last blemish when you sand it out with fine 'wet-or-dry' supported on a flat rubbing block.

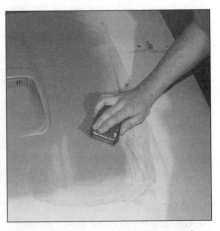

▲ AP6. We chose to spray on grey primer paint as a barrier colour between the yellow and the white top coat to follow. Red and yellow have a nasty habit of 'grinning through' white surface coats above them. When choosing your primer colour, use red for dark shades, grey for lighter coats, and grey or preferably white for white top coats and metallics. Plenty of water, a few spots of washing-up liquid and the finest grade of 'wet-or-dry' and the final primer coat was prepared for finish painting.

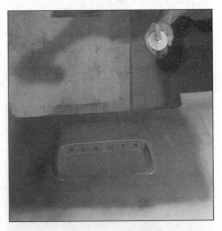

▲ AP7. Now here's a tip from the experts. Holding a tin of black spray paint about 12 in (30cm) or more away from the job, dust a light coat on to the work surface. The idea is not to change the colour of the panel but just to put an even sprinkling of paint over the whole panel.

▲ AP8. Sand the entire panel all over once more with the finest grade of paper and the guide coat, as it is called, will be sanded off in all but the low areas. After you wipe off with a dry cloth, any low spots and blemishes will stand out like a sore thumb!

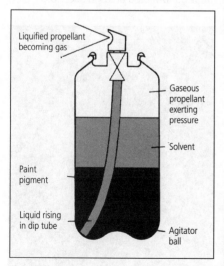

▲ AP9. How an aerosol works. The paint and pigment separate in the can. You have to shake and shake for that little metal ball to mix them thoroughly! This diagram also explains why paint stops coming out when you invert the can.

▲ AP10. If you do what comes naturally, the part of your finger sticking forwards catches the edge of the spray which builds up into a drip which is then shot forward as a blob on to your lovely handiwork. Most annoying! Hold the nozzle down with the top of your finger or, better still, buy an accessory trigger sold with some brands of aerosol paint.

▲ AP11. It's best to practice your spraying on a spare scrap of sheet metal. Hold the can too close and the paint will run; too far away and you'll have a 'dry' look finish.

▲ AP12. The first coat should be applied in regular strips up and down the bonnet, concentrating on obtaining an even coat without trying to blanket out the colour underneath. That's the way to achieve runs! You must leave a few minutes for the solvent in the first coat to 'flash off'.

▼ AP13. The second coat, as already suggested, follows in a pattern which crisscrosses the first and this time the colour beneath will usually disappear from view. Ideally, you may want to give another one or two coats. If any little bits of dust land in the paint surface, you may be able to polish them out with fine cutting compound, but be most careful not to go right through the paint and don't try it until the paint has had several days to dry really hard.

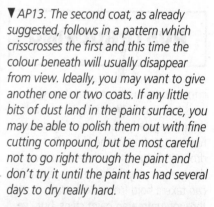

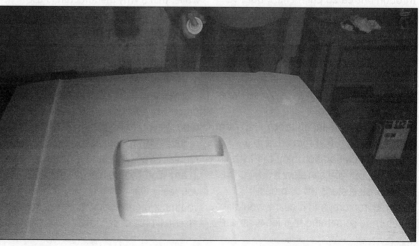

▲ *AP14. This shield does an excellent job of keeping the tyres clean while you* spray the wheels *in situ. You would be better off taking the wheels off the car so that there is no risk of overspray getting on to the bodywork. The outsides of the wheel flanges, covered by the shield, have to be brushed in later, by hand.*
(Courtesy: The Eastwood Company)

RUSTPROOFING

Most car handbooks give joke information on how to maintain your car's bodywork. They tell you to wash the car regularly, to oil the hinges and how to touch up stone chips. Dirt and dropped hinges have never sent a car to the great scrapyard in the sky yet! Rust *can* take a hold from the outside, through untreated paint chips, but I've never yet seen it send a car to the crusher! Ninety-nine point nine per cent of rusty cars are scrapped because of rust that starts on the inside and works its way out. If you understand the basic principles of rusting, it's easy to see what should be done about it.

Nothing is permanent: everything, from the moment it is first formed, is in a process of deterioration. You can't stop corrosion, but you can slow it down. After all, steel starts off as brown-coloured iron ore, and it dearly would like to return to something that looks similar!

Minute electric currents pass between areas of steel panels. This is known as electrolytic action – or rusting to you and me. Electrolytic action works best between dissimilar pieces of steel held close together. Separate sections held together with spot welds fit the bill admirably. Electrolytic action needs close physical contact, the presence of both air and moisture, and it loves a temperature which is just over freezing. Salt helps the process along wonderfully well.

Therefore, a perfect rust bath consists of mud from the road thrown up against joints in steel work, such as under wheel arches and in chassis sections. Then, in winter and the months that follow, salt water can soak in to form a damp poultice to work away when the temperature rises above freezing.

Also, a real boost to rust formation is a film of moisture trapped against the surface of the steel. Underseal (of the old-fashioned, paint-on variety) creates the perfect spot as it dries out and becomes brittle, trapping water beneath where it lifts from the steel it is meant to protect. Electrolytic action *hates* having water and air excluded, and it also thoroughly dislikes having salt water closed off. So, the basic principle of rust proofing is extremely simple: shut out air and water and you shut out rust!

On the outside of the bodywork, paint does the job of shutting out air and water. Paint underneath is fine – but only for a short while. Beneath the car there is a constant shot blasting factory at work. In addition, the salt and mud poultices work their way beneath the paint in a very short while: that's why manufacturers use underseal – it works for longer. But as I said before, when it goes wrong by drying out and going brittle, it adds to the problem that it was put there to solve.

When it comes to older cars, where rust will invariably have made a start, the process of rust prevention is simple, but it requires you to be thorough. It also requires you to repeat the treatment on a regular basis. Although it never appears in any workshop or service manuals, if you really want to keep your car alive, you must regard body maintenance as an essential part of servicing.

First of all, here's how to keep the car's outer panels in shape.

▲ *BM1. Paintwork will chip just about anywhere it can – not just on the leading edge of the bonnet, though that is obviously a major area. If you can't stop the paint coming off, at least you can stop the rust spreading outwards from the paint chips by using a suitable touch-up primer. In the top of the can is a handy brush made specifically for dealing with small areas. It unscrews and you can treat the affected areas in seconds.*

▲ *BM2. A skirmish with an unknown enemy in a car park has left this patch without paint. Application of primer will stop the rust spreading, though it is in your own interest to get some finish paint on the damaged area as soon as possible because primer is more porous than finish paint.*

▲ BM3. Another use is when you drill holes in the bodywork. You should always make a point of tidying up any burrs or rough edges from new holes you drill, and rustproof them – otherwise rust will get a hold and make the hole considerably larger! Once again, always cover primer paint with touch-up paint.

▲ BM4. Here some finish paint in an aerosol can is being sprayed into the cap from where it can be brushed on with a fine paint brush. Paint for spraying is too thin for brushing, so leave the cap to stand for a while to let the paint thicken. Alternatively, you can buy touch up paint in a small tube with an applicator, similar to that shown above.

Beneath the car, the process is a lot more 'earthy' and it becomes even more essential that you carry it out properly. None of the work is what you might call pleasant, but the first time is the worst. The majority of cars never receive this treatment, and the majority of cars rot away before they should. The choice is yours! A word of warning, however. Some manufacturers of rustproofing products make it sound as though, by using their process, you can effectively rust proof your car with very little effort. I'm sure it helps them to sell their product but I'm equally sure that it doesn't work that way.

Don't waste your time by rustproofing your car in the winter time. The underside will be wet, it will be unpleasant to work on and, worse still, the rustproofer is unlikely to work properly. This essential part of body maintenance should be carried out twice a year, however – once before the onset of winter and once at the end:

▲ BM5. Remove from beneath your car the mud that traps the salt water and you've removed a potent source of corrosion. You can scrape it off by hand, use a pressure washer such as the one shown here or even make your own by hammering the end of a length of copper tubing to create a thin, flat nozzle; then fitting a hose pipe to the other end, holding it in place with a jubilee clip.

Rust prevention should be regarded as a regular maintenance job, by which means you can extend the life of your car by many years. You'll have to inject rustproofing fluid into all the enclosed box sections and 'chassis' sections on your car. In many cases you'll find holes already in place; in others, you'll be able to take off a cover, a piece of trim or a door lock in order to gain access. But in quite a few cases, you'll need to drill holes to gain an entry. Decide on your drill size with reference to the size of the injector nozzle and the size of grommets that you can obtain for blanking the holes off again afterwards. (You only need bother if the hole faces forwards or up – in which case you will want to keep water out – or if it is visible, such as inside door openings.)

The hand pump injectors that you can buy from DIY shops are often worse than useless. They don't usually make a proper spray, but simply squirt a jet of fluid that does nothing to give the all-over cover required. Make a dummy 'box section' out of a cardboard box – cut it and fold to make it about 10 or 15cm square – and try a dummy run. Open up and see if it has worked. If you haven't obtained full misting of the fluid, you could be making the problem worse. Remember: if you only partly cover the internal areas to be protected, rust strikes even harder in those areas that aren't covered than it would have done previously, gathering all its force on the unprotected areas, as it were. So, consider investing in a full professional rustproofing gun. They are expensive but the cost is minute compared with the cost of replacing or repairing your car. Consider buying jointly with friends; persuade your car club to buy and hire out; attempt to hire from a local body shop; hire a compressor from a tool hire shop to keep the cost down. Alternatively, consider taking your car to a garage with suitable equipment and having them do the work for you. It may not be quite as thoroughly carried out as if you do the work yourself – unless you are allowed to 'lend a hand' and point out the areas where you would like fluid to be injected – but full, professional injection equipment as shown in the following picture sequences will make the fluid reach much further and deeper than amateur equipment.

If you carry out the work at home, place newspaper beneath the car to catch the inevitable drips that will flow out of bodywork drain holes – if you use enough fluid, that is! Make absolutely certain that you don't clog drain holes by injecting far too much fluid – especially in door bottoms where water could gather and form a veritable indoor pond.

Safety: Before using rust proofer, read the manufacturer's safety notes. Keep it off the exhaust or any other components where it could ignite. Keep it off and out of brake components – cover them up with plastic bags before starting work. Wear an efficient face mask so that you don't inhale vapour. Wear goggles to keep material out of your eyes. Follow the safety notes in the Appendix with regard to safe working beneath a car raised off the ground.

▲ BM6. Finnigan's Waxoyl underbody seal is much better than most underseal. It remains flexible, unlike the conventional type that hardens, becomes brittle and traps moisture beneath it. The aerosol type is easy to apply but some masking-off may be required – and see the Safety note above.

▲ BM7. Waxoyl is probably the best known make of rust inhibitor on the UK market, and it certainly seems to do the trick! Hand operated applicators are available, but they are very inefficient at injecting fluid in the right way. This is a different type of applicator, one that pumps up pressure rather like a garden sprayer. It is better, but is still not ideal.

▲ BM8. Best of all by a long way is the professional rustproofing gun such as the SATA shown here. It is quite expensive to buy but much less expensive than corrosion in your car. You will need a compressor to run it, but you may be able to hire one from your local tool hire shop.

Also note that the following areas on a car should *not* be treated with rust inhibiting fluid: engine; gearbox; back axle; prop-shaft and drive shafts; wheel hubs; brake drums and discs (*most important!*); brake cables; door mounted speakers. Mask them off with paper or plastic sheet and masking tape to keep fluid off them. A plastic bag will be fine for brake drums or discs. Also, if seat

belts of the retractable type are housed within box sections, pull them out and hold them fully extended before spraying. When you have finished, make sure that you have cleared out all bodywork drain holes to allow trapped water to disperse. Also ensure that door windows are wound fully up to avoid spraying rust inhibitor on to the glass.

▲ BM9. Another type of rust inhibiting fluid comes in aerosol cans. It is fairly expensive to buy but it is certainly less expensive than having to buy injection equipment. On the other hand, when it comes to re-treatment, or time to treat another car, it will cost you a lot less money to have the proper equipment to hand.

▲ BM10. There are many places where fluid can be injected through pre-existing holes but if you have to drill fresh ones, try to do so beneath trim or carpet so that they can't be seen. Otherwise, plug visible holes with rubber blanking grommets available from your accessory shop.

BM11. The author and Porter Publishing mechanic Graham Macdonald between them spent many hours with a sandblasting cabinet removing every trace of rust from under bonnet fittings and suspension components from an MGB used as a project car in another Haynes book.

Important Footnote: The author has restored a number of vehicles over the years and at one time ran a small restoration business, so he has seen the 'insides' of quite a number of vehicles, including rusty ones that had been treated with wax rust inhibitors. If fluid such as Waxoyl is sprayed on in cold weather, the rust inhibitor may simply sit on top of the rust instead of soaking into it, and it also seems to fail to soak into spot welded joints where there is dirt or more rust present. The first priority when treating a car that already has rust present is to use a fluid that will soak right into the rust and creep into every crack and crevice. One way to help rust inhibiting fluids to do their job is to stand the tin of fluid in a bowl of warm water for some time before commencing work so that the fluid becomes thinner. (Don't *ever* do so with pressurized or aerosol containers – only screw-top cans of Waxoyl.) Better still, mix the fluid 50/50 with new engine oil. This thins it down considerably and the oil will creep into all of the places where you need to exclude air and water. It is to be hoped it will take some of the rust inhibiting fluid with it; at least it won't leave it sitting on the surface. You can use the cheapest engine oil that you can lay your hands on for this, of course, but don't be tempted to re-use old engine oil since it contains contaminants that can cause more harm than good.

The rest of this section shows how a rebuilt MGB was thoroughly rustproofed before putting it back on the road. No two cars are the same, but this picture sequence gives an idea of what is involved.

BM12. All of these components were first of all painted with Würth zinc-rich primer (telephone your local professional paint factors to find a stockist) which is said to have the highest concentration of zinc in any paint primer available. This provides an excellent disincentive for rust to take further hold, especially when the components to be finished in black have been painted in Finnigan's Hammerite in a smooth finish which gives an exceptionally hard and long lasting finish. It also provides just the right shade of black for those under bonnet components that should be painted in black. Of course, it's not exactly an option unless you are repainting said component, in which case it's worth bearing in mind.

BM13. Before applying rust prevention to the project car, Graham applied Würth seam sealer to every single joint where water could find a way in. This involved some time crawling beneath the car and sealing off every access point. All of the enclosed box sections and the bottom of the doors as well as the insides of the framing in the bonnet and boot were injected with conventional Waxoyl rustproofing fluid – available in a yellowy wax colour or in black – and all of the exposed underbody areas were sprayed with Waxoyl underbody seal.

BM14. Graham used the spray lance to introduce ordinary Waxoyl into the insides of the crossmember prior to having it fitted. Nicol Transmissions, who rebuilt this car's gearbox and rear axle, had arranged for both the rear axle tubing and the crossmember to be plastic dip-coated, which gives an exceptionally durable and attractive finish.

BM15. The inside of the front valence was also sprayed with Waxoyl prior to fitting it to the body.

SAFETY NOTE: Wear an efficient face mask when injecting aerosol or pressure-injected rustproofing fluid.

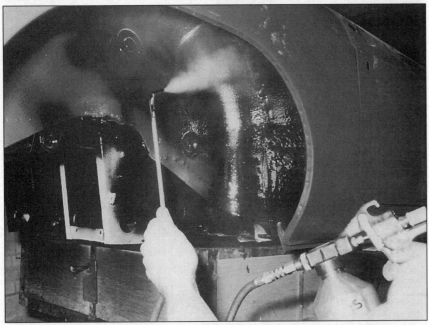

BM16. Beneath the wheel arches, Waxoyl underbody seal was applied. This never goes completely hard and is almost impervious to damage from stone chips. The sprayed-on appearance is quite attractive. Spend quite some time cleaning off mud, rust and loose paint from areas to be treated. Ignore any claims that it's acceptable to apply preservatives over damp or dirty metal. It's best to clean surfaces with nothing more penetrating than a garden hose. If you use a power washer, leave the car for a week or two in dry, summery weather for the innards to dry out before rustproofing begins.

BM17. The rear of the underbody was sprayed with the same underbody seal ...

BM18. ... and the bottoms of the floor panels were sprayed right up to the edge of the sills. Overspray was cleaned off later with plenty of rags and white spirit.

▶ *BM19. Access to the double skinned front bulkhead was easily found through various apertures cut beneath the scuttle top.*

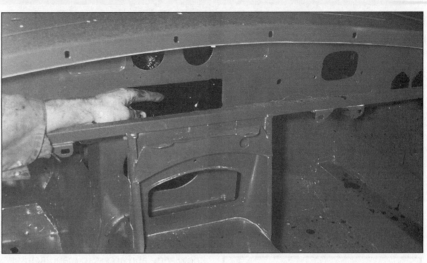

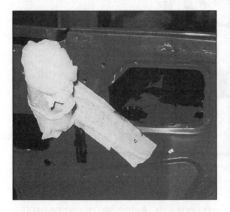

▲ *BM20. Parts of the insides of the rear wings could also be accessed through ready made apertures – but beware! Waxoyl does tend to slide uselessly off vertical surfaces of shiny metal if you put too much on.*

▼ *BM21. The injector lance was used to inject fluid into all of the enclosed sections. Whilst many of them could be accessed through existing holes, some new holes had to be drilled such as this one at the end of the toe boards – an easy spot to miss!*

▼ *BM22. All of the chassis rails and crossmembers have to be injected, of course. Access to the rear rails could only be obtained by drilling a hole at around the mid-point inside the boot. This enables the lance to reach full distance in both directions. The lance is inserted through the hole, and when it reaches the end of the chassis member the trigger is pressed on the gun. As the lance is withdrawn the inside of the box section is fully coated with Waxoyl which 'creeps' into all the seams.*

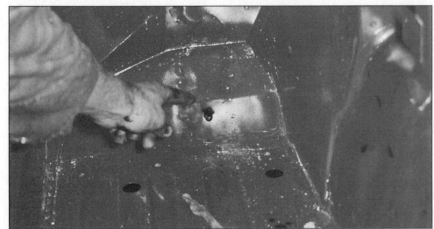

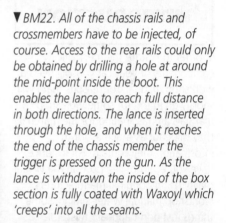

◀ *BM23. The tops of the wing beadings are prone to corrosion, but if they are sealed from above with paint and covered from beneath with fresh Waxoyl the problem should be deferred almost indefinitely.*

Chapter 4
Mechanical components

In order to restore the mechanical components of your car you will need a workshop manual, for reasons that I will shortly go in to. But some workshop manuals are fascinating for the material they miss out as much as for the information they contain. For instance, have you ever noticed how, in the virtual reality of the 'original manufacturers' workshop manual writer's mind, some things just don't appear? Rust, for instance. That never appears in a manual. Nor seized bolts; they don't exist. And as for a cylinder head that won't budge from the block – never heard of such a thing!

To be fair, there are good, practical reasons why this should be so. Most workshop manuals were either written by the manufacturers when the car was new, or they appear to be based on the manufacturer's manuals. For that reason, the stuff they contain is gold dust to the restorer of mechanical components. You'll find out the acceptable amount of crankshaft end-float, and the torque figures for tightening the main bearings. You'll learn the correct dismantling order for tricky components, correct suspension setting and how to rebuild a gearbox, which I have not included in this book for reasons that I will come to in a moment.

'Official' manuals almost never include DIY information, however, and they assume a professional level of knowledge and access to manufacturer's special tools. You might say that I *would* recommend Haynes manuals, *wouldn't I* – but they really do contain more information for the home mechanic, and tips on how to do the job without specials which, with older cars, you very often can.

Of course, Haynes manuals are not available for absolutely every classic car. If you own a '50s Vauxhall Cresta or a Ferrari, you will be forced to look elsewhere. First port of call should be your one-make club. When I needed a manual for my 1936 Vauxhall 14, the small but excellent Vauxhall Owners' Club supplied me with a photocopy of an original. If your club is not so excellent – and almost all are run by enthusiastic volunteers, so you will encounter problems from time to time – try the sellers of specialist manuals who advertise in the classic car magazines, especially in *Practical Classics*. Also, try the major autojumbles, where there are always stallholders with ancient second-hand and reprinted manuals for sale. Go to whatever lengths you must in order to obtain one. Even if your car is too old or too rare for you to be able to find a manual in print, beg the loan of one from another club member and photocopy it yourself. Without one, for all the figures and setting it will contain, you will be up against it.

The advice given in this section does not seek to replace the information that you will find in your manual but to add to it. You will find a number of 'case histories' selected to illustrate the sorts of problems that you are likely to encounter when restoring mechanical components. A number of components are not covered here: gearboxes are relatively complex to restore but by no means impossible. The supply of parts often is impossible – the market has frequently been cornered by the professional restorers, or they are the ones who know how to make or adapt other parts in order to make them fit. But the real clincher is that a rebuilt gearbox is often cheaper than the cost of buying, piecemeal, all the parts you require – *and* you will get a guarantee. Steering racks and steering boxes are often impossible to rebuild without special tools, and for safety reasons you are best advised to leave them to the experts, while differentials and overdrive units both come into the gearbox category: complex; expensive parts; cheaper to have reconditioned. Of course, you might be fully competent, with access to excellent engineering equipment, and the correct spares might be to hand, but for the majority of restorers that will not be the case. And the remainder probably won't need this book in any case!

ENGINE REMOVAL

Some engines can be removed either by themselves or in conjunction with the gearbox; others have to be removed either with or without the box of cogs, depending on the individual car. Check your manual. This section is based on the removal of one of the simplest engines to remove: the Morris Minor 1000. Whatever type of engine is involved, take a good hard look and think the job through before starting. Consider, for instance whether, as in this case, it may be best to disconnect a mounting tower or support from the car, leaving it attached to the engine until later. After consulting your manual, decide whether to leave the gearbox attached or not, if you have the option. Generally, they are best separated unless the bellhousing (engine-to-gearbox) bolts are impossible to reach. In the case of many cars fitted with transverse engines you may have no choice, of course. Decide also what you are going to leave on the engine until later and what to remove with the unit *in situ*. Almost impossible-to-reach mounting bolts will be left until later, but not at the risk of damaging a key component such as fuel pump or carburettor. In any case, *always* remove the glass bowl from a mechanical fuel pump that is so equipped. In general and if in doubt, remove components before engine removal rather than after. The unit will be lighter, you will give yourself more manoeuvring space and you'll reduce the risk of damage. Remember that, in restoration works, time is not the first priority; quality is! Before starting work, 'gunk' and wash the engine clean, scraping encrusted dirt from the lower reaches of the engine first. This will make the engine far more pleasant to work on, you will be able to see what you are doing, and the unit will be safer to handle.

TOOL BOX

Full range of socket, ring and open spanners; pliers; range of screwdrivers; large lever; engine hoist; self-grip wrench.

Safety: NEVER work or stand beneath an engine suspended on a hoist, or have an arm or hand in a position where it could be crushed. Even the sturdiest of hoists could give way, or ropes or chains could slip. When attaching to the engine, try to use mechanical lifting gear

rather than tying ropes. Always have someone with you to lend a hand.

With the engine out of the car ensure that, when working on it, that the block is securely chocked and that there's no danger of it toppling over. Don't trust anything but the stoutest of benches. Hire a purpose-built stand, or work on the floor. If garage roof timbers are used as a mounting for the hoist, ensure that they are REALLY strong. If in doubt, support them on either side of the car with 4"x4" timbers used as vertical baulks. Ensure that all lifting gear is sound and efficient. Watch out for trapped hands or fingers – engines rarely come out in one sweet movement – and keep children, pets and yourself from beneath the power unit whilst it is in the air. Make sure that batteries are disconnected. Work away from sources of ignition when disconnecting the fuel system and store carburettors, which invariably contain petrol, safely out of doors.

▼ *ER1. Fortunately for the Morris Minor owner, there is plenty of space in which to work, but not all cars are like this, of course. On early models such as this, remove the air cleaner and the battery as a first step. Also, drain the water out of the block and radiator using the taps provided. Drain the engine oil from the sump. Dispose of old oil at your local authority disposal centre.*

▲ *ER2. Pull out the split pin, remove the clevis pin from the bonnet stay and, with the aid of an assistant, remove the bonnet. Alternatively prop it fully open or even tie it with a piece of light rope to the boot lid handle.*

▲ *ER3. Disconnect the heater hose and heater cable (later models only) or, alternatively, leave both connected and remove the heater tap.*

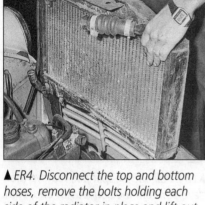

▲ ER4. Disconnect the top and bottom hoses, remove the bolts holding each side of the radiator in place and lift out the radiator, taking care not to damage it on the fan blades.

▲ ER5. Leave all the carburettor connections on the carb, unbolt it and place it out of the way. Take off the distributor cap, mark the leads and remove them from plugs and coil.

▲ ER6. Slacken the two exhaust clamp bolts (you'll probably need to grip the bolt head with a spanner, too) and let the exhaust pipe drop out of the way.

▶ ER7. Unbolt the engine tie-rod from the bulkhead and from the cylinder block and remove it.

▼ ER8. Take the wires off the coil. Tag them for identification but, since they are often incorrectly fitted, note that the white wire should go to the side marked 'SW' and the white and black wire to the side marked 'CB'. Remove them also from the starter motor.

▲ ER9. Remove the large nuts and bolts holding the starter motor in place ...

▲ ER10. ... and pull the starter motor out. You can now take out the ring of bolts around the bellhousing reached from inside the engine bay and from beneath the car.

▶ ER14. Prise up, twist and remove the exhaust-side engine mount.

Author's note: *What looks simple in ER14, I have found sometimes to be very tricky. It is then much easier to cut your losses and remove the four bolts that hold the engine mounting tower to the chassis/floorpan. You can then, if you wish, leave both engine mountings attached to the engine.*

▲ ER11. This is the Bath Minor Centre's own way of removing the engine: from the dynamo side, remove the engine mounting bottom nut and washers.

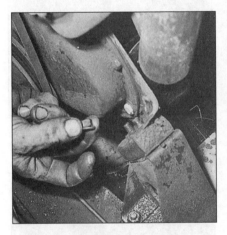

▲ ER12. Do the same to the other side, but also remove the top nuts and washers.

▼ ER13. Use your hoist to take the engine weight. Place a jack below the front end of the gearbox so that the weight is just taken.

▲ ER15. The other side will then come free allowing you to lift the engine up a touch, pull it forwards off the gearbox splines and lift it away, taking care not to place any pressure on the clutch or gearbox splines.

Follow your Haynes manual for detailed instructions on engine removal, but here is an overview. Note that another option is to remove the engine and gearbox together, although it is quite possible to remove the engine by itself. For clutch replacement, there is often little to be gained by leaving the engine *in situ*, since persuading the engine and gearbox to realign themselves is notoriously difficult on some cars, such as the MGB for instance! On other cars – Ford Escort I and II, for instance – clutch replacement with engine in place is much more simple.

On US cars and others fitted with the earlier type of emission control equipment, there will be other ancillary equipment such as air-conditioning and the air pump to be removed after disconnecting the hoses. If you can, remove air-conditioning equipment far enough out of the way to enable you to work on the car without disconnecting the hoses and allowing the gas to escape, although this is often not possible (see below).

Important note: Air-conditioning units *must* be depressurized by an air-conditioning specialist before removal. *Only* use a specialist who bleeds the gas off into a sealed container, *never* the air because of the severe ozone damaging nature of the older type of gas. *Only* have the air-conditioning recharged with the more modern ozone-friendly gas as used first by Saab and others. Contact your nearest Saab dealer if you have difficulty obtaining the correct gas. (Unfortunately, it does not work as well in older air conditioning systems and it

might cause seals to leak. Check with the original manufacturer, your one-make club or – most usefully – an air-conditioning system specialist.)

The pump itself is removed after loosening the pump bolts and removing the drive belt, then removing the top adjusting link bolt and the mounting bolt, after which the pump is free.

On many later cars, the restrictor connection must also be removed from the rocker box cover, and other components removed before the basic engine ancillaries become accessible for removal.

Other pointers to bear in mind when removing an engine are:

– Remove the water temperature gauge sender (if it is not of the electrical type), being careful not to damage the transmission tube. Coil the tube and place the whole unit out of harm's way in the rear corner of the engine bay.

– Drain the engine oil and the coolant, and disconnect all the hoses. If they are to be replaced, you may wish to cut through them with a saw, especially the bottom hose which is often difficult to get at.

– Unbolt the oil cooler (if fitted) from the car, leaving the hoses in place, disconnect the hoses at the engine end and lift all of the components away together. Disturbing the oil cooler connections at the oil cooler can easily result in damage to the cooler and is likely to cause leaks. Use two spanners if you have to remove the hoses to prevent shearing the union from the top of the oil cooler.

– Air cleaners will invariably have to be removed and you may wish to take off the carburettors.

– Undo the propshaft bolts at the gearbox flange and 'telescope' the propshaft splines backwards, and lower the shaft to the ground.

– Have a notepad and pencil to hand so that you can make lots of (greasy!) notes. They will be truly invaluable when it is time to put the engine back in!

ENGINE STRIPDOWN

ENGINE STRIP

This section shows how to strip a worn BMC/British Leyland B-series engine once removed from the car: it's a fairly typical overhead-valve, camshaft-in-block, cast-iron engine. If you're lucky enough to own an engine dismantling stand, use it; otherwise do the work on the floor, covering it first with an opened out cardboard box for cleanliness. It is much safer to work on the floor than on the bench from which the engine may topple!

CYLINDER HEAD REMOVAL

This can be carried out with the engine either in or out of the car. The following section contains photographs from a mixture of engine stripdowns: some of them with engine in car; some with engine out. The general principle remains the same.

If you are taking the cylinder head off with the engine still in the car, the first jobs are to: disconnect the battery; drain the radiator and block; remove the water temperature gauge sender unit, the heater tap, top hoses, the dynamo or alternator, and the spark plug leads.

▲ CH1. Start by taking off the rocker cover.

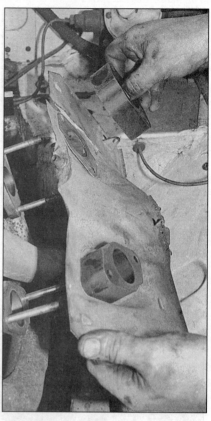

▲ CH2. And then the carburettors and heat shield.

▲ CH3. Take off the manifolds, although if the engine is to remain in the car, you can get away with leaving the exhaust manifold connected to the exhaust pipe, and tying it right back against the inner wing.

▲ CH4. Undo and remove the cylinder head nuts and those for the valve rockers ...

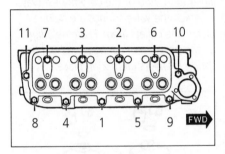

▲ CH5. ... following the tightening and loosening sequence shown here.

▼ CH6. Lift-off the rocker gear ...

▼ CH7. ... and where shims were fitted beneath the rocker posts, note where they come from and refit them on reassembly. They were not fitted in all cases.

▼ CH8. In a heavily sludged engine you will find it difficult to pull out the pushrods, but persevere! Poke eight holes into a piece of cardboard and number them one to eight. Insert the pushrods into the holes in the order in which they come out of the engine so that they can go back in the same place when rebuilding (or use masking tape tags – see next section). They will have bedded in to the rocker gear.

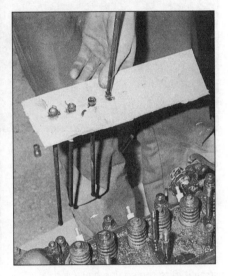

▼ CH9. If the head is totally stuck down and the engine is in the car, replace the sparking plugs (but not the plug leads – remove the distributor cap) and turn the engine over on the starter. The compression should help to lift it. Otherwise, use a soft faced mallet on the thermostat housing casting. **Do not** hammer a screwdriver or other blade into the gap between head and block.

▲ CH10. Lift the head away, but take care: (a) that you don't get your fingers underneath the head as you lift because it is easy for it to slip back down again and trap fingers between head and block, and (b) that you have the weight of the head supported adequately so that you do not injure your back as you stretch in to the engine bay. (With a cast-iron 6-cylinder head you might need assistance or to use the engine hoist.)

▲ CH11. With the aid of a valve spring compressor, you can squeeze the springs tight, remove the collets and withdraw the valves. Keep each collection of valve components together so that it can be reassembled from whence it came.

▼ CH12. You can best remove the head studs by locking two cylinder head nuts tightly against each other and then turning the bottom nut anti-clockwise with a ring spanner while keeping the pressure on the top nut with another spanner held in the other hand. If all else fails, use a proper stud removing tool or even, with enormous care, a Stillson (plumbers) wrench. Emery cloth the stud smooth afterwards – the jaws will have left marks. Take very great care not to break studs off. Work each one back and forth in a gingerly way until it begins to move. If you do have the misfortune to shear one, you could use a purpose-made extractor – they don't always work – or consider having an engineering shop drill and re-tap the hole, unless you have the facilities to do it yourself.

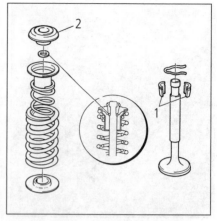

▲ CH13. This is the valve assembly for those engines with double coil springs. Note in this and the following illustration, two of the commonest ways in which the valve springs are held in place. The collets (item 1) are held light by the pressure of springs and hold the spring retainers (item 2) in place.

▲ CH14. Valve assembly, single coil spring engines.

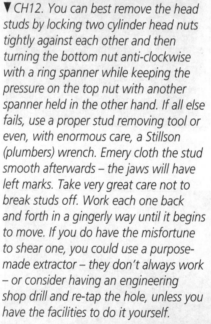

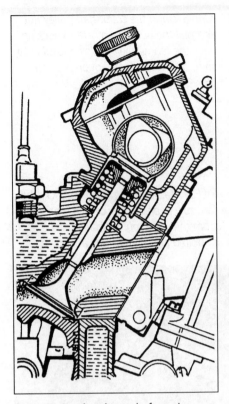

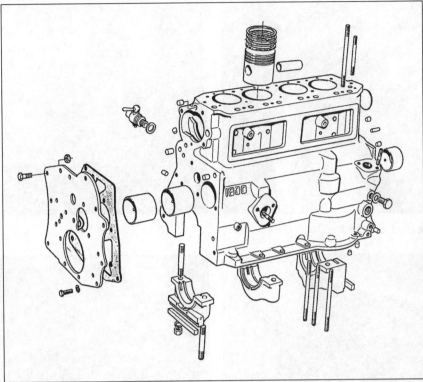

▲ CH15. Overhead-camshaft engines, such as this Fiat unit, are obviously more complex. Refer to your workshop manual for details.

▲ EBS1. The early, 3-main bearing engine cylinder block components. This is an example of the invaluable help and guidance you will receive from using a manual.

▼ EBS2. The early engine's internal components. If you can afford the cost, you might also consider buying a 'factory' parts book. The relative positions of many of the parts will be shown in more detail than in the manual.

ENGINE BLOCK STRIPDOWN
Safety: Do not lift excessive weight when moving the engine around. Enlist help and use a suitable trolley. Don't work where the engine can topple on you.
This section covers the stripdown of several different B-series engines, some 3-main bearing, some 5-main. The aim is to give the full story of what's involved in stripping down an aged engine. Use this section in conjunction with your workshop manual.

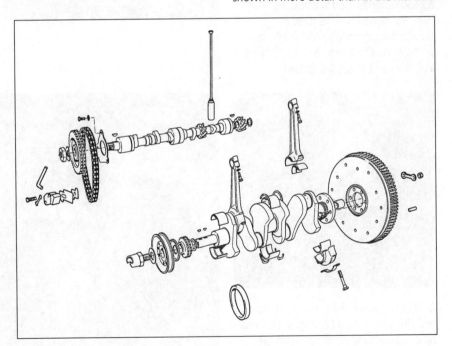

▲ EBS3. Remove the tappet chest covers ..

◄EBS6. Undo the crankshaft pulley nut and pull the pulley away after knocking back the tab washer. If it's impossible to shift, take a tip from caption number EBS29.

▲ EBS4. ... and reach inside to pull out the cam followers – like a set of thimbles. Long nosed pliers might be useful here. Obviously, this won't apply to overhead camshaft engines!

▼ EBS7. Tab washers knocked back, the fan, spacer and pulley can be removed from the water pump which can be unbolted and tapped free as shown.

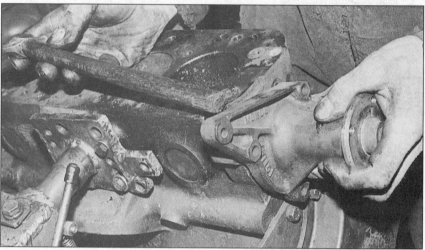

▼ EBS8. A ring of bolts holds the timing chain cover in place: it usually has to be prised off the block.

▲ EBS5. After removing the distributor and the plate found beneath it, secured by a countersunk screw, you can take out the distributor driveshaft. Screw in a ⁵⁄₁₆ in UNF bolt and lift out the driveshaft, turning slightly to free the skew gear.

▶ *EBS9. The oil thrower on this earlier engine is fitted with its concave side facing outwards. The oil thrower on later engines looks slightly different. The correct oil thrower has to match the correct timing chain cover. Early ones have a felt oil seal; later ones a neoprene seal. Make sure that the gasket set you buy for your car has all the correct bits and pieces, such as oil seals, for your engine. Indeed, make sure that your engine has not been adapted with parts from an earlier or later car.*

▲ *EBS12. Another tab washer ...*

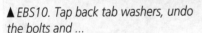

▲ *EBS10. Tap back tab washers, undo the bolts and ...*

▼ *EBS11. ... remove the timing chain tensioner. If it's too tight to remove, screw it back into its housing with an Allen key. Many engines (A-series units, for instance) are not fitted with a tensioner at all.*

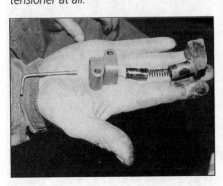

▲ *EBS13. ... another nut ...*

▼ *EBS14. ... and both timing chain cogs are free to be levered away.*

▲ EBS15. This later engine shows the single-row timing chain being removed.

▲ EBS16. Behind it, the camshaft retaining plate after which the camshaft can be eased out of the block, or you can leave it until ...

▲ EBS17. ... the bolts holding the engine front plate are removed ...

▲ EBS18. ... and the front plate lifted away.

▲ EBS19. When taking out the camshaft, it has to be 'jiggled' carefully so that the cams and, in particular, the skew gear do not damage the white metal bearings inside the block. They rarely wear and rarely require replacement so look after them!

▶ EBS20. At the back of the engine, tab washers and nuts removed. Some engines have wired-on nuts; some use locknuts.

▲ EBS21. The flywheel can now be lifted away. Don't let it drop; it's quite a weight!

▲ EBS24. In a different sequence, this early engine's backplate bolts are removed ...

▼ EBS22. More tab washers and more nuts ...

▼ EBS26. Wise mechanics do it kneeling down! (It's safer on the floor because the engine has less distance to fall and there is less risk of injuring yourself as you move the block around.)

▲ EBS23. ... and the five-main bearing engine's rear oil seal retainer can be removed.

▼ EBS25. ... and tapped free of the block.

▲ EBS27. With the innumerable sump bolts removed, the sump can be tapped smartly with a soft-faced hammer and lifted away.

▲ EBS28. Three long bolts hold the oil pump to the block. Lift it away complete. On some engines, the pump components come apart as it is removed: check your manual.

▲ EBS29. If it was not previously possible to undo the crankshaft pulley nut, wedge a piece of wood between crank and block, place a socket and tommy bar on the nut, and strike it smartly with a lump hammer. Take care that the spanner doesn't fly off, and that the block stays stable and does not topple. Don't use a ratchet wrench; you might break it!

▲ EBS30. Beneath the oil pump is the oil pump drive which can be lifted with a twisting motion using a pair of long-nosed pliers.

▼ EBS31. Undo all the nuts holding the main bearings in place, but first knock back tab washers (if fitted)!

▼ EBS32. Then, drift the end main bearings out of the block. You might have to make a special tool which consists of a stout 'bridge' over the bearing cap, a bolt passing through a clearance hole in the top of the 'bridge' and into the thread in the cap and a nut run down the bolt to bear downwards on the bridge, thus pulling the bearing cap out.

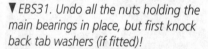

▲ EBS33. The centre main has a semi-circular thrust washer in a recess on each side, with another matching pair in the block. Retrieve them all.

▲ EBS34. Tab washers back; bolts out; big end caps lifted away with the aid of a tap from an engineer's hammer.

▼ EBS35. You can now lift the crank out of the block.

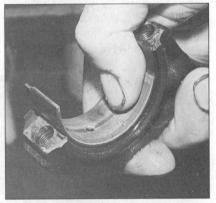

▲ EBS36. Reach up inside the block from beneath with a hammer handle and tap the pistons up and out.

◀ EBS37. Because of the surface tension of the oil, the only way to remove the bearing shell is to slide it out in the direction of the locating lug. You will try in vain just to lift it off!

▼ EBS38. Reassemble each con-rod with big end cap – it is **essential** that they are maintained as matched pairs.

▲ EBS39. Chisel into each of the core plugs ...

▲ EBS40. ... and lift each one out. This one was really ripe! Always replace them all as a matter of course.

▲ EBS41. On earlier engines, with a mechanical tachometer drive, undo the nut holding the drive in place at the back left of the engine and lift it away from the block.

CYLINDER HEAD OVERHAUL

With the engine stripped down you will want to overhaul the cylinder head, but you can carry out a certain amount of useful diagnostic checking while the engine is still running and in the car. Misfiring at low speeds is most likely to be caused by a fault in the ignition system but could also be caused by a burned out valve. It is a simple matter to check the compression of each cylinder. Remove the leads from the coil to the distributor so that the engine cannot start. Now, take out the sparking plugs and fit a compression tester to each sparking plug opening in the cylinder head in turn whilst spinning the engine over on the starter motor. In the majority of cases, the pressure should be between 8.2 and 13.8 bar (120 and 200 lbs per square inch) according to the engine's compression ratio, but more important, there shouldn't be a difference between the various cylinders of more than about

15 per cent. Poor compression can also be caused by badly worn piston rings or bores, however, so if the readings give cause for concern, squirt some oil in to each of the cylinders and run the test again. If you see no improvement, the fault lies with the valves.

After you have removed the valve rocker gear, the pushrods can be pulled out, although sometimes a build-up of deposits means that you have to give them a good tug! If the pushrods are good enough to reuse, make a tag out of masking tape and stick it to each pushrod. Write a number from 1 to 8, starting at the front of the engine (in the case of four-cylinder engines) showing which position the pushrod came from. This is perhaps preferable to the usually quoted method of pushing holes in a piece of card (see previous section) as there is always the possibility that the pushrods will fall through the holes if they are not stored carefully!

▼ CHO1. With the cylinder head bolts or nuts removed, the head can be lifted away.

▲ CHO2. The very best way to work on a cylinder head is by placing it on purpose-made cylinder head stands. A couple of blocks of wood would be almost as good, but note that clean surroundings are essential.

▲ CHO3. The thermostat housing fitted to BMC A-series engines is made of aluminium and is often reluctant to budge. Try tapping each of the lugs with a hammer; try soaking each hole in releasing fluid for 24 hours beforehand, if you can; try heating with a butane blow torch (**not** welding torch because the aluminium alloy will melt). If the worst comes to the worst, you may have to destroy the housing in order to remove it, although things are not often that bad!

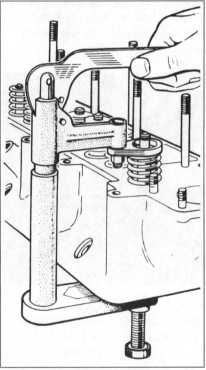

▲ CHO4. Before even attempting to remove the valve springs, strike the end of the stem of each valve sharply with a hammer. This will probably free the cotters and make the valve springs easy to remove. Valve spring compression tools come in all shapes and sizes.

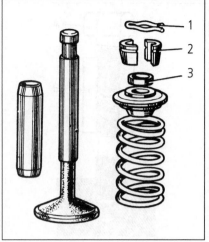

▲ CHO5. With this type of valve spring retaining system, a circlip has first to be removed (item 1) before the cotters (item 2) can be lifted out. Take care not to drop and lose them! It is worth noting now that if you forget to fit new oil seals (item 3) when the cylinder head is reassembled the engine will become a 'smoker' to the extent that you will imagine that something has gone terribly wrong!

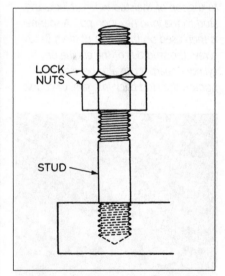

▲ CHO6. The classical way of removing studs from the cylinder head (or block) is to run a pair of nuts down each stud and to lock them together with a pair of spanners. When the bottom nut is turned in an anti-clockwise direction, the stud should come out of the hole.

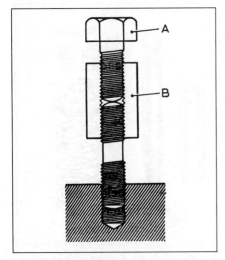

▲ CHO7. If you can find or make a long hexagonal nut (item B) you will be able to produce a stud removing tool which gives more grip than the system shown in CHO6, although it has to be said that the former system works in at least 90 per cent of cases. The long nut is screwed down on to the stud; a bolt of the same thread type is screwed in from the top (item A) and is tightened down hard on to the top of the stud where it locks the stud to the long hexagon nut. A spanner is then used on the long nut (item B) to screw the stud out of the engine or cylinder head. It can also be used to tighten the stud back in again, of course.

▲ CHO8. An array of valves standing to attention on a stripped down Lea Francis 1800cc cylinder head. Those on the left have been cleaned up ready for re-fitting (see later). Third from the left is a valve that has become pitted beyond saving. There was water in the engine while the car spent many years standing under a

hedge! The right hand valve is badly oiled and coated in carbon as a result of very badly worn valve guides and valve stem oil seals. The valve on the right could be cleaned with a scraper and a power wire brush. However, since the wear in the valve stem and guides is likely to have been quite severe in order to cause oiling to this degree, it would be best to at least replace the valves and to have the stems professionally checked before deciding whether to fit new valves.

With the head stripped down it can be checked visually for cracking. In some cases a cracked cylinder head could be welded after grinding out the crack, but if the crack is across valve seats, it will be necessary to use specially developed stitching. Ordinary welding in this position might not be enough to prevent the crack from reappearing and from spreading later on. This is a job that will have to be carried out by your engine reconditioning specialist.

▲ CHO9. Here is an old valve guide held against a new replacement. If the guide has a shoulder on it it will be obvious how far into the cylinder head it must be driven. If it has not, its position will have to be carefully measured as it is tapped into place. On VW Beetles, the guides are generally supplied oversize. Main agents re-mount the holes so that the guides are a tight fit; others turn down the guides on a lathe. This latter approach has the benefit that the valve guide hole retains its original size. If the guide is loose, you may be able to save

the day by putting the guide on a mandrel held in a lathe and lightly knurling (putting a raised diamond pattern) on to the part of the guide that fits into the cylinder head, and using some Locktite to try to ensure that the guide does not shift.

▲ CHO10. This guide is being fitted with the assistance of a purpose-made valve guide drifting tool. It should be fairly simple to create a suitable substitute in the home workshop. The most essential part of this job is that the guide is drifted in absolutely straight and to its correct height in the cylinder head.

▲ CHO11. Valve seats are often badly pitted when an engine is ripe for restoration, and a professional reconditioner will re-cut the seats to the correct angle.

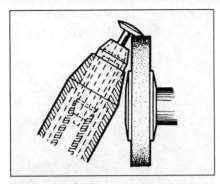

▲ CHO12. He will also be able to re-face the valve seats giving the two correct angles to be found on the seats, and leaving a minimal amount of hand grinding-in to be done. If seats are very severely eroded or even just slightly cracked, the head can usually be saved by letting in a new valve seat insert. This is a ring of hardened steel which is pressed into the cylinder head after the old seat has been precisely machined out ready to take the insert.

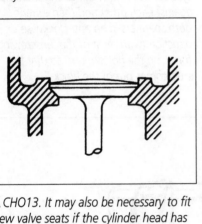

▲ CHO13. It may also be necessary to fit new valve seats if the cylinder head has received one overhaul too many, or too much is taken off the valve seat by machining. If the valve sits too deep it is said to be 'pocketed'. Efficient gas flow is discouraged and the engine will suffer from a loss of power and increased fuel consumption.

USE OF UNLEADED PETROL

Pocketing can also take place if an engine that is designed to run on leaded petrol is run on unleaded petrol for any length of time. Lead helps to prevent the valve seats from degenerating in use. Unfortunately, it also carries totally unacceptable health risks, especially for children and those who live in cities. Leaded petrol is not available in the United States; and even where it is available the onus is on the owner to convert his or her engine to run on unleaded petrol. Now, in the restoration process, is the time to do it!

In the pages of most classic car magazines are specialists who advertise exchange overhauled cylinder heads which have been fitted with suitable hardened steel valve seat inserts, and sometimes improved valve guides, to prevent the erosion that is otherwise set up by the lack of lead in petrol. Alternatively, your engine reconditioner may be familiar with the process of adapting your cylinder head so that your car can run on unleaded petrol. If your car is the type that previously was specified as having to be run on a higher octane petrol, you may have to use so-called super unleaded petrol. Less demanding engines may be perfectly happy with standard unleaded.

▲ CHO14. Moss Engineering in Ledbury, Herefordshire, where most of these photographs were taken, re-face a cylinder head with a fly cutter rather than a grinder. This puts a series of concentric cuts or tiny grooves in the surface of the cylinder head which, while it doesn't look quite as pretty as a newly ground surface, allows the gasket to 'grip' better. This is particularly useful for competition or diesel engines.

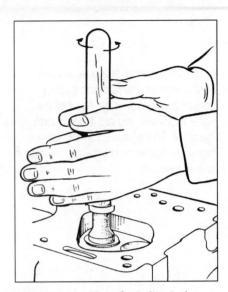

▲ CHO15. The idea of grinding in (or lapping in) is to produce a final gas-tight fit between valve and valve seat. When your reconditioner re-faced the valves and the valve seats, he did so in such a way that the angle on each is slightly different. If the whole of the width of the face of the valve and the valve seat was to touch, there would be too little pressure between the two and gases would escape. The idea of grinding is to produce a very narrow ring of contact between the two. Dip the valve stem in paraffin to give it some lubrication in the valve guide. Take a little fine grinding paste and wipe the merest touch of it around the face of the valve. Place the valve in the cylinder head and, using the hand grinding tool shown, work the grinding tool and valve to and fro like a caveman trying to light a fire. When you have done this for a minute or two, wipe off the grinding paste and put on a tiny touch of engineer's blue. (You can create your own checking paste by burning a candle underneath a piece of metal. Mix some of the resulting soot with a spot of thin engine oil and use the black paste in place of engineer's blue.) The aim is to produce a thin ring of checking paste, transferred from one surface to the other indicating a narrow but complete area of contact between the two. It is essential that you remove every trace of grinding paste from valve, valve guide and cylinder head. If any of it should get in to the engine it will wreak havoc with bearing surfaces!

▶ CHO16. After re-fitting each valve spring, collets and retainer, place a socket spanner over the head of the valve as shown and tap it down with a hammer. This ensures that the valve is correctly seated in its retainer and that it is free to move.

▲ SVS2. Remove the cylinder head, but note that two of the cylinder head bolts are not bolts at all but studs threaded at each end. Remove them by taking both cylinder head nuts, tightening them hard against each other and then turning both spanners in an anti-clockwise direction (with most of the 'unscrewing force' on the bottom nut) so that the stud comes out of the block.

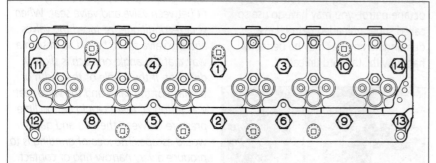

▲ CHO17. When re-fitting the cylinder head – and especially in the case of aluminium cylinder heads – it is important to follow the correct tightening sequence. The basic principle is that you start from the middle and work your way out, but the numbering system here gives the right idea.

SIDE-VALVE STRIPDOWN

▶ SVS1. The slightly eccentric overhead-inlet, side-exhaust valve layout was used in many Rover saloon cars from 1948-on and in the Land-Rover for decades to come! The side-exhaust valve part of the engine is quite typical of side-valve engines. (Courtesy: Land Rover Parts)

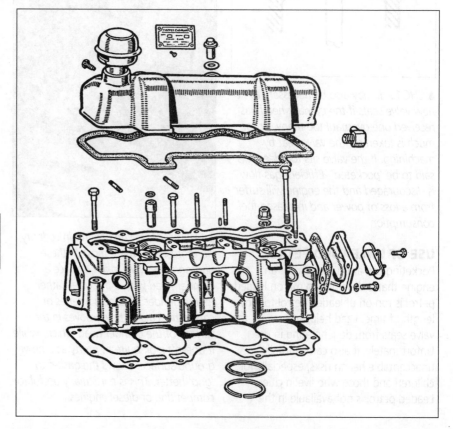

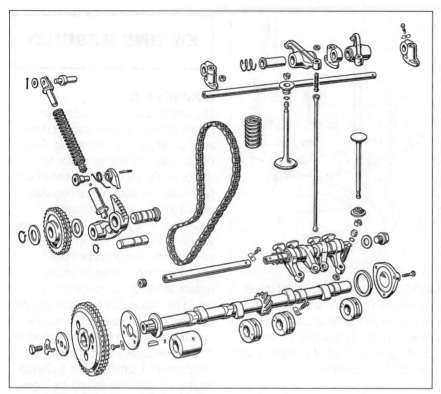

▲ SVS3. This is the layout of the inlet and exhaust valve gear in the four-cylinder engine and the timing chain and tensioner arrangement.
(Courtesy: Land Rover Parts)

▲ SVS6. It's then an easy matter to withdraw the exhaust valve itself, but take this opportunity to see whether there is any serious amount of lateral movement between exhaust valve and guide which is fitted into the block. If more extensive work is required, refer to the workshop manual.

▲ SVS4. To remove the exhaust valve, turn the engine over until the cam lobe is furthest away from the rocker.

▲ SVS5. Compress the valve springs with a compressing tool and remove the collets. Note that they are quite easily dropped when working in the lower confines of the engine bay!

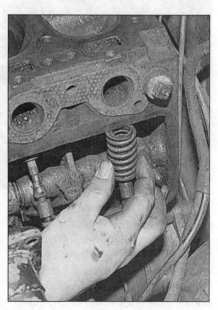

▲ SVS7. The double valve springs can also be lifted away at this stage but ensure that just as with the push rods for the overhead inlet valves, the exhaust valves and springs are saved in the correct order because the valves will have bedded into the place from whence they came and the valve springs are selected as matching pairs.

▲ SVS8. The valve can be ground into the new valve seat in the normal way, placing a smear of fine grinding paste around the valve seating area ...

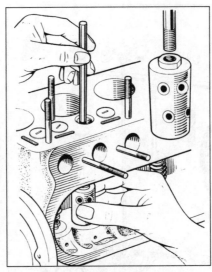

▲ SVS10. This is how the valve tappets are removed on some side-valve engines with concealed camshafts. After removing the tappet screw, the tappet can be taken out with the fingers or with the aid of a screwed rod.

ENGINE REBUILD

ENGINE FAULTS

This section shows how to check an engine once it has been stripped down, and how to carry out the rebuild. One option open to the enthusiast is to stripdown the engine him or herself and have whatever machining is necessary carried out by a specialist engine reconditioner. If you take this route, you will have to carefully inspect each of the components in your stripped down engine and decide what you must replace and what you can retain. It would be a good idea to go through the components with your chosen engine machine shop, who will be able to advise on the serviceability of your engine's components. Triumph 4- and 6-cylinder engines and the B-series unit are shown being followed through, although general principles are similar for most overhead-valve engines.

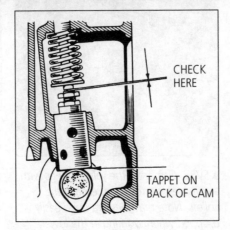

▲ SVS9. ... and then grinding the valve into the valve seat in the normal way. Be sure not to use too much grinding paste, so that none of it becomes transferred into the sump. It is difficult to imagine anything that could wear an engine more quickly then valve grinding paste circulating around it in the engine oil! Make doubly sure that you wipe all traces of it away with a rag dampened with paraffin, but once again be careful not to wash the grinding paste into the sump.

CHECK HERE

TAPPET ON BACK OF CAM

▲ SVS11. Setting a side-valve's valve clearances.

▲ EF1. Pulling against the force of the spring, pull each rocker along the shaft to expose its bearing surface on the shaft and examine it for wear. Then check bushes and shaft by taking hold of a rocker and attempting to rock it at 90 degrees from its normal action, i.e. in line with the shaft itself. You will probably find excess wear, and will need to replace the shaft and rebush the rockers.

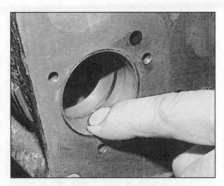

▲ EF2. Look at the ends of the pushrods and at their mating surfaces on the rockers. Pitting or 'nippling' indicate excess wear, and overhaul or replacement will be called for. Scrap and replace bent pushrods.

▲ EF5. Camshaft bearings are often stained but not often worn. New white metal bushes will have to be pressed in only if the bearings are scored.

▲ EF6. This is the amount of deflection you get with a new timing chain: any more means wear.

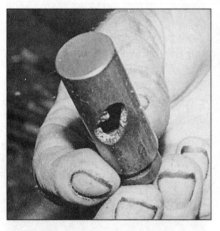

▲ EF3. Look for pitting or wear on the surface of the cam follower ...

▼ EF4. ... and for wear on the peak of the cam. You could replace or have the camshaft reground.

▲ EF7. Take a look at the innards of the oil pump. This is a badly worn outer rotor. Also examine the inside of the outer rotor and the outside of the inner rotor (if you know what I mean!) and look at

the peg on the end of the driveshaft where it locates into the slot on the inner rotor shaft. Severe wear can sometimes take place here. Any rebuild should include a new oil pump.

▼ EF8. Scoring on the end-plate in particular will cause a loss in oil pressure.

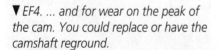

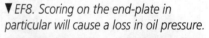

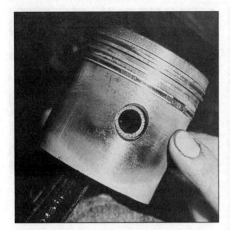

▲ EF9. Dark marks on the side of the piston indicate blow-by caused by worn rings and a worn bore.

▲ EF10. And crank regrind time! Your specialist will be able to measure the crank journals and advise on acceptable wear tolerances.

▲ EF11. Unacceptable wear on the bearing shells would be wear through to the copper backing. Even more dire is this complex maze of wear lines in the surface of the shell caused by water getting into the sump oil.

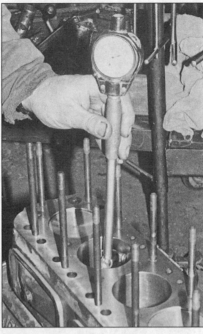

▲ EF12. Bore wear and bore ovality can only be measured with an internal micrometer or a dial gauge such as this one. More specialist advice required here.

REBUILDING THE ENGINE

When your machined engine components and replacement parts come back from the reconditioners, you will be anxious to get started! Before doing so, spend some time blowing out water and (especially!) oil passages with compressed air. WEAR GOGGLES! Swarf in bearings or bore could rip out all the good work! If you don't own a compressor, have the reconditioner do this for you, or ask if you can use their air line when you collect the components.

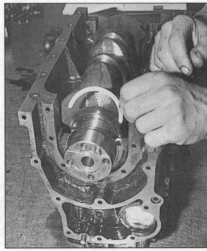

▲ RE1. Ensure all components are almost clinically clean. Fit new main bearings into the crankcase, ensuring that oilways in the bearing match with those in the engine, and that the tags shown positively lock into their recesses. Generously lubricate moving parts with fresh oil. Additionally, use some special assembly lubricant if available. Don't use Slick 50: it might prevent parts from properly bedding-in; rubbing together to a nice fit.

▲ RE2. Carefully lower the crankshaft into the block.

◀ RE3. Slide new thrust washers around each side of the rear main bearing so that they sit on top of the crankshaft (engine right side up). Ensure that their oil grooves face outwards and that the bearings positively locate.

▲ RE4. After applying lots more oil, fit the front and centre main bearing shells and caps and tighten to the correct torque. (See your workshop manual). Ensure everything turns freely.

▲ RE5. Check the crankshaft endfloat at the rear of the crankshaft by levering against any slack (again check the tolerances in your manual). A dial gauge would be useful here if available. Next, fit the rear main bearing and cap and tighten to the correct torque. Double check that the crankshaft rotates smoothly. Six-cylinder engines are very similar; it's just that they have an extra bearing. Apply more oil with every additional bearing cap.

▲ RE6. Fit the main bearing shells to the correctly ordered caps, taking the same care as detailed in RE1. Tighten to the correct torque. The endfloat could also be checked now. On Triumph engines, fit the front sealing bridge. Fit the small paper gaskets shown with a little sealing compound. If it hasn't been done already, remove the old wooden seals – one is shown here still in the end of the bridge and compared with a bright new one. Many engines have their own quirks – although it has to be said that the use of a piece of softwood in an engine takes some beating! – so consult your manual for details.

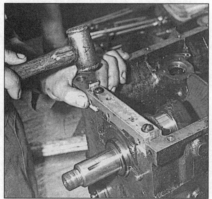

▲ RE7. Screw down the bridge, making sure while doing so that it lies flush with the face of the crankcase. A good metal straight edge is useful here. Coat each wooden block with a smear of jointing compound and tap in. They'll remain a little proud of the surface, so trim off the excess. If desired, the rear engine seal could now be fitted, though in this particular rebuild the timing gear and pistons were fitted next.

▲ RE8. The golden rule with any rebuild is to oil, oil and oil again ...

▼ RE9. Refit the front engine plate with a new gasket and a coating of jointing compound. Fit the camshaft holding plate and check for endfloat. Endfloat (check correct amount in your manual) is adjusted by fitting a new plate.

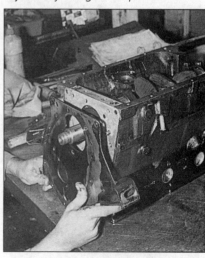

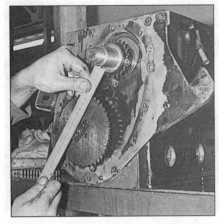

▲ RE10. Temporarily refit the timing sprockets and check that the two wheels are in exactly the same plane. Ensure that they are level with each other by fitting different thickness of shims behind the crankshaft sprocket. This is the sort of job that can hold everything up, as you have to order a set of shims, but it **must** be done in order to prevent premature timing chain wear.

▼ RE11. Once the correct shims have been fitted, remove the sprockets and refit the crankshaft Woodruff key.

▲ RE12. If fitting new con-rod bushes, ensure that the oilway in the bush matches the oilway in the top of the con-rod. Have the bush reamed to size – a job you can't do easily at home. You could have your specialist assemble pistons for you. Make sure that the pistons and con-rods are the correct way around to fit into the block – note the offset in the con-rod.

▲ RE14. Using a proper ring compressor tool (it's not worth trying without), tap the piston and con-rod assembly into the bore. Fit new big-end shells making sure that the tags locate in the con-rods and caps. Where relevant, refit locking tabs and tighten the new bolts to the correct torque. As necessary, tap over the locking tabs.

▲ RE15. Referring to the workshop manual, especially if fitting new timing wheels, refit the timing gear complete with new chain. fit a new locking tab plate, tighten the wheel bolts and bend over the locking tabs.

▼ RE16. Assemble the components, prime with oil and bolt into place.

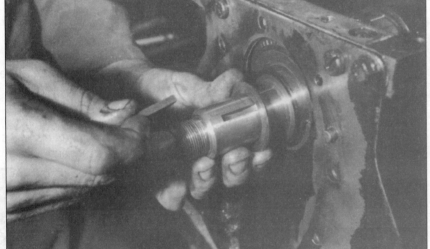

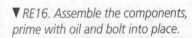

◄ RE13. Once assembled, lock in the gudgeon pin with new circlips noting that the load on the clips should be taken on the flat, not the curved side. When fitting to the piston, stagger each ring gap around the piston to cut down on compression losses and wear.

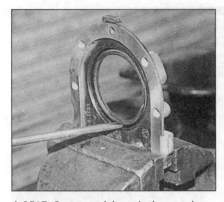

▲ RE17. Some models, as is the case here, are fitted with a flexible oil seal, whereas others are not. Tap out the old seal with a suitable drift. You'll have to 'find' the edge of the seal cup with the end of your drift, tight against the seal housing.

▼ RE18. Carefully push in a new seal and tap squarely home. Don't allow one side to go in and then try to hammer down the other side to match, it won't!

▲ RE19. Fit a new gasket, oil the seal and then carefully offer the assembly on to the block without damaging the seal lip. Hold in place finger tight with two opposing bolts. Rotate the crankshaft, adjusting the plate until it is properly centred.

Some Triumph engines without this flexible seal may either have the seal plates made from cast iron or aluminium alloy. Both types should be centred in the same way as above, but the seal should be centralized by inserting a feeler gauge between the seal and crankshaft journal. On some cars, the oil seal simply taps into a recess after the rear main bearing is fitted; on others there is no seal at all, but a scroll on the crank which 'screws' oil back into the engine as the crank turns. These engines invariably 'spot' oil – onto the garage floor!

▲ RE20. Ensure mating surfaces are free from all debris – not that there should be any around. Smear both sides with a little jointing compound ...

◄ RE21. ... and fit a new gasket. Put the sump in place and tighten evenly down.

▲ RE22. **Important!** *Steel sump joint leaks often occur because the flange is split or – as commonly happens – it becomes distorted. Weld up (and file flat) any splits; dress the flange flat with a hammer and check with the edge of a steel rule.*

▲ RE25. *Fit a new gasket. Often, it will be embossed with 'TOP'. If not, compare against the old gasket as removed.*

▲ RE23. *Back at the top end, refit new cam followers – plenty of oil again!*

▲ RE26. *The cylinder head can now be lowered into position.*

▼ RE27. *For the sake of a few pennies, replace the old stud nuts and washers with new ones.*

▲ RE24. *Replace the head studs with the correct tool or use the double lock-nut technique.*

▲ RE28. *Tighten in the correct sequence (from the centre working out) to the correct torque. The latter varies from model to model.*

▲ RE29. Refit the push rods in their respective holes ...

▲ RE32. Tap out the old oil seal in the timing chain cover taking care not to distort the cover.

▲ RE33. Tap in a new seal and fit a new spring tensioner if fitted. Note that many older cars used a felt seal. Soak overnight in oil before fitting.

▲ RE34. Slide on the oil thrower with its dished side outermost, i.e., so that the thrower is pointing towards the engine.

▲ RE30. ... followed by the rocker gear. Don't overtighten the pedestal nuts. They're made of alloy and may crack if treated roughly! Again check for the torque required.

▶ RE31. Finally set the rocker to the correct clearance – see your manual. Recheck this setting when, after the engine has run for an hour, you re-tighten the cylinder head nuts and again after the first 1,000 miles.

▲ RE35. A tip for those engines with a spring tensioner for the timing chain built into the cover. Having fitted a new gasket, loop a piece of thin wire or string around the spring tensioner and, pulling it towards the side of the cover, locate the cover on the block. With the cover just off the block, the string can be pulled out having done its job. In the case of engines with a slipper-type of tensioner (see strip-down procedure) you will have to compress the spring, fit the slipper then re-tension the spring.

▲ RE36. Secure the cover fixing screws, fit the pulley ...

▶ RE37. ... and replace the front nut to the correct torque. Fit locking tabs if relevant.

▶ RE38. Next, relocate the backplate and secure. Ensure the crankshaft spigot bush is fitted into the end of the crank. Always replace with new – and lubricate! Note that engine backplate (and frontplates) often have bolts of varying lengths. It is often **essential** that these go back from whence they came to give proper grip and, possibly, to avoid damage if a long bolt is fitted where a short one should be.

▲ RE39. Offer up the flywheel and locate it on to the crankshaft dowel, making sure that that is in good condition.

▲ RE40. Tighten up the fixing bolts and torque down. If the starter ring is worn, have it replaced by your specialist – or see how to DIY later in this chapter. Check that it is seated tight on the shoulder of the flywheel.

▲ RE41. *Finally, before engine and gearbox are ready to be united (conventional in-line units) the clutch must be fitted. Unless the 'old' one is virtually new, it would be false economy not to fit a complete new unit including thrust washer. Offer up the friction and pressure plates with the two plates located on an old input shaft (the best and cheapest tool for the job – usually easily available at one-make club autojumbles), alternatively buy or borrow a general purpose alignment tool. A universal model is produced by the S-P 'Speedline' brand. It's not worth trying to make one from a rod of wood because the hassle involved in an engine refusing to mate with its gearbox is disproportionate to the cost. The aim is to centralize the clutch splines with the engine such that the gearbox input shaft will pass smoothly through. Also ensure that the friction plate remains free of grease and that it locates properly on the flywheel. Friction plates are normally clearly labelled 'Flywheel Side'. If put on the wrong way round, the pressure plate might or might not fit but the clutch just won't operate so the job would have to be done again.*

STARTER RING GEAR

The starter motor on the author's pre-war Vauxhall 14 stuck every other throw of the starter motor. The usual culprit is a worn starter ring – it was! Check yours with the engine out and attend to it if necessary. The teeth on the flywheel starter ring were badly worn in three equally spaced-out positions, coinciding with the places where the 6-cylinder

engine came to rest. No replacement was available, so here is what the author decided to do, with the assistance of mechanic Sean Niescor. If a new starter ring is available, the conventional way of removing the old is by hacksawing through part of it, up to the shoulder of the flywheel, taking care not to cut into the flywheel. Then, wearing safety goggles, a sharp cold chisel is used to break through the ring.

▲ SR1. *The worn teeth can be clearly seen.*

▲ SR2. *A good, clear centre punch mark was made on the flywheel alongside the centre of one of the damaged parts of the ring gear. Then another clear mark was punched on to the ring gear itself, this time in the middle of a good section. The two were to be aligned!*

▲ SR3. *A 'Workmate'; a steel car ramp; a BOC Portapak gas welding set. With the largest nozzle, the ring was heated, round and round ...*

▲ SR4. *... then when really hot, a couple of sets of clamps were used to rapidly grip the flywheel (it's HOT!) turn it over and drift off the ring gear. It took a couple of separate heating sessions, the gear cooling, contracting and tightening again. (N.B. DON'T try cooling the flywheel. Thermal shock could damage it.)*

▲ SR5. Then the ring gear was heated separately ...

▼ SR6. ... popped back on to the flywheel with centre punch marks aligned and tapped down tight. N.B. It is essential that the flywheel is refitted to the engine in exactly the same position as it was before.

FINISHING TOUCHES AND TIPS

▶ FTT1. Earlier, I mentioned the need to obtain all the right gaskets for your particular engine. Sometimes that is just not possible and you may have to make your own. A gasket making kit, complete with a range of hole punches will help you to make a professional job of it.
(Courtesy: Frost Auto Restoration)

▲ FTT3. You then remove the nut and bolt used for installation and – voila! – a new thread!
(Courtesy: The Eastwood Company)

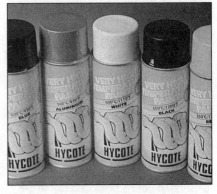

▲ FTT4. Manifolds are best treated with a brush-on or spray-on 'very high temperature' paint. The ordinary sort burns straight off, of course. Stick to silver, grey or black, depending on the original appearance and your preference.
(Courtesy: Frost Auto Restoration)

▲ FTT2. If you are unfortunate enough to strip a thread – especially annoying in a blind hole – or to shear a stud which needs drilling out and you then damage the thread, a thread repair insert will save the day. You drill out the hole and spanner in the insert.
(Courtesy: The Eastwood Company)

▲ FTT5. Under bonnet black items should never be painted in gloss black – it looks all wrong! Obtain semi-gloss from your specialist or local motorists' store.
(Courtesy: The Eastwood Company)

FRONT SUSPENSION OVERHAUL

Since the days when the first 'modern' classic cars began to appear after the Second World War, coil springs have been the most popular front suspension medium. There has been a large number of variations on the theme and a number of fairly unique systems such as those employed by the Mini (rubber springs on some cars; hydrolastic fluid-based suspension on others), the strange horizontal coil springs linking front and rear suspension on the Citroen 2CV, and the Rover knee-action linkage with its horizontal front spring. The great majority of cars have either a double-wishbone type of front suspension or a MacPherson strut arrangement first used by Ford and later adopted by a number of other manufacturers.

Safety: Take careful note of the usual safety requirements when working underneath a car supported off the ground. Coil springs contain an enormous amount of energy within them and so when they are being compressed or released they must be treated with great caution. Follow the instructions in the workshop manual for your particular car and in particular, only compress the springs using purpose-built coil spring compressors such as those available from Sykes-Pickavant. At least two compressors are needed for each spring and they must be in good condition so that the nuts move easily on their threads. Otherwise the clamping hooks might turn during tightening or releasing and become disengaged from the coils. DO NOT use if the threaded rods have become bent or if the hooked part of the clamp is damaged.

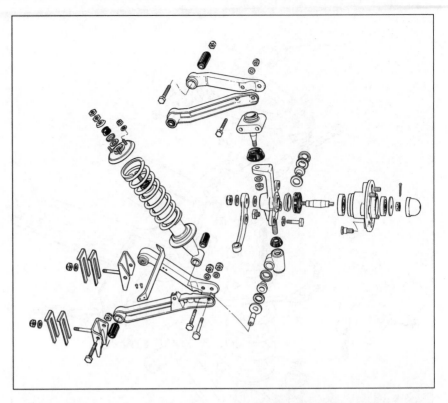

▲ FSO1. And here is just one of those variations on the themes mentioned above. On the Triumph Spitfire, GT6, Vitesse and Herald the spring and damper can be removed as a combined unit. However, when the spring is separated from the damper the spring must be compressed with clamps in the normal way.

▶ FSO2. The MGB is one of those cars where you can remove the front coil springs in relative safety without the need for special tools. With the road wheel removed, plus the brake caliper, mud shield, hub and the anti-roll bar disconnected, a trolley jack is placed under the spring pan towards the outer end in such a way that the jack is very securely positioned and cannot slip. The weight of the car is then taken on the jack sufficient to just compress the spring a little. N.B. it is not possible to carry out this job with an MGB unless the engine is in the car giving sufficient downwards force on the jack to compress the spring. You can then release and remove the upper pivot pin that passes through the

damper arm which means that the full force of the spring is now bearing on the jack and is not contained within the suspension. It is therefore **imperative** that the jack is lowered slowly and with great care to gently release the force within the spring.

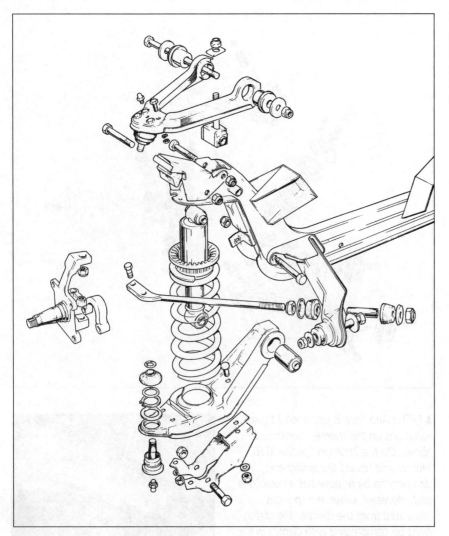

◀FSO3. This Jensen Healey front
suspension is of a relatively conventional
type, with shock absorbers contained
inside the coil spring. On some systems it
is possible to remove the shock absorber
without disturbing the coil spring.

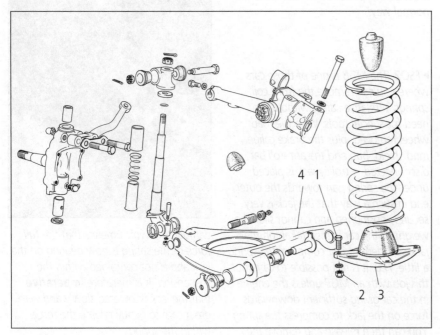

◀FSO4. With other systems, such as the
Austin Healey Sprite/MG Midget front
suspension (itself derived from the
Austin saloons such as A30, A35 and
A40), the spring can be removed with
the aid of two high tensile 'slave' bolts.
Two of the original short bolts (items 1
and 2) are removed from diagonally
opposite corners of the spring seat (item
3) which is held on to the bottom of the
bottom wishbone (item 4). The longer
bolts (about 100 – 150mm [4 – 6in]
long) are then fitted with the original
nuts – they must be threaded along their
entire length of course – and the two
remaining short, original bolts removed.

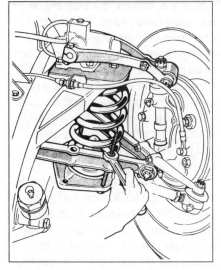

▲ *FSO5. The two dummy bolts can then be unscrewed a few threads at a time until all the tension is taken out of the spring. (This is from another but essentially similar car's front suspension.) Incidentally, note that this is yet another variation on the double-wishbone theme where the top link is in fact the shock absorber arm. This is essentially similar to the top link used on the Morris Minor and MGB.*

▶ *FSO6. With some other systems, such as those employed on MK1 and MK2 Jaguar saloons, Sunbeam Alpine, Minx and similar brethren, there is the facility to fit a long through-bolt up through the lower plate and the centre of the spring to hold the lower plate in place while the lower plate retaining nuts and bolts are removed. The through-bolt is then slowly withdrawn taking the pressure off the spring.*

▼ *FSO7. The MacPherson strut system as used on most Fords and an increasing number of vehicles thereafter was first introduced in the 1950s and is shown here as fitted to the Ford Consul and Zephyr. As can be seen by this illustration, the top suspension location is mounted directly to the bodywork while the bottom one consists of a pair of track control arms whose position is maintained by the use of a stabilizer bar or anti-roll bar. The MacPherson strut units can either be replaced complete or strut inserts can be obtained at far lower cost. Effectively, these inserts are the shock absorbers which are screwed in to*

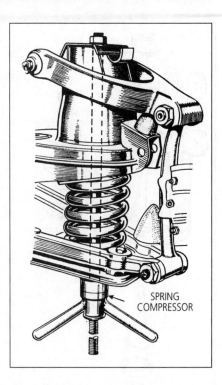

SPRING COMPRESSOR

the top of the MacPherson strut units and although you need to compress the spring and disconnect the unit, they are easier to fit and cheaper to buy than complete suspension legs because complete removal of the bottom of the strut is avoided.

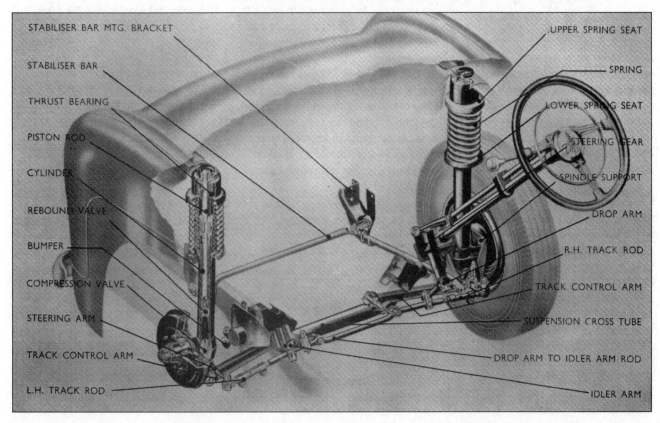

STABILISER BAR MTG. BRACKET

STABILISER BAR

THRUST BEARING

PISTON ROD

CYLINDER

REBOUND VALVE

BUMPER

COMPRESSION VALVE

STEERING ARM

TRACK CONTROL ARM

L.H. TRACK ROD

UPPER SPRING SEAT

SPRING

LOWER SPRING SEAT

STEERING GEAR

SPINDLE SUPPORT

DROP ARM

R.H. TRACK ROD

TRACK CONTROL ARM

SUSPENSION CROSS TUBE

DROP ARM TO IDLER ARM ROD

IDLER ARM

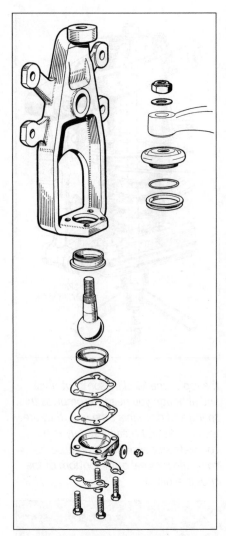

▲ *FSO8. The lower wishbone joint on many Jaguars appears to be adjustable, but in practice they do not wear in a concentric manner. If you try to adjust the joints, there is every prospect of the steering becoming stiff with dangerous consequences. Always replace with new when worn.*

▶ *FSO9. Some cars, such as the Morris Minor and Triumph Herald have kingpins which screw in to a top trunnion and swivel in their screw thread as the steering is turned. The threads wear badly – to the point where the suspension can jump apart, in fact. Very regular lubrication is essential; and replacement of both kingpin and trunnion is necessary when any looseness becomes apparent, after dismantling, degreasing and reassembling.*

DISMANTLING AND REASSEMBLING FRONT SUSPENSION

Beyond giving a long list of problems specific to individual models of car which there would clearly not be room to do here, the best advice is to contact your specialist supplier before beginning to strip down the suspension on your vehicle. In the case of vehicles fitted with the Austin A30/MG Midget type of front suspension, the specialist will undoubtedly advise you to leave the bottom wishbone connected to the kingpin and to purchase an exchange assembly. This would be extremely sound advice since the two are often inseparable without carrying out severe damage. The problem is that the fulcrum pin connecting the two is screwed into position and you are better off cutting out the potential problems and obtaining an exchange unit ready to bolt straight back on to your car. Your specialist will be able to advise whether your particular car has any similar problems and whether he has a ready solution to hand, such as that already described.

You will often have a problem with installing new rubber bushes, and it is not unknown for customers to return to their specialist suppliers and claim that they have been supplied with the wrong size! Attempting to hammer them into position rarely does any good for the simple reason that the hammer is more likely to bounce off the rubber than for the rubber to go in to its trunnion. A little lubrication *of an appropriate type* will work wonders! Do not use oil or grease because this might perish the

rubber and, similarly, it is probably best not to use hand cleaner since this could cause corrosion. I have always used Waxoyl to encourage suspension rubbers to go into place. Use a woodworker's clamp or a long nut and bolt and a pair of washers to draw the rubber into place – they will slip in much better that way than by attempting to hammer them into place – until they are far enough in to enable you to assemble whatever components have to go around them. In the case of the MGB, for instance, the top wishbone-cum-shock absorber arm is in two parts and should be split in to its two component pieces before being passed over the top suspension rubbers. Then, when the end of the wishbone arms are fully re-tightened, the rubbers will be pushed all the way into place.

Next, we'll take a look at the overhaul of the kingpin and front suspension on one of the most popular of all classic cars, the MGB.

Strictly speaking, of course, kingpins are part of the steering system, but since they form a logical part of suspension stripdown, they will be dealt with here. New kingpin bushes have to be reamered to size after being fitted to the stub axle, and so when buying a new kingpin and bushes you are strongly recommended to go for an exchange stub axle assembly with the new bushes correctly reamered to size.

Also note that it is almost universally recommended nowadays that MGB owners do not fit standard lower inner wishbone bushes but that they fit the reinforced ones as used on the MGB GT V8. Only two per side (four per car) are

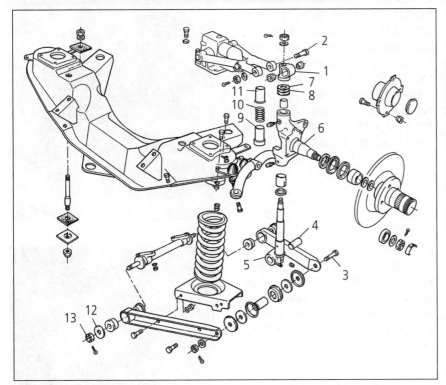

▲ DRFS3. The kingpin assembly was stripped down on the bench. The top swivel axle nut had been removed as part of the dismantling process and the top trunnion was removed after taking out the top fulcrum pin (Items 1 and 2).

needed because they are twice as long as the eight-per-car standard bushes. They provide more resistance to twisting between the shock absorber arms and the top trunnion.

Safety: Observe all the normal safety rules when working beneath a car suspended above the ground – see Appendix. Make 110 per cent sure that all the bolts and fittings are connected up – and that none is missed. Ensure that the kingpin clearance and free play are correct (see DRFS18) before trying the car on the road. DO NOT DRIVE WITH STIFF KINGPINS BECAUSE STEERING WILL BE STIFF AND UNSAFE. Have a specialist check your work before using the car on the road.

▲ DRFS1. The front suspension components (item numbers referred to hereafter in this section). Stripdown will be the reverse of the assembly procedure described in the latter parts of this section. **Take very great care when disconnecting the kingpin because of the enormous force contained within the front coil springs.** If the engine is in the car, you can place a trolley jack firmly and securely beneath the bottom trunnion and then lower the trolley jack very slowly and carefully whilst supporting the car itself on an axle stand, or you could use the Sykes-Pickavant spring clamps described later in this section. For safety's sake, we chose to use both together!

◀ DRFS2. Extracting the old bushes from the inner end of the wishbone arms can be tricky. We applied releasing fluid then used a pair of spanner sockets – one large and one small to force the bush right out of the end of the wishbone arm.

▲ DRFS4. This is the fulcrum pin and the old bushes as they came out of the trunnion. The bottom swivel bolt and bush (Items 3 and 4) often wear and the bush at least should be replaced.

▲ DRFS5. The kingpin (Item 5) slides easily out of the stub axle (Item 6).

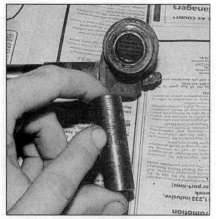

▲ DRFS6. This is an example of the wear that can take place in the swivel pin bush (item 4)...

▼ DRFS7. ... and of that which occurs in the top thrust washers (Items 7 and 8).

▶ DRFS8. The dust excluders can be extracted from the kingpin by pushing down against the force of the spring and taking all three components out together (Items 9, 10 and 11). Look after these components! Clean them up carefully, paint and grease them ready for re-use since, at the time of writing, they're not available as new items.

▶ DRFS9. The usual fate of aged bump stops! Not only does the bump stop rubber come adrift, but the aluminium packing piece corrodes heavily against the steel with which it comes into contact and the whole thing expands and buckles.

▼ DRFS10. Fortunately, MG specialists are able to supply (as with almost everything else!) new bump stops complete with top and bottom rubbers and new aluminium spacer blocks. Fit zinc-plated or even stainless steel bolts to cut down on corrosion. But **never** use stainless steel bolts in place of the correct high tensile steel load bearing bolts in the front suspension.

▲ DRFS11. The front shock absorbers were bolted down into the four large captive nut positions on top of the crossmember.

▲ DRFS12. A reversal of the previous process ensured that the new wishbone bushes were pushed fully home. **Don't** use grease – it rots rubber!

▲ DRFS13. The washer nut and split pin (Items 12 and 13) can next be fitted to the end of the wishbone pivots.

▲ DRFS14. Wishbone pans bolt between the wishbone pivots ...

▼ DRFS15. ... and the new road springs, are inserted between the wishbone pans and their housings in the crossmember.

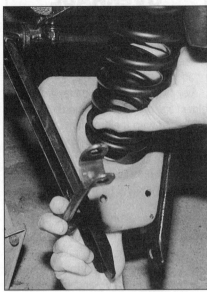

▼ DRFS16. Spring compressors ready in place, the kingpin can be re-fitted to bottom wishbones.

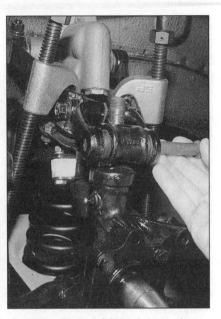

▲ DRFS17. A new fulcrum pin can be fitted (Item 2) after loosening the bolts holding the two halves of the top wishbone together, enabling them to be slipped over the bushes.

▲ DRFS18. The kingpin top nut, when tightened down to the torque recommended in the manual should also be fitted with a new split pin. Before doing so you should check that there is no more than 0.002 inches. ('Two thou') of play or up-and-down movement in the kingpin. Arrange to purchase a whole selection of thrust washers so that the right amount of play can be established. In practice, 'two thou' of play will mean that you can scarcely detect any up-and-down movement at all but – and this is important – there must be no stiffness when attempting to move the stub axle forwards and backwards through its full steering range.

▲ DRFS19. Always fit new split pins (and lock nuts, too) – this time in the bottom pivot bolt nut after, once again, tightening up to the recommended torque. The trick is to tighten up correctly and then back off the slot in the castellated nut by the smallest amount possible to expose the hole through which the split pin can be passed before being split open and bent in opposite directions on the other side. See your workshop manual for further details.

STEERING SYSTEMS OVERHAUL

Steering systems can be broken down into two broad types: those operated via a steering rack and those with one type or another of steering box.

Sloppy steering is the bane of many older cars, particularly when they are compared with their modern equivalents. Before blaming the steering rack or box, consider some of the alternative reasons for vague steering. Cross-ply tyres are far more likely to 'tramline' – to follow changes in the surface of the road – than radial-ply tyres. Most cars run far better on radials and they will corner and brake better, too. Morris Minor 1000s, for instance, ride more comfortably and are less prone to rear wheel hop when accelerating hard in a low gear up a steep incline. Discuss with members or officials of your club whether your car is likely to go with the majority on radial-ply tyres. Even more important, check that all of the tyres on your car are of the same size and type (you should never mix cross-ply and radial-ply tyres on the same car, nor steel braced and textile braced tyres). If you are not sure about the types of tyres fitted to your car – and classics can gather a motley assortment over the years – your local tyre centre will be able to advise. Tyre pressures that are too high or too low can also make a surprisingly big difference.

If your car changes direction when you accelerate or brake, then you are probably driving an early example of rear-wheel steering – one that shouldn't be there, of course!

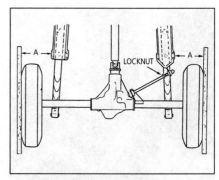

▲ STS1. Check that the rear axle is tight on the springs – look for obvious signs of movement and check mounting bolts for tightness. Check that the Panhard rod (shown above), if fitted, has not broken off its mountings. Check that the rear subframe (Minis, E-type Jaguars, for instance) is properly mounted with no corrosion, breakage or looseness in the mounting points. Check even that quarter-elliptic spring mountings have not corroded themselves into a state of terminal disconnection ('Frogeye' Sprites and Jaguar MKI/MK2 as shown above, for instance).

▼ STS2. All steering systems utilize a number of ball joints, and they are a common cause of wear and sloppy steering. And, of course, the more there are of them, the more wear will cause 'slop' to accumulate. Older cars with steering boxes often have a drag link (to transmit steering from one wheel to the other) with adjustable spring-loaded ball cups. When you have the tracking set by your local garage, these are what will be adjusted. Tracking provides the correct amount by which the wheels 'toe-in' – they very slightly both steer towards the centre of the car – during straight-ahead driving. The car's steering is stabilized (so it's worth checking!) and tyre wear is minimized.

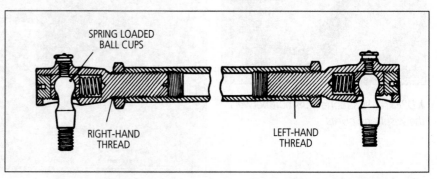

▶ *STS3. The ends of the track rods join to the steering arms via a ball joint of a non-adjustable type on the great majority of classic cars. If wear is detected, they are replaced with new ones. They fit to the steering arms through a tapered shank. The same method is also often used for other ball joints in the steering system.*

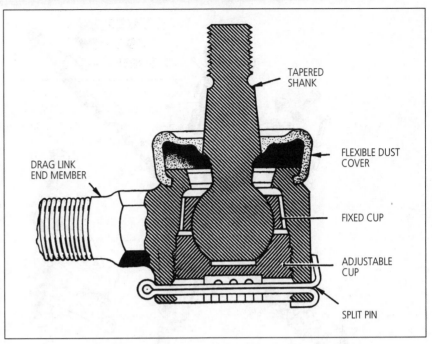

TAPERED SHANK

FLEXIBLE DUST COVER

DRAG LINK END MEMBER

FIXED CUP

ADJUSTABLE CUP

SPLIT PIN

▲ *STS4. The tapered shank system gives a very positive location but it also makes the ball joint very difficult to remove. There are ball joint removal tools available from your local motorists' store and there is the traditional way of doing the job. With the latter, you hold one hammer against one side of the eye (on the end of the steering arm, fitted over the taper) and hit the other side sharply with another hammer. This deforms the eye enough to loosen it on the taper. Theoretically! In practice, you may have to use a removal tool and a pair of hammers – and to strike the eye repeatedly until a good, sharp blow shocks the joint free. You will probably cut the rubber bellows on the ball joint as you hammer, so you will probably have to renew it even if you are just dismantling for another job. (Courtesy: The Eastwood Company)*

▼ *STS5. One fairly common type of steering box is the Marles steering gear, fitted to some of the more expensive cars such as the Aston Martin. The central roller unit can be moved closer to or further away from the spiral cam track which runs across the top of the drawing shown here. The cam can also be adjusted so that it rotates easily but without free movement. At worst, the* bearing surfaces between the cam gear and the roller break up – a terminal complaint! Don't use a box in this condition because it could possibly jam. (This is otherwise known as the hourglass or worm-and-roller steering box.) Description of how to carry out these adjustments – which will vary in detail – can be found in your workshop manual.*

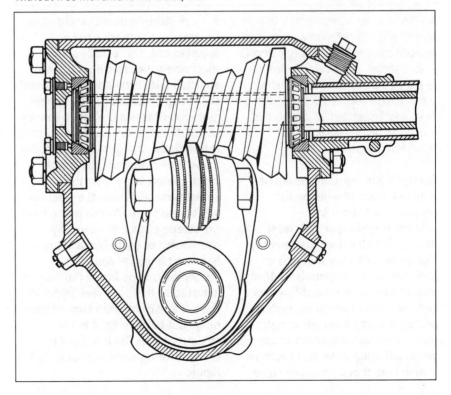

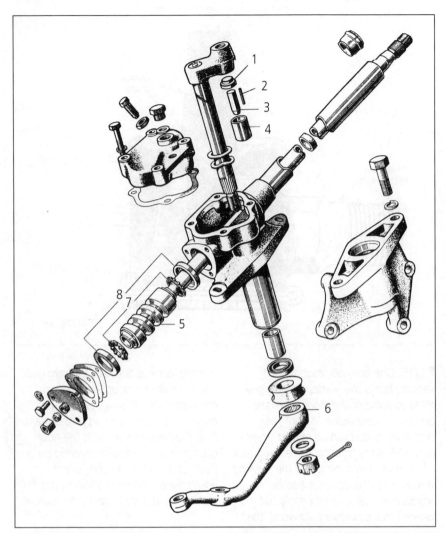

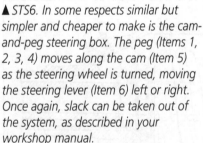

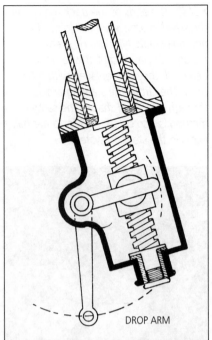

DROP ARM

▲ STS7. The worm-and-nut steering gear is one of the oldest-established and simplest systems. The adjustments available are to take up end-float in the long screw thread ('worm') by altering the thickness of shims in the end-plate and by taking end float out of the rocker shaft fitted to the 'nut'. If there is any more than slight wear between the components – after stripping the box, cleaning out and reassembling – it's time for a rebuild.

▲ STS6. In some respects similar but simpler and cheaper to make is the cam-and-peg steering box. The peg (Items 1, 2, 3, 4) moves along the cam (Item 5) as the steering wheel is turned, moving the steering lever (Item 6) left or right. Once again, slack can be taken out of the system, as described in your workshop manual.

Safety: If you are at all unsure of yourself, have all work on the steering carried out by acknowledged experts. *At least* ensure that all fixings are correctly tightened with new split pins or locknuts, where appropriate. *Always* ensure that there is no stiffness or tightness anywhere in the system and all the way from left to right lock – especially important to check when adjusting a steering gearbox.

Also note that a point will come

with all steering boxes where wear becomes too extensive to be adjusted out. This usually shows itself when the steering is correctly adjusted with little slackness around the straight-ahead position (where most wear takes place) but becomes stiff, difficult to turn and reluctant to return to the straight-ahead without a positive effort from the driver when turned away from the straight-ahead, where the steering will be less worn. At this point, have the steering box professionally overhauled or try to buy a second-hand unit in better condition. Incidentally, some boxes can be adjusted so that they feel 'right' at the left and right-hand ends of their range but become tight in the straight-ahead. The box *must* be checked for tightness across its full range.

General checks: As well as the general checks to be made on wear between components described earlier, check (where appropriate) for wear on steering shaft bearings or bushes, on the rocker shaft and its bearings, the cups and cones on the ends of the cam (STS6, Items 5, 7 and 8).

Wherever you see signs of breaking up of bearings or contact surfaces, or if the casing is cracked or broken, DON'T USE THE STEERING BOX. Broken up parts inside the box could cause steering seizure while, if the casing breaks through – more likely with an aluminium casing which could even corrode through – all steering would be lost.

How do you tell when wear in a steering box is too bad for a straightforward overhaul – new bearings

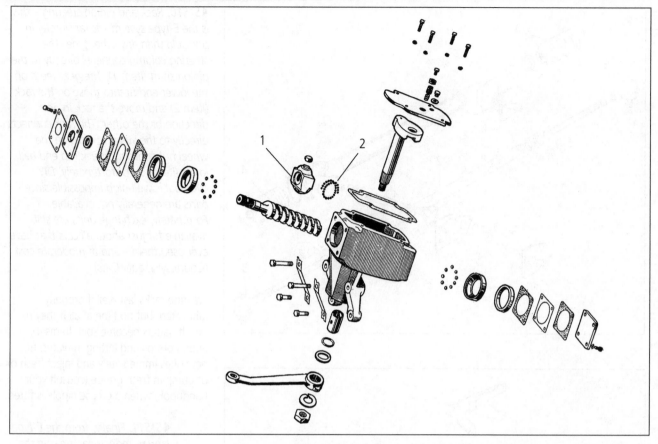

and gaskets plus adjustment – to be viable? Take the box off the car and degrease the internal components. Strip down and reassemble, if necessary. Hold the box in a vice via one of its mounting points and grasp the input shaft. Pull up and down; turn the shaft through its full range. (Also, if the box is dismantled, check the relationship between each of the internal components). If there is anything more than a very minimal amount of play with adjustments correctly taken up, the box is probably beyond repair. The rust and corrosion that forms over the years inside many steering gearboxes will have disguised the problem.

For many units, this gives a major problem since new internal components are rarely available. You will then have to look out for a second-hand unit that is good enough to overhaul.

▲ STS8. The recirculating ball steering box is a development of the worm-and-nut system. The nut (Item 1) is carried on ball bearings (Item 2) to minimize friction. Any balls or tracks that are pitted or rough should be replaced. Unfortunately, with advanced age, the worm in which the balls run is prone to breaking up. For safety's sake, the box will have to be scrapped if a new threaded worm cannot be found. Severe cases of breaking up could cause the box to seize solid.

▼ STS9. This drawing shows just how many places there are within the steering gear of a typical system for wear to take place. As well as the six ball joints, the steering box components and the mounting points, there is the steering idler (Item 1) that carries a twin version of the steering lever, or drop arm fitted to the steering box (Item 2), known as the idler arm or lever (Item 3). The bearings in the idler (when one is used) must also be checked for wear and either the slack taken up or the bearings replaced.

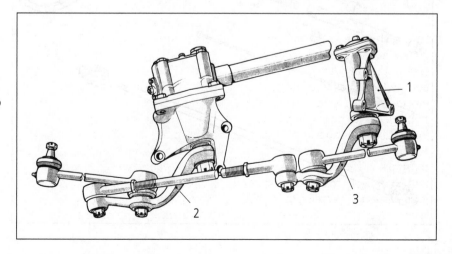

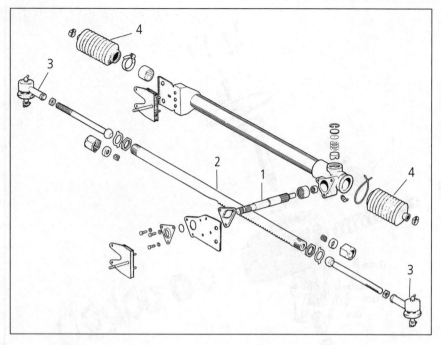

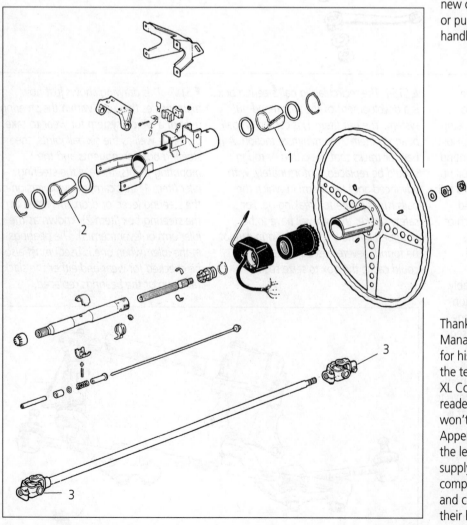

◀STS10. Rack and pinion steering – this is the E-type system – is far simpler in principle than any other type. The steering column connects directly to the pinion shaft (Item 1). The gear teeth on the lower end fit into those on the rack (Item 2) and move the rack in one direction or the other. The rack connects directly to the steering arms on the wheel hubs through track rod end ball joints (Items 3). Unfortunately, DIY overhaul is well-nigh impossible since parts are generally not available. Fortunately, exchange units are still available for just about all cars that have ever used them – and at moderate cost. (Courtesy: Jaguar Cars)

Steering racks last well if properly lubricated, but no time at all if they're not. If gaiters become split (Items 4), letting out oil and letting in water, fit new ones immediately and inject fresh oil or pump in fresh grease (consult your handbook) when a grease nipple is fitted.

◀STS11. Finally, from the E-type Jaguar, more wear areas in the steering department! When the felt bearings wear (item 1 and 2), the steering wheel will move up and down at right angles to its axis. Renew after soaking in oil for 24 hours, but beware! If the new ones are too thick, steering may be too stiff. If so, use thinner felts. If either of the universal joints are worn, (Items 3) the steering might feel loose and in extremis could fail totally. (Courtesy: Jaguar Cars)

Thanks are due to Mark Marwood, Managing Director of XL Components, for his company's kind assistance with the technical information in this section. XL Components, unfortunately for the reader, do not sell to the public, so you won't find their address in the Appendices. They are, however, one of the leading specialists in overhauling and supplying new steering and suspension components for sale to the motor trade and classic car specialist suppliers, and their help is much appreciated.

REAR SUSPENSION OVERHAUL

This section looks at the overhaul of the two main suspension systems used on classic cars: half-elliptic leaf springs, and coil springs. While there are many detail variations on the rear coil spring suspension, removal of dampers and the necessary compression of coil springs follows a similar pattern to that of the front suspension – see Section 6 for details. However, detail variations are such that you will need to refer to your manual for specific information.

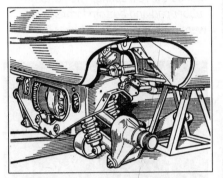

▲ *RSO1. The famous Jaguar rear suspension is mounted on a separate subframe – which need not be removed for damper/spring units to be taken off, by the way. Condition of the rubber mounting and structural strength of the bodywork around the mounting points is of paramount importance.*
(Courtesy: Jaguar Cars)

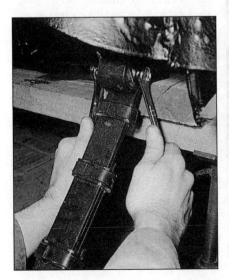

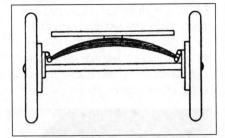

▲ *RSO2. Transverse leaf springs were fitted to cars before the First World War, to Ford Populars up to 1960 and even to some American cars – and ostensibly sports models, such as the Camaro – well after that. See Chapter 1, Section 3 for more information on changing a spring. The following sequence shows the fitting of new springs, dampers and other fittings to the highly conventional leaf spring suspension of the MGB.*

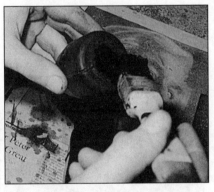

▲ *RSO3. Before fitting the bump stop to the chassis, lubricate the fitting hole with Waxoyl. Don't use grease because it causes rubber to go spongy.*

▲ *RSO4. The bump stop is a hard push on to the mushroom-shaped fitting peg inside the wheel arch.*

◀ *RSO5. A replacement spring is best fitted first at the front spring hanger.*

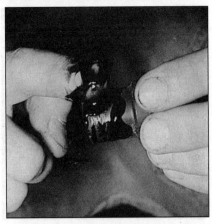

▲ *RSO6. Both front and rear spring mountings are fitted with a pair of rubber bushes, one from each side. Again, Waxoyl helps them to go in more easily.*

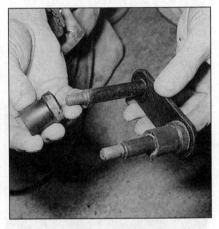

▲ *RSO7. The rear shackle pins are fitted with a pair of rubber bushes ...*

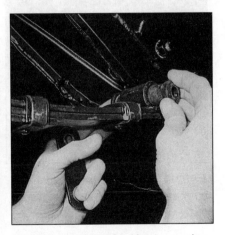

▲ *RSO8. ... and the shackle pins can be pushed through the rear chassis mounting point and the rear end of the spring with new rubber bushes fitted from inside the car.*

▼ RSO11. With the top rubber pad and top locating plate resting on top of the spring (and both springs fitted to the car!) the reconditioned axle was manhandled underneath the car and placed in position on top of the location plate.

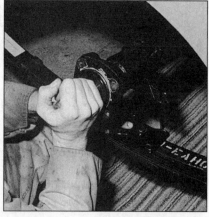

▲ RSO9. The new spring had to be jacked-up in the centre to take the weight off the springs so that Graham could carry out the fitting and concentrate on pushing the shackle pins and bushes into place. The shackle plate is next fitted over the inboard bushes – you may sometimes have to use a clamp to push it far enough on to get the spring washers and nuts started on the threads.

▼ RSO12. Bump rubber pedestals are notorious for rusting out, and for the MGB you can now purchase bright zinc-plated ones along with matching U-bolts, all of which are very resistant to future corrosion.

▲ RSO13. The bump stop pedestal and U-bolts were slipped into position through the top locater plates and around the rear spring. The bottom rubber pad and bottom locater plate were pushed on to the U-bolts ...

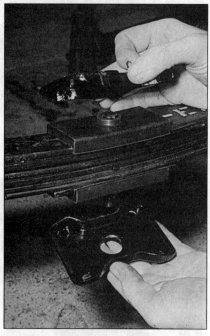

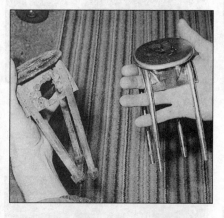

▲ RSO14. ... and the shock absorber link and plate added to the sandwich. New plain washers and lock nuts were tightened evenly, ensuring that the axle, the locater plates and the centre bolt which protrudes above and below the spring as a peg, were all seated snugly against each other. You will see that if you do so, it will be impossible to position the axle incorrectly on the spring.

▲ RSO10. New rubber pads were purchased to fit between the locating plates when the axle was fitted up.

◄ RSO15. The rear shock absorbers are simply located to the body with a pair of bolts, spring washers and nuts ...

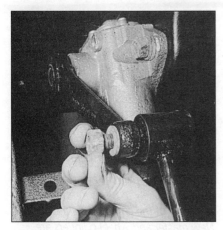

▲ *RSO16. ... and the shock absorber link described earlier is passed through the end of the arm and a plain washer, spring washer and nut fitted to secure it.*

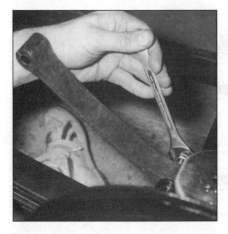

▲ *RSO17. Don't forget the rebound strap which bolts on to a special and rather flimsy mounting welded to the rear axle casing and to a bracket on the underside of the body through which a nut and bolt are passed.*

Note: When removing the old checkstrap, the nut holding it in place on the bracket on the rear axle frequently seizes solid, and the bracket itself is prone to shearing away. For that reason, if the nut is in any way difficult to remove, use a nut splitter, or saw through the outer edge of the nut so as to ensure its removal without damaging the bracket. In the past, MGB rear axles have been scrapped because of this bracket breaking off. Now, there is a repair kit which enables a replacement bracket to be clamped to the axle tube.

It must be quite obvious that correct operation and maintenance of the brakes is one of the most crucial safety aspects of your classic car. For that reason, this chapter does not seek to go into any detail relating to the braking system on your car. There must be no room for ambiguity when it comes to maintaining the brakes, and therefore you are advised to use your Haynes or manufacturer's workshop manual for information on your particular car's braking system.

Safety: Unless you are properly trained, you are strongly advised to have a qualified mechanic check over any work that you may have carried out on your braking system before using the car on the road.

It is crucially important that no dirt gets into the hydraulic side of the braking system and you must therefore work in the cleanest possible surroundings with clean hands and tools and take the greatest care not to introduce any dirt whatsoever into the system.

Normal brake fluid is hydroscopic, which means that it absorbs moisture from the air. This moisture has two effects. One is that it causes internal corrosion in master cylinder and wheel cylinders and even more dangerously, it can cause the brakes to fail when you need to carry out an emergency stop. When you apply the brakes hard, the brake fluid increases in temperature under the pressure applied: so much so that the temperature can exceed the boiling point of water. If there is a significant amount of water vapour in the brake fluid, the water vapour boils and turns to steam creating something similar to an air lock in the hydraulic pipe. If this happens, the brake pedal can go to the floor and the brakes will fail to operate. Most manufacturers now
recommend that you change the brake fluid every three years. An alternative – probably a better alternative for the owners of classic cars – is to use only silicone brake fluid. This more expensive fluid is not hydroscopic, does not absorb moisture from the air, will not cause internal corrosion and is not prone to brake failure in the way described. For cars that stand for long periods of time, brake wheel cylinders rusting and seizing then become a thing of the past.**

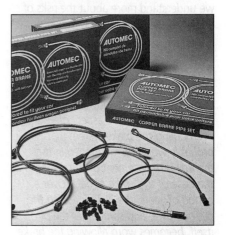

BS1. You are strongly recommended to fit copper alloy brake pipes such as these manufactured by Automec. They are ready-produced to length with the correct ends and fittings and all are labelled to show which part of the car they belong to. They are not, strictly speaking, original, but since they will never corrode out, they are much safer to use. Some cars, such as the Morris Minor with a brake pipe hidden away in one of the chassis legs, and the MG Midget with a brake pipe that crosses the front of the engine bay completely out of sight, are potentially death traps if the unseen steel brake pipes rot away.

Another tip almost certainly not to be found in the manuals but one that is crucially important from the point of view of the health of anyone working on the car is to ALWAYS use asbestos-free friction materials wherever possible. Asbestos is a cancer-inducing agent and should be avoided wherever possible. Where only asbestos friction materials are available, the greatest care should be taken when working on the braking system. Always wear an efficient particle mask, be sure to use a proprietary brand of brake spray which you can spray on to the inside of the drum and the shoes after taking off the drums to prevent dust from flying around, and dispose of old brake shoes and pads and all the dust that you will gather up safely in a sealed plastic bag.

NEVER file or sand brake shoes or pads. Old-timers suggest filing the leading edges of brake shoes, but now we understand more about the risks of asbestos, this can be highly dangerous advice!

▼ *BS2. This schematic view of a conventional drum brake system as fitted to many classic cars shows the layout of the components. One aspect of overhauling the brake system that probably won't be mentioned in the manual is replacement of the pivot pin at the base of the brake pedal.   Over a period of years, the bush in which the pin operates, and sometimes the pin itself, becomes worn allowing the brake pedal to move from side to side, and inducing some sloppiness into the pedal's movement.*

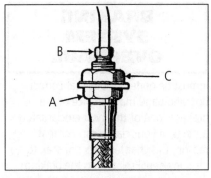

▲ *BS3. When replacing flexible brake pipes, be sure always to undo the metal brake pipe first (B) and to hold the nut on the end of the flexible pipe (A) with a spanner before undoing the nut that holds the pipe in place (C).*

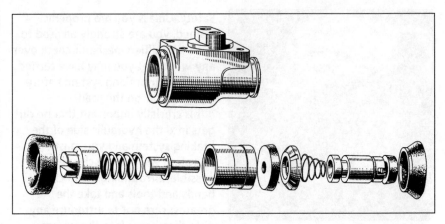

▼ *BS4. No matter what your manual might say, you are strongly advised to replace a faulty master cylinder or wheel cylinder rather than attempting to rebuild it with new rubbers. If the rubbers have worn, it is highly likely that the bores on the cylinders will also be worn, and in view of what was said earlier about the hydroscopic nature of brake fluid, they will probably be rusty as well. Rubber repair kits are available, but their life is likely to be short and the risk of failure of the components too high. New master and wheel cylinders are available for almost all the cars covered by this book. If you see any corrosion when you peel back the rubber on a wheel cylinder, replace it with new.*

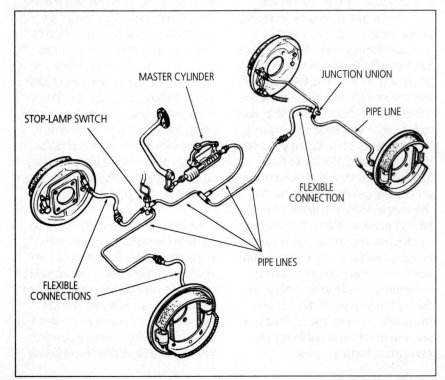

MASTER CYLINDER

JUNCTION UNION

PIPE LINE

STOP-LAMP SWITCH

FLEXIBLE CONNECTION

PIPE LINES

FLEXIBLE CONNECTIONS

▼ *BS5. A useful tip if you have to dismantle part of the braking system, and to prevent too much fluid from being lost from the system, is to first top up the master cylinder and then screw down the filler cap with a piece of plastic bag placed over the top of the master cylinder. This will partly seal the system, closing off, in effect, the air hole in the filler cap and prevent too much fluid from being wasted.*

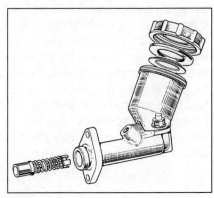

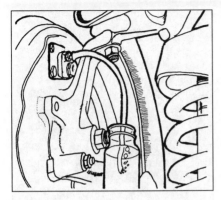

▲ BS6. Whenever you work on the hydraulic part of the system, or if you drain out the brake fluid in order to replace it with silicone, you will need to bleed it of air. Any air trapped in the system will cause the brake pedal to at least feel spongy, and could cause total brake failure, so this part of the work needs to be done with great care. Start by making sure that the master cylinder is full of fluid and is replenished regularly as air is bled from the system and fluid

pumped through it. If the master cylinder has a bleeder screw, slacken it and depress the brake pedal slowly by hand. Continue to do so until fluid comes out of the bleeder screw free from air bubbles. Then, whilst the next stroke is continuing, and before the pedal reaches the end of its stroke, tighten the bleeder screw securely. As in all brake bleeding, a tube fitted to the bleeder screw and outletting in a jar beneath the level of more brake fluid will prevent air from being drawn back in to the system. You will invariably have to carry out this operation with an assistant, although it is possible to purchase a 'one-man' (or woman!) brake bleeding kit which is fitted to each bleeding screw in turn and prevents any air from getting back in to the system.

You then continue around the four wheels of the car, bleeding the braking system at each wheel in turn. Start with the one furthest away from the master cylinder and then do the one on the

opposite side of the car and then turn your attention to the front wheel furthest away from the master cylinder and finally the one nearest to it. You may find that you have to carry out the job several times before the brake pedal responds with a feeling of solidity. But do take note that if you have also just fitted new brake shoes, there may be some 'phantom' springiness in the system that will go away once the brake shoes have bedded in. Only an experienced and trained mechanic can be sure to tell the difference, and it is for this sort of reason that your work should always be checked.

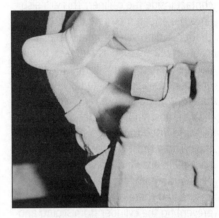

▲ BS7. Flexible brake pipes are best checked by grasping them and bending them double. Any signs of cracking will then become apparent and a pipe that is cracked, perished or chafed where it has rubbed against any part of the car should be replaced.

◀ BS8. When replacing the brake shoes, bear in mind the following points: With an older car you may well have to replace the brake adjuster. The adjuster key frequently is rounded off and the mechanism becomes seized internally. Adjusters are frequently riveted to the back plate, so file or grind the rivet heads off and fit a new one using suitable countersunk head bolts, ensuring that they do not foul the brake mechanism in any way, and fit lock nuts to prevent their coming loose. Always use a properly made tool rather than an adjustable spanner for adjusting brake adjusters and lubricate them internally with a copper impregnated lubricant. That way they will last for far longer.

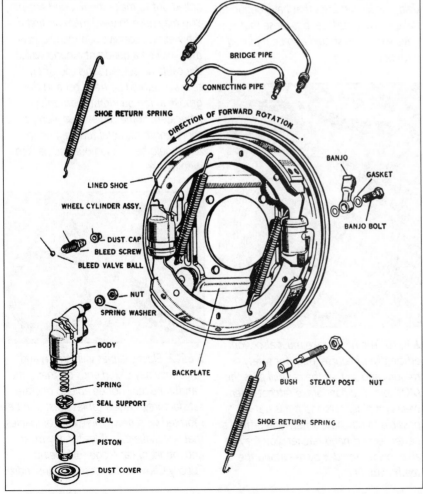

When you are buying parts for your brakes or you are at an autojumble, you would be well advised to obtain some spare brake return springs, bleed nipples and brake shoe steady bolts or clips. These can become broken, internally clogged or lost, in turn and prevent you from carrying out the work you intend to do. You are almost sure to use them sooner or later!

Use brake grease or copper impregnated grease *sparingly* on all metal-to-metal contacts, such as where the brake shoes rub on the back plate or on the back of a brake pad where it has contact inside the calliper. This will also have the effect of cutting down on chatter and noise. Automatic adjusters, as fitted to cars such as Jaguars, should also be treated sparingly with the same grease because otherwise they will be rather prone to seizure.

With most single cylinder brakes, such as those fitted to the rear of most cars, the cylinder must be free to slide on the back plate allowing the brake shoes to be centralized when they are operated. Ensure that there is no corrosion present preventing the cylinder from sliding and once again, use copper impregnated grease sparingly.

Do bear in mind when fitting new pads or shoes to worn but serviceable discs or drums that the new pads or shoes will have to take on the groves and contours of the surface on which they will press before they will operate properly. For that reason, you have to 'bed-in' new shoes and pads for several hundred miles before the brakes will work at full efficiency. Take note of this and drive even more carefully than normal until the brakes are up to full efficiency – after all, most classic cars' brakes are not as efficient as their modern counterparts in any case.

If brake pads or shoes are found to be one-third of their original thickness or less, renew them.

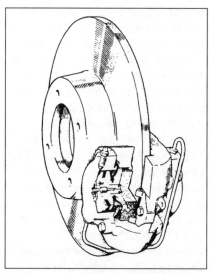

▲ BS9. When brake discs and brake drums wear, they become thin. They are then unable to dissipate the heat that they generate as efficiently as they were designed to do, which means that the brakes simply don't work as well as they should. Obviously, cracked brake drums and discs should be replaced without delay, as should discs that have begun to flake on their surface, but those that have worn thin should also be replaced with new.

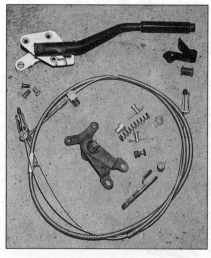

▲ BS10. The handbrake must also work efficiently, of course, both for safety reasons and so that the car will pass the MOT test. The handbrake ratchet often wears on older cars and if it is not possible to purchase a new one or find a better second-hand ratchet, you may be able to save the day by re-cutting the teeth with a file.

▲ BS11. Underneath the car at the rear, usually mounted on the rear axle if the car is rear-wheel drive, will be a brake regulator that separates the action of the handbrake cable to left and right rear wheels. The pivot pins often wear and often seize. Seized units should be freed off, cleaned and thoroughly greased – make it part of your maintenance schedule – and worn pins should be replaced after the holes have been drilled out to make them round again. You may have to weld them up first if the wear is excessive. On many cars there will be a quadrant around which the cable passes, and this too often seizes. It should be freed off and the groove in the quadrant thoroughly lubricated. Some cables pass along a short length of metal tubing, and this too should be cleaned out and packed with grease.

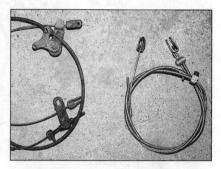

▲ BS12. Elderly cables will stretch and, since they have fixed ends on them, the handbrake may not be able to operate satisfactorily. Frayed cables must also be replaced with new. There are companies that will make up cables for any make and model of car – one such being Speedy Cables in London (see Appendix).

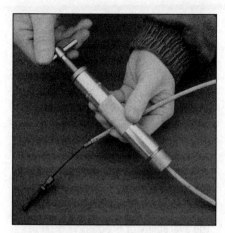

▲ *BS13. The insides of brake cables as well as throttle, choke and bonnet release cables should be lubricated, but it is usually difficult to do so. This lubricator, obtainable from Frost Auto Restoration Techniques Ltd (see Appendix), does the job of forcing lubricant all the way along the insides of the cable.*
(Courtesy: Frost Auto Restoration)

TYRES

Do you ever wonder what you would do if spares for your classic car completely dried up? Life would become pretty inconvenient and you might have to fit a 'later' dynamo, different light units and have panels and upholstery specially made. But what if the supply of tyres dried up? Then, you'd be completely stuck!

Most of us take for granted the round, black things that sit at each corner of the car. And the fact that we *do* take them for granted tells us just how good they are, and just how good supplies can be. There are even 'the right' tyres available for classics from the '60s (Cinturatos? Certainly, Sir!), right back to the pre-war days – pre-1914-18 War, that is! Which takes us back to the tyre's origins.

The humble tyre has come a long way since John Boyd Dunlop developed the first pneumatic example in 1888, tested first of all on his grandson's tricycle, and later being used on light cars and motorcycles by the end of the nineteenth century. (N.B. There is

considerable controversy about who *actually* invented the tyre. We'll stick with our story!) The pneumatic tyre was a revelation for the early motor industry, and without it the motor car might well not have developed as rapidly as it did. However, its design was not to be John Boyd's greatest challenge: that was to come later when the demands of motor manufacturers led Dunlop to continually redesign and improve upon the original pneumatic tyre in an effort to produce tyres capable of withstanding ever-increasing top speeds.

Thanks to early motor sport and attempts at the Land Speed Record, tyre design improved greatly in the early years. Without these two major incentives, the design would probably have remained basically unaltered for a long time; but with the Land Speed Record increasing from 39.24 mph in 1898 to nearly 400 mph by the time World War II broke out, the pressure was on to produce better and better tyres.

It is easy to underestimate the importance that tyre design had on the development of the car; after all, the pneumatic tyre is the ONLY major car component that didn't exist before the advent of the car itself. Think about it – it's true! And without it, the car could not conceivably have developed in the way it has.

While buying new tyres is rarely an experience to look forward to, mainly because of the consequential strain on your bank balance, it can be extra difficult for those of us who choose to drive older or classic cars. However, as we said earlier, *locating* original tyres for your car isn't too difficult nowadays, thanks to the efforts of Vintage Tyre Supplies. But still various questions need answering – such as whether your crossply tyres can be replaced with radials without any long-term adverse effects; whether a wider wheel and tyre combination will improve your classic's handling and roadholding, albeit at the expense of originality; and whether it is worth saving money by choosing retreaded tyres as opposed to brand new ones. What exactly do the numbers and letters on the side of each tyre REALLY

mean; is there any advantage in going for a well-known make rather than a cheaper alternative (should the latter be available for your particular car); and can drivers of older cars be assured of readily available tyres for many years to come, or is it worth investing in a spare set now, while stocks are still around? The list of queries stretches on....

Many tyres are still available from low-cost High Street outlets, although patterns have often changed. Assuming you are unlucky in trying to obtain tyres locally, do not despair! A quick phone call to a specialist such as Vintage Tyre Supplies (see Appendix) should work wonders and, thanks to their well organized mail order system, you can have the tyres of your choice (usually to original specification) within days.

The company was founded in 1962 by Philip Pollock and Lord Montagu of Beaulieu – even 30 years ago there was seen to be a need for a specialist supplier of tyres for old cars and for racing cars and, of course, that need is all the more intense now. The company now boasts a storage capacity for 8000 tyres, all of which are suitable for veteran, vintage and classic cars of all kinds. In fact, so vast are their stocks that Philip Pollock told us: 'We are able to supply tyres for virtually *every* vehicle that has ever been made. And if you do own a rare vehicle with a totally obsolete rim type, Vintage Tyre Supplies will advise on how to re-wheel or re-rim without detracting from the original appearance of your car's wheels and tyres.'

Most of Vintage Tyre Supplies' stocks come directly from Dunlop/SP Tyres, a company with a refreshingly positive attitude towards the old-car movement. Vintage Tyres hold the sole franchise for Dunlop's Vintage & Veteran tyre range, and any tyre sizes that are not manufactured by Dunlop, Vintage Tyres will commission to have manufactured abroad by other companies. The company's reputation is certainly spreading, with exports of tyres now reaching 27 countries.

Dunlop/SP Tyres are undoubtedly at the forefront of tyre manufacture for classic and obsolete vehicles. Many of

Dunlop's old designs have now been reintroduced and a great deal of money has been invested in expanding the range. Based on the assumption that cars will handle better and behave properly when fitted with original specification tyres rather than poorer substitutes, Dunlop aim to continue production of such tyres as a matter of course, using their racing tyre shop as the production base for the short runs required. The early Jaguar XJ-series cars are a case in point, with one of the original patterns of tyre now re-manufactured but with an up-rated, higher speed-rated casing. An instance of having your cake and eating it!

While owners of concours-potential cars will insist on fitting original tyres, what about those who use their classic every day and want tyres capable of coping with 1990s traffic conditions? There is unlikely to be any major problem should you decide to fit new radials instead of crossplies on your 1962 Hillman Minx. Indeed, the car should behave BETTER over uneven surfaces, where there is less likelihood of the radials 'tramlining' – you'll be able to drive in a straight line even if your local highways department have taken the top 'layer' off the road! Having said that, the car's suspension and steering were designed with crossply tyres in mind and should behave 'as original' if that is what you fit. The trouble is, 'original' handling is often dreadful! On the other hand, there's no doubt that a set of new crossplies (even whitewalls) will look rather nicer on a period car than radials. You pays your money and takes your choice.

It is advisable to stick to the original size of wheels and tyres in most instances (whether or not you choose crossplies), for similar reasons. While you may notice marginally improved roadholding if you do alter sizes, this will not be the case ALL the time, and your suspension and steering will have rather more to cope with, too.

If you can afford brand new tyres rather than re-treads, you are strongly advised to buy them. There's no doubt that re-treaded tyres are now a great improvement over their predecessors, but if you plan to keep your car for a while, it's worth the extra money that new tyres will cost. You'll be getting greater longevity and maximum safety thrown in with the price.

Once you've bought your new tyres, you'll want to look after them, so start by regularly checking their pressures – at least every fortnight. Over-inflated tyres will lead to a hard ride and premature wear of the centre of the tread, as well as less tyre contact on the road. Under-inflation causes excessive flexing and extra wear on the tread edges. And remember – if you're changing from crossplies to radials, the pressure required will now be different; check this out with your supplier immediately.

If you're curious to know what the profusion of numbers and letters on the side of your tyres means, it's a reasonably simple formula to work out. Take a 185/65R14 82H as an example: '185' refers to the nominal section width of the tyre, in millimetres; '65' represents the aspect ratio – the ratio of the tyre width to the section height (in this case, the distance from the bead of the tyre to the tread is 65 per cent of the tyre's width). 'R' refers to tyre construction (in this case, radial). '14' indicates the wheel diameter, in inches. '82' is the load index, a numerical code for the maximum load the tyre can carry at the speed indicated by the speed symbol (refer to manufacturers' recommendations here). 'H' is the speed symbol, another alphabetical code indicating safe maximum speed relating to the above load. In this case, 'H' means the tyre is capable of up to 130 mph at maximum load! Apply the above formula to your own

car and you'll find out most of what you need to know about your wheels and tyres – although do bear in mind that the symbols themselves were only introduced in the early '60s and that manufacturer's original data simply does not always relate to them, in the case of most classic cars.

If the manufacture and supply of tyres for classic cars is healthy at the moment, what does the future hold? According to Vintage Tyre Supplies, it's all good news! With interest in classic cars running high, the availability of previously obsolete tyres has increased dramatically in recent years ... and it looks set to stay that way. We can rest assured that we'll all be able to buy suitable tyres for our old cars almost indefinitely. Are there many other car components of which we can say the same? Probably not! In fact, were it not for the efforts of Vintage Tyre Supplies and Dunlop/SP, many of the classic and vintage cars currently on the road would either be standing still or running around on non-standard wheels and tyres. And there's not much appeal to a car sitting, static, on a set of bare wheel rims, is there?

Unfortunately, a small number of specialist tyres are not available for even the more modern cars – 'run flat' Dunlop Denovos, for instance – but Vintage Tyre Supplies can advise on replacement wheel rims for modern cars, too.

▼ T1. John Boyd Dunlop's prototype pneumatic tyre of the 1880s.

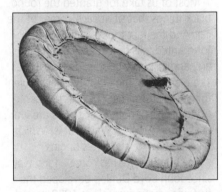

▲ T2. J.B. Dunlop's grandson tests his tricycle fitted with all-new pneumatic tyres.

▲ T3. Royal approval for Dunlop! King George's Daimler at the head of a procession during his visit to Fort Dunlop in 1933.

▼ T4. One of the original 'Cord' patterns, dating back to 1922.

▼ T5. For use with a 21" rim, the Dunlop F4 is a large diameter tyre for such pre-war cars as Lagondas, Bentleys, and so on.

▲ T6. The Dunlop SP Sport is just one of the company's old-design tyres that's still being produced – as fitted to certain E-type Jaguars.

▲ T7. A series 1 Jaguar XJ6 wheel and tyre, an SP Sport dating back to c. 1969.

▲ T8. The Dunlop Road Speed RS5, one of the Classic Car Tyres available from V&TS.

CARBURETTOR OVERHAUL

Most types of carburettors used on British cars have repair kits available for them, but before starting work ensure that the parts are available for your particular model. Any work to be carried out on a carburettor should be done in conditions of the strictest cleanliness, and you should always bear in mind that a carburettor is a precision instrument easily damaged by rough use, over-tightening or by maltreating internal components. You may be best working on a large sheet of card spread on the floor because then there is less likelihood of tiny components rolling away never to be seen again. Use an engine cleaner and a toothbrush as you dismantle the carb and if the unit is very badly corroded you could even leave it soaking for a week or so in a bath of releasing fluid – or even diesel fuel – to release stubborn and corroded threads and fixings.

Your workshop manual will be invaluable when it comes to stripping the carburettor, but service manuals are invariably written in fairly technical terms. Keep a notepad and pencil handy to make notes and sketches as the unit comes apart. You could even run a cheap film through the camera, photographing each component as you remove it. Where components can be fitted back together in more than one position, use an indelible marker pen to show where the parts should go back together again. The ink will wipe off later with a spirit wipe, whereas a scratch would be there for all time. You should also measure the position of adjustable items such as linkages and count the number of turns needed to unscrew any adjusting screws. Never dismantle anything until you understand how it works, otherwise you will be very unlikely to be able to put it back together again properly.

Nuts and bolts that remain stubborn could be heated if all else fails. Try boiling water first of all, and only as an absolutely total last resort should you turn to heat from a butane torch, but *never* a welding torch. The alloy from which the carburettor's body is made has a low melting point and you could easily destroy it. Patience will be your best ally!

Thoroughly clean the carburettor using a carburettor cleaning fluid available from your motorist store, and remove any stuck-on gasket material with a sharp knife. Before going any further you should now check all of the castings for cracks, which are most likely to be found around bolt holes, and are caused by over-tightening. If you find any, the carburettor should usually be discarded: find another second-hand unit to overhaul. Mounting flanges can also become distorted allowing an air leak, and you should check with a straight edge that they are true. If there is any distortion, it might be worth having a precision engineering shop skim off the tiniest amount necessary. You should also blow through all the tiny passageways in a carburettor with a foot pump or with compressed air – even borrowing the local garage's air line (always wear goggles), although it might politic to fill your car up with petrol at the same time!

If the spindle on the throttle or choke flap is worn you can get away with it by replacing it with a new one, but if the hole in the carburettor's body is worn you will have a bigger job on your hands unless removable spindle bearings are fitted. If they are not, you will have to get a specialist engineering shop to drill out the body and fit new steel bushes and ream them out so that the spindle turns perfectly in them.

With fixed-jet carburettors, the jets should be blown through but *never* poked through with a pin. If the jets appear to be damaged – and it's by no means uncommon for them to be drilled out in a crude attempt to overcome a flat spot or to gain more performance – replace them with new ones.

Inspect volume or air control screws for wear ridges on their points, and for the condition of their locking springs, and if the carburettor has a plunger-type of accelerator pump check that the plunger is not worn or scored and that its spring and operating rod are in good condition.

Carburettor linkages will also wear over a period of time, of course, and should be carefully examined, and replacement parts fitted where necessary. Check also for distortion through rough handling in the past.

When reassembling the carburettor, make sure that the gaskets you use are placed the correct way round so that they do not block off any important passageways. Instant gasket material should not be used because it will be prone to spreading to where it's not wanted. O-rings should be smeared with a little oil to aid seating, and all moving parts should be lightly oiled as they are put back together. If you are worried about any screws coming loose use a thread-locking compound such as Loctite. See the end of the section on engine rebuilding for how to make your own gaskets if new ones are not available.

The following sequence shows the rebuilding of a variable-jet SU carburettor as fitted to very many British cars. The photographs and information were supplied by Burlen Fuel Systems who now supply all new parts for SU carburettors and several other makes too. Contact them first for new carburettors or carburettor parts of all types (see Appendix), and in the event that they're not able to supply parts for a particular carburettor they may be able to put you in touch with someone who can.

▲ CO1. A Burlen Fuel System kit seen here alongside a dismantled SU HS4 carb.

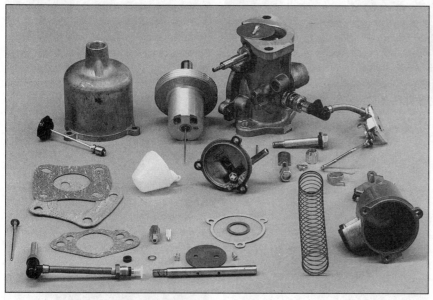

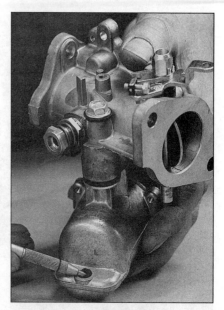

▶ CO4. Before putting the new jet in place, ensure that all of the old rubber gland is removed from the outlet at the bottom of the float chamber. It's easily overlooked!

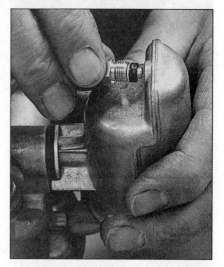

▶ CO2. When putting the HG4 back together again, don't forget to open the split screw end in order to lock the disc in place.

▶ CO3. Having replaced the throttle lever, interconnection lever tab washer and nut, and tightened them, don't forget to bend the tab washer down to lock the nut.

▶ CO5. When fitting the new jet, ensure that the gland nut, metal washer and rubber gland are in the correct order and tighten in place. It can be easy to put the nut in cross-threaded!

▶ CO6. If the carbs on your car have a wire jet linkage, push on the new retaining clip with a small socket spanner. Other flat linkages use a small self-tapping screw.

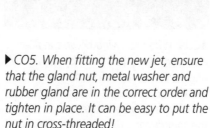

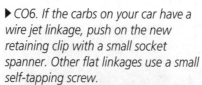

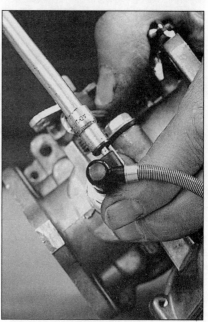

◀CO11. Take care to line up the keyway in the piston with the tag on the body and at the same time, ensure that the needle enters the jet.

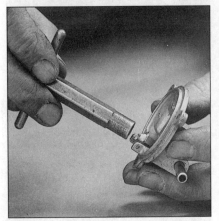

▲CO7. Ideally, the new needle valve should be fitted with the special Burlen Fuel Systems key, as shown here. However, a 'thin wall' socket spanner will do.

▲CO9. When screwing down the float chamber lid, replace the alloy tag which originally included the carburettor specification number. This is vital to enable the carburettor dealer to obtain the correct parts the next time the carb is serviced.

▲CO12. Don't forget the piston spring when reassembling the suction chamber. Then check that the piston lifts and drops smoothly. Early carbs with fixed needles may need the jet centering.

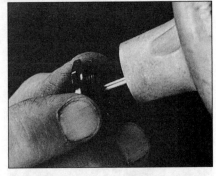

▲CO13. Finally, replace the damper in the dashpot.

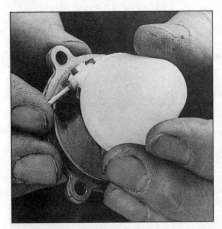

▲CO8. When refitting the float, be sure to push in the pin so that it is central.

▲CO10. Hold the needle with the base of the shoulder flush with the base of the piston, whilst tightening up the fixing screw.

▲CO14. Rather tasty: this pair of HS6 SU carbs is exactly the same as the originals from Leyland Special Tuning, and all SU carburettors are available today from Burlen Fuel Systems.

Chapter 5

Restoring interiors

INTRODUCTION

As a general rule, the outside of your classic car is what makes everybody else appreciate its appearance, but it's the inside that you, the owner, will appreciate most. At least, that is true if you use the car as it's meant to be used, and actually drive it regularly! Then, you'll see, feel, smell and be surrounded by the dashboard, steering wheel, door casings: the whole panoply of functional and decorative items that go towards making the interiors of older cars particularly special.

This chapter shows how to renovate or replace all the major trim items, whether leather or plastic, and it touches on the restoration of instruments, although that can be a bit tricky for most DIY restorers. As with other sections of the book, we cover a series of 'case studies' – sometimes on individual cars or components, more often on a group of cars or projects.

Included in this chapter is a section on headlining replacement. Some of it was photographed at the Morris Minor Centre in Bath where they actively discourage owners from attempting to fit their own. They reason that poorly fitted headlining can ruin the appearance of the car's interior. And, since it requires above-average ability to fit successfully, this might be a job that you would prefer to leave to a specialist. However, the work is certainly not beyond the careful and able home restorer – so the choice is yours.

The first Section covers that part of the car that seems to sustain most wear and damage in the shortest space of time: the seats.

SEAT REMOVAL AND RE-COVERING

FRONT SEAT REMOVAL

▼ SRR1. There can be nothing less 'high tech' than the simple, sensible way a Minor front seat is held in place, and yet it's typical, in essence, of most seat retaining systems. It's secured by a couple of steel straps which pass over the frame tubing and which are each held in place by two bolts and washers. There are actually two positions provided for these brackets. If you want to move the seat back, take out the bolts, find the alternative threads just a little way back, clean out the threads and refit the seat. Easy! But do remember to seal the original threaded holes with mastic. Unfortunately most cars don't have this simple but sensible provision.

Safety: Impact adhesive fumes can be dangerous in a confined area, and they are highly inflammable.

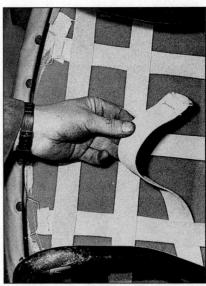

▲ SRR2. Sooner or later, most older-car owners come to know the undignified feeling of driving with their rear-end virtually on the floor, hands and feet stretching for the controls like some under-age joy rider. A piece of broken webbing is almost invariably the cause.

189

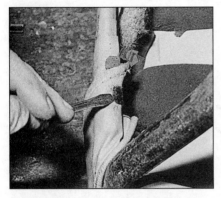

▲ SRR3. Along with broken webbing usually goes damaged seat covers. Start taking the old ones off by pushing off the clips holding the cover in position at the rear – underside of the frame. Most seat covers clip on in a similar fashion although there will be a huge range of variations, of course. For instance, if your car has reclining seats, you will have to unscrew and remove the recliner handle. Look out for trim fixing screws, too. Seat trim is rarely mysterious – a little searching will reveal all.

▲ SRR4. Once you have opened up the first access point, you will then be able to see that the front and back of the backrest cover were folded and clipped together on to the seat frame.

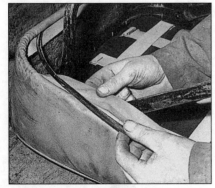

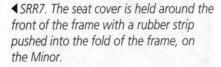

▲ SRR5. Unwrap them, then just pull the backrest cover up and off like an armless T-shirt.

▲ SRR6. Go back to the seat base and push off the clips holding the base cover in place. (Don't lose these clips!) Once again, fixing principles are often similar on different cars even if details differ.

◄ SRR7. The seat cover is held around the front of the frame with a rubber strip pushed into the fold of the frame, on the Minor.

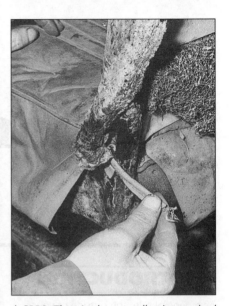

▲ SRR8. There's also a small strip attached to the frame tube, designed to pull the seat cover back nice and tight. You could tie it or glue it when refitting. Look out for individual features on your seats and make careful notes – take photographs, too – as you take the seat apart.

▲ SRR9. Quite often, the seat foam has been cut by the webbing. If the cutting action has been severe, it can go right through, necessitating renewal of the foam. It can be purchased through mail order suppliers, such as Woolies or through a local trimmer who may be able to cut it to shape and size. For the most popular classics, new replacements are usually available.

▲ SRR10. Now's the time to fit new webbing if necessary. The way it fits is self-explanatory when you examine it. Refit the foam and pull on new covers in the reverse of the order shown in the previous pictures. Of course, if your car has wire springing, this will be one job you won't have to worry about!

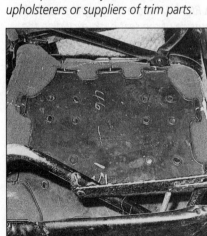

▲ SRR11. New foam, wadding, covers and webbing – in fact every part of the seat – is available as a replacement item for the Minor including single-colour and duo-tone styles of cover.

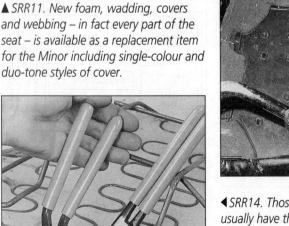

▼ SRR12. Later seats are held by clips all around the base instead of the rubber strip shown in SRR7 ...

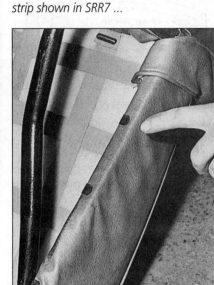

▼ SRR13. ... while the very latest seats had a one-piece rubber membrane, as shown here, and many were recliners, making them very much more comfortable. On British Leyland cars, membranes are held on via clips. If new membranes are not available, you may be able to convert your seat bases to the webbing type. New Pirelli webbing and wire clips are readily available from upholsterers or suppliers of trim parts.

◀ SRR14. Those seats with wire springs usually have the springs held to the seat frame with remove-and-discard fixing clips. Replacement rings are available and special pliers make installation far simpler. (Courtesy: The Eastwood Company)

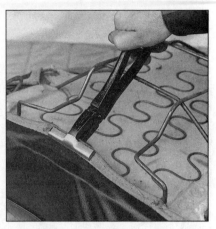

▲ SRR15. Another type of special pliers, known as stretching pliers, can be used to pull upholstery tight without damaging it. (Courtesy: The Eastwood Company)

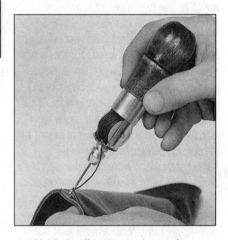

▲ SRR16. Small scale repairs can be carried out to car upholstery with this hand-operated lock-stitcher. You wouldn't exactly want to run up a set of new seat covers with this tool but it's excellent for repairs to seats, loose carpet edging, soft-tops and so on. (Courtesy: The Eastwood Company)

RE-COVERING SEATS

In 1984 and 1985, Practical Classics magazine – the magazine for classic car, DIY and restoration enthusiasts – restored their own Series I Land-Rover. Since, as you would expect, replacement seats are not available for Series I vehicles, Practical Classics carried out their own seat overhaul. The author is very grateful to Practical Classics magazine for giving permission for the use of their line drawings for this section. It shows how simple seat covers can be produced at home from scratch. You will need the use of a sewing machine capable of sewing through vinyl.

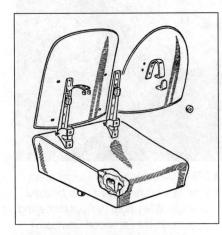

▲ RCS1. The two types of seat back fitted to Series I Land-Rovers 1948-53. 1954-58 model's seat bases had special tongues in their rear lower corners which slotted into the bodywork while the hinge brackets for the seat backs were of a slightly different construction. For a long time, new Series I seat bases were not available, owners having to resort to cutting up piece of foam to make substitutes. Now, however, through their connection with a well-established Birmingham company, by the name of Latex Cushion Ltd., Dunsfold Land-Rover can supply new, replacement seat bases, complete with the correct type of base board, for Series I Land-Rovers. Quite a breakthrough! (Courtesy: Land-Rover)

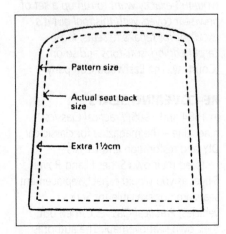

▲ RCS2. Lay seat back on to paper and draw around it – add 1.5cm all round and cut out.

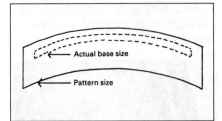

▲ RCS3. Hold the seat back vertically on to the paper, draw along the concave curve at the base of the back, extending the line 4cm beyond the sides. Draw a line parallel with this curve approximately 12cm away, then join these two lines to make the base pattern strip.

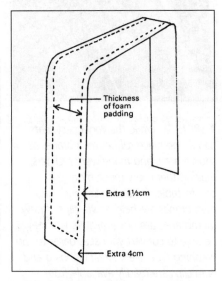

▲ RCS4. Measure the length around the outside of the seat back, excluding the base but adding 4cm either end to allow for 'neat edge' turning under. The width of this box section strip is the thickness of the foam padding, plus 1.5cm each side.

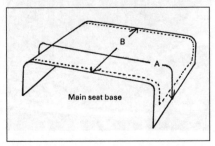

▲ RCS5. Measure the front-to-back length over the top of the seat base, adding 4cm to each end for turning under and stapling to the wooden base (dimension A). Measure the width of the seat, adding 1.5cm for sewing seams.

▼ RCS6. Hold the seat base on its side and draw round, adding 1.5cm to the top and sides for turning and 2cm at the bottom. In order to calculate the amount of material required, lay all the pattern pieces onto a table, or mark an area on the floor the same width as the fabric to be purchased (usually 150cm). Do not forget to include two seat backs and two seat base sides for each seat.

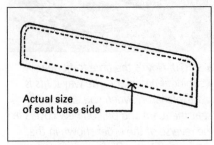

▼ RCS7. Make sure that all pattern pieces are parallel to the edge. Buy the correct amount of vinyl, using your rough layout as a guide. (It is also a good idea to draw it all out to remind you later where each piece goes). Lay all the pattern pieces out on vinyl – do not pin in place; pin holes will show. Sellotape can be used if necessary, but spreading the fingers of one hand to hold the patterns is probably easiest. Cut out using sharp scissors. First, set the sewing machine to the longest stitch, and note that in the following diagrams the 'wrong' side of the vinyl is shown as the tinted areas.

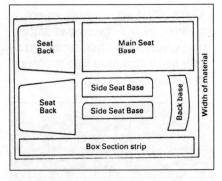

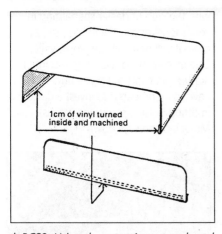

▲ RCS8. Using the extra 4cm at each end of the main seat base and the extra 2cm on the bottom of each side seat base, turn each up 1cm and machine down on to the 'wrong' side of the vinyl in order to neaten these edges.

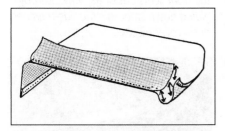

▲ RCS9. The two side seat bases are sewn to the main seat base, beginning with one or other as follows: Find the middle points of both pieces A & B (see next diagram) and paperclip or sellotape these points together ('right' sides of vinyl together).

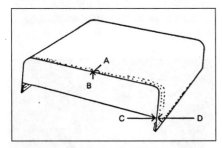

▲ RCS10. Continue to paperclip or pin both pieces together until points C and D are matched, with a small part of the main seat base extending beyond these points. (If pinning, make sure that the pins are inside the seam allowance of 1.5cm, so that they do not make holes that will be permanently visible in the vinyl).

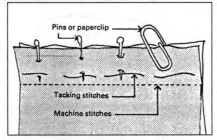

▲ RCS11. Tack, using large running stitches, inside the seam allowance, so that no marks will show and then machine 1.5cm from the edge. Repeat with the other seat side section.

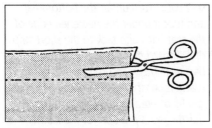

▲ RCS12. Once sewn, trim the seams down to about 7mm ...

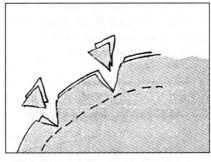

▲ RCS13. ... and cut 'V' shapes in the curved edges near to the stitching to avoid lumpy seams and pulling. Turn the seat cover 'right' side out, fold the excess seams (now underneath) towards the main seat base piece.

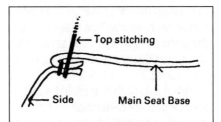

▲ RCS14. Stitch from the 'right' side close to the edge, stitching through all layers of seam. This is called 'top stitching' and is for strength as well as for decoration.

▼ RCS15. Place the seat cover over the foam-covered seat base and mark out the position of the wooden slats which protrude. Cut the vinyl 1cm smaller than the size of the slat to allow for turning under.

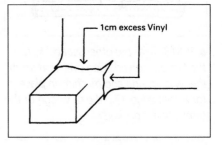

▼ RCS16. Cut into corner D, turn raw edges under and machine in place.

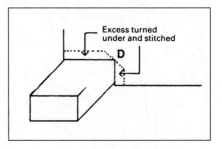

▼ RCS17. Sew the base section to the forward facing seat back along the curved bottom edge, keeping 'right' sides together. To help the curvature, cut towards seam stitching every 3cm. The base section should extend beyond the edges of the seat back.

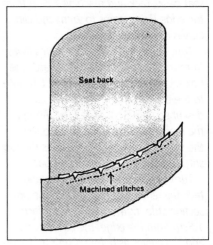

193

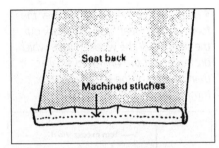

▲ RCS18. Take the other seat back, turn the bottom curved edge over 1cm on to the 'wrong' side and machine in place for a neat edge. Clip the raw edge of the turnback if it puckers.

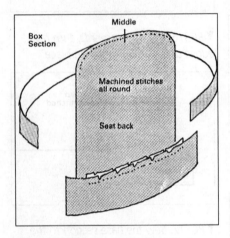

▲ RCS19. Find the middle of both the top of the seat backs and the box section strip and mark these points. Place 'right' sides together and, starting at the centre just marked, place the strip around the outside raw edge of the first seat back. Tack and machine 1.5cm from the edge. Trim seams to 7mm and clip curves as before.

Turn 'right' side out, push seams away from the seat back material towards the box section side strip, and top stitch close to the edge from the 'right' side as described in RCS14. Note that, though the main seat base is top stitched, it is the side box section which carries the top stitching in the case of the seat back.

Turn the work inside out again and tack the remaining seat back to the box section strip 'right' sides facing. Machine 1.5cm from the edge, then trim seams and clip curves as before. Don't try to top stitch; with the whole seat back cover turned correct side out, the envelope thus formed renders this impossible, except by laborious hand stitching.

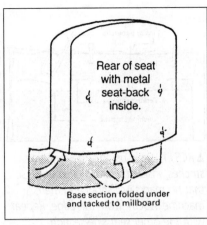

▲ RCS20. Place cover over the padded seat back. Turn under the bottom flap and tuck it under the neatened edge of the seat back and tack to the short strip of millboard rivetted to the metal backrest. This is secured by the metal brackets. At this stage the seat cushions can be offered up for a first fitting. From this the exact position for the leather straps, which secure to seat bases, can be established. At the same time the position for the rubber stops on the seat backs can be determined. The seats will then have to be removed for the fitting of the leather straps and the rubber stops. The seats are then ready for final fitting.

CARPET REPLACEMENT

Replacement carpets are available for a vast range of vehicles. The trouble is that the cheaper ones that you see advertised in Exchange & Mart are usually rubbish. Not only are the materials poor – not so important, since most were poor when the cars were new – but the fit is often dreadful! Before you buy, ask whether the section that goes over the gearbox tunnel has been machine pressed to give the correct shape or cut and sewn. If the latter, confidently expect a raised, ridged appearance.

Having said all that, it could be that poor carpets are better than no carpets – although many enthusiasts over the years have been so disgruntled by 'kits' that they have made their own from scratch.

The moral is: buy the best carpets that are available. You'll usually find them

with the club or dealer specializing in your model of car. If you have to pay more it will generally be worthwhile. One more word or warning, though: no matter what sort of kit you buy, you'll have to be prepared to invest a day or so in fitting it. Here's how the Morris Minor's carpets go down.

▲ FNC1. New carpets are installed with the front seats out of the way. Start by gluing down smoothly the side-member or sill cover pieces.

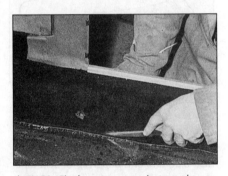

▲ FNC2. Fit the rear seat trim panel, make any necessary cut-out for the seat belt mounting, and use the back of your scissors to push the carpet neatly into the corner.

▲ FNC3. Place the gearbox tunnel piece in place after removing the gearstick gaiter. Refit the gaiter and trim, feeling through the carpet with a bradawl or nail to find the original screw holes.

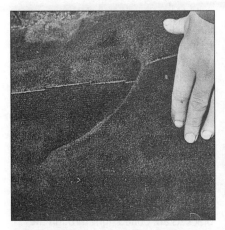

▲ FNC4. Today's carpets don't always perfectly replicate the old, so put a tuck into the carpet behind the handbrake to take account of the changing tunnel shape.

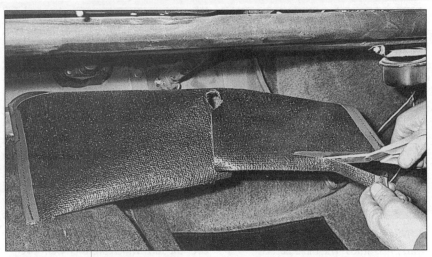

▲ FNC7. This carpet needed a shade trimming off it to make it fit properly up against the parcel shelf.

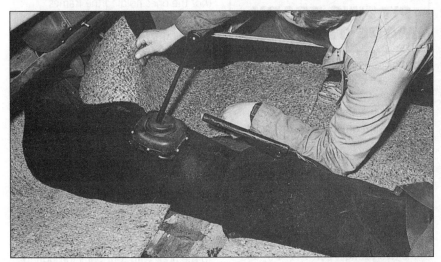

▲ FNC5. Original-type soundproofing 'underfelts' are next fitted into place ...

▲ FNC9. ... then the shape of the dipswitch was cut out of the slit one half at a time.

▲ FNC6. ... not forgetting the area beneath the rear seat.

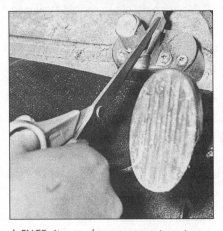

▲ FNC8. It was also necessary to cut pedal apertures and to fit the carpet around the dipswitch. A straight cut was made up to the end of the carpet in line with the middle of the switch ...

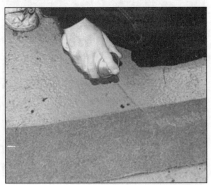

▲ FNC10. The most convenient way of applying adhesive is with an aerosol can.

▲ FNC11. Many carpets are held down with press studs. The male part is screwed down to the floor of the car with a self-tapping screw.

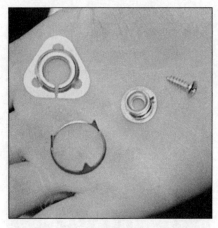

▲ FNC12. These are the components of each carpet press stud.

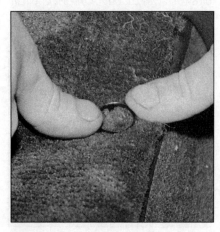

▲ FNC13. The locking ring is pushed through the carpet from above ...

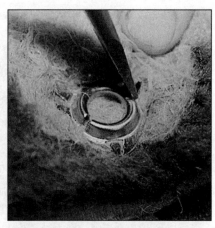

▲ FNC14. ... and the female part pushed over the tabs which are then bent over, securing it into place.

FITTING READY-MADE TRIM KITS

When most people think of trim, they think of seat covers, but in this section I've deliberately gone for all the stuff that surrounds the seats: the cockpit trim, for want of a better expression, whose appearance can make or break the look of the interior. I was fortunate to have the advice and assistance of Rees Brothers in Aldershot, where comprehensive pre-war car restorations co-exist with more modern classics such as MGBs and TR5s and 6s, favourite cars of the two younger partners Andy and Robin. It's a delight to see old-fashioned standards and abilities alongside a healthy, non-snobbish enthusiasm for classic cars of all sorts.

I followed the retrim of a TR6, a typical classic sports car of the era in a couple of respects. One is that the trim construction is similar to others, with lots of carpet and covered hardboard panels. The other is that just about every single part of the trim is available off the shelf – the same being true of the Triumph Spitfire and GT6 (and most models of Herald, too), MGB and MG Midget/Austin-Healey Sprite. The major difference between the trim panels currently available and those that were around when the cars were new, according to Rees Brothers' Andy, is that

today's panels are so much better made. But, then, that fits in with today's restoration trends, whereby properly restored '60s and '70s popular cars are invariably better fitted together, corrosion-proofed and better finished than they ever were when they were new.

STRIPPING OUT

The first job, in the case of the TR6, is to remove the hood and hood frame. The hood frame, or (in the case of fold-up and put-away hoods) the frame retaining brackets are bolted right through the side trim panels. Then you'll have to take out both of the seats. With each of the classics mentioned, you push the seats as far as they will go in each direction and undo the bolts holding them to the floor (*not* the ones holding the frames together; it can sometimes be confusing!). Seats that have been in place for some time will invariably be very difficult to move to the fullest extents of their travel. Start by pushing the seat right forwards – you may have to use a large hammer and a protective block of wood on the seat frame in order to move it all the way – and then, when the bolts are out, sit in the seat and push it back as far as it will go in the opposite direction. In the case of Triumphs, both the TR5 and 6 and the Spitfire/GT6 range, there is a gearbox saddle (usually housing the radio) fixed to the floor with four bolts through to captive nuts beneath on the chassis, and to the dashboard at two points at the top, and this, too, must be removed.

You can then take out the carpets, but take good care of them. Ignore your first instinct to scrap them straight away – they may turn out to supply you with one last invaluable service! In fact, all of the old trim could become your best friend, as a source of useful information, when it is time to put the new trim in place, so store all of it carefully for now, and try not to destroy its shape or its fittings. Next, you can take out all of the cockpit trim boards, working in the opposite order to the 'fitting up' procedure suggested later, and the door panels can be taken off.

On some cars, such as the early MGB,

window winder handles and door release catches are held on with cross-head screws, and their release couldn't be easier, although later MGBs have a door release latch that is held in place with a pair of plastic clips whose release can appear to be a Chinese puzzle at first sight. The two plastic clips surround the latch assembly and form part of the trim. Just push them together and the centre joint, made up of a pair of previously invisible 'hooks' in the ends of the plastic, will come apart. Ah So!

Triumphs, as was Canley's wont, are a little more complex than most MGs, but there is nothing to it. Each handle is pushed on to a square shaft and held there by a pin which passes through the back of the handle and the shaft. The pin is held from dropping out again by a round plastic disc called an escutcheon plate fitted between the handle and the trim board. You can't normally see the pin or get at it because the natural springiness of the door panel, assisted by a spring behind it, holds the escutcheon plate tight-ish up against the back of the handle. Just push the escutcheon plate and panel away from you in the vicinity of the handle and there you will see the aforementioned rear-of-handle, complete with holes, through one of which will be the pin which can be pushed or tapped out with a suitable piece of welding wire. The best way of not dropping it into that great black hole into which small but vital parts are prone to disappear is to ensure that the pin lies horizontally when you start tapping or pushing, making it less likely to fall right out. As soon as the pin appears, grab one end of it, using a pair of long-nosed pliers, and pull it out like an annoying splinter from a finger. Fold a piece of masking tape around the pin, making it less likely to go AWOL, and pop it into a plastic bag – in fact *the* plastic bag; the one you should be using for all the small odds and sods that will be taken off for re-use. If you are unfortunate enough to lose a handle retaining pin, cut yourself another one from a piece of appropriately sized welding rod. Into the bag also pop the escutcheon plate, handle and spring, lest they go missing or simply get forgotten.

The rest of the trim will probably be held in by one of the following means: There will be lots of self-tapping screws and cup washers; obvious and simple to deal with. There will be some clips, such as tonneau clips, also held in place with the same types of screws. Take very great care to hang on to the clips, and make notes and sketches – even take photographs – of what goes where. It really is all too easy to forget later! Other clips will be affixed with pop rivets, and to remove them you should drill the heads off their pop rivets, but take the very greatest of care not to slip with the drill. Some panels will be clipped into place behind metal brackets (although there is none of those on TRs, nor on the MGB) while others, and particularly those on the doors, will be held on with hidden spring clips. If ever you want to remove and re-use such trim boards, pull them away – they simply pull forwards and the clips 'spring' out of the holes which surround them – with the greatest of care. Once the trim board becomes old and damp, it weakens and the clips are prone to breaking away from the boards. An old screwdriver with a long wide blade – you know, the one at the bottom of your tool heap with the rounded smooth tip that did sterling service for your grandfather fettling steam engines but is too worn now to be of much use – slid up betwixt panel and door frame is ideal for lowering out the clips one by one without hurting the frame paint. Motto: Never throw any tool away, it'll always have a use eventually!

PREPARATION

Once the cockpit is down to bare essentials, you can do a bit of spring cleaning and prepare to fit the new trim. Unfortunately, the removal of trim all too often reveals some hidden horrors beneath, in the form of rusty inner sills or floor pans, but let's look on the bright side for now! You may well find that you have gained access to inner body panels, including the insides of the doors, that were previously a closed book. Why not carry out a bit of corrosion bashing while you can? Scrape and hoover out any loose stuff, and apply a good coat of

Waxoyl with spray or brush, mixing it with 50 per cent cheap but fresh engine oil so that it 'creeps' better. This doesn't suggest that Waxoyl by itself is no good; I swear by the stuff and regularly take it on toast for breakfast and soak my feet in it after a hard day at the office! I even apply it to every car I own. It does, however, suggest that it can be helped to insinuate itself into seams and rust.

You will have had to remove the seat belts in order to take out the trim, and now is a good time to take a look at them and decide whether they need replacing. Seat belt fabric does weaken with age and in the interests of safety, it might be time that they are replaced. You may also wish to consider changing to inertia reel seat belts for the added convenience and the extra safety they confer. Some cars will require an extra reinforced mounting point before this can be done, and Andy at Rees Brothers can recommend a way of converting TR5s and early TR6s to late TR6 seat-belt spec., and both he and I strongly recommend that the job is done professionally for safety's sake.

With all of the trim out, you can also take a look at a Triumph TR's transmission tunnel. The moulded cardboard from which they were originally made – what a totally unsuitable material to choose! – disintegrates totally where it goes over the gearbox, and the separate, rearmost piece behind the handbrake collapses because people will insist on putting their feet upon it. What a place to stand: on the floor! The front piece of nonsense is replaced by a GRP section, which requires slightly trimming down and drilling accurately so that it fits snugly when screwed down to the original captive nuts, and it also requires the transfer of two special little brackets and clips at the engine end that support the front end of the original 'mushboard' knee panels either side of the transmission tunnel.

Before you start work with the new trim, ensure that you have all the materials to hand that you will need. Note that, in the case of the TR at least, door trim boards come without new fixing clips, self-tapping screws and cup washers, while adhesive and underfelt are never supplied. You may also wish to purchase a tin of silicone masonry sealer from your local hardware store, and a sheet of clear plastic sufficient to cover both door trims. The mystery will be revealed. It seems crazy to me that we allow hardboard door trims to fall apart. Water is bound to get into any door, no matter how good the window seals, so why don't we do something about it? My wife and I both have modern everyday cars, and both of them have a sheet of plastic glued to the inside of the door frame, behind the door moulding. Why don't we fit the same when restoring classic cars? The fixing clips just push right through. Then, if you want a belt and braces approach, you can liberally paint silicone fluid over the back of the board, completely and effectively sealing the board against damp – I know because I've tried it.

FITTING UP

I make no apologies for having spent longer on preparation than on fitting up. Most successfully carried out tasks *are* nine-tenths preparation. C'est la vie!

One part of the trim that deteriorates through the harsh effects of heat and light, rather than through wear and tear, is the dash top. Andy had got hold of a replacement padded top from Moss Europe, while for the MGB, the same company do a padded dash top rail and a separate roll of dash top trim that has to be glued down. Andy took me over to another TR that Rees Brothers were working on, one with the screen removed, to show that the dash top is positioned by aligning it to the three holes which hold down the screen and the plates holding the tonneau clips. Then it's a matter of replacing and re-aligning the screen and getting on with the rest of the trim.

The wheel arch cover is in vinyl, but if it was glued straight down, imperfections in the shape of the pressed steel panel beneath would show through. Andy strongly recommends the use of foam, glued down first, to give a richer feel to

the job and to make the finish smooth and attractive. You have to buy the foam separately; it doesn't come with the kit, although perhaps it should.

Next, the new carpets can go in place, starting with the incredibly fiddly small pieces that go around the front end of the gearbox tunnel. One of them *should* have the reversing light and overdrive wires going through it and, although Andy insists on doing the job properly, it would be considerably easier to make a short cut, about two inches into the carpet – it can't be seen under the bulkhead – and slot the wires into the cut. Some of the carpet has to be glued down and Rees Brothers use spray-on adhesive (one of the new 'non-glue-sniffing' variety) bought from the local motor factors, which works splendidly without the dangers of the traditional stuff. The inner sill trim – carpet on the TR – is glued right down to the sill, not forgetting to cut out holes for the rear seat belt mounts.

The footwell side boards, as with most classic sports cars, are held in place with chrome plated self-tapping screws and Andy points out that the rear edge of the board must always be positioned, not against the edge of the A-post, as you might expect, but about half an inch back, so that you have room to push on the door seal. Also, Andy recommends buying enough foam for the bulge over the diff. while he used underfelt beneath the rear 'parcel shelf' carpet. Incidentally, any excess glue can easily be removed with white spirit but *don't* use cellulose thinners because of the risk of melting or marking your nice new trim.

There will be several fixing screw holes to find, and three seat belt mounting point holes to position on each side. The easiest way of finding any of them is to push something like an electrical screwdriver through the carpet or trim, from the other side of the panel. For cutting a neat, round hole in carpet or trim, Rees Brothers use one of a set of hollow round punches with a sharpened edge. You really couldn't begin to justify the expense of such tools for home working, so you will either have to

carefully cut with a sharp craft knife, or you could make your own punch from a piece of tubular steel. If you get hold of a piece of stainless steel tube from your local plumber, so much the better, because stainless is harder than mild steel and far harder than copper. You could then grind an edge all the way round the outside of one end of the tube and use it as a relatively short-lived but effective punch. Place the carpet or board on to a block of wood when punching through, and Andy recommends – a good idea, this! – that you should only punch down on to end grain. The punch will go into the end grain like a dart into the bristles of a dart board, protecting the edge on the punch and avoiding dicing the block into shreds. It's also worth offering the new boards up to the old – which you didn't throw away, did you? – to be 100 per cent sure which holes are used on your car. Not all the holes provided in the backing boards of the trim panels are used, so BEWARE – measure it twice and cut it once, as the saying goes.

Door window seals, which can be fitted with the door glass still in place on the TR6, come in a variety of types. Simplest to fit is the pop-rivet-on type; most difficult are the 'impossible' spring clips, which seem to require foot-long fingers to be pushed on to the door panel, and then the seals have to be pushed on to the clips. There are two different types of clip for the TR6 – one for the outer rubber seal and the other for the inner felt seal – but both fit the same way. An easy-to-make but invaluable service tool is the easy way to fit them. Take a strip of metal about 7 in long by 1 in wide, and roll one end of it around the shank of a ¼ in drill to form the letter 'J' shape. Balance a clip in the cup of the tool, lower it through the door top aperture and lift it up on to the lip edge. A little bit of experimentation will arrive at the best tool shape. Door seals have to be pushed under the end clips on the A-posts, pushed well around the door opening and then trimmed off *slightly too long at the top of the B-post*. The trim end clip, removed earlier, has to be placed over the end, concealing the end of the trim. But if the trim's too short.... Better by far to leave it long and have to take a little more off later.

The earlier type of door pull handle fitted to TRs was moulded into the foam door top trim. Of course, it breaks easily and, being moulded, could never be replaced by 'knife and fork' methods. Rees Bros. obtain theirs from Moss: a perfect case of a trim part that is so very easy to DIY fit but which actually couldn't be made by hand, no matter how high the level of skill.

The edges of the door top trim actually tuck under the felt inner window seal and under the door panel, so if they're going to be renewed, they must be done *before* these two jobs. They are glued on.

The quarter panel trim boards go on next, and they are cut out in such a way that they will follow the curvature at the rear corners of the cockpit, although the vinyl covering does crease in a rather disappointing fashion. The TR's fuel tank cover board is a tight fit and has to be pushed down hard on to the rear carpet, in such a way that the carpet remains flat and doesn't ruck, while the top edge of the board must be at the level of the rear decking; too high and the hood frame won't sit flat. This piece is the last section of board to fit in to the jigsaw puzzle, and covers up all the loose edges and flaps of trim that still remain on show – and then the job is done!

In the good old days, of course, it wasn't possible to buy 'off the peg' trim parts to allow you to do work such as this at home. In the good old days, replacement trim would usually have to be a close, often much simpler approximation of what the original looked like. Nowadays, retrimming one of the more popular classic cars is one of the more suitable jobs for a beginner (admittedly one with plenty of time to spare) to have a go at. For my money you can keep 'the good old days'.

▲ TK1. It's tricky to remove the pin holding the door handles in place on this TR6, although you could improvize with a couple of screwdrivers, a thick welding rod, long-nosed pliers and an extra pair of hands!

▲ TK2. One of the delights of restoring the more popular cars such as the TR series is that complete trim items such as this door trim panel are available. All that remains is to fit the clips to the rear of the panel and then pop it home. You would not be able to replicate the correct heat-formed patterns in the trim panel on a one-off basis.

▲ TK3. Door seals are not usually supplied as part of any kit, but you will need to buy new ones in order to finish the job off properly. They are remarkably expensive for what they are!

▲ TK4. If an original fibreboard transmission tunnel is complete and usable, you're very lucky! Fibreglass replacements are available for many sportscars so fitted

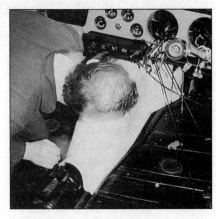

▲ TK5. This TR is being fitted with a new fibreglass gearbox cover. Alas, as so often happens with panels of this sort, the fit is not all it might be, and some cutting and shutting may be necessary.

▲ TK6. Here is another item that it would be impossible to produce as a one-off. Fortunately, new high-quality dash-tops are available for these cars.

▶ TK7. It is crucial when fitting this item that mounting holes and screen vent slots are aligned perfectly, as it is glued in place.

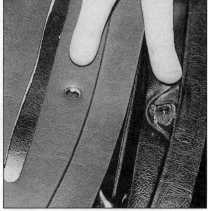

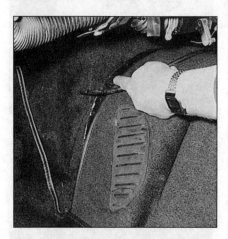

▲ TK8. These carpets are excellent! They are vacuum-formed, and fit the complex tunnel shape perfectly. Always check carefully to see if you have to make extra cut-outs, as in this case, for things like overdrive wiring or control cables. Important: *don't work in the depths of the footwell surrounded by a fug of adhesive fumes. It could be very dangerous! When applying adhesive in this area, work out of doors with hood down (if a sportscar) and all the doors open. Come up for fresh air every minute or two.*

MAKING A DOOR CASING FROM SCRATCH

In most respects the owners of modern classics thank their lucky stars that spares are easier to obtain than for many more modern 'ordinary' cars. But when it comes to classic car trim, the boot is on the other foot! Trim is always the first item in the stores to go 'NLA' (no longer available): dreaded words indeed! The only hope is that there is sufficient interest to make it worthwhile for specialists to commission production runs. But even if they don't, owners have the consolation that trim for older cars is far, far easier to replicate for both amateur and professional alike.

From the 'sixties onward manufacturers have commonly used heat-formed and welded plastic trim panels, and some of the shapes and special effects cannot be exactly reproduced by any other means. This problem will become increasingly acute with the passage of time, and the major factor in determining the value of what are today still quite modern cars might not be the condition of the bodywork but the condition of the irreplaceable interior trim. In this respect, the most popular classics such as Triumph Spitfire and Herald, MGB, Midget, VWs and most American classics are in an enviable position because the numbers of cars around makes trim production cost-effective.

Leaving out for the moment some of the complexities, it would be useful to go through the business of re-trimming a fairly straightforward door trim, such as that on the E-type Jaguar.

There are usually two sorts of damage to door trim, and one frequently precedes the other. Quite often damp gets inside the door because of a failed or missing door glass seal and then, either the plastic seal fitted to the door in order to protect the trim panel has been taken off and not replaced by someone repairing the door mechanism, or the car is from an age before such plastic sealing sheets were fitted. First, the door trim panel itself starts to warp and, quite apart from looking unsightly, it often bows the panel to the point where the window winder mechanism catches on the trim and scuffs the coloured covering from the vinyl or rexine, or whatever material has been used. More severe damage happens at the bottom of the panel, where the backing board and the covering sheet can rot away. If you're lucky the backing board may have rotted but not the covering trim, in which case it may be possible to peel it off and re-use it. However, since elderly trim is certain to be somewhat brittle and prone to tearing, you will have to take extreme care! If the trim is on a later car, you may have to be equally careful to peel off the seams welded through to the backing panel without ripping or stretching the trim. Remember to hang on to as many of the fixing clips as possible, or use the old clips as a pattern.

BACKING PANELS

Most modern cars use a type of compressed card called millboard, and it is sometimes possible to buy pre-cut sheets of millboard ready to take the trim covering, although this is only true of the more common classics. The next most common material, found on more up-market cars, is bitumen board. This is stiffer and less easy to work with than millboard, but it is a little more resistant to damp attack. Both of these materials are available from specialist suppliers, but a more suitable material would be 4mm hardboard, especially if it is the 'exterior grade' type which resists water quite well. You may be able to get hold of it from a chandler's (marine supplier), but if not use ordinary hardboard. I have made hardboard highly water resistant by giving it several coats of silicon fluid, designed for keeping the damp out of house walls, followed by a couple of coats of aluminium paint.

If you can't get hold of pre-cut boards, you can make your own without too much trouble. Place the old backing panel on to the sheet of new material and use it as a template to mark out the dimensions of the new panel. If the bottom of the panel has completely rotted away take a look at the clip holes, measure the amount by which the panel overhangs them on the sides and top of the panel and apply the same logic to the lower part of the panel. I said that you should use the old panel to mark out the dimensions of the new panel rather than draw around the old panel because if you do that, any inaccuracies or bowing will merely be replicated on to the new.

Millboard and bitumen board should be cut with a really sharp knife. Plywood and hardboard, on the other hand, are best cut with a power jigsaw or, since a jigsaw can be difficult to keep in a straight line, you may wish to use a tenon or panel saw for the straight bits. Smooth all the edges and the points of corners with a file and sandpaper. Holes in the panel can be cut with a craft knife, or be drilled and filed, whichever is appropriate to the material, and don't forget the holes around the edge of the panel which accept the retaining clips.

COVERING THE PANEL

Some door trims have upholstery material stuck straight on to the backing panel, but far more common is to cover first with a piece of thin felt (or 'wadding') which gives the panel a pleasant, plump feel to it and prevents the outlines of holes and clips showing or being felt through the trim. Use an adhesive such as Dunlop 1358 or Dunlop 758 which is heat resistant and can also be used for sticking underbonnet soundproofing in place. Neither of them melt foam or plastic, so they are quite versatile impact adhesives. It may be difficult to buy one of these adhesives other than through a professional upholsterer or through a specialist supplier. If you're sure that you're not going to be applying the adhesive to a plastic material, you could use any of the popular impact adhesives, but I would recommend one like 'Thixofix' which does not hold the two surfaces immovably in place right away, but gives you some 'shuffling time' before fully setting. For that reason it is not suitable as the sole means of gluing the outer trim to the panel, as it will allow any tension you may have put into the trim material to relax.

Impact adhesives are applied in a thin smear to both surfaces to be joined and then, when the surfaces are tacky, pressed together. You should stick felt down to the backing panel after spreading adhesive on to the panel only; felt is so absorbent that the adhesive will just soak in. Don't put adhesive around the trim clip holes because you have to be able to adjust the positions of the clips later. The felt will have been cut out a couple of inches oversize before being glued down, and it can now be trimmed to the size of the backing panel with scissors. Next comes the only demanding job in the whole operation. The trim material has to be placed over the front panel, wrapped around the edges and fixed to the back without any wrinkles or folds showing.

At this stage, take a hard look at the panel to see if there are any individual features to be borne in mind. The E-type, for instance, has door panels which display part of their backs when the doors are opened, making it important to cover part of the back of each panel as carefully as the front. There is no need to glue the trim material to the felt; indeed it would stop you from tensioning the trim properly. Place the trim material face down on a clean, flat work surface and place the trim board, felt side down upon it. The vinyl will have been previously cut to about two inches larger than the size of the trim board all round. The overlapping material has to be pulled over the edge of the board and stuck down with either adhesive or staples. Glue is messy to use and doesn't allow easy readjustment, whereas staples can be inserted in small numbers initially and removed for retensioning should the need arise. The only problem is that 4mm staples are not readily available other than through specialist trim suppliers, and longer staples can easily break through the front of the panel. Staple guns can be hired from most tool hire centres or purchased fairly reasonably. If you are using hardboard, aim to staple through the textured side of the board because staples often buckle against the harder, polished surface.

There is no hard and fast rule about where to start stapling. One approach is to staple one short end of the panel first, starting in the centre and stretching just a little sideways tension in the material as you go. Then the attention is turned to the opposite side, and the same approach is followed, except that a little side-to-side tension has to be added this time, but not too much – just enough to take out any wrinkles and sags. First one side and then the other of the longer edge can next be stapled and tensioned, but the corners and any curves – the tricky bits – can be left until later. When you come to clip holes close to the edge of the panel (you can have the clips in place by now if you want to) cut a vee in the folded over piece of material to clear the clip and hole.

GOING ROUND THE BEND

There are several ways of folding, cutting and fixing material into corners. If you devise your own system, be methodical; don't just carve material away in a haphazard fashion that you cannot repeat. But, before dealing with the corners, trim the surplus material from the sides of the panel. If you allowed two inches of overlap but stapled the material down ¾ in away from the edge of the panel, the rest of the fabric can be cut away. If you have decided to glue the material down (and that is the best way if the back of the panel is visible), the most satisfactory method of dealing with the corner is to mitre the material; cut a vee in it so that the two edges meet when they are glued down. Don't take the sharp end of the vee right up to the corner but leave it a fraction of an inch short so that there is no risk of the cut-out being seen on the front face. Natural stretch in the material will take care of the fraction of an inch not included in the vee. If you are using staples, cut a vee but also leave a tag of material which can be stapled down over the top of the mitre.

All that remains is to cut out the trim material to allow winders and the like to go through. Small round holes can simply be cut out carefully with a craft knife; larger, rectangular holes can be cut with a pair of corner-to-corner incisions and the four triangular flaps that are left folded through the panel and stapled down on the other side. Window winder holes don't have to be treated quite so fussily because they will be covered up by the escutcheon plates.

OTHER FLAT TRIM PANELS

A similar approach can be employed to replace other trim panels such as those fitted to the rear sides of two-door cars, or even the simply shaped panels that fit around the sides of the rear windows on Morris Minors, for instance. If the panel is flat, exactly the same approach as that described here can be used. But if the panel is held down with self-tapping screws and the covering material is a cloth fabric, particularly of the coarser weave modern type, don't try to drill through the fabric and board with an electric drill or there will be a strong chance of a ladder pulling right across the fabric. Pierce the fabric first with an awl, and use a hand drill.

Panels with simple shapes to enable them to fit around curves in the bodywork should be very carefully stripped and their concealed secrets studied. You must use millboard for this type of panel because it can then be scored with a craft knife and bent. On the bench, press a ruler on the scored line and lift the exposed section of board against the edge of the ruler for a really sharp fold. Plywood and hardboard are obviously too stiff for this task, and bitumen board is much too brittle and would break rather than bend. You'll also need to learn how the covering material was fitted. Use the original as a template for cutting out a fresh piece of material and try to follow the same folding pattern as that originally used.

THEME VARIATIONS

It is not beyond the amateur to add piping between two contrasting sections of trim. Fit the top section of materials in place on the panel first and staple the piping down to it after first measuring its exact position and marking it with tailors' chalk and a straight edge. You can buy ready made piping in standard colours or make your own by wrapping a strip of fabric around some upholsterers' cord. Then, once the piping is held in place, the fabric to cover the lower part of the panel is placed on the top but face down and with its lower edge running level with the lower edge of the piping strip. A narrow strip of millboard is placed above the piping, sandwiching the second piece of fabric in place, and staples are shot in through the top edge of the millboard, through the piping and both pieces of fabric. When the second piece of cloth is folded down, presenting its front face, the piping is revealed showing a narrow bead between the two pieces of cloth. Staples don't always hold through so many pieces of cloth, and it may be preferable to use tacks.

But, when hammering them in, hold a steel block against the back of the panel so that the ends of the tacks are clenched and prevented from pulling out of the material and damaging it.

CARPET ON DOOR TRIMS

Door casings sometimes have carpet covering the lower part. This can be fitted using the approach shown for adding piping – except that the piping itself is left out! In other words, you place the carpet, front face down over the upper section of door panel, staple or pin it into place with a piece of millboard as reinforcement and then flap the carpet over and into position. Some carpet trim sections, such as that on the Austin Ten, are pre-stitched all the way around the edge, and then the resulting rectangle of carpet is superimposed on to the bottom of the door trim.

So much for simple door trim panels. Some panels, as on the Lotus Elan and the Chevrolet Corvette, are based upon an intricately shaped backing (GRP and moulded firm foam respectively, in these two cases). They each demand considerable skill and/or persistence, but I'm told that they can be done at home by the amateur with a heavy duty sewing machine, considerable ingenuity to work out where to cut and fold and glue (you obviously can't staple to glass fibre or foam!), and who is prepared to accept a panel with sewn seams where there was none originally? More common cars from the sixties onward have a degree of heat-forming in them that can't be replicated. If you want originality, you'll have to be prepared to search and search for secondhand panels and to re-colour them if necessary. But, as I say, we may have to be prepared to accept a degree of non-originality in our trim panels eventually.

Thanks are due to Mr Langman of Coachtrimming & Supplies of Flaxley Road, Stechford, Birmingham for his help with this section.

▲ DC1. Using the old trim panel board as a template to mark out dimensions, make a new board from thin marine-grade (i.e. non-rotting) ply or hardboard.

▲ DC6. On corners, cut away surplus material leaving clearance for clips ...

▲ DC2. Most types of clip are available, but keep to old ones just in case.

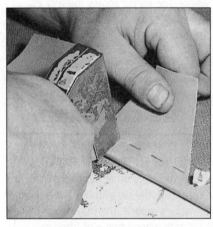

▲ DC4. Use enough overlap and just a little tension in fixing material.

▲ DC7. ... or fold surplus into a tag ...

▲ DC3. Thin felt, or wadding, gives a more luxurious feel when placed over the board beneath the finish trim material.

▲ DC5. E-type trim, partially exposed at rear. Glue down the long flap to conceal staples.

▲ DC8. ... staple and trim off excess material.

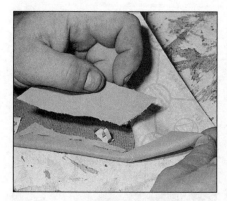

▲ DC9. Another alternative is to remove surplus and fold one flap down over the first, tucking under the raw edge of material before doing so.

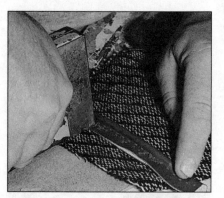

▲ DC10. Laying down your piping: fix it with just a couple of staples to hold it in place.

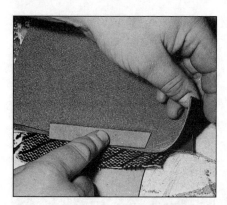

▲ DC11. Place lower section of fabric (i.e. to appear lower on the finished trim panel) upside down over piping, then staple through the fabric with a piece of millboard placed on top. The piping is here concealed from view by the 'lower' fabric (on top here!) and a small piece of millboard (upholsterer's cardboard). When the lower flap of fabric is folded down, the piping edge is revealed.

▲ DC12. When complete only the 'tubular' part of the piping remains visible. The mirror shows the way in which the rear of the panel has been finished off, as described earlier.

TRIM PANEL RE-COVERING

MAKING NEW TRIM PANELS

This is the story of an old trim panel taken from the car and used as a model to make a replica. The majority of older-cars' trim wasn't made or fitted by modern machine-intensive methods, so take the old trim apart with care, see how it's made up and make a new version of it using original covering.

▼ NTP1. Here's the old quarter-panel from the side of a rear window. The cover has been carefully stripped to be used as a model and the card is to be re-used.

▲ NTP2. After marking out the new cloth to suit the car, (referring to the old cloth as well) ...

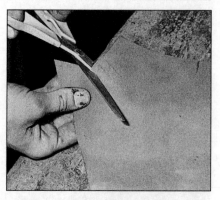

▲ NTP3. ... the new cloth is cut carefully to shape and glued to the card.

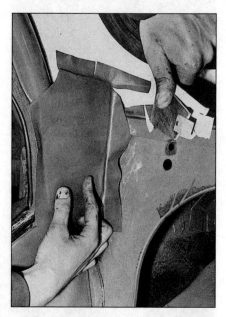

▲ NTP4. Then it's a simple matter of gluing, clipping, screwing, or folding the 'new' panel back in place as it was originally.

HEADLINING REPLACEMENT

Making a new headlining from scratch is probably beyond most home restorers, not least because you will need access to an industrial-type of sewing machine. The domestic type is simply not powerful enough to cope with the multiple layers of cloth that will have to be sewn (although I have heard of enthusiasts using the old-fashioned type of hand or treadle operated machine, but a lot must depend on the thickness of the cloth and the condition of the machine itself). It may also be beyond many restorers to make their own headlining because of the difficulty of making it fit the car without sags or wrinkles.

If you really do feel like having a go at making your own headlining you should first take down the old and examine the way in which it has been put together so that you can use the separate parts as a pattern for making your replacement.

An increasing number of classic cars have ready-made headlining replacement kits available for them through specialist suppliers, and if you can get hold of one of those kits, so much the better. And a plastic, rather than a cloth headlining, will be much easier to fit to most cars. The problem with headlining replacement is that it's not always clear how the old headlining must be removed! In general, it's not too much of a problem provided that you start by taking off any obviously screwed-on trim panels that butt up to the edges of the headlining, lights and grab handles and the like, at which point things should become a little clearer. When you start removing it, start from the lower edges which were under the side trim panels. They may be held down with a few dabs of adhesive or they could be tacked to a wooden strip running around the car on older models. The tacks themselves may be tricky to get out. Use an old wood chisel and ease beneath the fabric and underneath the head of the tack which should lift it sufficiently clear for you to be able to grab hold of the tack with pincers.

Obviously, the process will vary from car to car and you will have to carry out your own detective work to establish how the thing comes apart. But however 'hidden' fixings may look, you can rest assured that everything was once put together by hand and can just as easily be taken apart again by hand! In many cases, the headlining tucks behind the rear screen, side window and windscreen rubbers, and sometimes it fits behind finishing strips around the screens. On other occasions, it may be necessary to remove the screens completely. Either consult your manual or remove windscreen finishers and ease back the rubber to see how the headlining is fitted. If it has been glued to the screen aperture and wrapped around it, then you can be certain that the screens will have to come out. This will be far more likely with a plastic headlining than with the cloth type.

Other than in a few cases where the headlining is glued directly to the roof, or even consists of flock sprayed straight on to the roof – usually the province of sportscar hardtops or low production run cars where headroom is at a premium – the headlining is supported by steel bearers that run across the roof from side to side and tuck in behind side rails running over the doors. In a few cases, the side-to-side bearers are just held in place by the tension of the headlining, but in many the outer ends of the bearers are joined to each other by a wire which also extends down into the lower reaches of the car, front and rear, where it is pulled tight holding the bearers firmly in position and tensioning the headlining material. The fixing points for these wires are not always obvious, and you may have to grope about behind the rear seat and under the dash to find them, or consult your workshop manual where they should be clearly indicated. On some luxury cars, you will also find tapes sewn into the headlining in the rear corners so that the headlining can be pulled and tensioned smooth in that area.

One area that will almost never be featured in a workshop manual is the treatment of the metal bearers, and any other normally hidden metalwork, to prevent it from rusting in future. Cloth headlining in particular will become stained as the metalwork behind it goes rusty, so take particular care to clean it down, paint it with rust-inhibiting primer – such as a zinc-rich type from Würth – and then paint everything metal with Hammerite.

When you reinstate the headlining, your first priority will be to ensure that it is not sagged or wrinkled. If yours is a luxury car and you have never before fitted a headlining, you would be strongly advised to leave the work to a specialist, but the more straightforward vehicles such as Triumph Herald or Morris Minor should certainly be within your grasp. Note the comments in the section on how to fit a new soft-top, and if you have to use tacks, only use a few of them to start off with and don't drive them fully home so that you will be able to pull them out and reposition when (rather than if) you need to. Similarly, if the headlining is glued in place, use small dabs to start off with so that you can easily remove and re-adjust the headlining, using more adhesive later on when you are sure it is in the correct place. One extra tip: make sure that hammer heads, pincers, fingers and any other tools you use are scrupulously clean. There would be nothing more frustrating than to fit a new headlining only to irrevocably stain it even before it is in place.

If your cloth headlining has slight sags in it, remember what happens to cotton jeans when you wash them and try to apply the same principle to your headlining. No, don't put it in the washing machine: put a rubber or plastic pipe on the spout of your electric kettle and poke the tube up inside the headlining to squirt steam round the inside. This should only take a few seconds because you don't want to make the sagging headlining, soaking wet. This will not take out any wrinkles – indeed it is just as likely that it will emphasize any wrinkles that you may have left in place as the headlining shrinks – but it will help the headlining to become more taut.

The following sequence shows the replacement of a Porsche 911's headlining. There is no doubt that replacing the headlining for a 911 is a job that requires a lot of forethought and planning. It is necessary to remove all the glass, including the front and rear screens, before work can begin. If the car has a sunroof, this should also be removed.

Safety: Remember the hazards of contact adhesive and read the manufacturer's safety notes with care. Use in a well ventilated area and take a break if it causes a headache. Don't leave the adhesive lying around where curious youngsters might find it and be tempted to 'experiment' with it. Don't leave craft knives lying about with exposed blades if there are any small children around.

REMOVAL OF HEADLINING

With the glass out, remove the clips that hold the old headlining to the window recesses. Remove the interior roof fittings, making a rough sketch of where they are located relative to the door pillars, etc. Remove the door rubber surrounds.

As the old headlining is removed, note how it fits the roof, where adhesive has been used and the relative position of the sewn seams, stays, etc. If a sunroof model, note where the zip is positioned.

FITTING A NEW HEADLINING

Before starting to fit the headlining, which would be done after any paint restoration work, ensure that the inside of the car is as clean as possible and that paint dust, etc., is cleaned off the window recesses and adjacent areas. Do not allow adhesive to get on to your hands and then on to the headlining.

MODELS WITHOUT SUNROOF

Cars not fitted with a sunroof have transverse stays to tension the headlining across the centre roof section. Before the headlining is offered to the car, push the stays into the loops and place the caps on the wire ends.

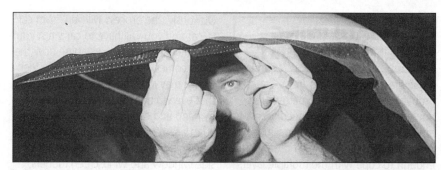

▲ HL1. Start by clipping the headlining to the door openings on each side in approximately the right location. Stretch the lining forwards to the windshield recess and place clips along the front seam to the pillars.

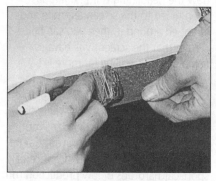

▲ HL2. Stretch the lining back to the rear window recess and similarly clip in position. Don't glue or cut yet!

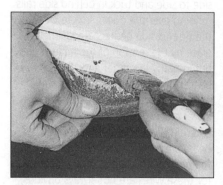

▲ HL3. Tension the lining out to each side, re-clip in place and check that the fit is good around the side windows and rear pillars down to the rear shelf. If happy with the positioning, remove the front clips and apply adhesive along the front strip. The adhesive will take a few minutes to cure, so this is a job that tests patience. Don't rush off to glue another section until the current one is completed. Use the clips to hold the lining in place at the top of the front screen recess, once glued.

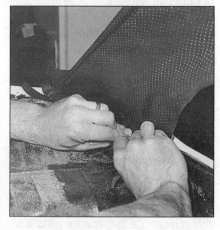

▲ HL4. Working towards the rear window, tension the lining evenly out to each side, across the rear window recess and down each quarter. This will involve removing and replacing clips until satisfied, and then applying a layer of adhesive.

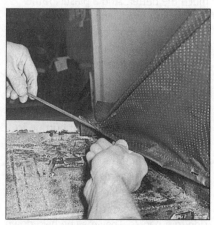

▲ HL5. At the base of each rear quarter, insert the stays into the loops in the lining and tuck the stays under the metal hooks on the shelf (to tension lining).

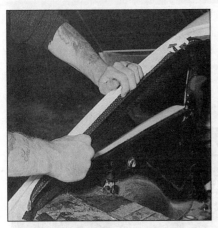

▲ HL6. The rear window recess will require gluing and clipping (so that the window moulding does not push the lining off the seam).

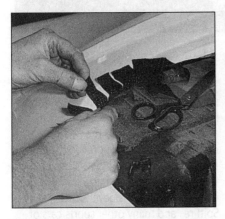

▲ HL7. Careful cutting of the lining will be necessary around the small radius of the rear side windows.

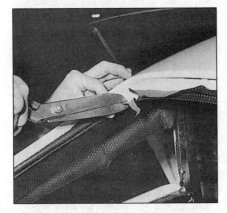

▲ HL8. When the glue has dried out, trim the excess lining off the front seams around the window recesses, taking care not to trim too much off. A craft knife is useful for this.

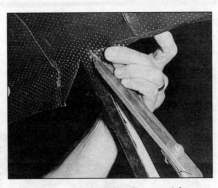

▲ HL9. Trim around the door and front screen pillars. If the pillar trim is to be replaced, this should be glued in position after the headlining. A small decorative fold back at the top of the leathercloth should be made, so as not to show the cut end of the material.

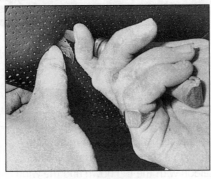

▲ HL10. With the lining in place and trimmed, use the craft knife to cut openings for the interior lights, sun visors etc. This process involved a lot of feeling around with fingers, so as to cut at the right place. Use the sketch made before removing the old headlinings as a rough guide.

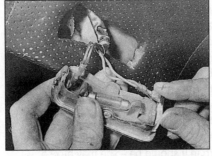

▲ HL11. With the interior lights, pull the leads through the lining and connect to the light assembly.

▲ HL12. Push into place, ensuring that the earth side is grounded onto the metal bracket in the roof.

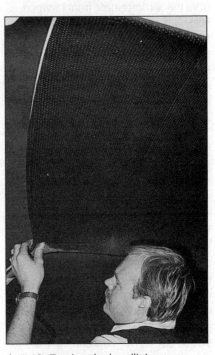

▲ HL13. Tension the headlining to remove any creases or wrinkles.

To finish off, the lining can be further tensioned by very careful use of a hair dryer, to pull in loose fabric. This technique should be used with special care as the lining can be damaged beyond repair. Don't expect large folds of material to magically tension themselves!

As was said earlier, the Morris Minor Centre in Bath does not even recommend the DIY fitting of a new headlining to as straightforward a car as a Morris Minor, although if you consider yourself more capable and competent than average, here is the outline of how to replace a Minor's headlining.

For those feeling adventurous, here is the procedure for removal and fitting of the rexine headlining fitted to later models (replacement of cloth headlining really is a job for a coach trimmer).

Take out the self-tapping screw holding the tensioning cable beneath the dash reinforcement panel on each side of the car. Tie a piece of wire to the end of the cable so that it can be reinserted through the front pillars when it is replaced.

The headlining is retained in the channel section above the windscreen by two concealed spring clips. Free them from the reinforcement front plywood fillet with a flat bladed screwdriver, taking great care.

Two more self-tapping screws are found holding the rear of the tensioning cable to the rear pillar flange behind the rear quarter liners. Unscrew, and again attach a length of wire to the cable.

On four-door models, remove the centre pillar trim pads. Where trafficators are fitted, a side tensioning screw is fitted to the top fixing screw; later models have a separate screw. The rear screws are fitted to the rear quarter inner reinforcement panel.

Slacken the self-tapping screw which secures the side tensioning cable which passes through each roof rear reinforcement and gusset plate.

Take out the top lining from the rear parcel shelf. The cable runs down each side of the rear window and there are two more screws to be removed. On most models the headlining is fixed to clips welded to the body and can be removed after folding the rear window rubber back as shown in the picture.

On early models, the rear screen has to be removed by pushing the glass and rubber inwards until it is free. Then the bottom edge of the headlining can be freed from the fibre strip to which it is held with tacks.

Remove the headlining from the rear of the car. IMPORTANT! Make sure that the wires which you fixed to the cables are removed from the ends of the cables before taking them right away, leaving the wires running through the front and rear pillar. When refitting, which is the reverse of the process given here, re-attach the cables and use the wires to draw them through the pillars.

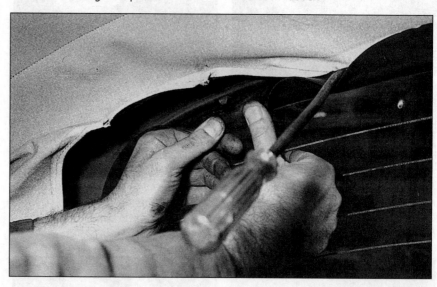

▼ HL14. Removing the rear of the Minor headlining from clips concealed behind the screen rubber.

SOFT-TOP REPLACEMENT

The romance of classic car motoring reaches its peak when you're bowling along in a sports car or convertible saloon with the top down and the wind rippling through the space that used to be occupied by your hair. Or at least, that's what you tell your better half when explaining why the Minor Convertible or the MGA, or whatever it is, can't possibly be sacrificed to the needs of the great god, Mortgage Repayment.

'In that case,' says she, 'why is it that romance on the classic car scale leads to a draught-induced crick in my neck, a damp patch on my shoulder when it rains and broken finger nails when I'm out in the damned thing and need to put the hood up?' And if it's true that your hood is ripped, fits badly around the window glasses and is awkward to handle – or is at least, more awkward than it should be – she may have a point. So, in the interests of marital harmony and the universal retention of beloved classic convertibles, here's how to fit a new soft-top and fix the frame.

TYPES OF SOFT-TOP
There are so many different types of soft-top, or hood if you prefer, and this list does not pretend to be definitive. It's also not chronological. The MGB has one of two broad types of soft-top fitted to it; or at least, there are two types of frame. The older type has a frame which, in common with 'Frogeye' Sprites, early Spitfires and many other sports cars of the early '60s and earlier, is lifted off the car and stored in the boot after the hood fabric has been removed and folded away. Then, in response to road testers and buyers who had been complaining about the crudity of it all for years, B.L. introduced folding soft-top frames to which the fabric remained attached after the frame was folded away.

Meanwhile, cars like the Morris Minor had been fitted with fold-down soft-tops from Day One, although they were originally of fabric and were held to the bodywork at the rear with good old-fashioned upholstery tacks, and to the header rail by the same method.

Meanwhile, the crafty Germans had been cheating all along by making soft-tops that were a delight to use, sealed out all the draughts and water, came fitted with a headlining and were even so well insulated that they were warmer and quieter than their saloon counterparts. Typical of a nation that never learned to play cricket! These soft-tops *are* a delight to use, but if replacement is required they are extremely demanding, both in terms of complexity and cost.

Before World War II, Salmons Tickford had led the way with their own so-called 'automatic' hoods. These had conventionally attached canvas material fitted over a frame which was folded by means of a winding handle, fitted to the side of the car's bodywork. In a Morgan 3-wheeler you'd enter a handle, wind away and, somewhere up front, the engine would start. With a Salmons-Tickford hood, you wind away and the frame rears up in front of your eyes to eventually flop itself down on to the rear of the automobile. When replacing the hood fabric, you just have to treat it like any other conventional soft-top, but pray that the cogs, cross-shafts, whistles and bells are all in place and fully functional. Mercifully, very few soft-tops – on the assumption that we are not here dealing with power hoods – stand comparison with the good old Salmons-Tickford patented device, in terms of complexity, so it's on with the show!

RESTORING THE FRAME

It can't be over emphasized that there is little point in putting time, money and effort into replacing your car's soft-top if the frame that supports it is in bad shape. And being in bad shape is, quite literally, what most of them are after a long period of time. It's no wonder that draughts and water may have appeared where none should be!

If your soft-top is of the fold-it-up-and-stow-it variety, there is little to go wrong, save the likelihood that the frame has become mis-shapen, in which case a little judicious bending will be called for. It is possible that the brackets fitted to the interior of the car, into which the frame tubes slot, will have become belled open, and in need of being closed up a touch, but not by so much that the frames are at all difficult to get in and out. The same applies to the joints in the middle of the frame if it is of the split type. Take a look at

contemporary publicity photographs of the car in a Collector's Guide, or at road test pictures in a Brooklands Book and compare the shape of the frame with that of your car. Pound to a penny, yours will be flatter than the original and not nicely curved over the width of the roof.

Mk I 'Frogeye' Sprite soft-tops are located, at the front, in the top of the screen surround with a specially shaped piece of 'flat iron', curved to the shape of the screen top. Ensure that it's flat and smooth, hammering out any kinks that may have got into it. The 'flat iron' is slipped into a narrow pocket along the front of the soft-top fabric and both are pushed into a slot in the screen surround top. If it's not a smooth shape, it won't easily slot in and out.

Folding frames are at least as susceptible to becoming mis-shapen as their simpler brethren, and the same advice about determining the correct original shape and restoring the old frame to the new shape applies equally here. You may have to use a little (judiciously applied) brute force and ignorance. Spitfire folding soft-tops, for instance, can sag at the outer edges, just behind the line of the doors, while all frames will tend to flatten out, as pointed out earlier, towards the centre of the sticks that run from side to side.

A much bigger problem with folding frame types, however, is the wear that tends to take place in the many hinges found in the frame. The typical B.L. type of frame has quite crude hinges – usually two pieces of 'flat' with a rivet through them both and a washer to separate the two flats. The rivets tend to wear, and so do the holes in which they turn; the frames themselves can crack, too. The cumulative effect of a large number of hinged joints, each with a little wear in them, is a frame that is noisy, awkward to erect and lower, and one that won't hold its proper shape under the tension of the vinyl soft top.

You may find that you can buy a brand new soft-top frame, and for B.L. sports cars, they are very good value indeed. On the other hand, you may want to repair the frame yourself. Oversized holes *could* be welded up, but

don't bother, unless you are going to use gas welding! Electric arc weld is generally far too hard to re-drill, particularly MIG weld. You could try filling the hole with braze, although that will be difficult, since the braze will not want to 'stay put' in such a large hole, although you may be able to build up the edges of the hole. A really classy way of repairing the frame would be to make, or have made, a set of simple brass bushes, with their internal hole sizes the same as the new pins which you will be fitting in due course. You can drill out the frames to accept the new bushes and then braze (taking care not to melt the bushes!) or solder the bushes into place. Where countersunk rivets were used previously, for reasons of clearance – because a domed head would have fouled on another bit of the frame – you could leave the bushes blank and then drill and tap them after fitting. The hinge pin could then be screwed into the bush and secured with Loctite. The new frame hinges would then be smooth and free of play and wonderfully wear resistant, because while steel-on-steel wears like crazy, steel on brass benefits from the self-lubricating qualities of the brass. The task could take a while, but you'd have the satisfaction of a better-than-new job carried out.

Last, don't forget to pay attention to the header rail, if your car is fitted with one. The header rail is the section that clips to the top of the screen surround. If it is made of steel, the chances are that it will have rusted out. If not, take this opportunity to inject my favourite rustproofing brew of 50 per cent *new* engine oil and 50 per cent Waxoyl. If it's too far gone, buy a new one (freely available for MGBs, etc.) or have it repaired by a specialist who knows how to weld without distorting the thing – otherwise you'll be in *trouble* because it won't follow the shape of the screen any longer! If the header rail is made of timber, you may have to repair the ends if the wood screws holding the frame in place have come loose (try plastic wall plugs before despairing, and if they fail, buy a plug cutter from the hardware store, drill the screw holes out oversize and glue fresh timber plugs into place). But if it's rotted out, you'll have to have a new one made. Insist upon well-seasoned ash and soak it in Cuprisol (as used by Morgan, nowadays) to ward off future rot. With a jig saw, a spoke shave, a length of seasoned wood and patience, a new header rail is something you could well make for yourself.

MAKING A SOFT-TOP

The majority of sports cars and convertible saloons have off-the-peg soft-tops available through one-make specialists. In the case of cars where there is insufficient demand for a production line to be set up, your one-make club should be able to put you in touch with a trimmer who has made a good job of fitting a soft-top to a similar car to yours and who may even have patterns to enable him to rapidly assemble a new top for you.

The creation of a soft-top from scratch is something of an art and should only be attempted at home by someone with good fabric-working skills and access to an industrial quality sewing machine. Domestic machines are simply incapable of dealing with the multi-thickness seams that a professional trimmer is called upon to handle.

If the soft-top is being created for a car with a fully folding hood, it is likely that, as with the VW Beetle, the hood sticks will be fitted with strips of webbing, running front-to-back to give the soft-top fabric extra support. In the case of the Beetle, a cloth or plastic headlining (dependent upon year) has to be fitted to the inside of the frame first. This is a kind of upside down version of the fitting sequence of a soft-top, except that the headlining has to be made in pieces corresponding to the distances between the hood sticks. When they are sewn together, these pieces are then left with generous seam edges which are wrapped around each of the hood sticks and glued or tacked on to the hood sticks.

Whatever the car, the soft-top itself is always constructed from several separate pieces. In the case of the Beetle, a single section of fabric runs from the header

rail at the front to the body at the rear, while the two side pieces are separate. Otherwise, it would be impossible to stretch and pull the fabric to the curvature of the hood sticks. The outer fabric of the soft-top has to be cut out, after being marked out with tailors' chalk, and then the sections sewn together and the edge seams sewn into place. Many traditionally built cars do not have edge seams at all, but the lower rear and front edges of the soft-top are pinned down and then the tacks covered with Hidem binding: the trimmer will make up whichever is necessary.

Plastic rear windows will be sewn directly in to the fabric of the soft-top, once it has been stretched, pulled and persuaded into shape, while glass rear windows will have a wooden surround which has to be pinned into the fabric whilst on the car. It must be said that the whole procedure is extremely complex in most cases, although if the old soft-top is available and could be used as a pattern, the most difficult part of the problem will be solved, provided that you have the necessary skills – and that the old soft-top fitted properly. Otherwise, leave it to the experts!

FITTING A TAILOR-MADE TOP

For the majority of us the more likely scenario is that we ring up Moss Europe, the MGOC or The Morris Minor Centre and buy the soft-top we want and then go ahead and fit it! However, it's *not* necessarily a good idea to buy from a cheap-skate supplier of soft-tops who happens to list your classic. I once bought a cheap 'Frogeye' soft-top and, for once, took my own advice! Before starting to fit the lift-the-dot fasteners supplied, I draped the new soft-top over the old and found that the new one was far too large, so much so that it wasn't possible to make it fit simply by fitting the fasteners in a slightly advanced position. Needless to say, it was returned to sender!

Most soft-tops sold through reputable suppliers are now made to a high standard, none more so than those made by CHS Industrial, formerly Coventry Hood & Seating, who made

most British sports cars' soft-tops when they were new. CHS still have most of the original patterns, as well as the 'bucks' on which the hoods are fitted with fasteners, so the shape is virtually certain to be right. It's best to specify one of these soft-tops if they are available for your car. They are only available through specialist suppliers and not direct from CHS.

Assuming that you have repaired the frame and taken delivery of the new soft-top, this is what you do. If it's a new CHS soft-top, complete with a new header rail already glued into place and clips already fitted, just go and put it on the car! But let's assume the worst.

First of all, don't fit a new plastic soft-top in the direct sunlight of a hot day. The plastic will become loose and floppy and you can easily distort it as you fit it. On the other hand, don't attempt to fit a plastic top if the temperature is less than a good, warm summer's day in the shade. The most economical way of raising the temperature in a cold garage in winter is by placing an electric fan heater inside the car. **Don't** use any form of radiant heater, because of the risk of overheating trim and damaging it or causing a fire. Moreover, ensure that the sparks from an electric motor inside the fan heater cannot ignite the gasses given off by car batteries, or petrol vapour, and don't allow the fan heater to blow directly on to trim because it, too, could cause damage.

Take the new soft-top and drape it over the hood frame, which must be clipped and fitted into its normal 'closed' position. Take a lot of care to ensure that the soft-top fits the shape of the door glasses as perfectly as you can make it. Now, start with the rear of the new top. If you're dealing with a pre-war or traditional fabric soft-top, such as the Minor, start by driving tacks through the fabric and, if necessary, through the metalwork at the top of the body, and into the ash framing beneath. If you're having to pin through panelwork, you will usually try to re-use existing holes. Will the tacks stay in? They will if you buy slightly longer ones than those you took out! Start in the centre and work to one side and then the other, a tack or two at a time. *Don't*, at this stage, drive the tacks fully home and don't fit more than the bare minimum needed for holding the top in place. The chances are that you will have to take them out again in order to adjust the fit a touch, pulling the hood downwards or sideways a whisker in order to adjust tension and remove creases. But that is for later.

If you're handling a plastic top with ready formed seams around the rear edges, 'find' the positions of the hood clips fitted to the car's body by feeling through the fabric, and fit the fasteners, one at a time; once again starting from the centre rear and working outwards. You'll have to get this right first time because you won't be able to refit these fasteners without defacing the soft-top material. One of the exceptions to this start-at-the-rear approach is the aforementioned 'Frogeye', and that's because of the flap which is sewn into the front of the top for the windscreen fixing bar. On these cars, you fit the soft-top at the front, and then pull the top quite firmly back, tensioning it over the frame, while an assistant 'finds' the fastener positions on the body and fits the lift-the-dot fasteners. It must be said that another school of thought dictates that, with any sports car, you fit the front of the soft-top to the header rail first, and then fit the clips to the rear. In the end, you should follow whichever approach you prefer.

If you have started with the rear clips, you will now have a soft-top that is fitted at the rear body, but which lies flaccid over the frame and to the front of the car. It's now that the heating of the fan heater will come in useful in the winter months, because you now have to stretch the soft-top forwards – not inordinately, but firmly, and taking care to pull over a wide area and not at specific points on the edge of the top, because it can become stretched and distorted if you don't take a modicum of care. Also bear in mind that, if you stretch the whole thing too far whilst it's warm, you won't be able to close the soft-top on a cold day! And then you'll be back to justifiable complaints about

broken finger nails – your own included – and a soft-top that takes three strong men and a horse to pull up to the windscreen frame.

Plastic tops are normally glued to the header rail, while canvas ones may be tacked to a wooden header rail. If you're gluing, you will have to pull the soft-top forwards and mark it with tailors' chalk at the position where it has to be glued to the header rail. You can't just try gluing it down under tension because fresh glue won't hold and the tension will be lost – sag, flap! After gluing the front of the top to the rail – use a quality impact adhesive – the material is cut and trimmed at the edges where necessary, then glued to the underside and further held with screws through a rail which also holds a rubber sealing strip in place. Replace this, too, as a matter of course.

them, obscuring them from view.

Fitting a new soft-top, provided that you can obtain a new one in ready-made form, is by no means one of the most difficult of all classic repair or restoration jobs, although it must be emphasized that every car seems to have its own quirks. Either buy one of the restoration guides that deals with your car (OK, we declare an interest – see the list of books in the Appendices!) or at least, take very careful notes and photographs of how your soft-top comes apart when you strip it down. And you never know, a well-fitted soft-top might just put some romance back into your classic car ownership. But perhaps we'd better not go in to that....

▼ *ST1. A restored Beetle, still in the workshop, resplendent with new soft-top.*

Cloth soft-tops should be tensioned, though not by as much as plastic, (heat is superfluous, of course) and then tacked down, low at the front of the timber header rail. After tacking, and when you are sure of the fit all round, the tacks can be driven fully home, and surplus cloth cut off (both front and back) just beneath the line of the tacks. The tacks and the ugly cut edge are then hidden behind the ancient and appropriately named Hidem binding, which opens up to allow the application of more tacks, but then closes over

▲ *ST2. This Triumph Spitfire hood frame rivet had sheared right through. The hood still closed but flapped badly.*

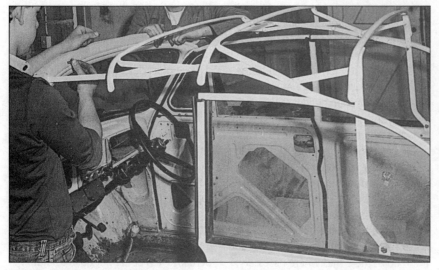

▲ ST3. Morris Minor hood sticks, checked to ensure that they are well clear of the doors.

▲ ST4. The Beetle hood sticks have been fitted with webbing, and the substantial hinges checked for wear. The webbing determines the hood stick positions – check carefully with a tape measure.

▶ ST5. New headlining is tacked to the wooden bearers on the hood sticks.

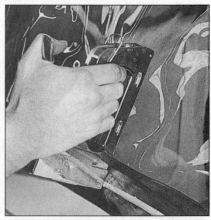

▲ ST6. The Minor soft-top is tacked at the rear, and clips fixed in place at the rear quarters.

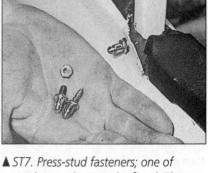

▲ ST7. Press-stud fasteners; one of several types that may be fitted. These are threaded and held on from inside the car with BA nuts.

▲ ST8. New press studs come in two parts, one passing through the material and fixing to the other by means of an in-built hollow rivet. You can spread the rivet – messily! – with a hammer and screwdriver. Or you could purchase an inexpensive special tool. (Courtesy: Frost Auto Restoration)

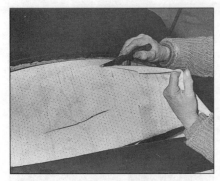

▲ *ST9. The Beetle's glass rear screen – an awkward-to-fit wooden screen surround has to be let in.*

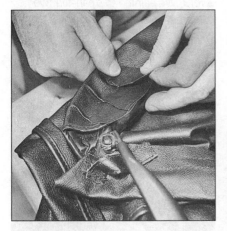

▲ *ST10. Where a soft-top is glued at the front, it has to be trimmed to wrap-around the header frame at the corners. The edges can be lifted after gluing, then cut and re-fitted so that they follow the header rail's curves.*

▲ *ST11. Tacked-down soft-tops use Hidem binding to disguise the tacks.*

▲ *ST12. The writer's 1937 Vauxhall soft-top was re-fitted to the ash header frame and then fitted to the back, over the 'automatic' folding frame. It was pinned through the top of the rear body and into the ash beneath – Hidem binding shown here at the ready.*

▲ *ST13. The 'automatic' part of the hood would be tricky to restore, but the frame itself has to be checked for distortion, just as any others.*

▶ *ST14. After a time, canvas hood material discolours, snags, becomes thin and eventually porous. Maxol canvas rejuvenating paint, available from classic car suppliers such as Paul Beck (see Appendices) will give a canvas hood a new lease of life.*

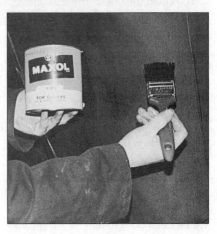

RE-FINISHING INTERIOR TRIM

Over the last few years, several improvements have been made in the area of classic trim. Some of the more complex heat-moulded plastic panels have been put back into production, for instance. Faded, jaded vinyl trim, and even leather, ABS plastic or UPVC can now be successfully recoated. However, it is essential that you check the instructions to make *certain* that the material to which the trim re-finisher is applied – as well as the coating applied by the manufacturer – is compatible with the re-finisher you choose. Also, note that the Vinylkote shown here will quite possibly *not* restore leather to a totally original appearance, particularly if your car is fitted with the highest quality hides, such as those from Connolly, fitted to Jaguars. The section looks at a refinisher called Vinylkote, one that has been tested and used with success by a number of magazines in the UK.

Vinylkote works by penetrating the surface of the material in question down to the substrate where it bonds itself to the molecules and changes the pigmentation. This means that it cannot crack, flake off or wear off. It is permanent and colour fast, and because it is not a surface coating or paint, the grain of vinyl or leather is left intact and in perfect relief. If required, natural leather can be 'fed' with hide food after application of Vinylkote and it even retains that lovely, leather aroma.

You could use one of the Humbrol spray kits shown here for spraying Vinylkote. This one, made with modellers in mind, is actually ideal for accurate spray work and, with the small glass jars, for using small amounts of several colours without wastage.

To allow Vinylkote to penetrate the substrate it is important to apply it in mist coats – do not try to cover in one coat. Applying too thickly can result in solvent trap which will leave the surface tacky for some time and prevent proper penetration. On completion, wipe over with a clean cloth to remove any dust or atomized spray that may have collected if the can was held too far away.

Vinylkote can be used to totally change the colour of an item or, in some cases, to bring back the original colour after it has faded. At the time of writing it is available in 27 standard colours and, if required, the manufacturers can colour match to your needs, although this has to be in one litre tins. You'll need space to work, and you must ensure that you will not be overspraying on to other equipment. Wear a suitable face mask and ensure that your work area is well ventilated. Practice on an unimportant panel first. Buy a couple from a scrapyard and try it out first.

▲ *RIT1. It is vital that the surfaces to be sprayed are absolutely clean, using Vinylkote's own 'Vinylprep'.*

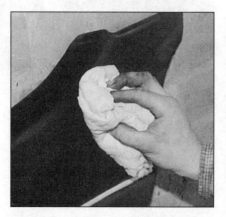

▲ *RIT2. If the surface has been previously painted or has a 'surface' (lacquer for example), then it must be removed by using Vinylkleen – follow Vinylkote's instructions with enormous care, so that you don't damage the vinyl surface.*

▲ *RIT3. We painted this panel in two colours which meant masking off, a job made tricky by the fact that there was a chrome strip along the trim. One inch tape was applied along the strip ...*

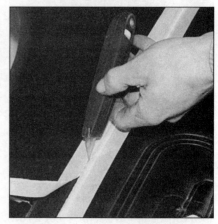

▲ *RIT4. ... and then the excess cut carefully away with a craft knife.*

▲ *RIT5. We used masking tape and newspaper to mask off the lower part of the trim (we decided to be outrageous on our practice run!) ...*

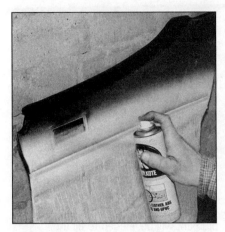

▲ RIT6. ... whilst we sprayed the top half white. The aerosol can has to be shaken for two minutes prior to spraying to ensure that the paint has mixed properly. The can should be held about eight inches away from the panel and paint put on in thin, even layers. Trying to get the whole coat on in one pass is a cardinal mistake and leads only to rivers of paint washing down the panel. Taking your time is the order of the day.

▲ RIT8. If you've got a large area to cover, it would probably be more cost effective to use Vinylkote as supplied in one litre tins. This Humbrol spray gun is ideal for the sort of work we're doing here, being small and light but offering much more control over the spray. After mixing the paint thoroughly ...

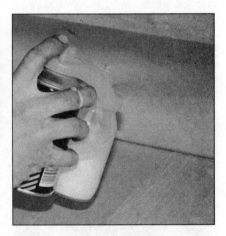

▲ RIT9. ... a quantity is poured into the glass jar (a messy job, even with a funnel!), and with the compressed air canister connected ...

▲ RIT10. ... the spraying technique is as before. Compare this old kick panel ...

▼ RIT11. ... with its cousin below.

▲ RIT7. The Vinylkote takes only 15 minutes to air dry, meaning that the process can quickly be repeated on the lower half of the panel. This rich brown colour gives a leather look to the vinyl trim and, with the masking tape and paper removed and the speaker grille replaced, it is hard to believe it's the same, ratty old panel!

▲ *RIT12. When you've finished spraying, you should clear the spray nozzles. With aerosol cans, invert it and spray until no paint appears. With the Humbrol gun used here, place the feed pipe in a can of thinners (or, in this case, Vinylprep), and 'fire' at the wall. These procedures prevent the build-up of paint in the gun.*

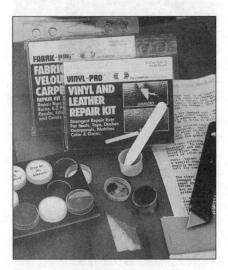

▲ *RIT13. Damaged vinyl trim can be repaired – before painting if you intend doing so – with patches, adhesive and repair paste which can be mixed to something as close as possible to the trim colour. It is also available for fabric, velour and carpets.*
(Courtesy: Frost Auto Restoration)

'CONNOLIZING' LEATHER

by Anthony Hussey of Connolly Leather. The only real problem about renovating the leather interior of a car lies in the mind of the aspirant renovator. It is a problem of self-doubt combined with the fear of failure. Be reassured. Should the worst happen and you be left with a sticky mess it can be put right. It may cost, but that's a risk everyone takes on board when they do any job for the first time. The physical acts of washing and re-colouring are not difficult, are not black arts, and can be performed by the most inexperienced DIY person. It is a job that thousands have performed to their own satisfaction. That being said, it should not be thought that the task is as easy or in any way similar to cleaning shoes, for it matters not if the colour comes off shoes, but it matters like mad if the finish comes off on a dress or shirt.

Renovation kits include colour combined with sealing lacquer in most cases, though there are some instances when a separate sealer is supplied. It is generally supposed that spray equipment is not available, and that swabs will be used, but there is no doubt that a better job can be done with a spray gun. A word on the making up of the swab. It should be smooth, and to achieve this the folding of the stockinette has to be done in a way that means that the internal folds do not form ridges, that could obtrude through the outer layer. The following sequence of photographs and captions detail the act of renovation.

Most British vintage, veteran and classic cars used Connolly leather, and Connolly's have kept pretty comprehensive records of what leather was fitted to which car, so a phone call is probably all that is needed to establish what the colour reference number is. As colours fade over the years, it may be necessary to send a small thumb-nail sized cutting, taken from under the seat. If the leather is to be restored to the original shade the alternative is to keep the existing colour, and this does mean

that a minimum of colour can be applied, which in turn means that the eventual effect will be less 'finished', less painted and most natural. This point is worth expanding on. There are a lot of people who want their leather to look new again. This is fairly straightforward to achieve. All it requires is liberal applications of pigment. Unfortunately, this can sometimes result in a very flat, over-painted appearance, particularly if not only the finish, but the surface of the leather as well, has cracked, as so much pigment will be needed to fill the surrounding surface that it will completely bury the grain of the leather. The sight of cars renovated like this, compared to some of the finished leather seen in modern cars, has brought about a demand for more sympathetic renovation. More and more people want their cars to look well-used and well cared for, rather than brand new again. This precludes filling cracks and accepts them as part of the natural ageing that occurs. It is of course a question of degree, but if the finish and surface of the leather has cracked badly then there is not a lot that can be done as a permanent repair. Filling cracks with pigment on leather that will flex, does not last and is a waste of time.

One final warning. At about the end of the '70s motor manufacturers decided to upgrade the specifications of their leather so as to make it wear longer. 150 years instead of 75!! At the same time health and safety rulings started to toughen up, which meant that many finish ingredients have become illegal. These two happenings mean that over the last 15 years finishes have changed frequently. For instance we have moved from cellulose through resin to aqueous pigments. If you try to renovate one with another, there is the possibility of a disaster. So far, to our knowledge, no one has yet caused the interior of a prized possession to turn into a fly-paper mess or a cracking ruin, but the possibility is there and the chances are increasing. Huge chemical firms spend millions researching flexible finishes for the leather industry, and the top sealer coat can change overnight as new harder wearing but softer feeling ones are developed. What, in renovation terms, would work on a car made on Friday might well be a disaster on a car made the following Monday. This, luckily, is a fear for the future and applies to the next generation of classics, but it's wise to check, where you can, even now.

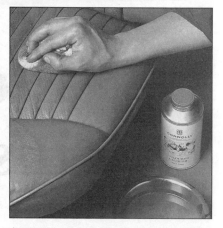

▲ CL1. Using Connolly leather cleaner, you should first wash the seat with some vigour, although it is as well not to saturate the leather. As can be seen the dirt rolls off! The corner of the seat nearest the lens shows typical wear characteristics. The dirt has worn through the finish leaving the grain layer exposed. If left like this the light will penetrate and cause the fibres to oxidize: go red, dry and crumbly. Once this has happened the days of that particular piece of leather are numbered and the application of enough lacquer to fill the break will cause the surrounding leather to look over finished. The crack will also reappear after a very short period of time.

▲ CL2. When the leather is nearly dry but just damp, apply Connolly Hide Food, gently but firmly making sure, in the case of pleated leather that it does not 'cake' in the folds or under the piping. Rub it well in and then leave it at least overnight, and preferably for 24 hours. This allows the hide food to be drawn into the fibres whilst the drying is taking place. Before lacquering, wipe over with a soft cloth to remove any surplus that may remain.

(Photos: Tom Miller)

▲ CL3. It is essential that the swab is folded in such a way as to present a smooth soft pad, with no underlying wrinkles which could cause lines in the finish. The lacquer should be rubbed in firmly until the pad starts to drag. This ensures that intercoat adhesion is taking place.

▼ CL4. The finished seat, looking wonderfully refreshed but not over-restored! It is important to note that all the operations shown here should take place in a warm, dry atmosphere. Cold and/or damp conditions can hinder drying and intercoat adhesion.

Chapter 6
Electrical & instruments

SPEEDOMETER RESTORATION

In general, the repair and restoration of an instrument such as this is best left to the experts, as the special equipment and spare parts required are not readily available to the home mechanic. Here is an overview of the way in which Renown Instruments restored this Land-Rover's speedometer. The following notes are by John Philpott, instrument restorer, of Renown Instruments.

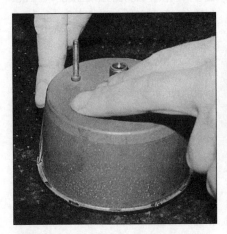

▲ SR2. The strip down begins with the removal of the bezel. The fixing lugs are easily broken, so great care must be taken at this stage if the bezel is to be re-used.

▲ SR4. ... followed by the inner spacer ring.

▲ SR1. The speedometer which is in need of refurbishment arrives at the instrument workshops for visual and mechanical check-over.

▲ SR3. The bezel glass is removed ...

▲ SR5. The movement mounting screws are removed.

▲ SR6. This now enables the entire mechanism to be removed from the case as a complete unit. At this point great care must again be taken. The unit comprises many small, delicate parts, which may be easily damaged. Also, the magnet assembly could be damaged. This would affect the calibration, and without specialist equipment it would be impossible to restore the instrument to its original accuracy.

▲ SR7. Here the instrument's main components are shown disassembled prior to cleaning and replacement of any worn parts.

▲ SR8. The main magnet drive spindle is refitted into the base casting ...

▲ SR9. ... and secured with the fixing screws – the unit must rotate freely.

▲ SR10. The spindle cup is reassembled on to the magnet top.

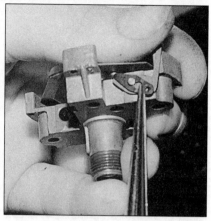

▲ SR11. Here, the clips which secure the cam gear and hold the operating arms for the odometer are being checked for security before the initial testing.

▲ SR12. The test shows some 5 mph high on the reading at 60 mph ...

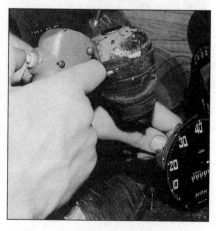

▲ SR13. ... so the magnet is de-magnetized using special equipment ...

▲ SR14. ... and the result is spot-on.

▲ SR15. The new, shining instrument with the old, rusty case alongside.

▲ SR16. The finished reconditioned and recalibrated instrument.

DASHBOARD AND INSTRUMENTS

Admittedly, removal of the Land-Rover's dash panel is easier than almost any other vehicle on earth, but once it's off, the way in which instruments are held in place is commonly seen on very many other vehicles. So, let's take a look behind the green door.

Safety: Always disconnect the battery before working behind the dash.

▼ DI1. Remove the five retaining screws securing the instrument panel to the dashboard. The top row are held in by captive nuts.

▼ DI2. The panel is then pulled forward to expose the wiring etc.

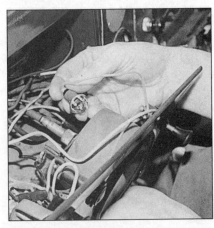

▲ DI3. The speedo lamp bulb is simply pulled out...

▲ DI4. and the speedo drive cable unscrewed and pulled away.

▲ DI5. Unscrew the knurled nuts securing the speedo to the instrument panel. This nut also attaches the earth wire.

▲ DI8. The warning lamps are simply pushed through the instrument panel and the bulb holder pulled out.

▲ DI11. The instrument is then pulled clear from the panel.

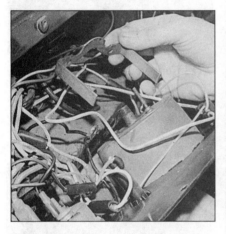

▲ DI6. Remove the speedo securing bracket.

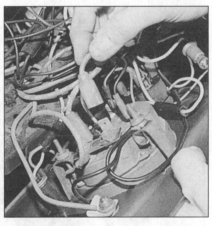

▲ DI9. Remove the wiring connections from the combined fuel gauge/ammeter, making sure to label every one in turn.

▲ DI12. Fitting the new speedometer, the procedure is a direct reversal of removal. You can then refit the instrument panel to the dashboard.

▲ DI7. The speedometer can now be pulled free from the instrument panel.

▲ DI10. The combined fuel gauge/ammeter is secured in a similar manner to that of the speedo, first unscrewing the knurled nut and removing the two separate retaining brackets.

OTHER INSTRUMENTS

Another leading restorer of classic car instruments of all types, including speedometers, is Vintage Restorations of Kent who specialize in the restoration of the esoteric and rare as well as the more modern stuff. John Marks, the founder of the company turned a hobby for the repair of old time-pieces into an extremely busy business restoring instruments. Vintage Restorations will sometimes use components that are brand new, and were made for instruments of the seventies, in order to repair instrument of the thirties – simply because some of the parts have not changed in that period of time!

▲ OI1. The first job when an instrument arrives in the workshop is for every speck of dirt to be removed in the ultrasonic cleaner.

▲ OI2. Here, a rebuilt electric clock is on test prior to being correctly regulated.

▲ OI3. Much of the work is of the same level of finesse as that required by a watch repairer. Here, the size of a balance staff is being measured.

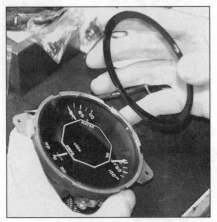

▲ OI4. This is an MGTF triple panel instrument being reassembled after a total rebuild.

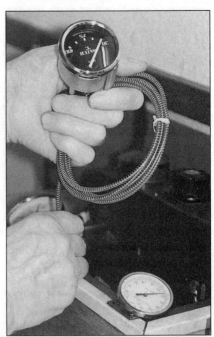

▲ OI5. This capillary type of water temperature gauge has to be carefully calibrated using special equipment – not exactly the sort of job that you could carry out at home.

▲ OI6. And, similarly, an oil pressure gauge received the treatment on special calibrating equipment: again something that is just not feasible for even the most enthusiastic of DIY repairers.

◄ OI7. Vintage Restorations make their own new instrument faces for the majority of popular instruments, and for the rarest ones of all they have a graphic artist create an instrument face from scratch.

DASHBOARD OVERHAUL

For vinyl dashboards, see 'Painting Vinyl' in this chapter. For veneered wooden dashboards, you are into a separate area of restoration but the three golden rules are: (1) rub down lightly with very fine sandpaper on a wooden block (*never* freehand and only *ever* moving the sandpaper in the same direction as the grain, *never* across the grain); (2) take *enormous* care not to go through the veneer, especially at the edges and round holes; and (3) apply the new varnish in a dust-free environment with a spray-on household semi-matt or gloss (depending upon what was original) thinned 50/50 with white spirit – first wiping *all* dust off the surface. Wear a suitable face mask.

▼ *DO1. The rules of rubbing down, stopping, priming and all the rest of normal respray skills apply equally to respraying a metal dashboard – but take even greater care because your handiwork will face you every hour you spend at the wheel.*

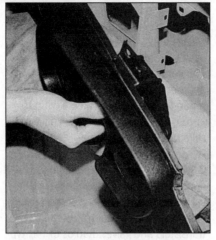

▲ *DO2. Some cars had a crackle-finish dash or dash components. You could have a bash at refinishing one yourself if you dash out to (Frost? Eastwood?) and buy a tin of their crackle finish paint. But follow the instructions on the can and practice on scrap metal first: it's dashed difficult to get right! (The 'crackles' can vary in size, even across the same panel, or even fail to appear at all, if you don't get it right.)*

WIRING

Most British cars use standard Lucas wiring, colour-coded in accordance with the Lucas wiring diagram. If you have to extend or replace wiring, or fit a 'period' accessory, the best approach is to use a suitable length of the correct wire from a scrap wiring loom. It is important that any cable you use is man enough for the job – see the wiring size and load chart below. If you are not sure about component load or about the size of any given piece of cable, seek advice from your local auto-electrical specialist – don't guess!

Number and diameter of wires		Approx. continuous amps
mm	inches	
14/0.25	14/0.010	6.00
14/0.30	14/0.012	8.75
28/0.30	28/0.012	17.50
44/0.30	44/0.012	27.50
65/0.30	65/0.012	35.00
84/0.30	84/0.012	45.00
97/0.30	97/0.012	50.00
120/0.30	120/0.012	60.00

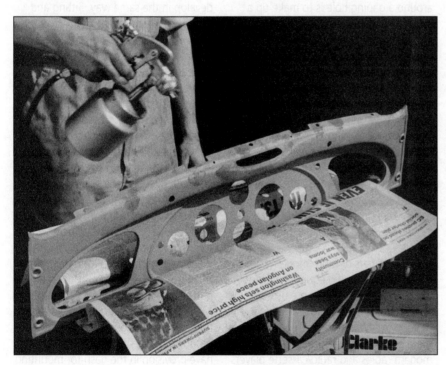

Frankly, the best sort of dashboard is a factory-made replacement, such as those for TRs, if your car has one available.

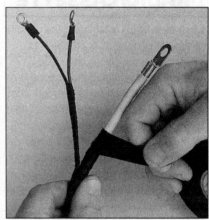

▲ *W1. The old-fashioned type of cloth insulation tape is better than the plastic type for repairing a damaged section in a fabric covered wiring loom, although you will need to glue down the end to stop it unravelling. Some tape, available from specialist outlets, actually fuses itself into a touch contiguous sheath once it is in place.*
(Courtesy: Frost Auto Restoration)

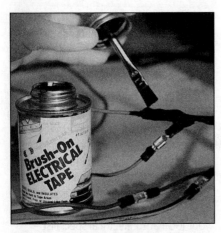

▲ W2. For insulating crimped ends or soldered wire joints, brush on insulation is neater and, especially where there is a bundle of joints, it is much easier to apply. You do have to be careful to cover completely and evenly, to avoid the risk of an electrical short.
(Courtesy: Frost Auto Restoration)

FITTING A RADIO OR RADIO/CASSETTE

Most of us enjoy listening to the radio or a cassette in our cars and there's no reason why your classic should be without a suitable unit, either ancient or modern. Car radios for classics run from the £2,000 worth of pre-war valve radio, surely the ultimate in period accessory, to the latest in FM stereo with Dolby tape facility. These are the options, and here's how to fit them.

Don't get hung up on tweeters and woofers, wow and flutter, crossover networks and physiological volume control. Just remember that all car radios consist of is a receiver, an aerial and a speaker. Then, when you've read all the brochures and had to go hide in bed to suck your thumb and stroke your favourite blanket, cling to that fact: it may help you to keep a grip on things!

In fact, it may help those of a nervous disposition if I deal with the earlier valve sets first. Although, it may not, since Car Radio Repair & Restoration Service in Frome, Somerset, tell me that the pre-war Radiomobile push-button can cost

£1,500, and Becker radios for early Mercedes £2,000.

Early units, right up to the early 1960s, used valves that had to run at around 200 volts DC, and to supply the appropriate HT voltage they used a separate box, usually called a 'vibrator' at that time, but now more likely to be called by its proper name – a 'synchronous vibrator unit'. I can't think why. By the 1960s, valve technology had improved to the point where 12 volt valves were available, and some sets were 'hybrids' using a mixture of transistors and valves. Radios of this type were invariably held in place by their tuning and volume control spindles, with an extra bracket at the rear for good measure. Fitting one of these units to a car of an appropriate age should present no problems at all, unless a hole has been cut in the dash to accept differently spaced spindles; or, horror of horrors, a front-fitted radio which demands a rectangular hole in the dash. Oddly spaced holes are usually covered by the radio face plate, while the only way around a gaping hole is to make up a mounting plate or have the dash repaired. Vibrator units can be mounted in a cool place in the bulkhead or in the boot, but a word of warning: because of the high-voltage, high-tension current inside the radio, don't try fiddling with its innards with the thing switched on unless you really know what you are doing. Early aerials and speakers are not much different in principle from their modern-day counterparts although under-car aerials of the type favoured by the makers of pre-war 'quality' cars are inherently less efficient than vertical aerials.

Some owners of more modern classics may wish to fit audio equipment into their cars for the much more prosaic reason that they want to listen to the radio, or a favourite tape. Then, the far more efficient and pleasant to listen to modern radios and radio/cassette players come into their own. And, while it can't be denied that some of the more sophisticated units are a little more time-consuming to fit, you don't need to be a skilled electrician to do it. However, you

do need to understand a few basic principles and to follow the instructions!

Philips Car Audio sent expert Peter Monk to talk me through the fitting process as it applies to a number of different cars. Peter always starts by fitting the speakers first because they are the items that can be most difficult to site. In many ways, they are all too often the weakest link in the audio chain and should be selected with at least as much care as is given to choosing the set itself. (Listening to superb stereo equipment through sub-standard speakers has been likened to gazing at the Mona Lisa through frosted glass!) It is theoretically essential that the impedance of the speaker, measured in ohms, agrees with that of the set, although in most cases manufacturers allow a range of impedances for their sets ranging from 4 to 8 ohms, with 6 ohms being the norm for some older Lucas equipment.

The physical size of the speaker is less important than those in the home hi-fi set-up because there isn't room inside the car to allow the bass notes to develop in the same way. Sitting and fitting are far more important! The speaker must be fitted on a baffle which insulates the front of the speaker from the back because then not only will the baffle vibrate with the speaker and give extra depth of sound but also the air, pushed forwards and back by the cone in the speaker as it rapidly vibrates, will then be unable to short-circuit into the air movements taking place in the opposite direction at the back of the speaker. A free standing speaker can give a power output of ½ watt but can then give as much as 10 watts when fitted into a sealed box! In most cases, there isn't much choice of baffle – the trim pad on the car door or the rear parcel shelf being all that is available. Metal does not make a good baffle, however, as it resonates and vibrates, producing a harsh sound. Many cars have provision in the dash for mounting a single speaker, and if you're fitting just a Long Wave/Medium Wave radio, that could be all you will need. It is usually necessary to fit the speaker from beneath the dash or gearbox tunnel cover, and you often have to fit a speaker of the correct shape. In general, the rear parcel shelf is a poor place to fit a speaker or speakers. In more up-market cars, especially those with headrests, a lot of sound is swallowed by the upholstery and, if the speaker lies horizontally, most of the treble notes will pass through the rear screen leaving only the booming bass notes in the car. Stereo speakers are best mounted in the doors or rear side trims of two door cars. Footwell mounted speakers are excellent for those with ears up their trouser legs, while one stereo speaker in the front and one in the rear will suit those who drive while gossiping and looking mainly in the direction of the passenger. Normal folk should go for side-to side stereo speakers mounted in a place from where most of the sound will 'get through'.

The ideal power capacity of the speakers selected will be just slightly over that of the radio or radio/cassette. If the unit gives 8 watts per channel, 15 watt speakers would be acceptable, but 50 watt speakers would be 'underdriven', as they say, and lose clarity.

When fitting speakers into a car door, you have to be careful to find a part of the door which is free from other protrusions. It is surprising how difficult this can be, even though top quality speakers are designed to give maximum output from the minimum physical depth. Older cars, those with quarter lights, are often a better prospect than later vehicles because there is usually a 'free' area beneath the quarter light. On the other hand, most modern cars will have some sort of provision in the shape of the door frame to allow speaker fitting – the 1972 Beetle Cabriolet featured in this section having holes in the door frame, and the Audi Coupé having pressed recesses. You must watch out for the intrusion of a stiff door stay, however! You don't actually notice it while the door is open, and Peter has come across cases where poor owners have fitted speakers in blissful ignorance only to smash one of them to smithereens the first time the door is slammed shut. And you must also watch that the speaker is not so deep that it is

struck by the window as it winds down. Also, beware the length of the speaker mounting screws; don't use screws so long that they foul on the window winder mechanism.

Most manufacturers supply a template on the speaker box which can be cut out and taped to the door or other trim in the place where the speaker is to be fitted. Template and trim can all be cut out together with a craft knife giving the correct shape to house the speaker. Spiral nuts are slipped over the edges of the trim panel and the self-tapping screws supplied pass through the speaker body and into the nuts. Some door-mounted speakers have their own grilles; others have to be fitted and then have a separate grille screwed over the top. If you can't stand the thought of cutting into your classic car's trim panels, there are speakers which are designed to be free standing in their own pods and with a high power output specially designed to give a strong stereo effect. You can screw them down or even fit them with Velcro, and they really do give the best of both worlds for the classic car owner who doesn't want to make any permanent changes to the interior of the car, although sound quality is rarely as good with this type of speaker.

Unless stereo speaker wires are correctly connected, the speakers can counteract one another, the cone of one 'pushing' air while the other is 'pulling' air, reducing both volume and stereo effect. Speaker wires are always colour coded. Decide which one you are going to term 'positive' and look for a '+' or a dot on one of the two terminals on the speaker. Connect the same wire to the same terminal on the other speaker, too.

Once the speaker is fitted and connected to a door, you have the problem of feeding the wiring through to the body of the car. It should go without saying that grommets must be used to prevent raw metal edges chaffing the wires where they pass through the door frame and the hinge pillar. (And DO remember to pop the grommets on at the appropriate time because they won't go on with all the wiring in place no matter how much

swearing you do!) The speaker wiring holes should be drilled so that they are NOT in alignment, thus enabling the wire to fold neatly out of the way when the door is closed. If the wire sticks out of the door gap on the inside or, worse still, the outside of the door when it is shut, put a twist in it until it agrees to stay hidden. Passing the wire through the hinge pillar can be a bit of a Chinese puzzle. Push greenhouse wire, which is both flexible and insulated, through the hinge pillar hole from the inside, twist the speaker cable round the end of it and pull through into the footwell or bulkhead. Some cars have a large interior light switch on the door pillar which can be easily unscrewed to give ease of access into the hinges pillar; others have rustproofing holes already drilled which can be used whilst yet others have gaiters fitted between door and hinge pillar carrying an umbilical cord of electrical power to the door's power windows, electric door mirrors or whatever other goodies the manufacturer may have fitted, and these give the neatest connections of all, naturally.

If you are fitting equipment which is contemporary to the age of your car, there should be no real problem, but if you attempt to fit modern equipment to an older car – by which I mean one with positive earth ignition – you will have difficulties. You can add a cassette player to an existing radio by insulating its mounting from the car's bodywork and running in wiring of the correct polarity (unless the insulation was 100 per cent foolproof, however, there would always be a risk of a dead short and a fire) but you can't normally insulate a radio or radio/cassette player in the same way. Aerials have to be 'earthed' to the car's bodywork in order to screen them from interference and, since the aerial connects to the body of the radio, you can't readily avoid earthing the radio set. You could insulate the radio from the car and fit a screen-mounted aerial, the sort that is simply stuck on to the inside of the screen, but they are far less efficient than body-mounted aerials and give greatly inferior reception.

In order to fit a radio built for negative

earth radio to a car built with positive earth you are left with two options, other than wrecking the set within seconds of connecting it up the 'wrong way round'. You can either convert the car to negative earth, or you can have the radio itself converted. The former option can actually be less dramatic to carry out than the latter, although it all depends upon the car. The more luxuriously appointed the car is, the more difficult it will be to convert. Things like lights, indicators and wipers (in most cases) work equally well no matter which way they are connected, and even equipment such as electric windscreen washers, heater motors, ammeters and wiper units with off-screen parking devices – the unclassical Austin 1800 is the only one that readily springs to mind – will work after the terminal positions have been simply reversed. However, alternators need a specialist's attention to be converted, if they can be converted at all, while clocks, air horns and electronic tachometers either cannot be converted at all or can only be converted after some difficulty. The ignition coil, incidentally, will appear to work perfectly well connected up the wrong way round, but there will in fact be a loss of efficiency. Assuming that there is no problem with accessories, all you have to do is change the battery leads over and turn the battery round and then repolarize the dynamo. Connect up the battery leads in their new positions but ensure that the fan belt is on the dynamo to stop it acting as a motor and running itself to destruction. Take a wire, which should previously have been connected up to the positive terminal on the battery, and brush it a couple of times on the small terminal on the dynamo (the one known as the field terminal) creating a good fat spark. This reverses the field in the dynamo and allows it to work perfectly in its new role. You can't, of course, carry out the same trick with an alternator, but the relatively few cars that were fitted with positive earth alternators can usually be given a negative earth alternator of a similar type. If your car has too many pieces of 'difficult' equipment to make

polarity conversion a sensible option, you could always pay to have the set itself converted by a specialist, although conversion is unlikely to be cheap.

If your classic still has 6 volt electrics, you may be able to buy a 6-to-12 volt converter either from a specialist or from an autojumble. If not, you can again have the set adapted by a specialist although, once again, at a price!

All modern radios and mountings in cars conform to DIN mounting standards. Deutscher Industrie Normenausschus were German national standards which have become international norms, accepted by all the leading radio makers (most of which, incidentally, are Japanese; with the European exception of firms like Philips and Blaupunkt. Even the Radiomobile name has been bought by the Japanese!). Modern classics often have a mounting slot covered by a plate or small storage slot into which the radio can fit. Others are made to be fitted with spindle mounted radios. These are fitted after clipping a special mounting plate to the mouth of the aperture, while slot-in type radios are preceded by a special cage which holds the radio in place.

All radios should be fitted with a separate fuse, although those with a built-in fuse are best of all because there is no external, unprotected wire. Those units with digital tuning and a memory, must be connected up to a permanent power supply and not through the ignition, or the memory will be lost every time the ignition is turned off. I can't see the point of wiring a transistorized set through the ignition at all because it effectively prevents you from listening to the radio with the engine turned off. On the other hand, valve sets take a great deal more power to run and are best used when the generator is putting plenty back into the battery!

Fortunately, older radios made to fit the 7 in x 2 in slot can be fitted to a slot opened out for a DIN-sized radio, so there's no need to worry about causing irreversible damage to a slot of that size.

Whichever type of set-up you want, it should be possible to fit it yourself. But once the thing is in, one problem

remains; how do you USE the TLCD or the Opto-Electronic Tape Transport Monitor? I think I'll have to go and stroke my blanket again.

Special thanks are due to Philips Car Audio for their assistance, and to audio specialist Peter Monk of Marpet Car Audio, advising on behalf of Philips.

▲ CR1. If you haven't got an antenna/aerial fitted, drill a fresh hole or take out the plug in the body and clean part of the hole to bare metal so that the fitting can make electrical contact. Protect against rust with a generous smear of petroleum jelly or better still, CopperEase, copper-impregnated grease. Generally, the aerial should be fitted at the corner of the car furthest away from the engine's ignition system.

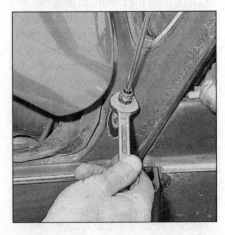

▲ CR2. Feed the wire towards the radio mounting, and tighten the antenna clamp down. Angle the antenna/aerial back because FM reception will be improved that way. Excess antenna/aerial wire should never be coiled.

▲ CR3. Take off part of the door trim and locate the cut-out in later doors where the speaker can be fitted, or a suitable site when there's no speaker provision already there. Use the template provided with the speaker to cut out a hole for the speaker, but be sure to use a craft knife that is really sharp.

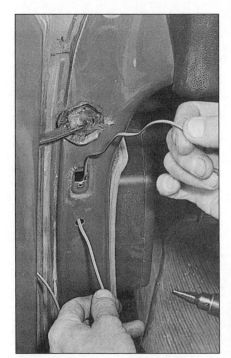

▲ CR4. If necessary, drill a hole in the door pillar and another in the door, but position them so that they don't line up. This allows the wire to tuck itself in. If it tends to stick out between door and wing, put a twist in it. Use an interior light switch opening to gain access to your drilled hole, if there's one fitted.

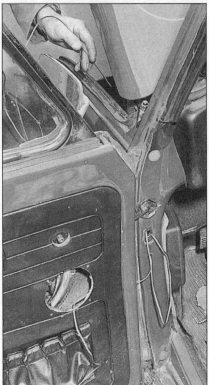

▲ CR5. Now feed the speaker wire through – into the luggage bay in this Beetle.

▼ CR6. The Beetle's heater can unit will have to come out to enable you to feed the wire through to the rear of the radio. You'll also need to check that the depth of the radio isn't too great for the limited amount of space available here. Many cars don't need any components to be removed: it's just a matter of feeding cables behind the dash.

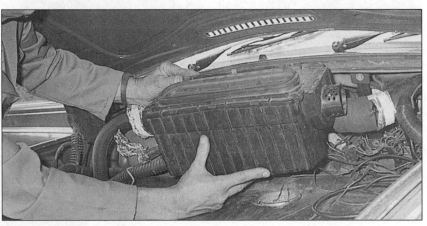

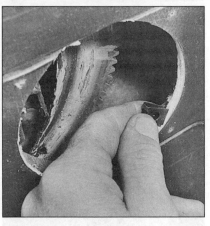

▲ CR7. But, back to the speakers. Philips supply screw clips which are pushed over the trim board.

▲ CR8. After piercing the board, the speaker can be fitted and the screws inserted. But, if you have cloth trim, don't use a power drill because you could easily 'ladder' the cloth and ruin it.

▲ CR9. Prepare the radio aperture by feeding through the speaker and power wires. Use a test lamp to discover whether the feed wire you have chosen works with or without ignition, and remember that where a radio doesn't have a built-in fuse (all of Philips radios do, it seems) you MUST include one in the line.

▲ CR10. Lay out the radio fitting kit so that you can see where everything goes. This is the Philips kit with spindle mounting plate which clips into the standard aperture.

▶ CR11. This much older set – a period accessory in this MGB – uses the same system.

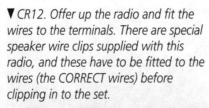

▼ CR12. Offer up the radio and fit the wires to the terminals. There are special speaker wire clips supplied with this radio, and these have to be fitted to the wires (the CORRECT wires) before clipping in to the set.

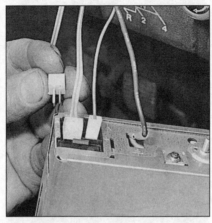

▼ CR13. Fit the mounting kit – this bracket just clips into the Din slot – and then the radio. There should be spacers supplied with the kit to pack the radio spindles so that not too much of the spindles show.

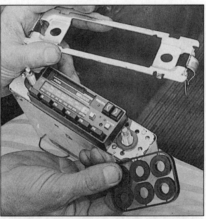

▲ CR14. Tune the radio to a weak station, low down on the frequency scale and turn the antenna/aerial trimmer until you achieve maximum volume.

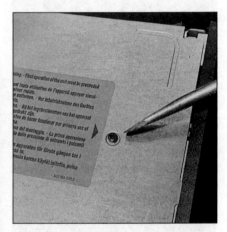

▲ CR15. Many radios have their trimmer mounted in the body, in which case it may be necessary to tune the trimmer before inserting the radio. The location of the trimmer will be described in the fitting instructions.

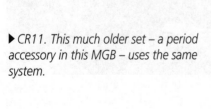

▲ CR16. Another common type of fitting system is the 'cage' type where a complete 'cage' is fitted into the mounting slot and the radio then pushes in, automatically clipping into place. It's then impossible to remove without the 'keys' supplied; theoretically, that's a great anti-theft device, but it's not so great if the frustrated thief starts carving the dash about in a desperate attempt to force the radio out!

▲ CR17. The MGB dash aperture has to be lightly filed to bring it out to the DIN size; this Audi Coupé has a DIN slot as standard, so later sets push straight in.

▶ CR18. Older car owners may wish to find the 'right' type of set for their car. This is a Radiomobile 100, made between 1946 and 1950 and fitted to a number of up-market British cars.

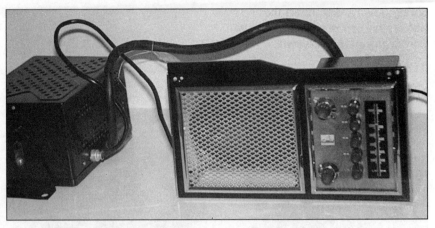

▲ CR19. For the next 15 years, the Radiomobile 4220 took its place.

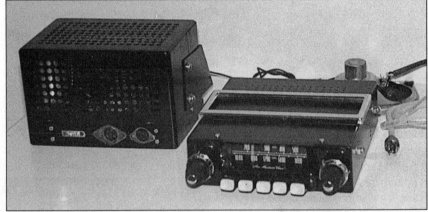

▲ CR20. Or, there was the Radiomobile 4000, another two-part unit, in common with most valve sets. Thanks to Car Radio & Restoration Service (see Appendix) for these three photographs.

FITTING AN ALARM

Top of the range of alarms marketed by Gamma in the UK is an alarm that speaks to would-be intruders, telling them to 'Move away from the car ...' when they get too close. For most classic cars that would have been just too much, although for a Ferrari GTO, you never know – it might be just the job! But with both feet on the ground, this section shows a simpler, though still relatively sophisticated unit, being fitted to an MGB.

It is important to only fit a system that cuts off its own siren after a given time (unless disturbed again) – 15 seconds, perhaps. False alarms are all too common and an alarm that sounds for hours is nothing but an anti-social nuisance.

Safety: Always disconnect the battery/ies before working on any part of the electrical system.

▲ AU4. The control box was found a convenient home beneath the dash.

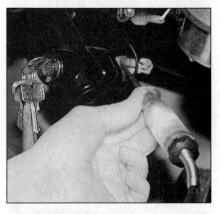

▲ AU5. The Gamma fitter used our Sykes-Pickavant test lamp to identify a source that was 'live' with the ignition turned off.

▲ AU1. The Gamma alarm unit that we chose to fit to this MGB was still full of microchip sophistication. It also contains a battery backup so that even if someone disconnects the batteries on the vehicle, the alarm's battery will take over and do its job.

▲ AU2. The Gamma alarm sensor sends out a microwave beam that can be adjusted to fill the cockpit of the MGB, but is not affected by air movement. Thus, it can be used with a soft-top car or even when the top is down. Mind you, we ended up adjusting the sensitivity right down because of the risk of the unit being set off by low flying butterflies!

▲ AU3. The sensor was to be placed behind the front console, and would be fitted beneath the radio set once that was installed.

▲ AU6. Almost as important as the alarm itself is this flashing light which tells all and sundry that the alarm is activated. Rather than drill into any integral part of the car, the fitter drilled and mounted the sensor in a prominent position on a switch blanking plate.

▲ AU7. This is what you call a siren! It comes with its own integral self-recharging battery pack. Where they are fitted, door switches and boot lid and cockpit doors can be wired into the system, and extra switches placed on the bonnet. The unit senses current drain from anywhere in the car and, in addition, there is the microwave movement sensor already described.

▲ AU8. The remote control that comes with the Gamma alarm causes the car's turn indicator lights to flash on and off once to tell you that the system is armed, and to flash three times when you turn the system off.

▲ AU9. The winking indicator on the dash confirms the status of the system and is a visual deterrent to any would-be thief. The only disadvantage we found was that the car's battery would run flat if the alarm was left on for more than a week or two – which is another good incentive to use your classic car on a regular basis!

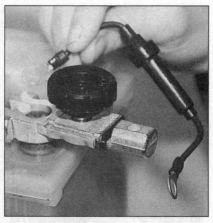

▲ AU10. Less sophisticated but probably useful where the small-time thief is concerned: the Dis-car-nect enables you to disconnect the battery feed, allowing enough current to get through the small, fused wire to power a clock – or alarm! It's also a useful way round those infuriating leaks-to-earth that drain batteries and drive you mad because you can't find the source.

ELECTRIC COOLING FAN

The advantages of an electric cooling fan over the mechanically driven variety are unarguable. You save energy (which means money!), cut down on noise and reduce warm-up times. The most well-known of the aftermarket cooling fan kits is made by Kenlowe and I recently fitted one to a Series II Land-Rover and one to an MGB. Three or four hours work would be about right for each, although 'thinking time' can be longer – it depends on the car!

Kenlowe supply different types of fitting kit, depending upon the model specified. The Land-Rover fitting kit supplied is not the one shown here. I used a spare kit from the MGB because its components seemed to make more sense to me. The L-R kit involved fitting the kit on the inside of the rad. (tricky, in my view); I placed it on the front, as recommended for the 'B. To ensure that the fan was changed from 'suck' to 'blow', it was necessary to pull the fan off the spindle, reverse it and replace the retaining clip. It's a *tight* fit on the spindle!

▲ ECF1. The MGB kit. It's very comprehensive, but with any vehicle you should add an in-line fuse near to the unit itself.

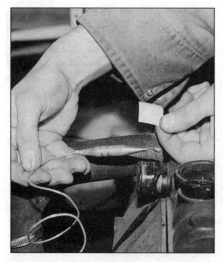

▲ ECF2. A sensor fits into the header tank via the top hose. A patented rubber sleeve, curved, tapering and with a slot down the middle, allows the capillary tube to fit inside the hose without causing a leak. You have to tighten the clamp well, and I used non-setting gasket paste.

▲ ECF4. ... and made new ones to fit the thermostat to the MGB's rad. surround on the inner, protected face. Of the two support bars provided, one was fitted with the bottom 'leg' facing forwards; the other sideways, for extra stability.

▲ ECF3. The thermostat has to be manually adjusted so that the fan comes on at the temperature of your choosing. I used existing bolt holes in the Land-Rover ...

▲ ECF5. On the Land-Rover, the 'legs' were suspended from the panel above. It is vital that the motor is fitted with the cable aperture/drain hole facing downwards. The instructions provided by Kenlowe are thorough, if a mite difficult to penetrate, but the job is not difficult. On any other car, don't forget to allow for that thinking time, so that you can work out in advance what goes where – and how!

IMPROVING HEADLAMPS

One of the curses of classic car driving is having to use a car with inadequate headlamps. We tend to assume that older cars inevitably fail to lighten their own darkness – and for many older cars, it's perfectly true! Series I E-types with those gorgeous glass headlamp covers have nowhere near enough headlamp power for the car's performance. Even one of the slowest classics on the road, the early 1200cc Beetle has headlamps that don't match its performance, but this time it's because the headlamps are only powered by six volts; and the same is true of upright Ford Pops. and their close cousins. But, then, any classic car with bulb headlamps will seem grossly inadequate when compared with its modern counterparts, and even many of those with sealed beam units seem to have a built-in dimmer switch. In fact, that's exactly what they have got! Most older cars have developed unwanted resistance through the lighting system, and this is probably the main reason for a lack of headlamp power, at least compared with the vehicle's potential.

Some time ago I spent a useful couple of hours talking to Stuart Rose of Cibie (SEV), the French company famous for those powerful rally lights many of us first noticed festooning Renault Alpines in the Monte Carlo Rally all those years ago. In common with all other major manufacturers, Cibie produce high-output replacement headlamps for most cars. I fitted a set to the Audi Coupé I then owned, but first of all Stuart talked me through the pitfalls and solutions to low headlamp power on older vehicles.

Stuart suggests that the enthusiast's first job is to spend a few pounds on a little multimeter with which voltage can be measured. Measure the voltage across the battery terminals and make a note of it. The rest of these instructions relate to negative earth cars. If your car is positive earth, reverse the polarity part of the instructions that follow. First of all, go to the lighting switch and connect one end of the multimeter to each of the positive switch terminals and the other to a very good, clean earth. The reading should be almost the same as that you obtained by taking a reading across the battery. Now follow the wiring along to the headlamps taking special note to check both sides of the dipswitch, particularly if it is of the older floor-mounted type. If you find that the voltage reading drops away considerably – say as much as two or three volts – after the power has gone through the dipswitch, you have found one of the 'dimmers' in your system! Carry on, ending up with the connection at the bulb or sealed beam unit. A total drop throughout the system of the aforementioned two or three volts hits headlamp performance to a considerable degree. The commonest culprits, apart from bad terminals on the dipswitch mentioned earlier, are likely to be the ends of the cables where they connect to metal terminals. The cable often becomes frayed and thinned in this area and that in itself will cause a voltage drop, akin to a drop in the amount of water flowing through your garden hose when someone stands lightly on it.

There would be absolutely no use whatsoever in fitting uprated headlamps if the system itself proves to be inadequate. Just by making the system work to its optimum efficiency you may be surprised to find that your headlamps are adequate for your needs. Stuart claims that an improvement in the order of 25 per cent can be obtained just by making sure that all the cables are properly connected and the dipswitch is working as it should. However, if you also want to uprate the output of the headlamps themselves, Stuart added some further advice.

There are so many different types of headlamp, mounting, side lamp bulb position, glass pattern and many other details, that it is impossible to be specific about every instance. Stuart says that SEV will be pleased to advise individual owners on which headlamps will suit their needs best – see Appendices for address and telephone number.

Fundamentally there are two types of system: sealed beam units and bulbs.

Sealed beam units have to be thrown away and replaced when they fail, of course, but the reflectors won't tarnish and the electrical connections are likely to be more durable. Reflectors in bulb-type headlamps tend to corrode – which in itself cuts down headlamp power quite dramatically – and the bulb connections are also prone to corrosion, leading to voltage drop. Over the years I have always converted my round headlamp English classic cars to sealed beam halogen units whenever possible because of the dramatic improvement that this seems to bring. You need to change the headlamp mountings and connectors, and you also have to make sure, if your car runs a dynamo, that the power is sufficient for the headlamps. Early Mini dynamos produce from 30 to 35 amps, while an H4 halogen headlamp conversion consumes about 10 amps on main beam. If the dynamo is in excellent condition and the regulator correctly set, you should just about be OK, but do bear in mind that you might have wipers running, side lamps will be lit, and the heater blower and radio might also be on. On the other hand, you probably won't be driving your 1959 Mini over great distances at night so, given all else is in good shape, it shouldn't be a problem.

One interesting oddity that Stuart told me about was the Cibie 410 Tungsten sealed beam unit that can be changed from left-hand to right-hand drive beam by flicking a switch on the back. If you can get hold of one of these units and it fits your car, it could be a godsend if you regularly take trips across the channel.

Whichever type of system you fit, have the beams set at an MOT testing station with the correct beam setting equipment. You might even say that this is yet another golden rule in ensuring that your standard headlamps work correctly: get them pointing in the right direction and at least they will be illuminating the part of the road that you want to see!

For those more concerned with visual originality than high light output, Marchal still carry 1950s headlamps as stock items, and people like Holden Vintage and Classic (see Appendices)

carry all of their Lucas equivalents. It is even possible to get hold of Marchal Ampilux which had phenomenal performance from two reflectors and two bulbs per unit. They were fitted to Le Mans cars, but you must make sure if you want to fit a unit of this sort that not only will it fit your car correctly but also that it will be legal in use. Ensuring that your headlamps do not dazzle oncoming traffic is a perfect case of enlightened self-interest, if you'll excuse the pun. There's not much point having the road ahead illuminated like the glare at a pop concert if the poor old-age pensioner coming towards you is blinded by the light and runs into you!

▲ IH1. This model of Audi Coupé is fitted with so-called 'small American rectangular' units. One pair of headlamps gives the dip beam the other the main beam. These Wipac replacements have their side lamp bulbs in a different position from the originals and you have to ensure that there is sufficient clearance.

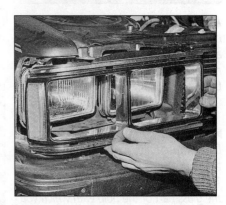

▲ IH2. After removing the trim, each unit was unscrewed from the car, taking care not to drop the tiny retaining screws.

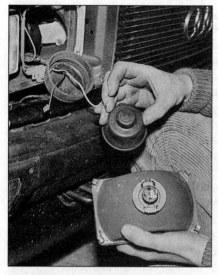

▲ IH3. A nice touch, this, and quite important for cars which throw a lot of mud and water on to the back of headlamps: the Cibie units have double rubber seals to keep out the moisture. You do, of course, have to fiddle the wiring through the seals and connect it up before the seals can be eased into place.

▲ IH4. All of the wiring and switches had been found to be in excellent condition, and the new headlamps made a big and noticeable improvement to what had been a particularly weak point on the car.

▶ IH5. If you fit headlamps with separate high output bulbs, be sure never to touch the bulbs with your bare fingers. There will often be a card sleeve around the glass part of the bulb with which you are supposed to handle it if you must.

DYNAMO, ALTERNATOR, STARTER MOTOR AND ANCILLARIES

Rebuilding a dynamo, an alternator or a starter motor is another one of those areas where you might, theoretically, wish to carry out all the work yourself. In practice, however, very few people have the access to special tools and special components, or have the inclination to spend large amounts of time in carrying out work that a specialist could carry out for you – and provide you with a guarantee! For those who want to strip down complete units, your Haynes manual goes into a surprising amount of detail on how to go about it. This section concentrates on showing you how to check the components, how to carry out simple repairs and how to find out whether, for instance, your battery keeps going flat because the battery is at fault or because the charging system isn't working properly.

DYNAMO

It is a basic rule of fault finding to check the obvious things first, so before you assume that either the battery or the dynamo is faulty, check the drive belt. Ensure that the inner surfaces of the belt are not cracked or glazed and that the belt is not frayed, and tighten its tension to that recommended in your handbook. With most systems, there should be about half to three-quarters of an inch (13 to 19mm) of movement in one direction on the longest run of the fan

belt, usually between bottom pulley and dynamo pulley.

If you still suspect that the dynamo is not providing enough charge, the following sequence of checks to be carried out on Lucas dynamos will help to tell you whether an exchange dynamo is necessary or whether the battery itself is in need of replacement.

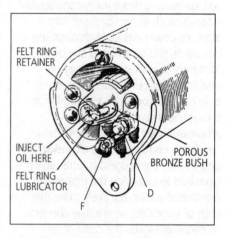

FELT RING RETAINER

INJECT OIL HERE

FELT RING LUBRICATOR

POROUS BRONZE BUSH

D

F

▲ D1. This Lucas drawing shows how to ensure that the dynamo bearing is lubricated, and also indicates the main output terminal (D) and the field terminal (F). On later models these have push-on Lucas terminals, but the principle is exactly the same. In order to check the dynamo, you will have to invest a few pounds in purchasing an inexpensive volt meter, calibrated 0 to 20 volts.

Now follow the following sequence:
A. Check that the dynamo and control box are connected correctly. The dynamo terminal D should be connected to the control box terminal D and the dynamo terminal F connected to its equivalent on the control box.
B. Disconnect the cables from the terminals D and F on the dynamo. Ensure that all lights and accessories (including interior lights) are turned off.
C. Connect the terminals D and F together with a short length of wire.
D. Clean a part of the body of the dynamo so that you can clip one lead of your volt meter to it, giving a good earth. Clip the other volt meter lead to one of the dynamo terminals D or F.
E. As you gradually increase the speed of the engine, the volt meter reading should

rise steadily and without fluctuation. You must not race the engine in an attempt to increase the voltage. It is, in fact, enough for the engine to run at between 1,000 and 2,000 rpm. Do not run the engine too fast because the dynamo is running entirely without load and too high a speed could damage it electrically. Do not allow the voltage to build up to above 20 volts on a 12 volt system, or 10 volts on a 6 volt system.

If your volt meter has shown a reading of about 12 volts, reconnect the terminals D and F at the dynamo and disconnect terminal D from the control box. Now reconnect the volt meter between the end of the cable D that you have just disconnected and a good earth point. You should obtain the same reading that you had at the dynamo when the engine is run again at the same speed as before. If not, you've found the problem: faulty wiring. If the reading is correct, test the control box – see below.

If there was no reading when you checked the voltage at the dynamo, check the brushes – see below.

If the reading is low, at around 1 volt, for example, the field winding may be faulty. You can check the field resistance by disconnecting the cables from terminals D and E as before, and connecting a good-quality ammeter

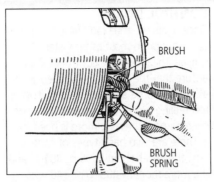

BRUSH

BRUSH SPRING

between the dynamo's two terminals. Increase the engine speed gradually once again so that it is turning over at the same speed as before, and this time the ammeter should read 2 amps, showing the correct field resistance.

If the volt meter reading at the dynamo is about 5 volts, this indicates a defective armature winding.

If you have found a problem with the field winding or the armature winding, you will need an exchange unit unless you can cannibalize an armature from another second-hand dynamo.

▼ *D2. This diagram gives you an idea of how the various parts of the dynamo fit together. There are, of course, two field coils, the lower one having been left out of this drawing so that you can 'see' the armature assembly. This is the model C42 dynamo.*

◄*D3. The brushes bear on the commutator (see D2) and carry the current generated by the armature as it spins inside the field coils. The current is carried to the commutator and then transmitted through the carbon brushes which rub on the surface of the commutator. Over a period of time, the carbon wears away and if the brushes are less than $^{11}/_{32}$ in (8.5mm) in length, they should be renewed. Incidentally, when you check the brushes, you should always return them into the slot from which they came because they will have bedded themselves in. As you lift out the brush – you have to pull the brush spring out of the way using something like a small Allen key, when you can then just pull out the brush with your fingers – you should ensure that it slides freely. If it is tight, lift it out and carefully clean out the collar in which it slides. Obviously, the dynamo will have to be removed and stripped down before you can get at the commutator.*

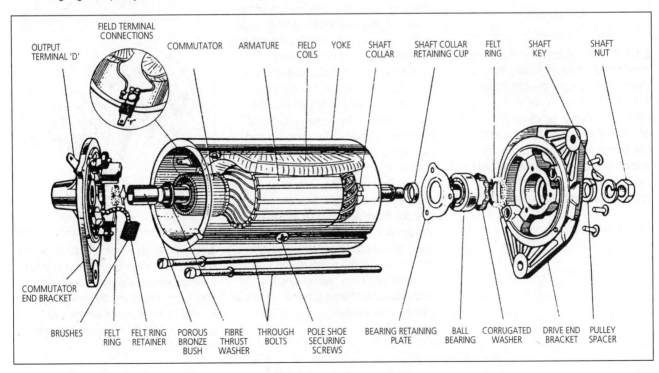

OUTPUT TERMINAL 'D'

FIELD TERMINAL CONNECTIONS

COMMUTATOR   ARMATURE   FIELD COILS   YOKE   SHAFT COLLAR   SHAFT COLLAR RETAINING CUP   FELT RING   SHAFT KEY   SHAFT NUT

COMMUTATOR END BRACKET

BRUSHES   FELT RING   FELT RING RETAINER   POROUS BRONZE BUSH   FIBRE THRUST WASHER   THROUGH BOLTS   POLE SHOE SECURING SCREWS   BEARING RETAINING PLATE   BALL BEARING   CORRUGATED WASHER   DRIVE END BRACKET   PULLEY SPACER

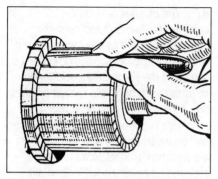

▲ D4. The commutator also wears down slowly as it spins against the brushes and the carbon from the brushes clogs the spaces between the segments. Since carbon transmits electricity, this reduces the efficiency of the dynamo. You could use a broken off piece of hacksaw blade to cut the packed-in carbon from the spaces between the segments.

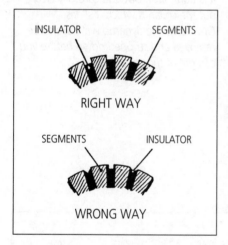

▲ D5. The spaces between the segments need to be cut away cleanly, leaving sharp edges. Even if the commutator looks to be physically sound it should be cleaned up with a rag dipped in a spot of petrol if its surface appears to be blackened. Have someone turn the engine over by hand whilst you hold a rag against the surface of the commutator with brushes removed.

CONTROL BOXES

Once again we shall look here at Lucas units, although most other systems are similar. The job of the control box is to ensure that the battery is supplied with as much charge as is available to it when it is feeling run down, and that it is not overcharged when no more is needed.

There are two basic types of control box: the two-bobbin RF95 or RB106 and the more modern RB310 or 340 with three bobbins. Control boxes are a fiddler's dream (or nightmare, depending on how you look at it) so it's quite possible that someone will have had a go at your control box in the past without having a full idea of what they are doing. Once you have established that the dynamo is working correctly, and with the same volt meter and ammeter that you used before, you should be able to set your control box for yourself. Full details of these time-consuming processes are given in your Haynes workshop manual, so there is no need to repeat them here especially since there are detail differences for different models. Suffice it to say that it is quite a tricky business which involves taking account of the ambient temperature and carrying out adjustments within 30 seconds of starting the engine and energizing the charging circuit, because heating of the shunt coil may cause false settings to be made. However, you simply cannot hope to have the control box working satisfactorily just by twiddling with the adjustments on a suck it and see basis. You will also need to ensure that the control box is in fundamentally sound condition. Remove it from the car and look at the rear surface of the box. Any blackened or burned out contacts suggest that the unit is in need of replacement, and new ones are certainly available from people such as Holden Vintage & Classic who specialize in older-type Lucas equipment. You can also check that the points in the regulator box have been cleaned, scrupulously following the instructions in your Haynes manual.

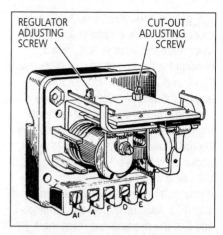

▲ R1. This is the two-bobbin RB106/2 control box.

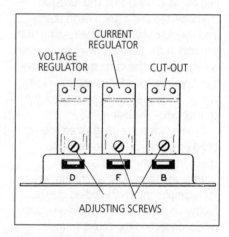

▲ R2. The three-bobbin RB310 control boxes have three standard adjuster screws.

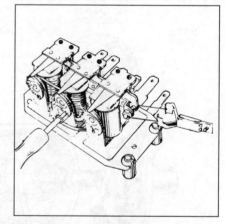

▲ R3. You need a special setting tool for the RB340 control box, although it has been suggested that you could use a chuck key, insulating the handle with several layers of insulation tape to avoid the otherwise inevitable 'tingly' electric shock.

ALTERNATORS

Apart from the fact that an alternator creates alternating current – as opposed to a dynamo's direct current – the main practical differences are that an alternator is much more efficient than a dynamo, and that it is even less suitable, in the main, for DIY repair. Your Haynes manual shows how you can check an alternator whilst it is fitted to the car, but there are many detailed differences appropriate to different models of alternator. Things start getting slightly esoteric – such as you are recommended, ideally, to have access to an ohmmeter and you would be best having an alternator checked over by an electrical specialist. You are also recommended to read carefully through the checking section in your Haynes manual to ensure that the specialist really does check the unit over correctly and doesn't just try to fob you off with a replacement. It has been known to happen!

If you have an earlier Lucas AC10 or AC11 type of alternator which has external components you will find it worthwhile, in practical terms, to switch to one of the later ACR models with all internal components, unless you are a stickler for originality. You will probably not be able to exchange one for the other, but you should be able to pick up an ACR unit second-hand. You will need a wiring diagram from a car that was fitted with an ACR as standard in order to work out how to convert the wiring. But first some words of warning with regard to all alternators: NEVER disconnect the battery while the engine is running and never run the engine with the alternator leads disconnected. Either would be a sure way to ruin the alternator. Also, remember to disconnect both the battery and alternator if you carry out any electric arc or MIG welding on the car because, once again, the alternator can be damaged.

STARTER MOTORS

In practical terms, overhaul of the starter motor is restricted to changing the brushes – in essence similar to those in the dynamo – and to washing out the mechanical starter gear with engine degreaser and a minimal amount of water. Make sure that the unit is completely dry and that no water whatsoever has got into the electrical components. Don't grease it.

It is theoretically possible to strip down the starter motor and rebuild it, but in practice you will probably not be able to get hold of the components you need. So, once again, it is probably better to cut your losses and purchase an exchange unit.

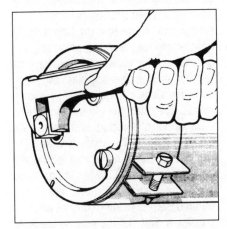

▲ SM1. Some starter motors have a squared pin on the end of the motor housing. If the starter motor 'sticks', turn the square with a spanner and you can 'wind' the stuck dog back down the pinion shaft. Try starting up again – it won't stick every time. If it sticks often, however, you may find that the starter ring on the flywheel is worn – see Engine Rebuild section for how to renew it.

DISTRIBUTOR OVERHAUL

The distributor is a vital part of any car's 'central nervous system' and most will continue to function when they are well past their best. Unfortunately, older classic cars, such as my pre-war Vauxhall 14, will show signs of having gone through several engine rebuilds – they'll have 40 or more thou. oversize pistons, and thrice-ground cranks, for instance – but both the distributor and the carburettor are usually left alone until they break. This is a Big Mistake!

I took a trip to Holden Vintage & Classic, leading specialists in all things British and electrical, to discuss with Managing Director Jeremy Holden what is involved in overhauling a 'dizzy'. First of all, as Jeremy pointed out, identify your problems! Symptoms include a general lack of 'go' because of a defunct advance mechanism, through to a spindle that can be waggled about, and 'fully floating' distributor bodies. Holden's have seen – and repaired – it all! Jeremy Holden took me round their distributor repair 'production line', but it's worth pointing out that Holden's are an Aladdin's cave of electrical components going back to the early years of motoring. When I asked if they had a bakelite upper distributor body for my 1937 car, they turned one up off the shelf! We decided to follow the rebuild process, following mainly an MGA distributor, just to see what has to be done.

It's worth saying now that to attempt to rebuild your own distributor can hardly be worth considering. First, you would need a well-equipped workshop, for reasons which will soon become obvious, and second, you would need access to – in this case – fairly obscure Lucas information on distributor types and their advance curves, as well as information on how to set them up. Holden's seemed more than happy to tell me what goes on behind the scenes; they can be content that 99.9 per cent of us could never consider even trying to rebuild our own distributors in any case!

Before rushing off to have your distributor overhauled, you will want to establish whether the expense will be necessary or not. The most 'external' of the external checks will be to see if the vacuum advance is working. Disconnect the pipe from the manifold end and suck hard. There should be almost immediate resistance, as if you have sucked a very small amount of air out of a sealed chamber – which you have. Then, as you let go, you should hear a small sound, a muffled 'click', as the spring inside the vacuum advance pushes the diaphragm back home. All suck and no stop means that the diaphragm has disintegrated; no return click, and the unit has seized. Also, if there is an external rod leading to the vacuum unit, try moving it manually. It should move (and automatically return) smoothly, not 'grittily'. Vacuum units are usually not interchangeable between different distributors, by the way. Holden's repairers actually cut the unit apart with a special tool, insert new diaphragm and spring into a new housing and refit to the distributor body. They say that it is very rare for an elderly vacuum advance to work perfectly, so they are renewed as a matter of course.

Other checks are best carried out with the distributor removed from the car. Take off the cap and rotor arm and try moving the spindle from side to side. (If you try this in the car, as some manuals suggest, the drive gears at the lower end of the unit can easily mask play in the spindle bushes.) If your distributor is more than a few years old, you can bet that the spindle bushes are worn! A waving spindle equals variable points gap, equals variable spark timing, equals lowering efficiency. And the same is true of a worn distributor drive slot at the bottom end of the unit. Holden's will put in a new spindle when wear is found; it will be up to you to replace the drive shaft in the block. Luckily, distributor drive shafts usually screw or pull up and out of the block once the distributor is out, depending on type, but consult your manual. Jeremy assures me that wear is virtually unknown with the geared type of distributor drive.

Incidentally, if you want to fit a distributor from a later model of car, do consult Holden's first, as advance curves can be very different. Earlier engines might 'pink' while later engines fitted with an earlier distributor might be down on power.

Vacuum advance mechanisms work directly on to the cam pillar and the plate at its base. When the vacuum inside the manifold reaches a certain point, the plate is pulled against the pressure of a pair of springs and this advances or retards the ignition,

according to the amount of acceleration. Also working on the same plate is the centrifugal advance mechanism. This consists of a pair of weights which push gradually outwards as the speed rises. Consequently, higher speeds and more centrifugal force will together cause the largest pull on the plate, advancing it furthest and fastest. To prevent things getting out of hand, the two coil springs can be 'tuned' to let the advance occur faster or slower, as required (the advance curve), and there is a stop to give the distributor its maximum advance. Holden's restorers fit new springs and ensure that the stop is the right length for the model of car in question – which is why you will have to tell year, engine size, and state of tune.

Holden's don't actually *start* here, of course! They strip the old unit down and send various bits, including the cam pillar away for plating. The shaft itself is checked for true running and reground 5 thou. undersize. Old bushes are pressed out of the cleaned body, and new sintered (self-lubricating) bushes are pressed in. Sintered material is especially prone to distortion or even disintegration, and simple but special press tools are required. Weights wear out and are always renewed while pivot posts, which almost never wear, are checked and only replaced if necessary. Finally, the rebuilt distributor is placed on the test rig and checked to ensure that the advance characteristics are exactly as required.

The newly rebuilt distributor will ensure that the engine's vital sparks are fed in at precisely the right time. In a nutshell, the bushes keep the spark exactly at the position you put it in; the correctly positioned stop ensures the optimum maximum *amount* of advance while the new springs control its rate. At the same time, the new weights and vacuum device ensure that the advance or retard is graduated correctly in accordance with the amount of acceleration and speed.

A distributor's innards are a brilliantly evolved piece of precision engineering. The most amazing thing of all is that the

whole thing works so precisely at such unimaginable speeds, which are mind-bogglingly high even in the typical classic car's engine. Small wonder that a badly worn unit carves into an engine's performance and makes the engine both more expensive to run and an unnecessary contributor to the frightening pool of pollution that we are all creating. And it's worth remembering that, if a good number of our classic cars are going to be able to pass today's MOT test, complete with emission checks, getting the sparks *and* the mixture spot on is going to require engines that run as the makers originally intended.

Thanks are due to Holden Vintage & Classic for their invaluable help. Their address can be found in the Appendices

▲ *DIS1. The author's Vauxhall, whose distributor was photographed for this article.*

▲ *DIS2. With the distributor out of the car, test for spindle and bush wear by rocking the top of the spindle.*

▲ DIS3. Check the drive slot in the base of the spindle. Wear is quite common here.

▲ DIS4. New bushes are of sintered construction – particles of metal and carbon compressed to form a perfect self-lubricating bearing material.

▲ DIS5. The old are pressed out; the new pressed in, using a special tool to prevent the sintered bushes from deforming or collapsing.

▲ DIS6. Some compression will invariably take place and the new bushes are reamered to size.

◀ DIS7. The newly reground spindle and base plate with new advance weights.

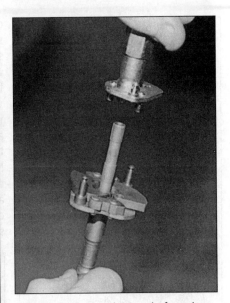

▲ DIS8. The replated rotor shaft pushes on to the spindle, and pegs in the base locate into the weights. As the weights swing out at speed, they advance the rotor shaft. The rotor shaft is held normally back at first base by a pair of springs which pull on posts mounted on the base plate. One of the posts is also the stop for the advance limiter built into the front of the rotor shaft. This can be added to by welding a bit on, in order to limit the advance, or ground off to increase it. The correct amount is stamped on to it.

▲ DIS9. The final step is to bench test the complete distributor to ensure that the lightning is striking where and when it is wanted.

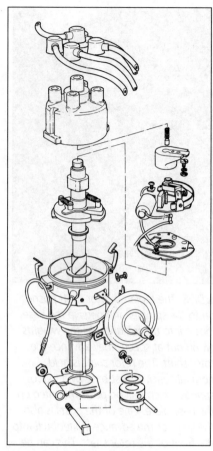

▲ DIS10. The MG Midget distributor is a typical Lucas unit with all of the standard features mentioned here.

STEERING WHEEL RESTORATION

Here is how to restore a steering wheel using a POR-15 Inc. restoration kit, and I am grateful for the assistance of Frost Auto Restoration Techniques in the writing of this section.

Most old steering wheel restorations are not very complicated, and you can use many of the same techniques in restoring dash knobs, gear shift knobs, radio buttons, and other hard rubber, bakelite, or plastic interior parts.

If any plating is required, it must be done prior to your steering wheel restoration. Ask your plater to completely mask the plastic from the harsh chemicals used in the plating process which could result in further

damage to your wheel. Very often the spokes of a steering wheel are made of stainless steel, which will clean up easily with a fine rubbing compound or with fine (000 grade) steel wool.

Before stripping the existing colour from your wheel, take it to your automotive paint store so you can match the original colour as closely as possible. Most colours can be closely matched to existing body colours from the same era and make of the car. We recommend cellulose paint because you can always sand out your mistakes and begin again.

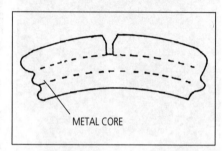

METAL CORE

▲ SWR1. Clean steering wheel completely with POR-15 Marine-Clean. Spray it on, rub it in, then rinse it away with plain water. This cleaner and degreaser has no petroleum additives and is environmentally safe to use and discard with your waste water. All cracks in your wheel must be sawn out and filled with POR-15 Putty. Saw out the cracks all the way to the metal core. This will allow the putty to completely fill the voids and make the wheel solid. Bevel or 'V' cut each crack a little. Don't over-cut. Use the file provided in your kit to make the bevels.

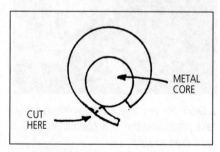

METAL CORE

CUT HERE

▲ SWR2. File or break off any hard rubber, bakelite, or plastic which has separated and curled away from the metal core. This happens quite often when the outer surface of the wheel is $\frac{1}{16}$ in or less from the metal core.

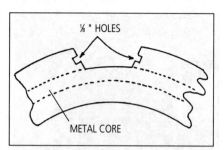

⅛ " HOLES

METAL CORE

▲ SWR3. If a large section of the wheel is missing drill several ⅛ in holes approximately ⅛ in deep into the wheel on both sides of the void. Use the file board with 100 grit to sand the edges. This procedure will allow the POR-15 Putty to form a strong bond with the wheel. The wheel must be clean and free of dust. You are now ready to use the POR-15 Putty. Cut equal parts of bar A and bar B. The easiest method is to place both bars side by side on your workbench with the ends lined up perfectly. Make a common cut through both bars. This will ensure you have equal amounts of each bar. Failure to mix equal parts of each bar may result in a mixture that does not harden completely. Now, wearing the gloves supplied, mix both parts together very thoroughly. Knead the putty and make sure it is totally blended. Failure to do this may result in soft spots in the finished job. Keep a dish of water nearby when using the putty. Dampen 'hands' of your gloves before kneading parts A and B together. If hands or fingers begin to feel 'sticky' while mixing, dip fingers in water again. Repeat if necessary until putty is thoroughly mixed.

NEVER HANDLE EPOXY PUTTY WITHOUT WEARING GLOVES!

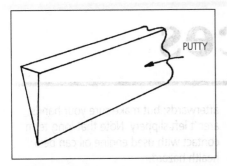

▲ *SWR4. Roll out a ¼ in rope-like section of putty and squeeze the bottom portion to form a wedge which can be forced into each crack. Use your thumbs to force the putty into the cracks. Use water on your fingers to feather and smooth the putty. You have plenty of time since the putty sets slowly, so don't rush! Rub your moist fingers across the crack to feather the edge. Remember, the smoother you make this job, the less time you will spend sanding later. If the putty does not feather out smoothly, use more water.*

If sections of the finger-grips are broken off the wheel, these can be moulded and formed with the putty. Once again, try to form them as fully as possible, because it's a lot easier to do this with moist putty than it is to sand or file a crudely-formed grip to the right shape later.

POR-15 Epoxy Putty will cure in 60 minutes at 75°F (24°C). Reducing the temperature by 5°F (3°C) will double the cure time. We recommend that you allow several days for curing if time is not important. After the putty is cured, you are ready to sand and shape the wheel.

Put a strip of 100 grit paper on the sanding board. Sand all filled areas with the sanding board except for the finger grips. Wrap 100 grit paper on the contoured (soft) sanding block; then squeeze this to the shape of the existing finger grips and sand your new grips to match them. Fill any low spots with POR-15 Putty, then feather. Allow the putty to cure, then re-sand with 100 grit.

Gradually reduce the sandpaper grit to a finer grade (100 grit to 220–240 grit to 320 grit). The rim must be smooth before priming. Use the red scuff pad

(360–400 grit) and go over the entire wheel just prior to priming. Mask off any areas that are not to be painted.

Now you must improvize and make a device on which to rotate the wheel. Use a pipe or dowel which will fit into the nailed-down block on the saw-horse or bench with either end. Push the pipe or dowel through the steering-wheel hub and wrap duct tape on both sides of the hub, or drill two holes in the pipe for pins.

Mount the wheel in block and wipe clean with the tack cloth. Now apply POR primer. **It is essential that you carefully read the instructions with this special primer.**

Sand the wheel with 320 grit until all the deep scratches and orange peel texture have disappeared. If you accidentally sand through the prime coat, re-spray with two more coats and allow to dry hard. Now watersand with 400 grit or finer wet-or-dry paper until all sanding marks are gone. The wheel must be smooth, with no scratch marks visible. Dry with a soft rag.

Wipe wheel again with tack cloth. You are now ready to apply several coats of your final colour. Do not touch the prepared surface with your hands, as that would leave an oily residue on the wheel, preventing the best possible

bonding between paint and the wheel. Spray several coats of your topcoat, allow flash-off between coats. Do not spray too heavily too fast, or it will take many days to dry. Allow the paint to dry thoroughly, then sand lightly using 600 grit sandpaper. Then use the grey scuff pad (1000 grit) over the entire wheel. N.B. Cellulose paint is not particularly hard. The painted surface will last *much* longer if you take the wheel to a professional re-finisher and have the wheel painted in 2-pack paint. For health and safety reasons, 2-pack is *not* suitable for spraying at home.

Wipe the wheel again with the tack cloth. Spray on the final coat or two. Allow approximately three days for drying. The final step is to buff the surface with POR-15 high gloss rubbing compound, using a soft cotton cloth. Wipe dry with a cotton terry cloth towel.

You now have a show-quality steering wheel. Polish it with your favourite wax after 60 days.

▼ *SWR5. The POR-15 kit contains everything you may need to restore your steering wheel, apart from finish paint. N.B. NEVER HANDLE EPOXY PUTTY WITHOUT WEARING THE GLOVES PROVIDED IN THE KIT.* (Courtesy: Frost Auto Restoration)

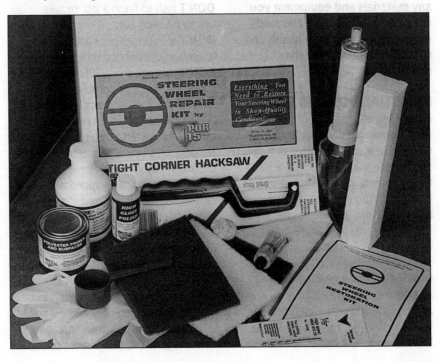

Appendices

WORKSHOP PROCEDURES & SAFETY FIRST

Professional motor mechanics are trained in safe working procedures, whereas the onus is on you, the home mechanic, to find them out for yourself and act upon them. However enthusiastic you may be about getting on with the job in hand, do take the time to ensure that your safety is not put at risk. A moment's lack of attention can result in an accident, as can failure to observe certain elementary precautions.

There will always be new ways of having accidents, and the following points do not pretend to be a comprehensive list of all dangers; they are intended rather to make you aware of the risks and to encourage a safety-conscious approach to all work you carry out on your vehicle.

Be sure to consult the suppliers of any materials and equipment you may use, and to obtain and read carefully operating and health and safety instructions that they may supply.

ESSENTIAL DOS AND DON'TS

DON'T rely on a single jack when working underneath the vehicle. Always use reliable additional means of support, such as axle stands, securely placed under a part of the vehicle that you know will not give way.

DON'T attempt to loosen or tighten high-torque nuts (e.g. wheel hub nuts) while the vehicle is on a jack; it may be pulled off.

DON'T start the engine without first ascertaining that the transmission is in neutral (or 'Park' where applicable) and the parking brake applied.

DON'T suddenly remove the filler cap from a hot cooling system – cover it with a cloth and release the pressure gradually first, or you may get scalded by escaping coolant.

DON'T attempt to drain oil, automatic transmission fluid, or coolant until you are sure it has cooled sufficiently to avoid scalding you.

DON'T grasp any part of the engine, exhaust or catalytic converter without first ascertaining that it is sufficiently cool to avoid burning you.

DON'T allow brake fluid or antifreeze to contact vehicle paintwork.

DON'T syphon toxic liquids such as fuel, brake fluid or antifreeze by mouth, or allow them to remain on your skin.

DON'T inhale dust – it may be injurious to health (see Asbestos below).

DON'T allow any spilt oil or grease to remain on the floor – wipe it up straight away, before someone slips on it.

DON'T use ill-fitting spanners or other tools which may slip and cause injury.

DON'T attempt to lift a heavy component which may be beyond your capability – get assistance.

DON'T rush to finish a job, or take unverified short cuts.

DON'T allow children or animals in or around an unattended vehicle.

DON'T park vehicles with catalytic converters over combustible materials such as dry grass, oily rags, etc. if the engine has recently been run. As catalytic converters reach extremely high temperatures, any such materials in close proximity may ignite.

DON'T run vehicles equipped with catalytic converters without the exhaust system heat shields fitted.

DO wear eye protection when using power tools such as an electric drill, sander, bench grinder etc., and when working under the vehicle.

DO use a barrier cream on your hands prior to undertaking dirty jobs – it will protect your skin from infection as well as making the dirt easier to remove afterwards; but make sure your hands aren't left slippery. Note that long term contact with used engine oil can be a health hazard.

DO keep loose clothing (cuffs, tie etc.) and long hair well out of the way of moving mechanical parts.

DO remove rings, wrist watch etc., before working on the vehicle – especially the electrical system.

DO ensure that any lifting tackle used has a safe working load rating adequate for the job, and is used precisely as recommended by the manufacturer.

DO keep your work area tidy – it is only too easy to fall over articles left lying around.

DO get someone to check periodically that all is well, when working alone on the vehicle.

DO carry out work in a logical sequence and check that everything is correctly assembled and tightened afterwards.

DO remember that your vehicle's safety affects that of yourself and others. If in doubt on any point, get specialist advice.

IF, in spite of following these precautions, you are unfortunate enough to injure yourself, seek medical attention as soon as possible.

FIRE

Remember at all times that petrol (gasoline) is highly flammable. Never smoke, or have any kind of naked flame around, when working on the vehicle. But the risk does not end there – a spark caused by an electrical short-circuit, by two metal surfaces contacting each other, by a central heating boiler in the garage 'firing up', or even by static electricity built up in your body under certain conditions, can ignite petrol vapour, which in a confined space is highly explosive.

Always disconnect the battery earth (ground) terminal before working on any part of the fuel system, and never risk spilling fuel on to a hot engine or exhaust.

It is recommended that a fire extinguisher of a type suitable for fuel and electrical fires is kept handy in the garage or workplace at all times. Never try to extinguish a fuel or electrical fire with water.

FUMES

Certain fumes are highly toxic and can quickly cause unconsciousness and even death if inhaled to any extent. Petrol (gasoline) vapour comes into this category, as do the vapours from certain solvents such as trichloroethylene and those from many adhesives. Any draining or pouring of such volatile fluids should be done in a well-ventilated area.

When using cleaning fluids and solvents, read the instructions carefully. Never use any materials from unmarked containers – they may give off poisonous vapours.

Never run the engine of a motor vehicle in an enclosed space such as a garage. Exhaust fumes contain carbon monoxide which is extremely poisonous. If you need to run the engine, always do so in the open air or at least have the rear of the vehicle outside the workplace.

If you are fortunate enough to have the use of an inspection pit, never drain or pour petrol, and never run the engine, while the vehicle is standing over it; the fumes, being heavier than air, will concentrate in the pit with possibly lethal results.

THE BATTERY

Never cause a spark, or allow a naked light, near the vehicle battery. It will normally be giving off a certain amount of hydrogen gas, which is highly explosive.

Always disconnect the battery earth (ground) terminal before working on the fuel or electrical systems.

If possible, loosen the filler plugs or cover when charging the battery from an external source. Do not charge at an excessive rate or the battery may burst.

Take care when topping up and when carrying the battery. The acid electrolyte, even when diluted, is very corrosive and should not be allowed to contact the eyes or skin.

If you ever need to prepare electrolyte yourself, always add the acid slowly to the water, and never the other way round. Protect against splashes by wearing rubber gloves and goggles.

MAINS ELECTRICITY

When using an electric power tool, inspection light etc., which works from the mains, always ensure that the appliance is correctly connected to its plug and that, where necessary, it is properly earthed (grounded). Do not use such appliances in damp conditions and, again, beware of creating a spark or applying excessive heat in the vicinity of fuel or fuel vapour.

Also, before using any mains powered electrical equipment, take one more simple precaution – use an RCD (Residual Current Device) circuit breaker. Then, if there is a short, the RCD circuit breaker minimises the risk of electrocution by instantly cutting the power supply. Buy from any electrical store or DIY centre. RCDs fit simply into your electrical socket before plugging in your electrical equipment.

IGNITION HT VOLTAGE

A severe electric shock can result from touching certain parts of the ignition system, such as the HT leads, when the engine is running or being cranked, particularly if components are damp or the insulation is defective. Where an electronic ignition system is fitted, the HT voltage is much higher and could prove fatal. Consult your handbook or main dealer if in any doubt. Risk of injury while working on running engines, e.g. adjusting the timing, can arise if the operator touches a high voltage lead and pulls his hand away on to a projection or revolving part.

WELDING AND BODYWORK REPAIRS

It is so useful to be able to weld when carrying out restoration work, and yet there is a good deal that could go dangerously wrong for the uninformed – in fact more than could be covered here. **For safety's sake** you are strongly recommended to seek tuition, in

whatever branch of welding you wish to use, from your local evening institute or adult education classes. In addition, all of the information and instructional material produced by the suppliers of materials and equipment you will be using must be studied carefully. You may have to ask your stockist for some of this printed material if it is not made available at the time of purchase.

In addition, it is strongly recommended that *The Car Bodywork Repair Manual*, published by Haynes, is purchased and studied before carrying out any welding or bodywork repairs. Consisting of 292 pages, around 1,000 illustrations and written by Lindsay Porter, the author of this book, *The Car Bodywork Repair Manual* picks the brains of specialists from a variety of fields, and covers arc, MIG and 'gas' welding, panel beating and accident repair, rust repair and treatment, paint spraying, glass-fibre work, filler, lead loading, interiors and much more besides. Alongside a number of projects, the book describes in detail how to carry out each of the techniques involved in car bodywork repair with safety notes where necessary. As such, it is the ideal complement to this book.

COMPRESSED GAS CYLINDERS

There are serious hazards associated with the storage and handling of gas cylinders and fittings, and standard precautions should be strictly observed in dealing with them. Ensure that cylinders are stored in safe conditions, properly maintained and always handled with special care and make constant efforts to eliminate the possibilities of leakage, fire and explosion.

The cylinder gases that are commonly used are oxygen, acetylene and liquid petroleum gas (LPG). Safety requirements for all three gases are: Cylinders must be stored in a fire resistant, dry and well-ventilated space, away from any source of heat or ignition and protected from ice, snow or direct sunlight. Valves of cylinders in store must always be kept uppermost and closed, even when the cylinder is empty. Cylinders should be handled with care and only by personnel who are reliable, adequately informed and fully aware of all associated hazards. Damaged or leaking cylinders should be immediately taken outside into the open air, and the supplier and fire authorities should be notified immediately. No one should approach a gas cylinder store with a naked light or cigarette. Care should be taken to avoid striking or dropping cylinders, or knocking them together. Cylinders should never be used as rollers. One cylinder should never be filled from another. Every care must be taken to avoid accidental damage to cylinder valves. Valves must be operated without haste, never fully opened hard back against the back stop (so that other users know the valve is open) and never wrenched shut but turned just securely enough to stop the gas. Before removing or loosening any outlet connections, caps or plugs, a check should be made that the valves are closed. When changing cylinders, close all valves and appliance taps, and extinguish naked flames, including pilot jets, before disconnecting them. When reconnecting ensure that all connections and washers are clean and in good condition and do not overtighten them. Immediately a cylinder becomes empty, close its valve.

Safety requirements for acetylene: Cylinders must always be stored and used in the upright position. If a cylinder becomes heated accidentally or becomes hot because of excessive backfiring, immediately shut the valve, detach the regulator, take the cylinder out of doors well away from the building, immerse it in or continuously spray it with water, open the valve and allow the gas to escape until the cylinder is empty. If necessary, notify the emergency fire service without delay.

Safety requirements for oxygen are: No oil or grease should be used on valves or fittings. Cylinders with convex bases should be used in a stand or held securely to a wall.

Safety requirements for LPG are: The store must be kept free of combustible material, corrosive material and cylinders of oxygen.

Cylinders should only ever be carried upright, securely strapped down, preferably in an open vehicle or with windows open. Carry the suppliers safety data with you. In the event of an accident, notify the Police and Fire services and hand the safety data to them.

DANGEROUS LIQUIDS AND GASES
Because of flammable gas given off by batteries when on charge, care should be taken to avoid sparking by switching off the power supply before charger leads are connected or disconnected. Battery terminals should be shielded, since a battery contains energy and a spark can be caused by any conductor which touches its terminals or exposed connecting straps.

When internal combustion engines are operated inside buildings the exhaust fumes must be properly discharged to the open air. Petroleum spirit or mixture must be contained in metal cans which should be kept in a store. In any area where battery charging or the testing of fuel injection systems is carried out there must be good ventilation, and no sources of ignition. Inspection pits often present serious hazards. They should be of adequate length to allow safe access and exit while a car is in position. If there is an inspection pit, petrol may enter it. Since petrol vapour is heavier than air it will remain there and be a hazard if there is any source of ignition. All sources of ignition must therefore be excluded.

LIFTING EQUIPMENT
Special care should be taken when any type of lifting equipment is used. Lifting jacks are for raising vehicles; they should never be used as supports while work is in progress. Jacks must be replaced by adequate rigid supports before any work is begun on the vehicle. Risk of injury while working on running engines, e.g. adjusting the timing, can arise if the operator touches a high voltage lead and pulls his hand away on to a projection or revolving part. On some vehicles the voltage used in the ignition system is so high as to cause injury or death by electrocution. Consult your handbook or main dealer if in any doubt.

WORK WITH PLASTICS
Work with plastic materials brings additional hazards into workshops. Many of the materials used (polymers, resins, adhesives and materials acting as catalysts and accelerators) readily produce very dangerous situations in the form of poisonous fumes, skin irritants, risk of fire and explosions. Do not allow resin or 2-pack adhesive hardener, or that supplied with filler or 2-pack stopper to come into contact with skin or eyes. Read carefully the safety notes supplied on the tin, tube or packaging.

JACKS AND AXLE STANDS
Special care should be taken when any type of lifting equipment is used. Any jack is made for lifting the car, not for supporting it. NEVER even consider working under your car using only a jack to support the weight of it. Jacks are only for raising vehicles, and must be replaced by adequate supports before any work is begun on the vehicle; axle stands are available from many discount stores, and all auto parts stores. These stands are absolutely essential if you plan to work under your car. Simple triangular stands (fixed or adjustable) will suit almost all of your working situations. Drive-on ramps are very limiting because of their design and size.

When jacking the car from the front, leave the gearbox in neutral and the brake off until you have placed the axle stands under the frame. Make sure that the car is on level ground first! Then put the car into gear and/or engage the handbrake and lower the jack. Obviously DO NOT put the car in gear if you plan to turn over the engine! Leaving the brake on, or leaving the car in gear while jacking the front of the car will necessarily cause the jack to tip (unless a good quality trolley jack with wheels is being used). This is unavoidable when jacking the car on one side, and the use of the handbrake in this case is recommended.

If the car is older and if it shows signs of weakening at the jack tubes while using the factory jack, it is best to purchase a good scissors jack or hydraulic jack – preferably trolley-type (depending on your budget).

WORKSHOP SAFETY – SUMMARY

1 Always have a fire extinguisher at arm's length whenever welding or when working on the fuel system – under the car, or under the bonnet.
2 NEVER use a naked flame near the petrol tank.
3 Keep your inspection lamp FAR AWAY from any source of dripping petrol (gasoline); for example, while removing the fuel pump.
4 NEVER use petrol (gasoline) to clean parts. Use paraffin (kerosene) or white (mineral) spirits.
5 NO SMOKING!

If you do have a fire, DON'T PANIC. Use the extinguisher effectively by directing it at the base of the fire.

PAINT SPRAYING

NEVER use 2-pack, isocyanate-based paints in the home environment or home workshop. Ask your supplier if you are not sure which is which. If you have use of a professional booth, wear an air-fed mask. Wear a charcoal face mask when spraying other paints and maintain ventilation to the spray area. Concentrated fumes are dangerous!

Spray fumes, thinners and paint are highly flammable. Keep away from naked flames or sparks.

Paint spraying safety is too large a subject for this book. See Lindsay Porter's *The Car Bodywork Repair Manual* (Haynes) for further information.

▶ 6.1 Invest in a workshop-sized fire extinguisher. Choose the carbon dioxide type or preferably, dry powder but never a water type extinguisher for workshop use. Water conducts electricty and can make worse an oil or petrol-based fire, in certain circumstances.

FLUOROELASTOMERS – MOST IMPORTANT! PLEASE READ THIS SECTION!

Many synthetic rubber-like materials used in motor cars contain a substance called fluorine. These substances are known as fluoroelastomers and are commonly used for oil seals, wiring and cabling, bearing surfaces, gaskets, diaphragms, hoses and 'O' rings. If they are subjected to temperatures greater than 315°C, they will decompose and can be potentially hazardous. Fluoroelastomer materials will show physical signs of decomposition under such conditions in the form of charring of black sticky masses. Some decomposition may occur at temperatures above 200°C, and it is obvious that when a car has been in a fire or has been dismantled with the assistance of a cutting torch or blow torch, the fluoroelastomers can decompose in the manner indicated above.

In the presence of any water or humidity, including atmospheric moisture, the by-products caused by the fluoroelastomers being heated can be extremely dangerous. According to the Health and Safety Executive, 'Skin contact with this liquid or decomposition residues can cause painful and penetrating burns. Permanent irreversible skin and tissue damage can occur.' Damage can also be caused to eyes or by the inhalation of fumes created as fluoroelastomers are burned or heated.

If you are in the vicinity of a vehicle fire or a place where a vehicle is being cut up with cutting equipment, the Health and Safety Executive recommend the following action:

1 Assume unless you know otherwise that seals, gaskets and 'O' rings, hoses, wiring and cabling, bearing surfaces and diaphragms are fluoroelastomers.
2 Inform firefighters of the presence of fluoroelastomers and toxic and corrosive fume hazards when they arrive.
3 All personnel not wearing breathing apparatus must leave the immediate area of a fire.

After fires or exposure to high temperatures
1 Do not touch blackened or charred seals or equipment.
2 Allow all burnt or decomposed fluoroelastomer materials to cool down before inspection, investigation, tear-down or removal.
3 Preferably, don't handle parts containing decomposed fluoroelastomers, but if you must, wear goggles and PVC (polyvinyl chloride) or neoprene protective gloves whilst doing so. Never handle such parts unless they are completely cool.
4 Contaminated parts, residues, materials and clothing, including protective clothing and gloves, should be disposed of by an approved contractor to landfill or by incineration according to national or local regulations. Original seals, gaskets and 'O' rings, along with contaminated material, must not be burned locally.

Symptoms and clinical findings of exposure:

A Skin/eye contact
Symptoms may be apparent immediately, soon after contact or there may be considerable delay after exposure. Do not assume that there has been no damage from a lack of immediate symptoms; delays of minutes in treatment can have severe consequences:

1 Dull throbbing ache.
2 Severe and persistent pain.
3 Black discolouration under nails (skin contact).
4 Severe, persistent and penetrating burns.
5 Skin swelling and redness.
6 Blistering.
7 Sometimes pain without visible change.

B Inhalation (breathing) – immediate
1 Coughing.
2 Choking.
3 Chills lasting one to two hours after exposure.
4 Irritation.

C Inhalation (breathing) – delays of one to two days or more
1 Fever.
2 Cough.
3 Chest tightness.
4 Pulmonary oedema (congestion).
5 Bronchial pneumonia.

First aid

A Skin contact
1 Remove contaminated clothing immediately.
2 Irrigate affected skin with copious amounts of cold water or limewater (saturated calcium hydroxide solution) for 15 to 60 minutes. Obtain medical assistance urgently.

B Inhalation
Remove to fresh air and obtain medical supportive treatment immediately. Treat for pulmonary oedema.

C Eye contact
Wash/irrigate eyes immediately with water followed by normal saline for 30 to 60 minutes. Obtain immediate medical attention.

APPENDIX 2

BRITISH AND AMERICAN TECHNICAL TERMS

English	American
Accelerator	Gas pedal
Aerial	Antenna
Alternator	Generator (AC)
Anti-roll bar	Stabilizer or sway bar
Battery	Energizer
Bodywork	Sheet metal
Bonnet (engine cover)	Hood
Boot (luggage compartment)	Trunk
Boot lid	Trunk lid
Bottom gear	First gear
Bulkhead	Firewall
Cam follower or tappet	Valve lifter or tappet
Carburettor	Carburetor
Catch	Latch
Choke/venturi	Barrel
Clearance	Lash
Crownwheel	Ring gear (of differential)
Disc (brake)	Rotor/disk
Drop arm	Pitman arm
Drophead coupé	Convertible
Dynamo	Generator(DC)
Earth (elec)	Ground
Engineer's blue	Prussian blue
Estate car	Station wagon
Exhaust manifold	Header
Fast back	Hard top
Fault finding/ diagnosis	Trouble shooting
Float chamber	Flat bowl
Free-play	Lash
Freewheel	Coast
Gudgeon pin	Piston pin or wrist pin
Gearchange	Shift
Gearbox	Transmission
Halfshaft	Axleshaft
Handbrake	Parking brake
Hood	Soft top
Hot spot	Heat riser
Indicator	Turn signal
Interior light	Dome lamp
Layshaft (of gearbox)	Countershaft
Leading shoe (of brake)	Primary shoe
Locks	Latches
Motorway	Freeway, turnpike
Number plate	License plate
Paraffin	Kerosene
Petrol	Gasoline
Petrol tank	Gas tank
'Pinking'	'Pinging'
Propeller shaft	Driveshaft
Quarterlight	Quarter window
Retread	Recap
Reverse	Back-up
Rocker cover	Valve cover
Roof rack	Car-top carrier
Saloon	Sedan
Seized	Frozen
Side indicator lights	Side marker lights
Side light	Parking light
Silencer	Muffler
Sill panel	Rocker panel
Spanner	Wrench
Split cotter (for valve spring cap)	Lock (for valve spring retainer)
Split pin	Cotter pin
Steering arm	Spindle arm
Sump	Oil pan
Tab washer	Tang; lock
Tailgate	Liftgate
Tappet	Valve lifter
Thrust bearing	Throw-out bearing
Top gear	High
Trackrod (of steering)	Tie-rod (or connecting rod)
Trailing shoe (of brake)	Secondary shoe
Transmission	Whole drive line
Tyre	Tire
Van	Panel wagon/van
Vice	Vise
Wheel nut	Lug nut
Windscreen	Windshield
Wing/mudguard	Fender

APPENDIX 3

SPECIALIST SUPPLIERS FEATURED IN THIS BOOK

Automec Equipment & Parts Ltd,
36 Ballmoor, Buckingham, MK18 1RQ.
Tel: 01280 822818
Non-corroding copper brake, clutch and fuel pipes. Silicone D.O.T.S. brake fluid. Rubber lined 'P' clips, pipe flaring and pipe bending tools, ABA stainless steel hoseclips.

Blaupunkt, Robert Bosch Ltd,
PO Box 98, Broadwater Park, North Orbital Road, Denham, Uxbridge, Middx, UB9 5HJ.
Tel: 01895 834466
High quality range of in-car entertainment systems.

BOC Gases, The Priestley Centre,
10 Priestley Road, The Surrey Research Park, Guildford, Surrey, GU2 5XY.
Tel: 01483 579857
Welding gases and DIY 'Portapak' gas welding equipment.

Bosch, Robert Bosch Ltd, PO Box 98, Broadwater Park, North Orbital Road, Denham, Uxbridge, Middlesex, UB9 5HJ.
Tel: 01895 834466
Very wide range of high quality D.I.Y. and professional power tools (and large range of Bosch automotive parts and accessories).

Burlen Fuel Systems, Spitfire House, Castle Road, Salisbury, Wiltshire, SP1 3SA.
Tel: 01722 412500
Full restoration service on all SU, Zenith, CD and Weber carburettors and fuel pumps. Backed up with full availability of new units, repair kits and parts.

Castrol (UK) Ltd, Burmah Castrol House, Pipers Way, Swindon, Wiltshire, SN3 1RE.
Tel: 01793 512712
Consumer Technical Department can supply full information on all lubrication requirements.

Chubb Fire Ltd, Racal-Chubb House, Sunbury-on-Thames, Middx, TW16 7AR.
Tel: 01932 785588
Fire extinguishers for workshop and car.

Cibie, Ring Automotive, Geldered Road, Leeds, LS12 6NB.
Tel: 01132 279 1791
Manufacturers of a wide range of original and replacement electrical equipment.

Clarke International, Hemnall Street, Epping, Essex, CM16 4LG.
Tel: 01992 565 300
Huge range of workshop equipment – everything from MIG welders to air compressors, bench grinders to power washers, and much more besides.

Comma Oils & Chemicals Ltd,
Lower Range Road, Gravesend, Kent, DA12 2QX.
Tel: 01474 564311
Motor oil, Copper Ease grease, X-stream corrosion resistant coolant.

Connolly Leather Ltd, Wandle Bank, Wimbledon, London, SW19 1DW.
Tel: 0181 542 5251
World renowned for the supply of highest quality leather to top manufacturers and of leather renovation kits for DIY use.

Coventry Hood & Seating (Part of Tickford Ltd), Tickford House, Tanners Drive, Blakelands, Milton Keynes, MK14 5BN.
Tel: 01908 614688
Manufacturers of original equipment soft-tops for most British cars. Available only through specialist outlets.

The Eastwood Company,
Unit G, Millbrook Road, Stover Industrial Estate, Yate, Bristol, BS17 5PB.
Tel: 01454 329900
A huge range of specialist tools, materials and equipment purpose made for the classic car restorer.

David Felton, Vintage & Prototype Car Panels, Brook Farm, Rushton Spencer, Nr Macclesfield, Cheshire, SK11 0RU.
Tel: 01260 226451
Panel repair or reproduction, in steel or aluminium, complete bodies, including ash frames to the highest standards yet seen by this author.

Frost Auto Restoration Techniques Ltd,
Crawford Street, Rochdale, OL16 5NU.
Tel: 01706 58619
A huge range of specialist tools, materials and equipment purpose made for the classic car restorer. Mail order catalogue available.

Hammerite Products Ltd, Acorn House, Prudhoe, Northumberland, NE42 6LP.
Tel: 01661 830000
Waxoyl, Hammerite hammered and smooth metal finishes – available from all high street auto accessory stores.

Holden Vintage & Classic Ltd, Linton Trading Estate, Bromyard, Herefordshire, HR7 4QT
Tel: 01885 488000
Suppliers of obsolete Lucas electrical equipment of all types. Excellent for overhaul of elderly distributors, especially where new replacements are no longer available. Mail order catalogue available, containing electrical, period accessories, etc.

Kenlowe, Burchetts Green, Maidenhead, Berkshire, SL6 6QU.
Tel: 01628 823303
Electric cooling fans.

Lucas Aftermarket Operations, Stratford Road, Shirley, Solihull, Warks, B90 4LA.
Tel: 0121 627 6000
Original braking, diesel, electrical and electronic equipment for the world's vehicles.

Macdonald Classic Cars, Unit 8, Linton Trading Estate, Bromyard, Herefordshire.
Tel: 01885 482042
Graham runs his own restoration business – highly recommended!

Machine Mart, (Head Office), 211 Lower Parliament Street, Nottingham, NG1 1GN. Tel: 0115 956 1805
The best range of workshop tools and equipment with outlets throughout the UK.

Marpet Car Audio, 16 Bourne Vale, Hayes, Bromley, Kent, BR2 7JW. Tel: 0181 462 6859
Cheerful and efficient installer of in-car entertainment and other electrical equipment. Agents for Cobra and Philips alarms.

Moss Engineering, Lower Road Trading Estate, Ledbury, Herefordshire, HR8 2DJ. (No connection with Moss Europe or Moss Motors.) Engine reconditioning to a high standard.

Moss Europe, Victoria Villas, Richmond, Surrey, TW9 2JX. Tel: 0181 948 8888
Quality parts and expertise for Triumph, MG and Austin Healey sports cars. Branches throughout the UK. Contact Moss Europe for details of your nearest branch.

Murex Welding Products Ltd, Hertford Road, Waltham Cross, Hertfordshire, EN8 7RP. Tel: 01992 710000
Suppliers of welding products available through BOC Centres nationwide.

Namrick Ltd, Nut & Bolt Store, 124 Portland Road, Hove, Sussex, BN3 5QL. Tel: 01273 736963
Nuts, bolts, washers; a full range of fixings in plated and stainless steel.

Philips Car Stereo & Automotive Systems, PCS House, Talisman Road, Bicester, Oxon, OX6 0JX. Tel: 01869 320333
Wide range of high quality in-car entertainment systems.

Pirelli Tyres Ltd, Derby Road, Burton-on-Trent, Staffs, DE13 0BH. Tel: 01283 566301

Pound Garden Buildings, Lye Head, Bewdley, Worcestershire, DY12 2UX. Tel: 01299 266337/266000
Excellent quality timber garages and workshops in a wide range of styles and sizes. Specials a pleasure.

PP Video Productions, The Storehouse, Little Hereford Street, Bromyard, Herefordshire, HR7 4DE. Tel: 01885 488800
Producers of 'classic' motoring videos. For all UK and overseas outlets, contact above address.

SATA, Saxham Business Park, Saxham, Bury St. Edmonds, Suffolk, IP28 6RX. Tel: 01284 760791
Rust prevention injection equipment.

SIP (Industrial Products) Ltd, Gelders Hall Road, Shepshed, Loughborough, Leicestershire, LE12 9NH. Tel: 01509 503141
Britain's largest manufacturers of welding equipment and air compressors with over 200 distributors nationwide.

Speedy Cables (London) Ltd, The Mews, St. Pauls Street, Islington, London, N1 7BU. Tel: 0171 226 9228
Speedo, brake, throttle, choke and other cables to pattern or specification. Also: repair and recalibration of post-1950 speedos, rev counters and clocks.

SP Tyres UK Ltd, Fort Dunlop, Erdington, Birmingham, B24 9QT. Tel: 0121 384 4444
Manufacturers of Dunlop Classic Range tyres. See Vintage Tyre Supplies Ltd.

Sykes-Pickavant Ltd, Kilnhouse Lane, Lytham St Annes, Lancashire, FY8 3DU. Tel: 01253 784800
Manufacturers of specialist automotive service and hand tools.

Vintage Restorations, The Old Bakery, Windmill Street, Tunbridge Wells, Kent, TN2 4UU. Tel: 01892 525899
Restoration and supply of vintage and classic vehicle instruments and dashboard fitting: temperature gauges rebuilt; speedometers recalibrated.

Vintage Supplies, Folgate Road, North Walsham, Norfolk, NR28 0AJ. Tel: 01692 406343
"Slosh Tank" fuel tank sealant and a wide range of specialist materials for the 'vintage' owner.

Vintage Tyre Supplies Ltd, At the National Motor Museum, Beaulieu, Brockenhurst, Hampshire, SO42 7ZN. Tel: 01590 612261
Worldwide distributors of Veteran, Vintage and Classic car and motorcycle tyres. Over 16,000 in stock including Dunlop, Pirelli, Michelin, Avon and Puma.

Wurth UK Ltd, 1 Centurion Way, Erith, Kent, DA18 4AF. Tel: 0181 319 6451
Zinc-rich primer and a vast range of other workshop materials.

Haynes
Restoration Manuals

Haynes Restoration Manual
MGB (2nd Edition)

History · Mechanics
Buying · Interior
Specification · Electrics
Bodywork · Modifications

Lindsay Porter

For more information on books please contact: Customer Services,
Haynes Publishing, Sparkford, Nr Yeovil, Somerset BA22 7JJ
Tel. **01963 440635** Fax: **01963 440001**
Int. tel: **+44 1963 440635** Fax: **+44 1963 440001**
E-mail: **sales@haynes-manuals.co.uk** Web site: **http://www.haynes.com**